TWO ZEN CLASSICS

TWO ZEN CLASSICS

Mumonkan and Hekiganroku

translated with commentaries by
KATSUKI SEKIDA

edited and introduced by
A. V. GRIMSTONE

New York • WEATHERHILL • *Tokyo*

First edition, 1977

Published by John Weatherhill, Inc., of New York and Tokyo, with editorial
offices at 7-6-13 Roppongi, Minato-ku, Tokyo 106, Japan. Copyright © by
Katsuki Sekida and A. V. Grimstone; all rights reserved. Printed in Japan.

Library of Congress Cataloging in Publication Data: Main entry under title:
Two zen classics. / Includes index. / 1. Hui-k'ai, Shih, 1183–1260. Wu-mên
kuan. 2. Hsüeh-tou, 980–1052. Pi yen lu. 3. Koan. / I. Hui-k'ai, Shih, 1183–
1260. Wu-mên kuan. English. 1977. II. Hsüeh-tou, 980–1052. Pi yen lu.
English. 1977. / BQ9289.H843T94 / 294.3'8 / 77-2398 / ISBN 0-8348-0131-0 /
ISBN 0-8348-0130-2 pbk.

CONTENTS

HEKIGANROKU

8 • *Contents*

PREFACE

IN MY PREVIOUS BOOK, *Zen Training: Methods and Philosophy*, I tried to explain some aspects of the theory and practice of Zen in a way that would be intelligible to a contemporary Western reader. My approach in that book was deliberately not a traditional one but made use of current ideas in philosophy, psychology, and physiology. My reason for this was that I believe the time has come for Zen to move on from the positions in which it has been firmly entrenched for many years. However, I do not wish to imply that the classic teachings can now be set aside. Zen will no doubt develop, and perhaps in time new Zen literature will appear. It has not done so yet. Before any such development can take place, Zen students must master the traditional teachings. I have therefore translated the two famous texts *Mumonkan* and *Hekiganroku* and have tried, by supplying appropriate interpretive notes, to make them approachable to Western students of Zen. The general nature of these texts, and the ways in which they may be studied, are outlined in Dr. A. V. Grimstone's introduction to this book.

I am deeply grateful to Dr. Grimstone, who, as with my previous book, has patiently turned my uncertain words into good English, written the introduction, and generally attended to all the problems involved in producing a book. The reader owes much to his labors. I must also thank most warmly Mr. Robert Aitken and Mr. Terence Griffin, who assisted me at an earlier stage with my translation of *Mumonkan*.

K. S.

INTRODUCTION

THE TEXTS TRANSLATED HERE by Katsuki Sekida, *Mumonkan* and
Hekiganroku, are among the great classics in the literature of Zen Buddhism. They were composed in China in the Sung dynasty (960–1279),
and are the two best known and most frequently studied collections of
koans. The aim of this introduction is to explain what manner of texts
these are and to give the reader some indication of the ways in which
they may best be approached. At the outset we should say that anyone
beginning the study of Zen will find this book more readily comprehen-
sible if Mr. Sekida's earlier book, *Zen Training: Methods and Philosophy*,*
has been read first.

Koans are a highly distinctive element in the literature of Zen Buddhism. There is no obvious parallel to them in the literature of other re-
ligions. They contain a message, but it is not a message that is expressed
by way of direct instruction or exhortation. Case 30 in *Hekiganroku*, for
example—and it is a quite typical sample—reads: "A monk asked Jōshū,
'I have heard that you closely followed Nansen. Is that true?' Jōshū said,
'Chinshū produces a big radish.' " An uninitiated reader perusing these
texts would probably learn rather little about the nature of Zen Buddhist teachings. This is as we should expect, for in Zen each of us must
arrive at his own directly experienced understanding. It cannot be transmitted to us by the words of others. The prime function of the koan is

*Katsuki Sekida, *Zen Training: Methods and Philosophy* (New York and Tokyo:
Weatherhill, 1975).

to serve as the medium through which this understanding may be reached. A koan is a problem or a subject for study, often, at first sight, of a totally intractable, insoluble kind, to which the student has to find an answer. This answer is not to be reached by the ordinary processes of reasoning and deduction. Indeed, to speak of an "answer" is perhaps inappropriate, since it suggests finding a solution to a problem by those methods. A koan is not an intellectual puzzle. We shall discuss shortly what it is and how it is to be approached, but to illustrate the point that a koan is no ordinary sort of problem we may note that the answer which is accepted by the student's teacher may be as seemingly irrational as the koan itself: a word or phrase, or an action, which shows that the student has experienced for himself the element of Zen of which the koan treats. There is, too, no single, approved answer to a koan. What a teacher will accept as satisfactory depends on the student he is dealing with, the stage of progress of the student's training, and so on.

Koans are by no means all of the same kind, as will probably be obvious to anyone who samples the ones in this book. Some are intended chiefly for the earliest stages in training, others for later ones. Case 1 of *Mumonkan*, for example—Jōshū's "Mu"—is the koan most commonly given to the beginning student, who has made some progress with controlling his thoughts by such preliminary exercises as counting or following the breath. *Mu* means "nothing" or "nothingness," and ultimately, by dint of long practice, the Zen student comes to grasp this nothingness, but when he is actually working on this koan he is not directly contemplating or inquiring into nothingness, nor is he trying to decide whether or not the dog has Buddha Nature (which was the question that elicited Jōshū's "Mu"). He is using the word "Mu," rather, as a meaningless sound on which to concentrate and with which to still his ordinary thought processes until he reaches the state of *samadhi* (see the notes to *Mumonkan*, Case 6). Some other koans are also used in these earliest stages of training. The majority, however, refer to later stages, when the student has attained some experience of samadhi, has achieved at least a preliminary sort of enlightenment, and is embarking on the long process of subsequent training—the cultivation of Holy Buddhahood, as it is called—which may lead him to maturity. Many koans deal with the application of Zen teaching to the ordinary situations of daily life. Koans have been classified into different types, relating to different aspects of

Zen and their suitability for students at different stages in their training.*
It must be noted, too, that koans often contain layers of meaning that
can be exposed by deeper and deeper study. A mature student returning
to a koan may discover more in it than he did when he first studied it.

The most general feature of a koan is that it cannot be approached by
the ordinary reasoning operations of the mind. Yet it is not a piece of
nonsense. Embodied in it there is invariably some element of Zen
teaching, which it is open to the student to extract if he approaches the
koan in the right way.

We might draw an analogy and say that a collection of koans is like
a well-equipped gymnasium in which the Zen student can train himself. He can start with fairly simple exercises and progress to more difficult ones. What he achieves depends on his own efforts. The gymnasium
is useless unless he gets to work in it.

Many koans are based on actual incidents in the lives of Zen masters.
These relate the answers the masters gave to questions put to them by
their monks or the questions they themselves asked their monks, or
describe the occasions on which the masters or their students achieved
enlightenment. Others describe exchanges (*mondō*) between mature Zen
masters. In the early days of Zen, teaching was no doubt largely spontaneous. In the course of time, however, the doings and sayings of the great
Zen masters were recorded and handed down, and were given to students as material on which to practice. The compilation of collections of
such koans followed naturally.

Koans are used to a greater or lesser extent for training students in all
schools of Zen. Of the two major sects today, the Rinzai places greater
emphasis on them than does the Sōtō, but they have their place in the
latter. They are not, however, a wholly indispensable element of Zen
training, and the student who finds himself unable to take the plunge into
paradox and illogicality that koans at first sight seem to constitute should
not suppose that he is thereby debarred from practicing Zen or from
deriving profit from *Mumonkan* and *Hekiganroku*.

Traditionally, the method of working on koans is that the student is
assigned one by his teacher and has to resolve it satisfactorily before being
allowed to pass on to another. Some Zen masters make their students

*See Isshū Miura and Ruth Fuller Sasaki, *Zen Dust* (New York: Harcourt, Brace &
World, 1966); C. C. Chang, *The Practice of Zen* (New York: Harper & Row, 1959).

work through all the koans in both *Mumonkan* and *Hekiganroku*, as well as other collections. Among the readers of this book there will no doubt be some Western Zen students who have access to a master and who are able to work on koans in this traditional way. They should find it convenient to have available English translations of these basic collections. Most readers, however, will not be in that fortunate position and will need some guidance on how to approach this book. The following remarks are largely based on Mr. Sekida's replies to questions I put to him.

It needs to be emphasized at the outset that the study of koans can yield a great deal to anyone who undertakes it seriously enough, even if he lacks the help of a Zen teacher. Mr. Sekida's notes on each case should be of much help to such readers. These notes, apart from elucidating textual obscurities and explaining allusions and so on, indicate the general nature of the problem with which each koan deals and discuss relevant parts of Zen theory. In the latter aspect the notes are a development of ideas contained in Mr. Sekida's *Zen Training*. The notes demonstrate the detailed application of these ideas to particular situations, and they show how recent ways of thinking about Zen can be applied to traditional teachings. Anyone who simply reads these texts, together with the notes, sufficiently seriously should learn a great deal about Zen, even though the koans themselves remain intractable. At the outset, undoubtedly, one will be at a loss to know what it is all about, but as one goes on, reading patiently, things should become clearer, and repeated rereadings should deepen one's understanding. I may say that I found this happening myself as I was revising Mr. Sekida's translation. Mr. Sekida himself believes that the sort of conceptual understanding of Zen to which such a study may lead can be of great value, even though it stops short of being complete Zen experience.

From this sort of immersion in the text, which can be undertaken by anyone interested in Zen as an object of study, one may, as a more deeply committed student of Zen, go on to deal with individual koans in a yet more detailed way. Such a student may learn these texts by heart. Indeed, if one studies them seriously enough, one inevitably will. The koan one is working on at the time should become deeply embedded in one's mind. It can be the subject of zazen practice. Here, seated in the posture for meditation, the student repeats his koan to himself over and over again. Mr. Sekida has described in *Zen Training* how this is done: "Recite it, exerting all your mind. . . . Take it syllable by syllable, word by word, and say it with all your attention, dwelling at length upon each word." The recitation is slow, and the inward voicing of each word or syllable may be done in phase with the slow, intermittent exhalation practiced in zazen (see *Zen Training*, chapter 4). The koan infiltrates the mind. And it remains with the student not only when he is seated in formal zazen posture but at all times. Koans can be worked on in whole or in part. Sometimes the entire koan may be studied, together with the material appended to it (introduction, verse, and so on), while at other times individual words or phrases or sentences may be singled out for study as they strike the attention. It is not possible to lay down rules for this: the student must find his own methods. The essential is to immerse oneself patiently and wholeheartedly in the koan, with unwavering attention. One must not be looking for an answer but looking at the koan. The "answer," if it comes, will come of its own accord. Whether the answer is "right," in the sense that the student has come to a true understanding of some aspect of Zen, can be determined only by a Zen teacher. No doubt such a teacher is highly desirable, just as in any other field of study, whether it be mathematics or horseback riding. But such teachers are at present few in number, and much can be done without their help. There are numerous instances of Zen students who have found their own way to enlightenment.

Mumonkan is usually studied before *Hekiganroku*, and it is customary to take the cases in the order given here. However, all the cases are independent, and they can be studied in any sequence.

We may now turn to consider in more detail the two texts translated here. *Mumonkan* is the later of the two. It is placed first in this book, and is usually studied first, because it is a shorter, simpler text than *Hekiganroku*. It was composed in 1228 by the Zen monk Mumon Ekai and is a collection of forty-eight koans, to each of which Mumon added a comment and a verse. The title *Mumonkan* is usually translated as "The Gateless Gate" (but see the notes to the preface of *Mumonkan*). *Mumonkan* is by now a relatively well-known text in the West. At least four complete translations into English are known to us.* Of these, the first two are

---

*Nyogen Senzaki and Paul Reps, "The Gateless Gate," in *Zen Flesh, Zen Bones*, ed. Paul Reps (Rutland, Vermont, and Tokyo: Tuttle, 1957). Sohaku Ogata, "The Mu Mon Kwan," in *Zen for the West* (London: Rider, 1959). R. H. Blyth, *Zen and Zen Classics*, vol. 4, *Mumonkan* (Tokyo: Hokuseido Press, 1966). Zenkei Shibayama, *Zen Comments on the Mumonkan*, trans. Sumiko Kudo (New York: Harper & Row, 1974).

simply translations of the text, without any attempt at annotation or interpretation. The third, by R. H. Blyth, is accompanied by extensive interpretive commentaries on each case. Blyth's translation is excellent, but his interpretations are often of a highly individual and unorthodox kind. As a guide to *Mumonkan*, and to Zen, his book must be treated with some caution. The most recent version, *Zen Comments on the Mumonkan*, contains an excellent translation by Sumiko Kudo and valuable commentaries by Zenkei Shibayama. This is an altogether admirable book. There is also a translation into German by Heinrich Dumoulin.*

With so many translations already available, the production of another might seem unnecessary. However, it is justified on two grounds. First, with a difficult text full of subtle allusions and implications, no one translation can ever convey the whole meaning; comparison of different renderings can be a real help to the English reader in approaching the meaning of the original text. Second, Mr. Sekida's notes contain a great deal of interpretive material which is not otherwise available and which should help to make this text more approachable than hitherto.

Hekiganroku was composed about a hundred years earlier than *Mumonkan*. Its original basis was a collection of one hundred koans compiled by Setchō (980–1052), an outstanding Zen master and a poet of great accomplishment. To each koan (here termed the "main subject") Setchō appended a verse which pointed to its meaning. The whole book was called Setchō's *Juko* (*ju*, verse; *ko*, old koans). It achieved great popularity, embodying as it did the essentials of Zen. About a century later another Zen master, Engo (1063–1135), added brief comments on each phrase or sentence of the main subject and Setchō's verse, and a long commentary on each case. He also provided a short introduction to most of the cases. It is to this work of dual authorship that the name *Hekiganroku* applies. The title derives from the fact that in Engo's room there hung a piece of calligraphy consisting of the two characters *heki* (blue) and *gan* (cliff or rock). *Roku* means "records." Hence, the usual translation of the title is "The Blue Cliff Records."

Engo's aim in adding to Setchō's text was to try to render it more approachable and intelligible. Full of paradoxical expressions and all manner of allusions, it employs a condensed, often involved style, while

---

*Heinrich Dumoulin, *Wu-mên-kuan: Der Pass ohne Tor*, Monumenta Nipponica Monographs 13 (Tokyo: 1953).

treating of matters of great subtlety and difficulty. Even in Engo's day, Zen students needed help. Yet then, as now, there were those who believed that "one should not make a picture book of Zen." Engo's long commentaries, in particular, tempted students to try to understand Zen conceptually, by the exercise of the intellect alone, instead of on the basis of their own immediate experience. For this reason, Daie (1089–1163), who succeeded Engo and was himself a great Zen master, destroyed the original edition of Engo's text. The book which we now know as *Hekiganroku* resulted from the work of a monk, Cho-mei-en, who in about 1300 collected all the surviving manuscript copies of the text that he could find and from them restored the original book as nearly as he could. In the interval which had elapsed, the original text had suffered additions and corruptions, especially in Engo's notes and commentaries. The main parts of the book, however—the main subjects, Setchō's verses, and Engo's introductions—are believed to be substantially free from such alterations. It is these parts of the text which are translated here. Engo's notes and commentaries are omitted, as is usually done now in printed versions of the text, though they have been taken into account in Mr. Sekida's notes. Where there is no introduction, it is probably because it has been lost.

Hekiganroku is a challenging book for a translator, and it is not surprising to find that only one attempt has hitherto been made to render it into English. This was by R. D. M. Shaw.* Shaw himself acknowledged that his was no more than a preliminary attempt on a difficult text. It served to draw the attention of English readers to this great work, but his translation must be termed inadequate. We have in general not been able to make a great deal of use of it. Occasionally, however, it has supplied a felicitous word or phrase. Apart from Shaw's version, we know of no other complete translation of *Hekiganroku*, though translations of some of the cases have appeared in various English works on Zen.

The two texts are markedly different in style. *Mumonkan* is brief and to the point. It is written, for the most part, in a terse, pithy style, the work, it would seem, of a practical man aiming to provide a text pared to essentials for the use of monks in their training. Setchō, on the other hand, seems to have been much more attracted by philosophical aspects of Zen, and was also a poet. *Hekiganroku* is correspondingly longer and is written

---

*R. D. M. Shaw, *The Blue Cliff Records* (London: Michael Joseph, 1961).

in a more subtle, literary style which is full of allusions and symbols. It treats of some of the deepest aspects of Zen theory, notably in connection with perception and cognition. Setchō's poems are very different from Mumon's verses. The former are literary productions in their own right, often of great beauty, and their translation cannot be simply a matter of providing a literal rendering of their content. We have done our best with them but are conscious of not having done them justice. We hope that in time a true poet with the necessary knowledge of both Chinese and Zen will give them the attention they deserve.

It will be noted that a few cases are common to both *Mumonkan* and *Hekiganroku*. Mumon may have drawn on *Hekiganroku* in compiling his own collection.

The teacher-disciple relationships between the various Zen masters and monks who appear in these texts (some of whom appear over and over again) are shown in the genealogical table at the end of this book. The reader will not find it difficult to discover the characteristic flavor associated with the teaching of different masters: Jōshū, Baso, Ummon all have their inimitable styles, which come through in even the briefest incident.

The reader will appreciate by now that neither of these texts is at all easy. Apart from the fact that they are collections of koans, which ultimately are not amenable to conceptual understanding, the texts contain much that is ambiguous, paradoxical, and illogical. This is not, as the reader might be tempted to suppose, the fault of the translation. The texts present the same problems to the reader of Chinese. Indeed, translated into English they are in some ways easier to understand than they are in the original, because by its very nature the English language imposes a degree of clarity that is avoidable in Chinese. (The price of such a gain in clarity is some loss of richness and depth.) In any case, the reader must not expect to find everything straightforward—he is not supposed to. Mumon, in particular, quite often says the exact opposite of what he means, no doubt as a means of keeping his readers alert.

One other general feature that perhaps requires comment is that some of the cases may appear to be very similar in content. In *Mumonkan*, for example, Cases 17 and 22 both deal with calling and responding, and in Cases 18 and 21 we have two instances of immediate, unpremeditated replies that come shooting out in response to stock questions. But in all such instances of seeming overlap we will find that there are subtle differences of emphasis. In Case 17, for example, the person called is already enlightened, while in Case 22 he is just reaching enlightenment. Cases 40 and 43 both deal with the same topic, but the one treats it as drama, the other as philosophy. Each case, ultimately, is individual.

In preparing Mr. Sekida's translation and notes for publication my aim has been to produce a text that is as lucid as is compatible with the nature of the subject matter. Mr. Sekida has checked my version with the greatest care, and the final text has been agreed upon between us.

A. V. G.

NOTE Chinese names and terms are generally given in their Japanese form. The Chinese equivalents of personal names can be found in Miura and Sasaki, *Zen Dust*. Non-English terms are italicized where they first appear but thereafter are treated as English words, with the addition of macrons where appropriate. However, certain common Zen and other Buddhist terms, such as koan, zazen, and karma, are handled as English words throughout.

A reference in the notes to another case without qualification (e.g., "see Case 20") denotes a case in the same text.

MUMONKAN

Memorial to the Throne

WE RESPECTFULLY GREET the Imperial Commemoration Day of January 5, the second year of Jōtei [1229]. Your humble servant, the monk Ekai, on November 5 last year published a commentary on forty-eight cases of the spiritual activities of the Buddha and the patriarchs, dedicated to the eternal health and prosperity of Your Majesty.

I reverently express my desire that Your Majesty's wisdom may illuminate all as brightly as the sun and your life be as eternal as that of the universe, that all the eight directions may sing and praise your virtue and the four seas enjoy happiness under your peaceful reign.

Written by Transmitter of the Dharma, your humble servant, the monk Ekai, formerly head monk of Hōinyu Zen Temple, built for the merit of Empress Jii

NOTES *The Imperial Commemoration Day of January 5, the second year of Jōtei.* This was the fifth anniversary of Emperor Risō's accession to the throne. Mumon was forty-six years old.

• *Ekai* was Mumon's name as a monk. Mumon Ekai (1183–1260) studied Zen with Getsurin Shikan. He struggled for six years with the koan "Mu." One day he heard the sound of a drum and suddenly gained enlightenment. He succeeded his teacher when thirty-six years old. The verse he wrote on his enlightenment runs:

> Blue sky, broad daylight, and a peal of thunder,
> The earth and creatures' eyes are opened;
> All the universe is making profound bows,
> Mount Sumeru dances to the ancient music.

Mount Sumeru, in the traditional Buddhist world picture, is the central and highest mountain of the universe.

• *Empress Jii* was Emperor Risō's mother. It was customary to build a temple for the repose of the spirit of a deceased emperor or empress. The first head of the temple was Getsurin, Mumon's teacher.

Mumon's Preface

BUDDHISM MAKES mind its foundation and no-gate its gate. Now, how do you pass through this no-gate? It is said that things coming in through the gate can never be your own treasures. What is gained from external circumstances will perish in the end. However, such a saying is already raising waves when there is no wind. It is cutting unblemished skin. As for those who try to understand through other people's words, they are striking at the moon with a stick; scratching a shoe, whereas it is the foot that itches. What concern have they with the truth?

In the summer of the first year of Jōtei, Ekai was in Ryūshō Temple and as head monk worked with the monks, using the cases of the ancient masters as brickbats to batter the gate and lead them on according to their respective capacities. The text was written down not according to any scheme, but just to make a collection of forty-eight cases. It is called *Mumonkan*, "The Gateless Gate."

A man of determination will unflinchingly push his way straight forward, regardless of all dangers. Then even the eight-armed Nata cannot hinder him. Even the four sevens of the West and the two threes of the East would beg for their lives. If one has no determination, then it will be like catching a glimpse of a horse galloping past the window: in the twinkling of an eye it will be gone.

> The Great Way is gateless,
> Approached in a thousand ways.
> Once past this checkpoint
> You stride through the universe.

NOTES *Mumonkan*. This title is usually translated as "gateless gate" or "gateless barrier" (*mu*, nothing, no; *mon*, gate; *kan*, barrier). The latter would suggest a barrier with no passage through it. However, the ideograph *kan* may also refer to a checkpoint on national or prefectural boundaries where travelers' credentials are examined by police, so that a possible interpretation of *Mumonkan* is "a checkpoint that is not blocked in any way." Hence, the title might also be translated as "open checkpoint."

• *Eight-armed Nata*. In Indian mythology Nata is a demon-king with three faces and eight arms; he is the eldest son of Vaisravana, one of the twenty *devas* (gods or, as here, demons). "Nata" is also pronounced "Nada" in Japanese.

In Case 87 of *Hekiganroku*, Engo says in his introduction, "When he displays the wrath of Nada, he is three-faced and six-armed." Six arms may seem more logical than eight, and Zen students generally follow Engo's version.

• *The four sevens of the West*. The twenty-eight Indian patriarchs from Shakyamuni Buddha to Bodhidharma.

• *The two threes of the East*. The six Chinese patriarchs from Bodhidharma to Enō.

Case 1 Jōshū's "Mu"

A monk asked Jōshū, "Has a dog the Buddha Nature?" Jōshū answered, "Mu."

MUMON'S COMMENT In order to master Zen, you must pass the barrier of the patriarchs. To attain this subtle realization, you must completely cut off the way of thinking. If you do not pass the barrier, and do not cut off the way of thinking, then you will be like a ghost clinging to the bushes and weeds. Now, I want to ask you, what is the barrier of the patriarchs? Why, it is this single word "Mu." That is the front gate to

Zen. Therefore it is called the "Mumonkan of Zen." If you pass through it, you will not only see Jōshū face to face, but you will also go hand in hand with the successive patriarchs, entangling your eyebrows with theirs, seeing with the same eyes, hearing with the same ears. Isn't that a delightful prospect? Wouldn't you like to pass this barrier?

Arouse your entire body with its three hundred and sixty bones and joints and its eighty-four thousand pores of the skin; summon up a spirit of great doubt and concentrate on this word "Mu." Carry it continuously day and night. Do not form a nihilistic conception of vacancy, or a relative conception of "has" or "has not." It will be just as if you swallow a red-hot iron ball, which you cannot spit out even if you try. All the illusory ideas and delusive thoughts accumulated up to the present will be exterminated, and when the time comes, internal and external will be spontaneously united. You will know this, but for yourself only, like a dumb man who has had a dream. Then all of a sudden an explosive conversion will occur, and you will astonish the heavens and shake the earth.

It will be as if you snatch away the great sword of the valiant general Kan'u and hold it in your hand. When you meet the Buddha, you kill him; when you meet the patriarchs, you kill them. On the brink of life and death, you command perfect freedom; among the sixfold worlds and four modes of existence, you enjoy a merry and playful samadhi.

Now, I want to ask you again, "How will you carry it out?" Employ every ounce of your energy to work on this "Mu." If you hold on without interruption, behold: a single spark, and the holy candle is lit!

MUMON'S VERSE
　The dog, the Buddha Nature,
　The pronouncement, perfect and final.
　Before you say it has or has not,
　You are a dead man on the spot.

NOTES　*Jōshū* (778–897) is one of the greatest Chinese Zen masters. He had his first experience of *kenshō*, or realization, when he was seventeen years old. His description of this experience was "Suddenly I was ruined and homeless." That is to say, he was thrown into a great emptiness. This emptiness has a special meaning in Zen. It can be a matured emptiness only when one has acquired the four wisdoms: the Great Perfect Mirror Wisdom, Universal Nature Wisdom, Marvelous Observing Wisdom, and Perfecting of Action Wisdom. Jōshū put the finishing touches to his enlightenment when he mastered "Ordinary mind is the Way," the story of which is told in Case 19.

• *The barrier of the patriarchs.* No one but yourself has put up the barrier that keeps you from understanding, although it may seem as though other people have erected it.

• *Mu* is nothingness. When you realize Mu you realize Zen truth. "Mu" is the word most commonly used in zazen practice. It is not said aloud but is concentrated upon in time with one's breathing.

• *Three hundred and sixty bones and joints.* How to adopt a correct posture is the first problem of zazen practice. Continued practice brings increasing awareness of the subtleties of one's posture and allows one to correct such faults as may occur.

• *Eighty-four thousand pores of the skin.* The breathing in zazen practice controls the pores of the skin, the circulation of the blood, and even the activity of the capillary vessels. Zen breathing and posture control skin sensation, which in turn controls the peace of both heart and mind. The quietness of absolute samadhi (see the notes to Case 6) comes from pacified skin sensation. This is a very important point to keep in mind. Never neglect it. Beginners will not understand, when they start to practice, how to control their breathing and pacify the skin, but do not let this deter you from practicing zazen in your own way. If you persevere, you will undergo many experiences and through these you will contrive, of your own accord, your own system and method. You will experience failures and frustrations, and will often be bewildered. Do not be discouraged. Those very frustrations and failures will prove to be valuable assets. In *Zen Training*, a book written specifically on this subject, you will find extensive information concerning posture and breathing. The following are the essentials. Sit with your back and waist straight. Push the lower part of your belly forward and your buttocks back until your upper body sits comfortably erect. Breathe in normally and exhale in a long, slow, quiet breath. Follow this simple practice until your own method develops from within yourself. Do not be impatient; even some of the great Zen masters took many long years to understand Zen truths.

• *Great doubt.* Summoning up a great doubt means generating a great driving force toward the realization of enlightenment. Never for a moment doubt its possibility.

• *Conversion.* Conversion often occurs in the human mind. Religious devotees usually give it a dogmatic interpretation according to their own beliefs. Saint Paul, for instance, experienced his conversion in terms of the Jewish faith. To discern the mental and spiritual coloring of one's dogmatic understanding is difficult and requires prolonged study.

• *Kan'u* was a famous Chinese general of heroic stature. Standing nine feet five inches and carrying his great sword Green Dragon, he was a leading figure in the history of the Three Kingdoms of China. He died in A.D. 220 and was enshrined as a god. He is still a very popular figure among the Chinese.

• *When you meet the Buddha, you kill him; when you meet the patriarchs, you kill them.* Your understanding must be your own. While you are under any other person's influence you are not standing on your own feet.

• *Sixfold worlds. Devas* (gods), human existence, *asuras* (malevolent spirits), animals, hungry ghosts, and hells. These represent all the conditions and situations of life.

• *Four modes of existence.* Live-born, egg-born, born from moisture, and born through metamorphosis. These represent all classes of living creatures and therefore also stand for all possible situations in life.

• *Merry and playful samadhi.* A merry and egoless activity of mind, such as that of an actor who, playing a part on stage, is freed from his own ego-centered thinking. In just this way, when a student of Zen fully realizes that there is no constant ego to which he can attach his notions of self and identity, the constrictions of egotistically motivated behavior and thinking are broken. Activity in this free frame of mind is called playful samadhi.

• *How will you carry it out?* Mumon says, "Employ every ounce of your energy." But how? Mumon did not go into the details of technique and practice. To Zen Buddhists in the East such things are a part of their general cultural background. Westerners, however, do not have this cultural heritage. Those who would like to find out more about the practical aspects of the subject may consult *Zen Training.*

Case 2 Hyakujō's Fox

When Hyakujō Oshō delivered a certain series of sermons, an old man always followed the monks to the main hall and listened to him. When the monks left the hall, the old man would also leave. One day, however, he remained behind, and Hyakujō asked him, "Who are you, standing here before me?" The old man replied, "I am not a human being. In the old days of Kashyapa Buddha, I was a head monk, living here on this mountain. One day a student asked me, 'Does a man of enlightenment fall under the yoke of causation or not?' I answered, 'No, he does not.' Since then I have been doomed to undergo five hundred rebirths as a fox. I beg you now to give the turning word to release me from my life as a fox. Tell me, does a man of enlightenment fall under the yoke of causation or not?" Hyakujō answered, "He does not ignore causation." No sooner had the old man heard these words than he was enlightened. Making his bows, he said, "I am emancipated from my life as a fox. I shall remain on this mountain. I have a favor to ask of you: would you please bury my body as that of a dead monk."

Hyakujō had the director of the monks strike with the gavel and inform everyone that after the midday meal there would be a funeral service for a dead monk. The monks wondered at this, saying, "Everyone is in good health; nobody is in the sick ward. What does this mean?" After the meal Hyakujō led the monks to the foot of a rock on the far side of the mountain and with his staff poked out the dead body of a fox and performed the ceremony of cremation. That evening he ascended the rostrum and told the monks the whole story. Ōbaku thereupon asked him, "The old man gave the wrong answer and was doomed to be a fox for five hundred rebirths. Now, suppose he had given the right answer, what would have happened then?" Hyakujō said, "You come here to me, and I will tell you." Ōbaku went up to Hyakujō and boxed his ears. Hyakujō clapped his hands with a laugh and exclaimed, "I was thinking that the barbarian had a red beard, but now I see before me the red-bearded barbarian himself."

MUMON'S COMMENT   Not falling under causation: how could this make the monk a fox? Not ignoring causation: how could this make the old man emancipated? If you come to understand this, you will realize how old Hyakujō would have enjoyed five hundred rebirths as a fox.

MUMON'S VERSE
Not falling, not ignoring:
Two faces of one die.
Not ignoring, not falling:
A thousand errors, a million mistakes.

NOTES *Hyakujō Oshō* (720–814), one of the greatest Chinese Zen masters, was the teacher of Ōbaku, who was the teacher of Rinzai. Hyakujō laid down the rules of conduct for Zen monasteries, although his work on the subject has not survived. He is also regarded as the originator of the Chinese tea ceremony. Oshō is a general title of respect used for a Buddhist priest.

• *Standing.* In the old Chinese monasteries the monks stood in rows to hear their master's lecture.

• *Kashyapa Buddha.* The sixth of the seven ancient Buddhas. They are Vipasyin, Sikhin, Visvabhu, Krakucchanda, Kanakamuni, Kashyapa, and Shakyamuni. In this context Kashyapa Buddha represents the remote past of human history.

• *Causation.* This word has a particular moral meaning in Buddhist philosophy. To explain its meaning here requires a brief excursion into what might be called Zen theory. The word *nen*, which has no equivalent in English, means either a unit of thought or a steadily willed activity of mind. Zen theory sees the activity of consciousness as a continuous interplay between a sequence of nen. Thus, the first nen always acts intuitively and performs a direct, pure cognition of the object. The second nen immediately follows the first and makes the first its object of reflection. By this means, one becomes conscious of one's own thoughts. The successively appearing secondary nen integrate and synthesize preceding nen into a continuous stream of thought. It is these nen which are the basis of self-consciousness and ego-activity. The integrating, synthesizing action of consciousness is the third nen. Reasoning, introspection, and so forth come from the third nen. But this third nen, clouded by its ego-centered activity, often argues falsely and draws mistaken conclusions. This delusive thinking in turn interferes with the pure cognition of the first nen. Zazen practice, when it leads to absolute samadhi, cuts off delusive thoughts. The activity of the second and third nen ceases, and gradually, through constant practice, the first nen is freed to perform its inherently pure and direct cognition. (See the notes to Case 47.) Each nen is accompanied by internal pressure, which remains behind and affects the ensuing thoughts. So causation here represents the effect of each nen-thought on the next. It is not so much the actions of killing, stealing, wronging others, and so on that give rise to evil karma as it is the delusions of the nen-thought, which thinks of killing, stealing, or wronging others. (See the notes to "Mumon's Zen Warnings" for a discussion of karma.)

When a phenomenon appears, it is there; when it disappears, it is not there. Everything is in constant mutation. But when your mind attaches itself and makes a problem of what there is or is not, then the feeling comes of being a victim of events, of falling under the yoke of causation. A child does not feel such a yoke. He simply lives life as it happens and enjoys it because he lives in samadhi. Animals, plants, and minerals too are all in a samadhi of their own. Only adults have lost the Eden of samadhi because of their deluded thinking. To free your own mind from delusion is the only true emancipation and freedom.

• *Turning word.* A word that changes the course of one's mind and directs it toward true understanding.

• *Ignore causation.* In the old man's question and Hyakujō's answer the master makes it clear that nen-thoughts always occur, that they necessarily leave their traces in the subconscious, and that hence karmic causation must occur. Thus, to ignore causation only compounds one's malady. To recognize causation constitutes the remedy for it.

• *The whole story.* Hyakujō happened to find the dead body of a fox and invented the whole story.

• *Ōbaku* (d. 850) had the personal name Kiun. He was a disciple of Hyakujō and the teacher of Rinzai. He stood seven feet tall and had a powerful voice. He cuts a brilliant figure in Zen history.

• *I will tell you.* Perhaps Hyakujō wanted to give Ōbaku a slap on the ear and say, "Don't mind going to hell!" In a playful samadhi, one can enjoy even hell.

• *Ōbaku went up to Hyakujō and boxed his ears.* By this Ōbaku was saying, "I know what you are going to do and say, but I want to get in first."

• *Red-bearded barbarian.* The Chinese of those days thought of China as the cultural center of the world. Indians and Persians were considered barbarians. But Shakyamuni and Bodhidharma, whom the Chinese revered, were both Indians. "Barbarian" therefore acquired a new meaning. The text might be paraphrased like this: "I thought Bodhidharma was red-bearded, but now I see before me a red-bearded Bodhidharma himself." The original text consists of ten syllables and was uttered in one breath, to powerful effect.

• *Enjoyed five hundred rebirths as a fox.* An enlightened man enjoys any condition of life in his playful samadhi.

• *Two faces of one die.* He does not ignore causation; at the same time, he does not fall under the yoke of causation. Both are one and the same thing.

• *A thousand errors, a million mistakes.* While he rebels against causation, whatever he says is mistaken.

Case 3   Gutei Raises a Finger

Whenever Gutei Oshō was asked about Zen, he simply raised his finger. Once a visitor asked Gutei's boy attendant, "What does your master teach?" The boy too raised his finger. Hearing of this, Gutei cut off the boy's finger with a knife. The boy, screaming with pain, began to run away. Gutei called to him, and when he turned around, Gutei raised his finger. The boy suddenly became enlightened.

When Gutei was about to pass away, he said to his assembled monks, "I obtained one-finger Zen from Tenryū and used it all my life but still did not exhaust it." When he had finished saying this, he entered into eternal Nirvana.

MUMON'S COMMENT   The enlightenment of Gutei and of the boy does not depend on the finger. If you understand this, Tenryū, Gutei, the boy, and you yourself are all run through with one skewer.

MUMON'S VERSE
Gutei made a fool of old Tenryū,
Emancipating the boy with a single slice,
Just as Kyorei cleaved Mount Kasan
To let the Yellow River run through.

NOTES   *Gutei Oshō.* Little is known of Gutei except the present case and his habit of reciting an incantation from the *Saptakotibuddhamatr Dharani.* Gutei was a nickname derived from the sound of *koti* in the dharani's title. The dates of Gutei's birth and death are not recorded, but he is thought to have been contemporary with Ōbaku.

• *He simply raised his finger.* Hakuin asked the meaning of "the voice of one hand." Bankei advocated "unborn" and "unborn" alone. Gutei simply raised his finger on every occasion. Each of these demonstrations of the truth was the same; and all were, at the same time, different. Gutei's was the samadhi of the intuitive first nen; Bankei's, the samadhi of the intuitive third nen; Hakuin's, a combination of both.

Man is absorbed in his own actions in the moment of sitting down, standing up, taking a step, opening a door, or raising his hand or finger. But is he really acting in a state of true samadhi? True samadhi controls not only momentary attention but also the whole stream of consciousness: that is, the trend of the mind. In samadhi also, each and every moment is independent. Gutei's samadhi was a demonstration of this. Although he always raised his finger, he never raised the same finger. He was always new.

• *Gutei cut off the boy's finger.* There is no point in asking whether this story is factually true. Zen stories are full of metaphor and are also often improved upon in the telling.

• *I obtained one-finger Zen from Tenryū.* Before Gutei had any real experience of Zen he lived alone at the foot of a mountain. It was a quiet twilight, a good time for meditation, and Gutei had been sitting for a long time in his hut. Outside, the dry fallen leaves were stirred by the winter wind and rustled softly on the ground. The dusk gathered; a new moon shed her dim light. A figure appeared from the dark and silently walked toward the hut. This was the nun Jissai, dressed in the clothes of a traveling priest, with a broad hat, black robe, and pilgrim's staff. She entered the hut, walked around Gutei's seat three times, and then, standing straight in front of him, threw her staff down on the ground, saying, "Say a word—then I will take off my hat." This phrase is a challenge to a Zen mondō, an exchange in which each participant demonstrates his understanding of Zen. In the old days, whenever traveling monks met they fought these "Dharma battles," training themselves never to be caught off guard.

Gutei on this occasion was at a complete loss for words. Jissai once more walked around Gutei's seat three times and again asked her question. Three times she did this, and finding that Gutei could still return no answer, she began to leave. Gutei said, "It is already dark; please stay here the night." Jissai replied, "Say a word and I will stay." Gutei could say nothing, and Jissai walked out into the night. That night Gutei tossed and turned in his bed, saying to himself, "What a stupid fellow I am. This will never do. Early tomorrow I will set out in search of a teacher who can give me instruction."

There is a crucial moment in one's life when determination decides one's destiny. Jissai's identity is not known. Perhaps she was a messenger sent by the Bodhisattva Kannon (Avalokitesvara) to awaken Gutei to a new determination. However, as Gutei dozed, the guardian deity appeared in a dream and said to him, "Do not leave this mountain. A living Bodhisattva is coming to visit you. He will give you instruction." Sure enough, within a few days Tenryū Oshō came to visit his hermitage. Gutei told Tenryū the whole story and asked him, "What is the essence of the Buddha's teaching?" No sooner had Gutei said this than Tenryū raised one finger. Gutei suddenly gained enlightenment. This is how Gutei inherited Tenryū's one-finger Zen. Little is recorded of Tenryū's life except a few anecdotes and his Dharma lineage.

• *Did not exhaust it.* One cannot exhaust Dharma treasure. It is never ending.

• *Gutei made a fool of old Tenryū.* In the end, Gutei made even greater progress than his teacher, Tenryū.

• *Kyorei.* Kyorei is a deity who cleaved Mount Kasan to let the Yellow River run through.

Case 4   The Western Barbarian with No Beard

Wakuan said, "Why has the Western Barbarian no beard?"

MUMON'S COMMENT   Study should be real study, enlightenment should be real enlightenment. You should once meet this barbarian directly to be really intimate with him. But saying you are really intimate with him already divides you into two.

MUMON'S VERSE
   Don't discuss your dream
   Before a fool.
   Barbarian with no beard
   Obscures the clarity.

NOTES   *Wakuan* (1108–79) was the disciple of Gogoku, who in turn was the disciple of Engo, the compiler of *Hekiganroku*. It was customary for Zen masters, when dying, to compose a short poem. Wakuan's death poem runs:

> The iron tree blossomed,
> The cock laid eggs;
> Seventy-two years,
> The cradle string snaps.

• *The Western Barbarian.* The Western Barbarian here stands for Bodhidharma, who brought Zen to China from India. He is always depicted with a beard. The case therefore means, "Why does Bodhidharma, who has a beard, have no beard?"

• *Meet this barbarian directly.* This is not really a meeting but a becoming. You should yourself become Bodhidharma. Then if you have a beard, Bodhidharma has a beard; if you have no beard, then neither has Bodhidharma. But can you say that you are in truth Bodhidharma?

• *Don't discuss your dream.* The way to enlightenment is beset with mirages. Do not attach yourself to experiences which may prove to have been merely dreams.

• *Before a fool.* Who is the fool? Zen involves every part of yourself. It is your very life itself. This is not a matter for discussion.

• *Barbarian with no beard.* To draw a distinction between beard and no beard is already straying from the point.

• *Obscures the clarity.* Words, concepts, and other inventions of the mind only obscure the truth. Do not cling to shadows, but catch hold of the truth itself.

Case 5 Kyōgen's "Man up in a Tree"

Kyōgen Oshō said, "It is like a man up in a tree hanging from a branch with his mouth; his hands grasp no bough, his feet rest on no limb. Someone appears under the tree and asks him, 'What is the meaning of Bodhidharma's coming from the West?' If he does not answer, he fails to respond to the question. If he does answer, he will lose his life. What would you do in such a situation?"

MUMON'S COMMENT Even if your eloquence flows like a river, it is of no avail. Though you can expound the whole of Buddhist literature, it is of no use. If you solve this problem, you will give life to the way that has been dead until this moment and destroy the way that has been alive up to now. Otherwise you must wait for Maitreya Buddha and ask him.

MUMON'S VERSE
Kyōgen is truly thoughtless;
His vice and poison are endless.
He stops up the mouths of the monks,
And devil's eyes sprout from their bodies.

NOTES *Kyōgen Oshō* was a disciple of Isan (771–853). The dates of his birth and death are not recorded, but since he studied earlier under Hyakujō, who was also Isan's teacher, he may not have been much younger than Isan himself.

Kyōgen stood seven feet tall and was a scholar of great erudition. His learning for a long time stood in the way of his enlightenment, but Isan recognized his innate ability. One day Isan asked Kyōgen, "When you were with our teacher Hyakujō, you were clever enough to give ten answers to a single question and hundreds of answers to ten questions. However, sagacity does not help you in studying Zen; in fact it stands in the way of your enlightenment. Now, I am not going to ask you about what you have learned from your reading or from your study of the sutras. Instead, tell me this: What is your real self—the self that existed before you came out of your mother's womb, before you knew east from west?"

At this question Kyōgen was stupefied and did not know what to say. He racked his brains and offered all sorts of answers, but Isan brushed them aside. At last Kyōgen said, "I beg you, please explain it to me." Isan replied, "What I say belongs to my own understanding. How can that benefit *your* mind's eye?"

Kyōgen went through all his books and the notes he had made on authorities of every school but could find no words to use as an answer to Isan's question. Sighing to himself, he said, "You cannot fill an empty stomach with paintings of rice cakes." He then burned all his books and papers, saying, "I will give up the study of Buddhism in this life. I will remain a rice-gruel monk for the rest of my life and avoid torturing my mind." Sadly he left Isan, and coming to Nanyang, where the remains of the National Teacher Chū (see Case 17) were buried, he took on the self-appointed job of grave-keeper. In his spirit of dejection he found this humble task best suited to him. Blessed are the poor in spirit, for they are freed from their own deluded egos.

One day, when he was sweeping the ground, a stone struck a bamboo. The sound echoed through his mind as the sound of a falling nut rings through the empty valleys and hills at midnight. This was the intuitive first nen ringing through his cleared mind and making a direct, pure cognition of the object. Kyōgen stood speechless, forgetting himself for a while. Then, suddenly bursting into loud laughter, he became enlightened. Enlightenment is consummated when pure cognition is reflected upon by the purified action of the third nen, which is henceforth the master of the mind.

Returning to his hut, Kyōgen performed the ceremony of purification, offered incense, paid homage to his teacher, Isan, and with the deepest sense of gratitude said, "Great master, thank you! Your kindness to me is greater even than that of my parents. If you had explained the profound cause to me when I begged you to give me an answer, I should never have reached where I stand today." Kyōgen's verse on this occasion runs:

> One stroke and all is gone,
> No need of stratagem or cure;
> Each and every action manifests the ancient Way.
> My spirit is never downcast,
> I leave no tracks behind me,
> Enlightenment is beyond speech, beyond gesture;
> Those who are emancipated
> Call it the unsurpassed.

• *A man up in a tree hanging from a branch with his mouth.* Kyōgen is driving you here into the same predicament he found himself in with Isan. Isan deprived Kyōgen of all his clever learning by asking the question, "What is your real self—the self that existed before you came out of your mother's womb?"—in fact, before he had learned anything at all.

• *His hands grasp no bough.* Kyōgen found nothing to which he could cling. His books and sutras gave him no answer to Isan's question.

• *His feet rest on no limb.* No notes from the lectures of the masters helped him in his predicament.

• *What is the meaning of Bodhidharma's coming from the West?* The answer to this question is that there is "no meaning." If you can directly grasp this "no meaning," then all problems are instantly solved. This "no meaning," intellectually explained, means emptiness: the emptiness of ego which is accompanied by emptiness of attachments, devices, purposes, and objects. Bodhidharma came from the West, but he came without being attached to a single purpose. Buddhist emptiness is not a nihilistic emptiness; it is not the bitter emptiness of frustration and despair which come from a mistaken attachment to constancy in a world which is ever changing. On the contrary, Buddhist emptiness is the ancient Way, before the "ten thousand myriad objects" of the mind were born.

• *If he does not answer.* If he can make a no-answer with a truly empty mind, then even if he cannot utter a word he is making a great answer.

• *If he does answer.* However eloquently he speaks, without an empty mind he is a dead man.

• *He will lose his life.* Once lose your life as Kyōgen did. Let go the branch, the bough, the limb, and a whole new life opens up before you.

• *Even if your eloquence flows like a river.* Mumon underlines Kyōgen's own lesson at the hands of Isan, when his eloquence was of no use to him . . .

• *Though you can expound the whole of Buddhist literature.* . . . and his learning of no avail.

• *The way that has been dead.* The way of truth, which, in a worldly sense, has been dead.

• *The way that has been alive.* The way of illusion, on which so many lives are based.

• *Maitreya Buddha.* According to Buddhist tradition, Maitreya is the Buddha to come. He is now living in heaven and will come to earth 5,670,000 years after the Nirvana of Shakyamuni Buddha.

• *Devil's eyes sprout from their bodies.* When Kyōgen was thrown into desperation and despair, his whole being suffered from a great oppression and demonic rage. This Kyōgen is inflicting on you in turn, in order to drive you to desperate lengths.

Case 6   The Buddha Holds Out a Flower

When Shakyamuni Buddha was at Mount Grdhrakuta, he held out a flower to his listeners. Everyone was silent. Only Mahakashyapa broke into a broad smile. The Buddha said, "I have the True Dharma Eye, the Marvelous Mind of Nirvana, the True Form of the Formless, and the Subtle Dharma Gate, independent of words and transmitted beyond doctrine. This I have entrusted to Mahakashyapa."

MUMON'S COMMENT   Golden-faced Gautama really disregarded his listeners. He made the good look bad and sold dog's meat labeled as mutton. He himself thought it was wonderful. If, however, everyone in the audience had laughed, how could he have transmitted his True Eye? And again, if Mahakashyapa had not smiled, how could the Buddha have transmitted it? If you say the True Eye of Dharma can be transmitted, then the golden-faced old man would be a city slicker who cheats the country bumpkin. If you say it cannot be transmitted, then why did the Buddha approve of Mahakashyapa?

MUMON'S VERSE
Holding out a flower,
The Buddha betrayed his curly tail.
Heaven and earth were bewildered
At Mahakashyapa's smile.

NOTES *Mount Grdhrakuta.* The Vulture Peak, near the town of Rajagaha in northern India. It was the haunt of many ascetics and religious teachers, and Shakyamuni Buddha stayed there for some time teaching his early followers.

• *He held out a flower.* Shakyamuni Buddha in this case is demonstrating his state of samadhi. "Samadhi" is usually interpreted as the state of total involvement of the whole personality with whatever it is that the person is doing. But what is not usually explained is that there are many different kinds of samadhi. Absolute samadhi is a total involvement and integration, with no object and no activity. Positive samadhi is a total involvement with some object or activity. Thus a painter, as he picks up his brush, will become completely concentrated in his involvement with painting—his painting samadhi. A musician will be in his playing or listening samadhi. But these are involuntary states. Voluntary samadhi can be attained first through absolute samadhi, which constitutes the essential foundation for all samadhi. Being well practiced in absolute samadhi, you can enter positive samadhi at will. Truly, it is a delightful thing! Fixing your eyes upon it, a blade of grass, even a stone at the roadside, begins to shine with the beauty of its essential nature. You are in the closest intimacy with the object.

In this case the Buddha held out a flower as a demonstration of his positive samadhi: his oneness, his closest intimacy, with the flower and through it the universe.

• *Everyone was silent.* The audience did not understand the Buddha's samadhi and so remained silent.

• *Mahakashyapa broke into a broad smile.* Mahakashyapa fully understood the Buddha's samadhi, and he involuntarily expressed himself in a smile.

• *The True Dharma Eye.* The original text says *shō-bō-gen-zō.* Analyzed into its components, this reads: *shō,* true or genuine; *bō,* law, teaching, Dharma; *gen,* eye; *zō,* treasure store. Hence, an approximate meaning is "the truth of the universe."

• *The Marvelous Mind of Nirvana.* The original text reads *nehan-myō-shin.* This can be translated: *nehan,* Nirvana; *myō,* wonderful or marvelous; *shin,* mind.

• *The True Form of the Formless.* The original text reads *jis-sō-mu-sō* (*jitsu* [*jis-*], true; *sō,* form; *mu,* no; *sō,* form). A literal translation would therefore be "true form, no form."

• *The Subtle Dharma Gate.* In the original this reads as *bi-myō-hō-mon* (*bi,* undisclosed; *myō,* subtle; *hō,* Dharma, law, teaching; *mon,* gate). In this instance the gate itself represents the treasure store of the Buddha's teaching.

• *Independent of words.* One should not be controlled by words, terms, and concepts, but should oneself control them.

• *Transmitted beyond doctrine.* Mahakashyapa understood directly from his own experience the truth that the Buddha was demonstrating. This attainment to the truth is beyond doctrine. Doctrine only follows as a conceptual paraphrase of the experience itself.

• *Why did the Buddha approve of Mahakashyapa?* The Buddha approved of the attainment of Mahakashyapa that had resulted from his own efforts. The transmission was automatic, and if Mahakashyapa had not earned it personally, no transmission would have been possible. This is the reason behind the apparent rudeness of Mumon's comments. The Buddha was not "giving" anything, nor was he "teaching" anything, although it may have appeared as though he were.

• *The Buddha betrayed his curly tail.* He revealed the secret, betraying the curly tail of his devilry and trickery.

• *Heaven and earth were bewildered.* Because of their ignorance and delusion, no one could comprehend the meaning of Mahakashyapa's smile.

Case 7   Jōshū's "Wash Your Bowl"

A monk said to Jōshū, "I have just entered this monastery. Please teach me." "Have you eaten your rice porridge?" asked Jōshū. "Yes, I have," replied the monk. "Then you had better wash your bowl," said Jōshū. With this the monk gained insight.

MUMON'S COMMENT   When he opens his mouth, Jōshū shows his gallbladder. He displays his heart and liver. I wonder if this monk really did hear the truth. I hope he did not mistake the bell for a jar.

MUMON'S VERSE
Endeavoring to interpret clearly,
You retard your attainment.
Don't you know that flame is fire?
Your rice has long been cooked.

NOTES   *Jōshū* has already appeared in Case 1. In fact he appears seven times altogether in *Mumonkan* and twelve times in *Hekiganroku*. Jōshū's Zen is called lip-and-tongue Zen because, although his words appear ordinary, they warrant very close attention and study. The present case is a good example of how he disguises profound truth in the garb of a trite commonplace.

• *I have just entered this monastery.* The beginner in Zen is in a flexible frame of mind. He is naive, sensitive, and humble. Because of the freshness of his attitude toward Zen the teacher's words, the manner of the senior monks, even the sounds of the temple's many bells penetrate his mind. In this state he is already halfway toward his goal, though he is not aware of it. He has not become habituated to his immediate world; everything appears to him as though seen for the first time. A thoughtful monk, however advanced he may be in his training, tries to keep himself in this state of pure innocence. The monk in this story is just such a monk, humble and questioning.

• *Have you eaten your rice porridge?* To understand this reference one must know something of the schedule of the Zen monastery. Monks get up at four in the morning. They start the daily routine with sutra chanting. This chanting is done on a single low note, and the vibration which it sets up throughout the body is good preparation for entering absolute samadhi in the meditation period which follows. At six o'clock breakfast is served, which includes the hot rice porridge mentioned by Jōshū in this case. The samadhi which has been reached by the monks in the meditation period is maintained throughout breakfast, which is therefore a solemn occasion. Every movement is made in hushed silence and with keen attention. Thus, implicit in Jōshū's question is the meaning, "Have you eaten your rice porridge in samadhi?"

• *Yes, I have.* Perceiving the inner meaning of Jōshū's question, the monk affirms that he was able to maintain his samadhi while eating breakfast.

• *Then you had better wash your bowl.* These words of Jōshū's are a Zen proverb. In samadhi every moment is independent, cut off before and behind. The monk is no longer at breakfast; he should pay attention to the present. What is past is past: wash it away, good or evil.

• *When he opens his mouth, Jōshū shows his gallbladder.* Every word of Jōshū's, though seemingly commonplace, exposes the resources of his mind.

• *I wonder if this monk.* Mumon is not talking about the monk: he is talking to you and about you. All Zen stories are about you, not other people.

• *Mistake the bell for a jar.* Be especially on your guard when you think you have attained a true understanding.

• *Endeavoring to interpret clearly.* Conceptual interpretation can clarify a subject and therefore is useful. But such interpretation often fails to communicate a real experience of the subject—the direct cognition by the intuitive action of the first nen. My own notes in this book are intended to be amenable to conceptual understanding, which Mumon denounces. You must go beyond my interpretations and explanations and reach the truth yourself.

• *You retard your attainment.* First you must reach pure, direct cognition. Then the conceptual demonstration serves to verify your experience.

• *Don't you know that flame is fire?* Look! Understand it directly!

• *Your rice has long been cooked.* As a child you were in moment after moment's samadhi. Getting older, getting cleverer, you have lost your samadhi. Your rice has grown cold.

Case 8   Keichū the Wheelmaker

Gettan Oshō said, "Keichū, the first wheelmaker, made a cart whose wheels had a hundred spokes. Now, suppose you took a cart and removed both the wheels and the axle. What would you have?"

MUMON'S COMMENT   If anyone can directly master this topic, his eye will be like a shooting star, his spirit like a flash of lightning.

MUMON'S VERSE
  When the spiritual wheels turn,
  Even the master fails to follow them.
  They travel in all directions, above and below,
  North, south, east, and west.

NOTES   *Gettan* was Mumon's great-grandfather in Dharma lineage. Little is known of him except this case and his lineage.

• *Suppose you took a cart and removed both the wheels and the axle.* In this analogy your body is the wheels, your brain the axle. Now suppose you have discarded them both. This is a description of what actually happens in absolute samadhi. Both bodily sensation and mental activity fall away.

• *What would you have?* The answer to this question is *jishu-zammai* (*ji*, self; *shu*, being one's own master; *sammai* [-*zammai*], samadhi). In absolute samadhi, the action of consciousness ceases and absolute stillness reigns throughout the body and mind. But the master of the mind is still aware. Thus, it is different from sleep or lethargy, in which you drift in a condition of blurred activity of consciousness or fall into a comatose state.

• *His eye will be like a shooting star.* This describes your condition as you come out of absolute samadhi and are freed from your deluded condition of mind. You have regained pure consciousness, positive samadhi. "Eye" here represents the quality of cognition of the enlightened consciousness, which penetrates the universe like a shooting star.

• *His spirit like a flash of lightning.* Spirit represents *Zen-ki*, that is, the keen spiritual power (*ki*) of the Zen mind. This is the instantaneous action of a Zen master's mind, his Zen-ki illuminating everything about him as does lightning on a dark night.

• *When the spiritual wheels turn.* The "spiritual wheels" represent the action of the free Zen mind, which knows no restriction.

• *Even the master fails to follow them.* No one can follow his own samadhi, let alone another's.

• *They travel in all directions.* Samadhi transcends time and space. There is no time in an everlasting present. There is no fixed point in boundless space.

Case 9   Daitsū Chishō Buddha

A monk asked Kōyō Seijō, "Daitsū Chishō Buddha sat in zazen for ten *kalpas* and could not attain Buddhahood. He did not become a Buddha. How could this be?" Seijō said, "Your question is quite self-explanatory." The monk asked, "He meditated so long; why could he not attain Buddhahood?" Seijō said, "Because he did not become a Buddha."

MUMON'S COMMENT   I allow the barbarian's realization, but I do not allow his understanding. When an ignorant man realizes it, he is a sage. When a sage understands it, he is ignorant.

MUMON'S VERSE

Better emancipate your mind than your body;
When the mind is emancipated, the body is free,
When both body and mind are emancipated,
Even gods and spirits ignore worldly power.

NOTES   *Kōyō Seijō*. This master's monastic name was Seijō. Kōyō, the name of the place where he lived, was added to his name, a common practice among Zen masters. Little is known of him except the present case and his Dharma lineage.

• *Daitsū Chishō Buddha*. Dai, great; *tsū*, penetration; *chi*, wisdom; *shō*, superb: hence, this name translates as "the Buddha of Great Penetration and Perfect Wisdom."

• *Kalpa*. A kalpa is the period of time, hundreds of thousands of years long, which stretches between the creation and re-creation of a universe. It is divided into four stages: formation, existence, destruction, and annihilation.

• *Sat in zazen for ten kalpas*. In the state of absolute samadhi there is no time. Countless kalpas are just this moment, and this moment fills countless kalpas.

• *Could . . . not attain Buddhahood*. Furthermore, in absolute samadhi there is no realization, no enlightenment, no Buddhahood: just this samadhi.

• *He did not become a Buddha*. Buddha is Buddha from the beginning; there is no becoming a Buddha.

• *Barbarian's realization*. "Barbarian," in this context, has many possible meanings. It may mean anyone: sage, ignoramus, Bodhidharma, Shakyamuni, a foreigner, a fellow countryman. "Realization" means the direct realization and experience of the truth.

• *Understanding*. In the sense of conceptual understanding.

• *Ignorant man*. An unenlightened person.

• *Sage*. An enlightened person.

• *Better emancipate your mind than your body*. Zen asserts that body and mind are one. Conceptually, however, there appear to be two separate entities. In zazen practice it is through training the body and one's breathing that one can pacify the mind. Pacification of the mind is the only true emancipation.

• *When the mind is emancipated, the body is free.* At the same time it can also be said, body and mind being one, that when the body is free the mind is free. This leads to the next two lines.

• *When both body and mind are emancipated, / Even gods and spirits ignore worldly power.* If you achieve the mind-and-body peace of absolute samadhi and then come out into the world of positive samadhi, you will enjoy the freedom of mind of the gods, sages, spirits, and patriarchs, to whom the worldly power of princes is of no interest whatsoever.

Case 10 Seizei Is Utterly Destitute

Seizei said to Sōzan, "Seizei is utterly destitute. Will you give him support?" Sōzan called out, "Seizei!" Seizei responded, "Yes, sir!" Sōzan said, "You have finished three cups of the finest wine in China, and still you say you have not yet moistened your lips!"

MUMON'S COMMENT Seizei pretended to retreat. What was his scheme? Sōzan had the eye of Buddha and saw through his opponent's motive. However, I want to ask you, at what point did Seizei drink wine?

MUMON'S VERSE
  Poverty like Hantan's,
  Mind like Kōu's;
  With no means of livelihood,
  He dares to rival the richest.

NOTES *Seizei.* Little is known of him, but from the context of this story he was clearly a monk of some attainment.

• *Sōzan* (840–901) was an outstanding Zen master who helped his own master, Tōzan, to lay the foundations of the Sōtō Zen sect. The name Sōtō is thought to have come from the combination of the *Sō* of Sōzan and the *Tō* of Tōzan.

• *Seizei is utterly destitute.* He has lost all his "property," that is, his deluded thoughts, self-centered ego, and so on.

• *Sōzan called out, "Seizei!" Seizei responded, "Yes, sir!"* This is an exercise in positive samadhi, calling and responding, the answer coming like an echo to the call:

> The mirrors reflect the lights of the golden palace,
> The hills respond to the note of the moonlit tower's bell.

• *You have finished three cups of the finest wine.* From second to second Seizei is enjoying the fine wine of samadhi; it is complete, finished, in every second, and yet also ever present.

• *You say you have not yet moistened your lips.* Sōzan is saying, "Why do you feign ignorance of what you know perfectly well, the experience of positive samadhi?"

• *Seizei pretended to retreat.* Mumon gives us the explanation. Seizei was subtly challenging Sōzan to Dharma battle, that exchange in which Zen masters and students try their spiritual mettle. Seizei was taking the offensive, but his strategy was to feign retreat by begging obsequiously.

• *Sōzan . . . saw through his opponent's motive.* Sōzan was on the defensive, but his was the defense of the master player, which is also attack.

• *At what point did Seizei drink wine?* When one truly attains to genuine poverty (the Great Death, nothingness) and comes back again to positive samadhi, one understands how the finest wine of Zen tastes.

• *Hantan* was a famous Chinese scholar who was appointed to the high post of governor. He did not take up his post, however, but instead took care of his sickly mother. His contentment with honest poverty and his filial devotion made his name renowned.

• *Kōu* was a great hero in Chinese history. The commander of a large army, he fought the eventual founder of the Han dynasty (206 B.C.–A.D. 220) and won every battle but the last. Surrounded by the enemy's forces, he sat in his tent with his beloved mistress Gu, unmoved by the approach of death, and sang the song which afterward became famous:

> Strength to move mountains,
> Spirit to cover the world,
> Now all is lost;
> Sui, my horse, not yet dead.
> Gu! Oh Gu! What should I do with you?

The point of the reference to Hantan and Kōu is to draw an analogy with the condition of Seizei: poverty (nothing) and the grandeur of the Zen mind.

• *He dares to rival the richest.* There is no need for you to concern yourself about whether Seizei was rich or poor. Look to yourself. Are you so poor that you can rival the richest? "The richest" is a reference to Sōzan.

Case 11   Jōshū Sees the Hermits

Jōshū went to a hermit's cottage and asked, "Is the master in? Is the master in?" The hermit raised his fist. Jōshū said, "The water is too shallow to anchor here," and he went away.

Coming to another hermit's cottage, he asked again, "Is the master in? Is the master in?" This hermit, too, raised his fist. Jōshū said, "Free to give, free to take, free to kill, free to save," and he made a deep bow.

MUMON'S COMMENT   Both raised their fists; why was the one accepted and the other rejected? Tell me, what is the difficulty here? If you can give a turning word to clarify this problem, you will realize that Jōshū's tongue has no bone in it, now helping others up, now knocking them down, with perfect freedom. However, I must remind you: the two hermits could also see through Jōshū. If you say there is anything to choose between the two hermits, you have no eye of realization. If you say there is no choice between the two, you have no eye of realization.

MUMON'S VERSE
   The eye like a shooting star,
   The spirit like lightning;
   A death-dealing blade,
   A life-giving sword.

NOTES   *Hermit.* Zen students often used to live in small hermitages in some isolated place.

• *Is the master in?* The "master" in this context is the master of the mind. This is *shōnen* (*shō*, undeluded, mindful; *nen*, nen-thought). So a constant state of mindfulness is the condition of "master of the mind." It is in this sense that Jōshū asks, "Is the master in?" or, "Is there a constant state of mindfulness?"

• *The hermit raised his fist.* He raised his fist to demonstrate constant mindfulness.

• *The water is too shallow.* Practice in zazen must be a matter of ceaseless improvement. Speaking from the point of view of possible improvement, one's condition always remains shallow. The recognition of one's shallowness is important in zazen practice.

• *Free to give, free to take, free to kill, free to save.* He is free in every way because he is in a state of constant mindfulness, which is the only true freedom.

• *Why was the one accepted and the other rejected?* Since there is always room for improvement, no one is yet satisfactory in his attainment. At the same time, judging on merit, one may be admirable.

• *A turning word.* See the notes to Case 2.

• *Jōshū's tongue has no bone in it.* His tongue is unfettered by any intellectual rigidity. He is in complete command. He knows Zen fully.

• *The two hermits could also see through Jōshū.* Whether or not Jōshū praised or blamed them justifiably did not affect the two hermits; they were well aware of Jōshū's devious methods.

• *Anything to choose.* Every person stands upon his own two feet and is worthy of respect.

• *No choice.* Advancement in Zen practice never comes to an end; there are endless steps, phases, and grades in achievement, even among the most outstanding Zen masters.

• *The eye like a shooting star.* As an accomplished Zen master, Jōshū's eye works like a shooting star. A blink and you miss it . . .

• *The spirit like lightning.* . . . a moment off guard and you find you have been knocked down.

• *A death-dealing blade, / A life-giving sword.* In Case 5, Isan dealt Kyōgen a seemingly death-dealing blow, but it proved eventually to be a life-giving action. So too Jōshū, though appearing to reject, is nevertheless always constructive.

Case 12   Zuigan Calls His Master

Zuigan Gen Oshō called to himself every day, "Master!" and answered, "Yes, sir!" Then he would say, "Be wide awake!" and answer, "Yes, sir!" "Henceforward, never be deceived by others!" "No, I won't!"

MUMON'S COMMENT   Old Zuigan buys and sells himself. He takes out a lot of god-masks and devil-masks and puts them on and plays with them. What for, eh? One calling and the other answering; one wide awake, the other saying he will never be deceived. If you stick to any of them, you will be a failure. If you imitate Zuigan, you will play the fox.

MUMON'S VERSE
  Clinging to the deluded way of consciousness,
  Students of the Way do not realize truth.
  The seed of birth and death through endless eons:
  The fool calls it the true original self.

NOTES   *Zuigan.* The dates of his birth and death are not known. Since he was the disciple of Gantō, who died in 887 at the age of sixty, and since he studied with Kassan (805–80), he must have been a somewhat younger contemporary of theirs.
  • *Master.* The master of his own mind.
  • *Be wide awake.* Be constantly in the state of jishu-zammai. (See the notes to Case 8.)
  • *Never be deceived.* The Chinese character for "deceive" can also be translated as "delude," thus, "Never be deluded."
  • *By others.* Who are the others? In the end it is only our own delusions that delude us.
  • *No, I won't.* The following story suggests that as a young man Zuigan had had a bitter experience. When he was still a monk undergoing training, he had an interview with Kassan, who asked him, "Where are you from?" "From Lying Dragon Mountain," answered Zuigan. Lying Dragon Mountain was where his former teacher, Gantō, lived. "Did the

dragon rise up when you left there?" Zuigan in answer looked about him. Kassan then said, "You apply a burning moxa cure to skin which is already burned." (Moxa is a dried and refined herb which is burned at various points on the body as a cure for certain conditions and ailments.) "What's the use of your undergoing such torture?" Zuigan replied. Kassan said nothing. Perhaps Zuigan thought Kassan was not a strong enough opponent for him and that he was winning this Dharma battle. He continued to press Kassan, saying, "Thusness is easy to deal with, not-thusness is difficult to deal with. If you are in a state of thusness, you are wide awake. If you are in not-thusness, you are in emptiness. Are you in thusness or in not-thusness, say quickly!" "Today," replied Kassan, "you have made a fool of me."

Zuigan must have felt triumphant. In later years, however, he must have remembered this dialogue and said to himself. "Was it not I, after all, that was made a fool of? In those days I was too green to appreciate Kassan's maturity." This must have been a bitter recollection for Zuigan. The word for "deceive," which Zuigan used to call to himself, is almost interchangeable with a virtually identical Chinese word meaning "make a fool of," the word Kassan used. So Zuigan's "Never be deceived" can also be translated as "Never let yourself be made a fool of." With this explanation Zuigan's reply to himself, "No, I won't!" gains weight.

• *Old Zuigan buys and sells himself.* Introspective people buy and sell themselves so much of the time. But their buying and selling is not the same as Zuigan's. Zuigan was always at one with the master of his mind.

• *God-masks and devil-masks.* One nen-thought asks and another nen-thought answers. Then the next nen calls and the following nen responds. Such nen-actions are here called god-masks and devil-masks. "God" and "devil" have no particular meaning; one might also say "this mask" and "that mask."

• *If you stick to any of them.* You have, in truth, no constant self which you can stick to. When self appears, it appears; when it has gone, it has gone. All things are in perpetual motion and flow, but in sticking to your concept of ego and thinking of it as a constant entity, delusions appear.

• *If you imitate Zuigan.* If you act from the bottom of your mind as Zuigan did, then it is your own action and there is no imitation.

• *Clinging to the deluded way of consciousness.* Consciousness by its very nature is impermanent, but consciousness builds up and believes in a permanent ego. Dependence on that ego is the source of all delusions.

• *Do not realize truth.* As long as you adhere to your notions of ego you can never realize the truth.

• *The seed of birth and death.* Belief in the ego is the origin of suffering.

• *The fool calls it the true original self.* The deluded action of consciousness makes you believe in the permanency of your self-constructed ego and think of it as your original self.

Case 13　Tokusan Holds His Bowls

One day Tokusan went down toward the dining room, holding his bowls. Seppō met him and asked, "Where are you off to with your bowls? The bell has not rung, and the drum has not sounded." Tokusan turned and went back to his room. Seppō mentioned this to Gantō, who remarked, "Tokusan is renowned, but he does not know the last word." Tokusan heard about this remark and sent his attendant to fetch Gantō. "You do not approve of me?" he asked. Gantō whispered his meaning.

Tokusan said nothing at the time, but the next day he ascended the rostrum, and behold! he was very different from usual! Gantō, going toward the front of the hall, clapped his hands and laughed loudly, saying, "Congratulations! Our old man has got hold of the last word! From now on, nobody in this whole country can outdo him!"

MUMON'S COMMENT　As for the last word, neither Gantō nor Tokusan has ever dreamed of it! When you look into the matter, you find they are like puppets on the shelf!

MUMON'S VERSE
　If you realize the first,
　You master the last.

The first and the last
Are not one word.

NOTES *Tokusan* (780–865) was two years younger than Jōshū. At first
he made a special study of the *Diamond Sutra* and himself wrote a commentary on it. But when he came to study under Ryūtan he gave up his
scholarship to study Zen. His experience of realization under Ryūtan
forms the subject of Case 28. He was famous for using his stick, saying,
"Thirty blows if you speak, thirty blows if you don't." He was a hero
in Zen circles in his day. In his later years he displayed a mellow maturity, as shown in the present case.

• *Seppō* (822–908) was a persistent and painstaking man. He spared no
effort in his study of Zen. He volunteered to work in the kitchen and did
not mind hard labor. He was six years older than Gantō, but enlightenment came to him later than to Gantō.

Once the two of them, traveling together, were overtaken by a snow-
storm and forced to spend a few days at a wayside inn. Seppō as usual sat
assiduously in zazen. Gantō asked Seppō about his understanding. Seppō
answered that he had not yet attained peace of mind. Gantō said, "I
thought you had already attained such an understanding, but since you
say otherwise, let me ask you this: What use is there in learning from
other people's lectures and from the sutras? It is what you produce from
the bottom of your mind that moves heaven and earth." At this Seppō
suddenly became enlightened. His was a great talent but slow to mature.
In his later years he taught his own students with great conscientiousness,
and is said to have had over fifteen hundred monks in his assembly, the
reward of his painstaking labor throughout his life. He appears in five
cases in *Hekiganroku*.

• *Gantō* (828–87) was known for his sharpness and sagacity. When
Tokusan died, Gantō was thirty-seven years old. Two years later, accompanied by Seppō and Kinzan, he set out on a journey to visit Rinzai.
Hearing of Rinzai's death while they were traveling, they decided to
separate, each going his own way. At first Gantō lived by himself, but
many monks were attracted to him and he became the master of a large
temple. He was finally killed by looters who plundered his temple and,
finding Gantō alone doing zazen, all the other monks having fled, mur-
dered him. As he was killed he gave a great shout, which is said to have

resounded for ten Chinese leagues. This shout proved a great problem to monks in later years, including Hakuin Zenji (1685–1768), who could not understand its meaning. The problem was solved for Hakuin at the moment of his enlightenment, and he cried out, "Oh! Gantō is still alive, strong and healthy." For further details on Gantō see the notes to *Hekiganroku*, Case 66.

• *Tokusan went down toward the dining room.* The *Record of the Transmission of the Lamp* has the story like this: "Seppō was in charge of the kitchen. One day dinner was delayed. Tokusan went down toward the dining room carrying his eating bowls. Seppō, seeing Tokusan, said, 'The bell has not rung, the drum has not yet sounded, where are you going?' Tokusan turned around and went back to his room."

Tōzan categorized the states of enlightened consciousness in five ranks. The first rank (the apparent within the real) represents absolute samadhi. The second rank (the real within the apparent) represents positive samadhi. The third rank (coming from within the real) stands for the combination of both absolute and positive samadhi. The fourth rank (arrival at mutual integration) is the cleansed and shining activity of consciousness. The fifth rank (unity attained) stands for the mellow maturity of consciousness. In the present case Tokusan is in this fifth rank. Each rank is independent. None can be said to be superior or inferior. There is, however, a sequential order in their development. (For further discussion of Tōzan's five ranks see the notes to *Hekiganroku*, Case 61, and *Zen Training*, chapter 17.)

• *Seppō met him and asked.* He was challenging Tokusan to a Dharma battle.

• *Tokusan turned and went back to his room.* This was Tokusan's answer. He was not saying, "I cannot answer your question." He simply returned to his room.

• *Seppō mentioned this to Gantō.* Thinking, no doubt, that he had been victorious.

• *Gantō . . . remarked.* Gantō seemed to be speaking against Tokusan, but in reality he was setting a trap for Seppō.

• *The last word.* There are four wisdoms: Great Perfect Mirror Wisdom, Universal Nature Wisdom, Marvelous Observing Wisdom, and Perfecting of Action Wisdom. When you first attain realization, the first, Great Perfect Mirror Wisdom, appears. This is the fundamental wisdom. Usually, however, this wisdom is still dim. As you make progress, polishing the other three wisdoms, this Great Perfect Mirror Wisdom becomes ever more brilliant. That final state of great brilliance is the ultimate fulfillment of subtle enlightenment. Of course, it scarcely needs to be said that these wisdoms are simply names for aspects of actual experience. There are gradations in the development of these wisdoms, from which comes the idea of first and last.

• *Gantō whispered.* What intrigue was Gantō plotting with Tokusan?

• *Our old man has got hold of the last word.* As is so often the case in Zen stories, this remark is not what it seems. Gantō is not making a judgment but asking a question. He is saying to the other monks, and to Seppō in particular (for it was he who prompted Gantō to arrange this little episode with Tokusan), "Have you got hold of the last word?" That is the only important thing as far as you are concerned.

• *Neither Gantō nor Tokusan has ever dreamed of it.* Mumon is speaking of neither Gantō nor Tokusan but to his disciples and to you, telling them and you to attain a true understanding.

• *They are like puppets on the shelf.* Gantō and Tokusan were both acting out a little drama.

• *If you realize the first, / You master the last.* Shakyamuni Buddha enjoyed the beautiful landscape from the top of the hill. You may also see the same landscape from halfway up the hill, a view glimpsed through the shrubs and trees. Yours may be only a partial view, but it is true to say that you have seen the same landscape that the Buddha saw . . .

• *The first and the last / Are not one word.* . . . and yet it is also true that though the landscape is the same, the views of it enjoyed by you and by the Buddha are not the same.

Case 14   Nansen Cuts the Cat in Two

Nansen Oshō saw monks of the Eastern and Western halls quarreling over a cat. He held up the cat and said, "If you can give an answer, you will save the cat. If not, I will kill it." No one could answer, and Nansen cut the cat in two.

That evening Jōshū returned, and Nansen told him of the incident.

Jōshū took off his sandal, placed it on his head, and walked out. "If you had been there, you would have saved the cat," Nansen remarked.

MUMON'S COMMENT   Tell me, what did Jōshū mean when he put the sandal on his head? If you can give a turning word on this, you will see that Nansen's decree was carried out with good reason. If not, "Danger!"

MUMON'S VERSE
   Had Jōshū been there,
   He would have done the opposite;
   When the sword is snatched away,
   Even Nansen begs for his life.

NOTES   *Nansen* (748–834) was an outstanding Zen master. He was a disciple of Baso and the teacher of Jōshū. Nansen's words and actions, like Jōshū's, are full of originality. We find in them an inexhaustible fountain of Zen spirit. Nansen appears in three other cases in *Mumonkan* and in six cases in *Hekiganroku*. The present case appears in *Hekiganroku* as two cases, 63 and 64.
   • *The Eastern and Western halls.* In a monastery there were two groups of monks: those who looked after the daily administration and running of the monastery and those of the meditation group. The arrangement of monastery buildings in Nansen's day is not well known, but perhaps the two groups of monks lived in separate halls. Periodically the monks moved from one group to the other, changing their activities. When people are divided into groups in this way, a partisan spirit often asserts itself and quarrels arise between members of the different groups.
   • *Quarreling over a cat.* What they were quarreling about is not known and is unimportant. The point is that they were quarreling, and in this instance the object of the quarrel is personified by a cat. At the bottom of all disputes, egocentric thinking is invariably present. Even though there seems to be no egotism, and one may suppose oneself to be acting objectively, differences of temperament, ideals, understanding, and background inevitably bring about subjective—that is, self-centered—

thinking. How is the dispute to be settled? Kill the cat. But what is the cat?

• *If you can give an answer.* How will you answer? Can you say, "Don't worry, the cat is already cut in two; there is no need to use the knife; give it to me"? Dōgen Zenji (1200–1253) says of this case, "If I were Nansen I should say, 'If you answer, I will kill it; if you don't answer, I will kill it.' If I were the monks I should say, 'We cannot answer; please cut the cat in two.' Or I should say, 'The master knows how to cut it into two pieces, but he does not know how to cut it into one piece.'" And again Dōgen says, "If I were Nansen and the monks could find no answer, I should say, 'You could not answer,' and put down the cat."

• *No one could answer.* People are not awakened until they have gone through disastrous experiences, as we did in the World Wars.

• *Nansen cut the cat in two.* What kind of cutting did Nansen perform? With a threatening expression, brandishing his knife, he was killing the cat. He is always in samadhi. When killing, he is really killing; when releasing, he is really releasing. However, at the last moment, as Dōgen says, he must have put down the cat.

• *Jōshū took off his sandal, placed it on his head, and walked out.* What did Jōshū mean? Was he saying that he was no longer concerned with battling against self-centered thinking? Jōshū very simply took off his sandal, put it on his head, and went away. The whole action was performed as smoothly and as naturally as water running in a stream. A certain thought must have been in Jōshū's mind, but it was a thought that came prior to reasoning, that is, an intuitive action. Jōshū was famous for his so-called lip-and-tongue Zen, in which he expressed the most profound meaning of Zen in the simplest daily language. "The oak tree in the garden" was his answer to the question, "What is the meaning of Bodhidharma's coming to China?" (Case 37). This oak tree was the direct translation into words of his prereasoning thought. In the present case, Jōshū translated his intuitive thought into his action of taking his sandal off and so on. If we were to paraphrase it, we might say: When I was studying Zen there were many difficult and serious problems, but now that I have forgotten Zen, everything has become upside down.

• *If you had been there, you would have saved the cat.* Had Jōshū been there, he would have said a word that would have made Nansen drop his knife.

• *Nansen's decree.* To understand Nansen's decree you must formulate one of your own. What is your decree? Zen stories are always to be taken as your own stories.

• *Good reason.* You must do what you have to do purposefully, otherwise you will invite disaster.

• *Danger!* Can you say you are not in danger?

• *He would have done the opposite.* Can you snatch the sword away from Nansen?

• *When the sword is snatched away, | Even Nansen begs for his life.* If you can give an answer to Nansen strong enough to make him drop the sword, then he will be delighted to surrender.

Case 15   Tōzan's Sixty Blows

Tōzan came to study with Ummon. Ummon asked, "Where are you from?" "From Sato," Tōzan replied. "Where were you during the summer?" "Well, I was at the monastery of Hōzu, south of the lake." "When did you leave there?" Ummon asked. "On August 25" was Tōzan's reply. "I spare you sixty blows," Ummon said.

The next day Tōzan came to Ummon and said, "Yesterday you said you spared me sixty blows. I beg to ask you, where was I at fault?" "Oh, you rice bag!" shouted Ummon. "What makes you wander about, now west of the river, now south of the lake?" Tōzan thereupon came to a mighty enlightenment experience.

MUMON'S COMMENT   If Ummon had given Tōzan the true food of Zen and encouraged him to develop an active Zen spirit, his school would not have declined as it did. Tōzan had an agonizing struggle through the whole night, lost in the sea of right and wrong. He reached a complete impasse. After waiting for the dawn, he again went to Ummon, and Ummon again made him a picture book of Zen. Even though he was directly enlightened, Tōzan could not be called brilliant.

Now, I want to ask you, should Tōzan have been given sixty blows or not? If you say yes, you admit that all the universe should be beaten. If you say no, then you accuse Ummon of telling a lie. If you really understand the secret, you will be able to breathe out Zen spirit with the very mouth of Tōzan.

MUMON'S VERSE
The lion had a secret to puzzle his cub;
The cub crouched, leaped, and dashed forward.
The second time, a casual move led to checkmate.
The first arrow was light, but the second went deep.

NOTES   *Tōzan* (910–90). This is not Tōzan Ryōkai, the founder of the Sōtō branch of Zen, but Tōzan Shusho, who also appears in Case 18. He was born in the province of Shensi in northern China and traveled the vast distance from there down to Kwangtung to study under Ummon. He must have experienced indescribable hardships, for there was no method of travel other than by foot. Although a Chinese adage of the time declared, "Blessed are a thousand days at home, cursed is one day of traveling," it was a characteristic of Zen monks that they roamed the length and breadth of China seeking masters under whom they could study.

• *Ummon* (d. 949) was the founder of one of the five major schools of the Zen sect. His sayings have always been greatly admired for their depth of meaning. He appears five times in *Mumonkan* and eighteen times in *Hekiganroku*. His style of teaching was called "scarlet banners sparkle," and he was given the nickname Ummon the Emperor, while Rinzai was called the General and Sōtō (Sōzan and Tōzan) was called the Peasant (because of the steady and simple method of practice). Ummon was master to over forty outstanding Zen students, Tōzan of the present case being one of the four most distinguished. Ummon's Zen school became extinct two hundred years after his death, but his words and his great spirit have continued to inspire and instruct Zen students down to the present day.

• *Where are you from?* When a newcomer presented himself before a teacher he was usually asked this question. The question can be understood in a number of ways: What is your true origin, identity, experience, former teacher, monastery, and so on? The student's response revealed his condition to the master's keen eye. Monks who knew something of Zen were sometimes inventive in their answers: some affected, some simple, some counterattacking to test the master, each according to his level of attainment.

• *From Sato.* Nothing is known of Sato, but one can understand from the context that it was the name of a place. The Chinese character *sa* means a raft, and *to* means a ferry. Sato could have been a ferry that Tōzan had crossed a few hours before. If so, and if Tōzan was intentionally using a simple geographical term, then he was a tricky customer for Ummon to deal with.

• *Where were you during the summer?* Ummon tests Tōzan with another question. This time Tōzan must reveal something. The question here relates to the ninety-day summer session of a monastery: that is, at which monastery did you spend the summer session?

• *I was at the monastery of Hōzu.* This answer and Tōzan's manner betrayed that he was a novice. Some say that at this point Tōzan should have introduced a new topic, while others argue that there was nothing wrong in an honest answer. Ummon, however, was quick in every way. He was like a tiger scenting his prey.

• *When did you leave there?* Ummon was preparing his stick to give a blow.

• *On August 25.* Tōzan was just too simple-minded.

• *I spare you sixty blows.* For Tōzan this was more humiliating than the blows themselves would have been. A novice with a proper attitude toward his teacher is always powerfully affected by his words.

• *The next day Tōzan came to Ummon.* All night Tōzan had tossed and turned sleeplessly, trying to work out where he had gone wrong. He could find no answer to his rigorous self-searching and came to Ummon in a desperate state of mind. This is the condition that the skillful Zen master brings about by timely beating or harsh words. When the student has been brought to this extreme an explosion occurs, just as a ripe pea pod bursts open at the touch of a finger.

• *Oh, you rice bag!* A greedy good-for-nothing who cares more for worldly pleasures than for his great task.

• *What makes you wander about . . . ?* Ummon is saying, "What use is there in wandering about, now listening to Master Wang of West-of-the River, now to Master Chang of South-of-the Lake? What you are seeking you already possess. Why don't you bring it up out of the bottom of your heart and mind?"

• *Tōzan . . . came to a mighty enlightenment.* The deeper the devotion, the greater, when it comes, is the realization.

• *If Ummon had given Tōzan the true food of Zen.* Mumon is not talking of Ummon and Tōzan; he is talking to his own students, to you. He is saying, "If you are alert enough to benefit from this story which so clearly offers you the true food of Zen . . .

• *Develop an active Zen spirit.* . . . and you are sufficiently awakened to develop an active Zen spirit . . .

• *His school would not have declined.* . . . then you will be free from the ups and downs of life." In fact, Ummon's school did decline, and it died out within two hundred years because capable successors did not follow him. Rinzai was fortunate to have competent students coming after him. Will you not number yourself among them?

• *Tōzan had an agonizing struggle.* You must undergo an agonizing struggle in your study of Zen.

• *Made him a picture book of Zen.* You must be able to grasp Zen before being given a picture book of it.

• *Tōzan could not be called brilliant.* Mumon is asking you to be brilliant.

• *Should Tōzan have been given sixty blows?* Like Ummon, Mumon is taking the opportunity to lay a trap for you.

• *Breathe out Zen spirit with the very mouth of Tōzan.* "You will . . . go hand in hand with the successive patriarchs, entangling your eyebrows with theirs, seeing with the same eyes, hearing with the same ears," and breathing, too, with the same mouth (see Case 1).

• *The lion had a secret to puzzle his cub.* Tradition has it that a lion throws its cubs from the top of a precipice and takes the trouble to look after only those who manage to clamber back up the cliff. As training, too, the lion sets puzzles for its cubs, forcing them to be alert. This was also the technique of the old Zen masters, who forced their students into a dilemma. Mumon's comment, full as it is of illogicalities, is a good example of this method.

- *The second time, a casual move led to checkmate.* Ummon's second move seemed heedlessly made, but it was in fact strong and decisive.
- *The first arrow was light, but the second went deep.* In point of fact both arrows were effective.

Case 16   When the Bell Sounds

Ummon said, "The world is vast and wide. Why do you put on your seven-piece robe at the sound of the bell?"

MUMON'S COMMENT   In studying Zen, you should not be swayed by sounds and forms. Even though you attain insight when hearing a voice or seeing a form, this is simply the ordinary way of things. Don't you know that the real Zen student commands sounds, controls forms, is clear-sighted at every event and free on every occasion?

Granted you are free, just tell me: Does the sound come to the ear or does the ear go to the sound? If both sound and silence die away, at such a juncture how could you talk of Zen? While listening with your ear, you cannot tell. When hearing with your eye, you are truly intimate.

MUMON'S VERSE
With realization, things make one family;
Without realization, things are separated in a thousand ways.
Without realization, things make one family;
With realization, things are separated in a thousand ways.

NOTES   *The world is vast and wide. Why do you put on your seven-piece robe at the sound of the bell?* The four Dharmadhatu of the Kegon doctrine are the realm of the absolute, the realm of the relative, phenomenal world, the realm of the unhindered mutual interpenetration of these two, and the realm of the unhindered mutual interpenetration of phenomena. For convenience we may call these the first, second, third, and fourth categories. To demonstrate this doctrine Hōzō once set up in the center of a hall a Buddha image illumined by a lantern and arranged around it ten mirrors all facing each other. Each mirror was then seen to reflect not only the central image but also the reflection in each of the other mirrors and the reflections of the reflections.*

The world that is vast and wide corresponds to the realm of the absolute, where perfect freedom reigns over everything. But at the sound of the monastery bell you obediently put on your robe. Are you not therefore restrained? This is Ummon's question.

In everyday life we are in the world in which individual beings co-exist, and there, of necessity, the problem of liberty and restraint arises. An enlightened man also lives in this world of liberty and restriction, but he lives in the third category as far as his pure being is concerned and in the fourth category in his relations with other beings, that is, in the realm of mutual interpenetration of liberty and restriction. So when he puts on his robe at the sound of the bell, he is indeed restricted; but since he is also acting in positive samadhi, he is also perfectly free. Who would not say, with Huxley, "Let me be wound up every day like a watch to go right faithfully and I ask no better freedom"?

• *You should not be swayed by sounds and forms.* Sounds and forms represent outward circumstances. If you want to enjoy absolute freedom of mind, you should not be controlled by circumstances.

• *Even though you attain insight when hearing a voice or seeing a form.* Even if you attain kenshō by hearing a sound, just as Kyōgen did when he heard the sound of a pebble striking bamboo, or as Shakyamuni did when he saw the morning star, it is only a common occurrence. Mumon is emphasizing that the attainment of kenshō is only the beginning of zazen practice.

• *The real Zen student commands sounds, controls forms.* The Zen student controls circumstances, not in the worldly meaning but in the spiritual.

• *Clear-sighted at every event and free on every occasion.* His insight penetrates every event, and he enjoys freedom at all times.

• *Does the sound come to the ear or does the ear go to the sound?* Neither comes and neither goes. Pure cognition brings about interpenetration of subjectivity and objectivity.

*See Miura and Sasaki, *Zen Dust*, p. 181.

• *Sound and silence die away.* In pure cognition, objectivity (sound) and subjectivity (silence) are forgotten.

• *Listening with your ear.* In positive samadhi, you forget your listening while you are hearing.

• *When hearing with your eye.* In positive samadhi, all experiences of sensation and all mental activities are concentrated into one act of pure cognition. That is to say, mutual interpenetration of hearing, viewing, touching, smelling, and tasting is realized.

• *With realization, things make one family.* When you attain realization, universal oneness is understood. This line corresponds to the first category of the Kegon doctrine.

• *Without realization, things are separated in a thousand ways.* When you have not yet attained realization, the world appears separated in a thousand ways. However, from the viewpoint of the enlightened eye, this line corresponds to the second category of the Kegon doctrine.

• *Without realization, things make one family.* While you stick to your realization, you are under the sway of your own realization. You must outgrow your realization. When you are mature, you become forgetful even of your realization. That is true enlightenment. This "without realization" means such an enlightenment, in which things make one family. This line corresponds to the third category of the Kegon doctrine.

• *With realization, things are separated in a thousand ways.* With a realization like that described in the third line, things, in truth, are separated in a thousand ways at the same time that they are unified in a universal oneness. There is a Zen saying that unity without differentiation is a false unity. Things are separated, but they are in unhindered mutual interpenetration. Their individuality is preserved, and at the same time they are unified. This line corresponds to the fourth category of the Kegon doctrine.

Case 17   Chū the National
Teacher Gives Three Calls

The National Teacher called his attendant three times, and three times the attendant responded. The National Teacher said, "I long feared that I was betraying you, but really it was you who were betraying me."

MUMON'S COMMENT   The National Teacher called three times, and his tongue fell to the ground. The attendant responded three times, and he gave his answer with brilliance. The National Teacher was old and lonely; he held the cow's head and forced it to eat grass. The attendant would have none of it; delicious food has little attraction for a man who is satiated.

Tell me, at what point was the betrayal? When the country is flourishing, talent is prized. When the home is wealthy, the children are proud.

MUMON'S VERSE
He carried an iron yoke with no hole
And left a curse to trouble his descendants.
If you want to hold up the gate and the doors,
You must climb a mountain of swords with bare feet.

NOTES   *Chū the National Teacher.* Echū (d. 775) was generally called Chū the National Teacher, or Chū Kokushi. It is not known when he was born, but he seems to have lived for more than a hundred years, dying in 775. He was given the Seal of the Transmission of the Dharma by his teacher, the Sixth Patriarch, Enō. At first he lived in his temple on Mount Hakugai, which he did not leave for forty years. But his fame had long been known to the imperial court, and the emperor invited him three times to come and teach there. At length he was prevailed upon, and it is said that on his arrival at the palace the emperor came out to meet him and with his own hands grasped the shaft of his carriage and helped pull it along. He was teacher to the emperor for the rest of his life. The title National Teacher (Kokushi) has been given to many Buddhist teachers, but Echū was the first to be accorded this honor, and he was so highly regarded in this respect that a reference to "Kokushi," without qualification, is taken as applying to him. He appears in three cases in *Hekiganroku*.

• *The National Teacher called his attendant three times, and three times the attendant responded.* The National Teacher wanted to transmit the Lamp of the Dharma, and he had marked out his attendant as his successor. This calling was by way of a final test. The attendant's name was Ōshin. "Ōshin," called the teacher. "Yes, sir!" the attendant responded, and kneeling at the doorway of his master's room, he made obeisance. "Oh, you are here. All right, go back to your room." No sooner had the attendant returned to his room than the master called again, "Ōshin!" "Yes, sir!" Once more the attendant came to the teacher's room, knelt, and bowed. As before, the master merely told him to return to his room. Immediately, however, the teacher called again, "Ōshin!" For the third time the attendant came, knelt, and bowed. At this the teacher said to him, "I long feared that I was betraying you, but really it was you who were betraying me."

What does all this calling and coming and going mean? Calling and responding: nothing comes between. Pure cognition is effected. Between husband and wife, boss and secretary, every day and everywhere the calling and responding is carried on, and people are not aware of the secret of cognition. When you once experience samadhi, you will understand it. Look at the oak tree or anything else in the garden, and, if you have trained yourself in entering samadhi, you can immediately achieve pure cognition of the tree: that is positive samadhi. Listening to a sound is just the same. Ōshin heard the teacher's calling and answered with the responding samadhi. The second time and the third time he did not change. Suppose you called a waiter at a restaurant and repeated the same nonsense three times: what do you think would happen?

• *I long feared that I was betraying you.* I had long feared that because of my poor instruction, you were not making good progress in zazen practice.

• *But really it was you who were betraying me.* But in truth, you were betraying me. In the original, the characters for "betraying" are read *kofu*. *Ko* means to sin, and *fu* means to rebel against. The meaning of *kofu*, therefore, is to act against the teacher's instruction. But the National Teacher is here using the word as the certification of Ōshin's passing the last test. In Zen the disciple is expected to progress further than the teacher. The National Teacher once answered the emperor's question, "What is the Buddha?" by saying, "You should go trampling on Vairocana's head." (Vairocana is the Dharmakaya Buddha. See the notes to *Hekiganroku*, Case 39.) A Zen proverb says, "When your view is the same as your teacher's, you destroy half your teacher's merit; when your view surpasses your teacher's, you are worthy to succeed him." In this case Ōshin was quietly enjoying his leisure time in the arbor, without troubling himself about his teacher, who was so busily occupied with beating about the bush. That was "betraying" his teacher.

• *His tongue fell to the ground.* To call three times was to behave like a fussy old grandmother. His tongue must have rotted from talking so much and fallen to the ground.

• *The attendant responded three times . . . with brilliance.* Every time, he answered brilliantly.

• *The National Teacher was old and lonely.* Growing old, the National Teacher was worried about finding a competent disciple to whom he could hand on the Lamp of the Dharma.

• *He held the cow's head and forced it to eat grass.* He resorted to the cramming system of education. This refers to the three callings.

• *The attendant would have none of it; delicious food has little attraction for a man who is satiated.* Ōshin had already eaten his fill.

• *At what point was the betrayal?* Ōshin had trampled on the teacher's head.

• *When the country is flourishing, talent is prized.* Echū's kingdom of Zen was pure and flourishing, and excellent disciples appeared.

• *When the home is wealthy, the children are proud.* Echū's household was wealthy, and the children did not care for petty presents.

• *He carried an iron yoke with no hole.* He had the responsibility of handing on the lamp to the next generation. The yoke corresponds to the responsibility. The yoke is, more precisely, a cangue which, in ancient China, was locked around a criminal's neck; it had a hole in the middle for the head. But this yoke has no hole and is made of iron—a stubborn and unwieldy thing. The unwieldiness refers to the heavy responsibility of the transmission.

• *And left a curse to trouble his descendants.* In Case 41, Mumon has a verse which speaks of Bodhidharma:

> Coming east, directly pointing,
> You entrusted the Dharma, and trouble arose;
> The clamor of the monasteries
> Is all because of you.

• *If you want to hold up the gate and the doors.* If you want to support the Buddha's teachings . . .
• *You must climb a mountain of swords with bare feet.* . . . you must be determined to bear infinite hardship.

Case 18 Tōzan's "Masagin"

A monk asked Tōzan, "What is Buddha?" Tōzan replied, "Masagin!" [three pounds of flax].

MUMON'S COMMENT Old Tōzan attained the poor Zen of a clam. He opened the two halves of the shell a little and exposed all the liver and intestines inside. But tell me, how do you see Tōzan?

MUMON'S VERSE
  "Three pounds of flax" came sweeping along;
  Close were the words, but closer was the meaning.
  Those who argue about right and wrong
  Are those enslaved by right and wrong.

NOTES *Tōzan.* This is the Tōzan who appears in Case 15, Tōzan Shusho. He was enlightened by Ummon's shout of "Rice bag!" which can be seen, therefore, as the real origin of his own cry, "Masagin!" (*ma*, flax;

sa, three; *gin*, pound). This case also appears in *Hekiganroku* as Case 12.

You may have enjoyed entering positive samadhi when you become one with a sound or an object. But the problem is how to enter such a state of samadhi independently of external circumstances. "Masagin" is the appreciation of the moment of asking and responding with nothing coming between. The apparently meaningless word "masagin" suddenly appears and pierces you through. It is immaterial what the actual, historical circumstances of the case are: whether Tōzan was weighing flax, seeing others doing it, or just remembering a certain occasion. In answer to the question, the "masagin" intuitively sprang up in him and came bursting forth. "Masagin" was just a projection of Tōzan's mind.

• *The poor Zen of a clam.* "Poor" here of course means rich.

• *Exposed all the liver and intestines.* Tōzan revealed his whole substance.

• *How do you see Tōzan?* The original text says, "Where do you see Tōzan?" This means that he exposes himself so clearly, but you cannot see him. He is nowhere. Now, how do you find him and identify him? A guardian deity once wanted to see the other Tōzan—Tōzan Ryōkai, founder of the Sōtō sect. In order to make Tōzan visible to him, the deity laid a trap by strewing rice and wheat in the monastery courtyard. Tōzan, finding the rice and wheat, said to himself, "Who could be so careless as to do such a wasteful thing?" In that moment Tōzan became visible to the watching deity. Perhaps Mumon was remembering this story when he asked, "How do you see Tōzan?"

• *Close were the words, but closer was the meaning.* The words and the meaning are intimately combined. When you grasp the meaning, "masagin" and you are indivisibly one.

• *Those who argue about right and wrong.* Many people argue about this case, or about other things, using conceptual understanding. This is because they have no direct experience. In understanding based on direct experience, however, there is no right or wrong, no good or evil. When spring comes, spring comes; when winter is gone, winter is gone.

• *Enslaved by right and wrong.* While you remain attached to notions of right and wrong, you stand caught in the world of good and evil. But everything is all right to an enlightened person. Hell or heaven: he doesn't mind which he goes to.

Case 19 Nansen's "Ordinary Mind Is the Way"

Jōshū asked Nansen, "What is the Way?" "Ordinary mind is the Way," Nansen replied. "Shall I try to seek after it?" Jōshū asked. "If you try for it, you will become separated from it," responded Nansen. "How can I know the Way unless I try for it?" persisted Jōshū. Nansen said, "The Way is not a matter of knowing or not knowing. Knowing is delusion; not knowing is confusion. When you have really reached the true Way beyond doubt, you will find it as vast and boundless as outer space. How can it be talked about on the level of right and wrong?" With these words, Jōshū came to a sudden realization.

MUMON'S COMMENT Nansen dissolved and melted away before Jōshū's questions, and could not offer a plausible explanation. Even though Jōshū comes to a realization, he must delve into it for another thirty years before he can fully understand it.

MUMON'S VERSE
  The spring flowers, the autumn moon;
  Summer breezes, winter snow.
  If useless things do not clutter your mind,
  You have the best days of your life.

NOTES *What is the Way?* There may be the way of the universe; the way of the progress of individuals; the way of the progress of human society, of civilization, of culture, of economic, sexual, and human relations; and the way of peace of mind. But they are all interrelated. When one experiences kenshō, one understands the way of the universe, the Dharma, and all. The progress, or evolution, of the human race has led to consciousness, which gave being its own eye to look into itself and realize its own nature. The progress of human society, of civilization and culture, of economic, sexual, and human relations are topics which require the combined efforts of scientists, philosophers, thinkers, and practical minds. However, the question asked by Jōshū in the present case is the fundamental one and is directed to the problem of peace of mind. The answer to the question is samadhi. If only you attain samadhi, you can solve the tantalizing problem instantly.

• *Ordinary mind is the Way.* Children are in samadhi in their play, work, and daily routine. Animals, plants, and minerals are also in samadhi, in their way. The adult alone has lost samadhi. If he can only rid himself of the deluded way of thinking of ordinary consciousness, he can act like a child, whose mental condition we call innocent. In short, innocence is ordinary mind. When you are innocent, your internal pressure is in a state of equilibrium, and that is the condition of ordinary mind. In your daily life, you often enter a well-balanced, harmonious state of mind, for instance, when cooking, working in the garden, even getting up in the morning, putting on your clothes, going downstairs, or fastening your shoelaces. If only you could do these things in positive samadhi! Ordinary mind is realized in your samadhi, and that is the way of peace of mind.

• *If you try for it, you will become separated from it.* When you are in samadhi, you are simply in samadhi, and your mind is peaceful. There is no seeking after the Way, nor separation from it. If you are not in samadhi, you are separated from the way to peace of mind, and you are tantalized and frustrated.

• *How can I know the Way unless I try for it?* Once you have experienced samadhi, you know it is the Way.

• *The Way is not a matter of knowing or not knowing.* Samadhi does not belong to conceptual understanding; it is to be experienced.

• *Knowing is delusion.* If you try to know it through conceptual manipulation, you will simply be deluded. But once you have experienced samadhi, it is indeed to be explained by conceptual understanding. Conceptual understanding must follow experience.

• *Not knowing is confusion.* Eventually you must come to a clear understanding.

• *You will find it as vast and boundless as outer space.* Samadhi is, by nature, vast and boundless.

• *How can it be talked about on the level of right and wrong?* Samadhi transcends the level of right and wrong.

• *Jōshū came to a sudden realization.* Jōshū was a great master, but he always said that he would ask even an eight-year-old boy to teach him if the boy were superior to him in understanding. Jōshū had his first experience when he was eighteen years old. He was assiduous in his training in Zen all through his life.

• *Nansen dissolved and melted away before Jōshū's questions.* One may deploy all the resources of a well-stocked mind and yet fail to persuade those who stand on a lower level. Nansen gave a fine answer, but it does not reach those whose ears are not trained to hear.

• *Could not offer a plausible explanation.* This in itself constitutes a koan. A master will say to you, "Tell me, what really do you make of this 'could not offer a plausible explanation'?"

• *He must delve into it for another thirty years.* Not Jōshū but *you* must delve into it for another thirty years. Zen is a matter of lifelong training.

• *The spring flowers, the autumn moon; / Summer breezes, winter snow.* If you are prepared, you can enjoy it all.

• *If useless things do not clutter your mind.* If only you could throw away the delusive thinking of the mind.

Case 20   The Man of Great Strength

Shōgen Oshō asked, "Why is it that a man of great strength does not lift his legs?" And he also said, "It is not the tongue he speaks with."

MUMON'S COMMENT   It must be said that Shōgen shows us all his stomach and intestines. But alas, no one can appreciate him! And even if someone could appreciate him, let him come to me, and I'll beat him severely. Why? If you want to find pure gold, you must see it through fire.

MUMON'S VERSE
    Lifting his leg, he kicks up the Scented Ocean;
    Lowering his head, he looks down on the fourth Dhyana heaven.

There is no space vast enough for his body—
Now, somebody write the last line here.

NOTES   *Shōgen Oshō* (1132–1202) is the latest of all the masters who
appear in *Mumonkan*. He was a contemporary of Mumon. The present
Japanese Rinzai school traces its descent through him.

• *A man of great strength does not lift his legs.* "A man of great strength"
is a man of great enlightenment. He fills all space; he is as boundless as
the universe. There is no space vast enough for him to move about in.
But if he is a man of great enlightenment, he should be able to move
freely, because he must be free in every way. How, then, will he move?
That was Shōgen's question. But no one could answer it.

• *It is not the tongue he speaks with.* Shōgen has three problems, of
which this is the second. It gives us a clue to help solve the first. A skilled
professional storyteller once told a story before a special gathering to
which a certain famous Zen master was invited. Later the master said,
"The storyteller was good, but he was still speaking with his tongue.
There is a Zen saying, 'It is not the tongue he speaks with.' " Hearing
these words, the storyteller taxed his ingenuity to work out a way of
talking without his tongue. On another occasion, he again had a chance
to tell a story before the master, who said, "Oh, this time he has lost his
tongue." The narrator became the master's disciple, and later he became
a most distinguished storyteller. When a sprinter runs, he forgets his legs;
when an invalid walks, he uses his legs consciously.

Shōgen's third problem is "Why does a man of enlightenment not
cut away the red strings dangling from his legs?" The red strings are one's
attachments. Why does he not cut these away? The enlightened man
spares no pains for the good of those who have not yet attained realization. That is his attachment. Shōgen produced this third problem when
he was dying. It must have been his last instruction. But Mumon does not
use it in this case. Why? See the last line of Mumon's verse.

• *If you want to find pure gold.* If you want to find a student who can be
compared to pure gold.

• *You must see it through fire.* You must give him hard training. The
student, also, will find the gold of samadhi only through the fire of hard
training.

• *He kicks up the Scented Ocean.* According to the ancient Buddhist cosmology, the Scented Ocean surrounds Mount Sumeru, which is in the center of the universe. This is like saying that he kicks up the whole universe.

• *He looks down on the fourth Dhyana heaven.* He looks down on the highest of the heavens.

• *There is no space vast enough for his body.* He is as vast and boundless as the whole universe.

• *Now, somebody write the last line here.* You are asked to complete the verse with a turning word.

Case 21   Ummon's "Kanshiketsu"

A monk asked Ummon, "What is Buddha?" Ummon replied, "Kanshiketsu!"

MUMON'S COMMENT   Ummon was too poor to prepare plain food, too busy to speak from notes. He hurriedly took up *shiketsu* to support the Way. The decline of Buddhism was thus foreshadowed.

MUMON'S VERSE
  Lightning flashing,
  Sparks shooting;
  A moment's blinking,
  Missed forever.

NOTES   *Kanshiketsu.* A *shiketsu,* or "shit-stick" (*kan*, dry; *shi*, shit; *ketsu*, stick), was used in old times instead of toilet paper. It is at once both private and polluted. But in samadhi there is no private or public, no pure or polluted.

• *What is Buddha?* As with many Zen questions, even such a simple and straightforward question as this can be asked in a number of different contexts:

1. A beginner seriously asks what is the fundamental principle of Buddhism.
2. A monk who has achieved advanced understanding demonstrates his condition by asking a question.
3. In Dharma battle the questioner tries to examine his opponent's condition. At the same time, however, he reveals his own condition by his choice of question and his tone of voice and manner.
4. Such questions and answers form a means of intimate exchange between a teacher and his principal disciple.

In the present case, each of these contexts is possible. In the first the student asks seriously, "What is Buddha?" Perhaps he is imagining the glorious image of the Buddha pervading the whole universe. The answer "Kanshiketsu" comes like a blow to smash such an image. This kind of answer is called "breaking the thinking stream of consciousness." In the second category Ummon adapts himself to the condition of the questioner. This kind of answer is called "following the ebb and flow of the tide." In the third context Ummon partly adapts himself to the question and partly counterattacks. In the fourth context Ummon and his questioner are chatting pleasantly. Questions and answers of that sort are called "heaven meets earth as the lid does the chest." Both minds are in unison; "kanshiketsu" corresponds to the Buddha as a lid fits the chest it was made for. Heart meets heart in warmth and intimacy.

• *Kanshiketsu!* The shout followed the question as the echo of a bell comes back from the hillside.

• *Too poor to prepare plain food, too busy to speak from notes.* Ummon has nothing prepared, no set opinion or fixed frame of mind. He is entirely innocent. He adheres to nothing. He is supremely free.

• *He hurriedly took up shiketsu.* Unflustered, as quick as lightning, Ummon answered.

• *The decline of Buddhism.* Mumon is always saying the opposite of what he means.

• *Lighting flashing, / Sparks shooting.* Ummon's quick eye took in the questioner instantly; his answer came with the speed of a shooting star.

• *A moment's blinking, / Missed forever.* If you stop for a moment to think, everything will be gone.

Case 22   Kashyapa's "Knock Down the Flagpole"

Ananda asked Kashyapa, "The World-honored One gave you the golden robe; did he give you anything else?" "Ananda!" cried Kashyapa. "Yes, sir!" answered Ananda. "Knock down the flagpole at the gate," said Kashyapa.

MUMON'S COMMENT   If you can give a turning word at this point, you will see that the meeting at Mount Grdhrakuta is still solemnly continuing. If not, then this is what Vipasyin Buddha worried about from remote ages; up to now he has still not acquired the essence.

MUMON'S VERSE
    Tell me—question or answer—which was more intimate?
    Many have knit their brows over this;
    Elder brother calls, younger brother answers, and they betray
       the family secret.
    They had a special spring, not one of yin and yang.

NOTES   *Ananda* was the nephew of Shakyamuni Buddha and was more than thirty years younger than Shakyamuni. He entered the Buddha's Way when he was around twelve years old. He was fair of face and figure, and had an exceptional memory. He was the Buddha's attendant from his twenties until the death of the Buddha. He constantly followed Shakyamuni and kept in mind his every word and act and every sermon. When the Buddha passed away and the collection and compilation of his teachings was effected under the leadership of Mahakashyapa (also called simply Kashyapa, as in this case), Ananda recited from memory the Buddha's sermons and talks, reproducing them with wonderful accuracy and with the dignity that the Buddha had displayed when he was alive. It is said that so magnificent and majestic was Ananda's deportment that those present at the meeting wondered if the Buddha had reappeared before them. Certainly Ananda behaved remarkably in his trance,* in which all his past memories returned to him. Ananda did not attain his enlightenment while the Buddha was alive; he accomplished it under Mahakashyapa, whom we met first in Case 6. The present case tells how Ananda's enlightenment came about.

• *The World-honored One.* This is one of the ten titles of the Buddha.

• *The golden robe.* The Buddha gave Mahakashyapa his robe and bowl as the token of the Transmission of the Lamp. The robe was not really gold, but as a token of the transmission it is accorded great value.

• *Did he give you anything else?* Ananda thought that, besides the robe, something spiritual must have been transmitted.

• *"Ananda!" cried Kashyapa. "Yes, sir!" answered Ananda.* In Case 10 we have: "Sōzan called out, 'Seizei!' Seizei responded, 'Yes, sir!' Sōzan said, 'You have finished three cups of the finest wine in China . . .'" Again, in Case 17, the National Teacher called his attendant three times, and three times the attendant responded. At what point did Seizei drink the wine? And what does all the National Teacher's calling and the attendant's responding mean? Calling and responding: nothing comes between. Pure cognition is effected. This is an exercise of positive samadhi.

The mirrors reflect the light of the golden palace,
The hills respond to the note of the moonlit tower's bell.

Ananda's samadhi was mature, and through this calling and responding he suddenly came to enlightenment.

• *Knock down the flagpole at the gate.* When a master's lecture was going to take place, a flag was hoisted on the pole at the gate of the temple. But now the pole was to be knocked down. Kashyapa's lecture was over. Knocking down the pole is a dramatic confirmation of the transmission of the Dharma to Ananda. Knocking down the flagpole has another important implication. Knock down your own ego, knock down what you treasure: enlightenment, Zen, your teacher, the Buddha, everything. This knocking down is used as an independent koan. The teacher will ask, "How do you knock down the flagpole?"

---

*An example of such a trance is described in "A Special Inquiry with Aldous Huxley into the Nature and Character of Various States of Consciousness" by Milton H. Erickson, reprinted in *Altered States of Consciousness*, ed. Charles T. Tart (New York and London: Wiley, 1969).

• *The meeting at Mount Grdhrakuta is still solemnly continuing.* "The meeting at Mount Grdhrakuta" refers to the incident recorded in Case 6, in which the Buddha demonstrated his positive samadhi and Mahakashyapa showed his understanding of it. When you have realized the Buddha's Way, you will find that the meeting at Mount Grdhrakuta is still solemnly continuing at this very moment.

• *What Vipasyin Buddha worried about.* Vipasyin is the first of the seven Buddhas of the past (see the notes to Case 2) and lived countless eons ago. But Mumon's way of speaking is peculiar; he is using Vipasyin to remind you of endless time, and Vipasyin is none other than yourself. You have worried yourself since remote ages past.

• *He has still not acquired the essence.* So long as you are worried in the wrong way, you have no time to acquire the essence. This saying is used as an independent koan. The teacher will ask you, "Why has Vipasyin not yet acquired the essence?" (See Case 9.)

• *They betray the family secret.* It is no secret to those who have once experienced it, being a secret only to those who have not yet glimpsed it.

• *Special spring.* Spiritual spring.

• *Yin and yang.* A spiritual spring is independent of yin and yang, the forces that form the foundation of the calendar of seasons.

Case 23 Think Neither Good Nor Evil

The Sixth Patriarch was pursued by the monk Myō as far as Taiyu Mountain. The patriarch, seeing Myō coming, laid the robe and bowl on a rock and said, "This robe represents the faith; it should not be fought over. If you want to take it away, take it now." Myō tried to move it, but it was as heavy as a mountain and would not budge. Faltering and trembling, he cried out, "I came for the Dharma, not for the robe. I beg you, please give me your instruction."

The patriarch said, "Think neither good nor evil. At this very moment, what is the original self of the monk Myō?" At these words, Myō was directly illuminated. His whole body was covered with sweat. He wept and bowed, saying, "Besides the secret words and the secret meaning you have just now revealed to me, is there anything else, deeper still?" The patriarch said, "What I have told you is no secret at all. When you look into your own true self, whatever is deeper is found right there." Myō said, "I was with the monks under Ōbai for many years but could not realize my true self. But now, receiving your instruction, I know it is like a man drinking water and knowing whether it is cold or warm. My lay brother, you are now my teacher." The patriarch said, "If you say so, but let us both call Ōbai our teacher. Be mindful to treasure and hold fast to what you have attained."

MUMON'S COMMENT   The Sixth Patriarch was, so to speak, hurried into helping a man in an emergency, and he displayed a grandmotherly kindness. It is as though he peeled a fresh lichi, removed the seed, put it in your mouth, and asked you to swallow it down.

MUMON'S VERSE
You cannot describe it; you cannot picture it;
You cannot admire it; don't try to eat it raw.
Your true self has nowhere to hide;
When the world is destroyed, it is not destroyed.

NOTES   *The Sixth Patriarch.* Enō (638–713) was the thirty-third patriarch descending from Shakyamuni Buddha and the sixth patriarch of Chinese Zen. Beginning with him, Zen developed in a new way. He is one of the three great figures in Zen history, the other two being the Buddha and Bodhidharma, who was the founder of Chinese Zen. Enō's father, a government official, was reduced in rank and sent to Nanhai in present Kwangtung Province. He died when Enō was three years old, and Enō was brought up by his mother. As he grew up, the family became more and more poverty-stricken, and he supported his mother by gathering and selling firewood.

One day he delivered a load of wood to a customer's house and happened to overhear a man reciting a sutra. When the man came to the passage, "Without abiding anywhere, let the mind work," Enō was suddenly illuminated. The man told Enō he was reciting the *Diamond Sutra*, given him by the Fifth Patriarch, Ōbai. Enō wanted to visit the Fifth Patriarch. People gave him some money to support his mother while he was away. He made the long journey from southern China to the northern provinces. A long story is told of his meeting the Fifth Patriarch, the conversation between them, and his subsequent doings.

After staying with the Fifth Patriarch for eight months, the famous midnight transmission of the Dharma Seal was performed by the patriarch. (See the notes to *Hekiganroku*, Case 5.) Before dawn, the Fifth Patriarch conducted Enō to the nearest ferry, where they parted, and Enō went southward. As soon as it was known that the Dharma Seal, the robe, and the bowl had been carried off by a layman whom they had not much respected, there was a great commotion among the monks, and a band of several hundred, led by one named Myō, set out after Enō. During the two-month pursuit many of the monks dropped out of the chase, and in the end it was Myō alone who succeeded in overtaking Enō at a pass on Taiyu Mountain.

• *The monk Myō.* As a layman he had been a general of the fourth rank. In manner he was rough and outspoken. In his practice of Zen and in other ways, however, he seems to have been assiduous.

• *The patriarch, seeing Myō coming.* The Sixth Patriarch chose, as the scene for his meeting with Myō, the mountain pass of Taiyu, which formed the border between Kwangtung Province and northern China. He placed the robe and bowl on a rock, and saying, "This robe represents the faith . . . ," hid himself among the bushes, leaving Myō to decide what to do.

• *Myō tried to move it.* To Myō, the robe and bowl were the most holy things—the Dharma itself. He knew that an unenlightened man should not touch them. He held out his hands but trembled and faltered, and could not even touch the robe.

• *As heavy as a mountain.* Mentally, he found the robe as heavy as a mountain. Even granted that he could touch the robe, he could not raise it. He knew clearly the difference between himself and Enō. Overwhelmed by the tremendous solemnity of this fact, he broke down and asked for help, calling Enō his teacher. Truly, he had found a patriarch in Enō. The Sixth Patriarch came out from among the bushes and asked Myō to sit in meditation. As he had thrown away all his ego's stubborn way of thinking, Myō was able to enter true samadhi. He was humble.

His mind was empty. Then came the Sixth Patriarch's words, "Think neither good nor evil . . . ," sounding like thunder in Myō's ears.

• *Think neither good nor evil. At this very moment, what is the original self of the monk Myō?* Myō's mind had already been emptied. There was no thinking of good or evil: no Myō, no others. With the Sixth Patriarch's words, Myō's emptied mind resounded as an empty cave resounds to a shot. Now realization had to occur, because the original self is nothing but the emptied mind. And that emptied mind was mobilized and made to rush to the threshold of consciousness, to be recognized by consciousness itself.

• *Myō was directly illuminated.* The resounding report in the cave is translated into the vision of a flash of lightning. At the moment of realization, the phenomenon of hearing with the eyes and seeing with the ears often occurs.

• *His whole body was covered with sweat.* Such a phenomenon may well occur at one's realization. Mental exaltation is necessarily expressed by some such bodily manifestation.

• *Besides the secret words and the secret meaning.* "Secret" is now no longer secret; it is as clear as daylight.

• *Is there anything else, deeper still?* When one experiences kenshō, one generally thinks one has seen into the whole secret of Zen. But the more you proceed, the deeper the world of Zen becomes. Myō felt the truth of this, which reveals his sincere character.

• *Whatever is deeper.* The deeper you go into your samadhi, the more profound you will find it becomes.

• *Be mindful to treasure and hold fast to what you have attained.* The original text says *zen-ji-go-ji* (*zen*, fully; *ji*, yourself; *go*, treasure; *ji*, hold by). "Treasure it yourself" is the meaning.

• *Don't try to eat it raw.* Don't try to go through it superficially.

Case 24 Fuketsu's Speech and Silence

A monk asked Fuketsu, "Both speech and silence are faulty in being *ri* or *bi*. How can we escape these faults?" Fuketsu said,

"I always remember the spring in Kōnan,
Where the partridges sing;
How fragrant the countless flowers!"

MUMON'S COMMENT Fuketsu's Zen spirit was like lightning and opened a clear passage. However, he was entangled in the monk's words and could not cut them off. If you can really grasp the problem, you can readily find the way out. Now, putting language samadhi aside, say it in your own words.

MUMON'S VERSE
He does not use a refined phrase;
Before speaking, he has already handed it over.
If you chatter on and on,
You will find you have lost your way.

NOTES *Fuketsu* (896–973) was Rinzai's great-grandson in the Dharma lineage. When young he studied the Confucian classics, as did most Chinese; later he turned to Buddhism. At first he entered the Tendai sect but at the age of twenty-five began Zen training. He appears twice in *Hekiganroku* (Cases 38 and 61).
• *Both speech and silence are faulty in being ri or bi.* Ri and bi are Buddhist terms meaning inward and outward action of the mind, respectively. They first appeared in the work of Sōjō, who was one of the four great translators of the Buddhist scriptures working under Kumarajiva and who died in about 412, more than a hundred years before Bodhidharma came to China.
Inward alone is faulty; outward alone is also faulty; speech is outward, silence is inward, and both are faulty; how can we be faultless? That is the monk's question. This question is concerned with the problem of the real and the apparent, equality and difference, freedom and restriction, absolute samadhi and positive samadhi, and so forth.
• *I always remember the spring in Kōnan.* Fuketsu quoted these lines of a famous ancient poet. They were from a favorite poem of his, so he spontaneously recited them when the monk asked his question. Kōnan

is a district stretching south of the Yangtze River, between Nanking and Payang Lake, famed for its beautiful scenery.

• *Partridges sing.* Partridges were the best loved songbirds of the people of the Kōnan district. Many poets composed verses about them. Fuketsu himself was born in Hangchow in Chechiang Province, which is in Kōnan, and he must have loved the partridge's song. The monk came asking Fuketsu how to be above speech and silence, real and apparent, and so on. But Fuketsu was not limited by the monk's question; he simply kept himself in his own samadhi. Positive samadhi is, in a sense, outward, but when you are in samadhi you transcend inward and outward.

• *Fuketsu's Zen spirit was like lightning and opened a clear passage.* Zen spirit comes flashing out like lightning, and the way through is immediately opened.

• *He was entangled in the monk's words.* A question was asked and Fuketsu answered; he was entangled. It is true that Fuketsu opened a passage for himself and held his own. But why did he merely remain on the defensive? That is Mumon's complaint. But was Fuketsu really (or merely) passive?

• *Could not cut them off.* Before the monk opened his mouth, why did you not cut off the source of his question? Mumon demands that you (not Fuketsu) eradicate the root of all your struggling and wriggling.

• *If you can really grasp the problem.* If only you have a deep understanding of your own samadhi, you can see right through the problem.

• *You can readily find the way out.* The passage will naturally be opened. Ordinary mind is the way. "If you try for it, you will become separated from it" (Case 19).

• *Putting language samadhi aside.* When you throw the whole of your mind into composing a poem, you find that a certain pure serenity pervades your mind. But Mumon says: Put aside this sort of samadhi. Attain the true language samadhi of Zen.

• *Say it in your own words.* Say it in your own true language samadhi of Zen.

• *He does not use a refined phrase.* Mumon is here using a verse of Ummon's. Ummon is saying: He does not use an elaborate phrase, but a direct one.

• *Before speaking.* Transcending the use of language.

• *He has already handed it over.* He transmits truth from mind to mind.

Case 25   Kyōzan's Dream

In a dream Kyōzan Oshō went to Maitreya's place and was led in to sit in the third seat. A senior monk struck with a gavel and said, "Today the one in the third seat will speak." Kyōzan rose and, striking with the gavel, said, "The truth of Mahayana is beyond the four propositions and transcends the hundred negations. Taichō! Taichō!" [Hear the truth!]

MUMON'S COMMENT   Now tell me, did Kyōzan preach or did he not? If he opens his mouth, he is lost; if he seals his mouth, he is lost. Even if he neither opens nor shuts his mouth, he is a hundred and eight thousand miles away from the truth.

MUMON'S VERSE
In broad daylight, under the blue sky,
He forges a dream in a dream;
He makes up a monstrous story
And tries to deceive the whole crowd.

NOTES   *Kyōzan* (814–90) became a monk when he was seventeen years old. At first he studied under Master Ōshin, who had formerly been an attendant of Chū the National Teacher (see Case 17). After Ōshin's death, he went to study with Isan, a distinguished teacher, and found he was in full accord with Isan in thought and temperament. He helped Isan develop his school, which was later called the Igyō branch of Zen. Many anecdotes are told of Kyōzan, generally in association with his teacher Isan, in which Kyōzan's Zen spirit is demonstrated. The relationship of the two was so intimate that it is often difficult to tell which was the teacher, which the disciple. Engo, the compiler of *Hekiganroku*, once said of them: "Teacher calling, disciple responding; father and son forming a family; light and shadow showing fine effects; in speech and silence they established perfect harmony."
One day when Isan and the monks were engaged in picking tea leaves, Isan called to Kyōzan, "All day I have heard your voice and not seen

you." Kyōzan, instead of saying anything, shook a tea plant. Isan said, "You have got the use, but not the subject." "I ask you, what do you say?" said Kyōzan. Isan kept silent. Then Kyōzan said, "You have got the subject, but not the use."

• *In a dream.* Dreams reveal the innermost secrets of one's mind. Every nen-action is accompanied by its own internal pressure, which is one's ego. Each internal pressure demands to be resolved or discharged; if it is not so resolved, it is retained as undisposed-of pressure stored in a secret corner of the mind. Why secret? Consciousness is often placed in a dilemma and has to conceal forbidden thoughts from itself. But the stored internal pressure does not remain dormant; it constantly knocks at the door, asking to be admitted once again onto the stage of consciousness and thereby to have itself discharged.

Dreams were invented—this is part of nature's wisdom—to provide a stage where internal pressures can find embodiment. Secret internal pressures undergo a profound distortion before being allowed on this stage, where they appear in symbolic form. There thus arises the necessity of dream-reading. These facts were first discovered and expounded by Freud, who states in *The Interpretation of Dreams*, "A dream is a [disguised] fulfillment of a [suppressed or repressed] wish." Some dreams are truly a disguised fulfillment of one's secret desires. But speaking more generally, we may say that dreams are an attempt to discharge internal pressures. Confucius once said, "Lately I do not dream of Gyō [a saintly ancient emperor]. I am on the decline." Confucius may have been aspiring after the condition of the sage. A composed mind will dream a composed dream, a disturbed mind a disturbed one. A sage is said to have no dreams, but that may mean no dreams so shocking that they remain in the memory after awakening.

Returning to Kyōzan's dream in the present case, it was simply the realization of the Zen saying, "With holy ones, dreams and wakefulness make one and the same stream." An enlightened mind is always in playful samadhi, in which medicine and sickness cure each other (see *Hekiganroku*, Case 87), and ego (internal pressure) is each moment neutralized and melted away, leaving behind no vexations and frustrations to be discharged in dreams. When Kyōzan told Isan of his dream, Isan said, "You have entered the holy rank."

• *The four propositions.* These are existing, non-existing, both existing and non-existing, and neither existing nor non-existing.

• *The hundred negations.* The four propositions are multiplied in Indian philosophy, eventually reaching one hundred negations. "One hundred," in this instance, means an infinite number. When one comes to think of negation, one has to repeat it endlessly. But in the Zen way of thinking, everything is direct, immediate, and intimate, and transcends endless negations.

• *Taichō.* Tai, clearly; *chō,* hear.

• *Did Kyōzan preach or did he not?* Any and every action of his is preaching, only you do not hear. Once a monk asked Kyōzan, "Who is he that delivers the sermon?" Kyōzan thrust a pillow in front of the monk.

• *A hundred and eight thousand miles.* If you are not enlightened, you are infinitely far from the truth. But if you only attain to the truth, the distance will disappear in a moment.

• *In broad daylight, under the blue sky.* If you only attain absolute and positive samadhi, everything will become as clear as if it were seen in broad daylight.

• *He forges a dream in a dream.* We have dreams in the world of dream. Don't dream a deranged dream.

• *He makes up a monstrous story.* It is a wonderful story.

• *And tries to deceive the whole crowd.* This is Mumon's old trick of generating doubt in you by seemingly illogical words. He is actually talking about you, not Kyōzan.

Case 26   Two Monks Roll Up the Blinds

When the monks assembled before the midday meal to listen to his lecture, the great Hōgen of Seiryō pointed at the bamboo blinds. Two monks simultaneously went and rolled them up. Hōgen said, "One gain, one loss."

MUMON'S COMMENT   Tell me, who gained and who lost? If you have an eye to penetrate the secret, you will see where Seiryō Kokushi failed. However, I warn you strongly against discussing gain and loss.

MUMON'S VERSE

Rolling up the blinds, the great sky is open,
But the great sky does not come up to Zen.
Why don't you throw them all down from the sky,
And keep your practice so close that no air can escape?

NOTES   *Hōgen* (885–958) was the founder of the Hōgen school of Zen. Seiryō was the name of his temple. He was well versed in the *Avatamsaka Sutras*, which were regarded as among the standard texts of Buddhist philosophy. But he also attached great importance to practice. When a monk asked him, "What is Buddha?" he answered, "First I want to ask you to practice it, second I want to ask you to practice it." On another occasion, a monk named Echō asked, "What is Buddha?" And this question was echoed by the famous answer, "You are Echō!" (See *Hekiganroku*, Case 7.)

When he was young, Hōgen traveled about visiting teachers. One day his journey was interrupted by rain and floods, and he stopped at a temple where Jizō, who later became his teacher, was living. Jizō said, "Where are you going, and what is the reason for going on a journey?" "I don't know," answered Hōgen. "Not knowing is most intimate," said Jizō. This remark aroused Hōgen's curiosity. Later, when they came to a gate and were parting, Jizō pointed to a stone by the gate and said, "It is said, 'The three worlds return to mind only, things to consciousness only.' Tell me, is this stone inside your mind or outside it?" Hōgen answered, "It is inside." Jizō said, "What makes you carry this stone around in your mind?" Hōgen could not answer. He accepted Jizō as his teacher and remained at the temple to study under him. In his interviews with Jizō, Hōgen often quoted from the *Avatamsaka Sutras* or the philosophy of the Consciousness Only school. Jizō always rejected Hōgen's answers, saying, "Buddhism is not that sort of thing." Finally Hōgen broke down and said, "I can have no words, no reasoning." Jizō said, "Speaking from the point of view of Buddhism, everything directly presents itself." At this, Hōgen suddenly came to realization.

• *One gain, one loss.* The original text says *ittoku, isshitsu* (*itsu* [*it*-], one; *toku*, a gain or to gain; *itsu* [*is*-], one; *shitsu*, a loss or to lose). This phrase can be translated either as "one gained, one lost" or as "one gain, one loss." Monks generally think in terms of the first translation and are puzzled. In our translation, there is no puzzle, so the true significance of the statement is lost. Everything has two sides; that is, every advantage has its disadvantage (gain and loss). The two monks' rolling up of the blinds is to be praised, as they showed their shrewdness in understanding the teacher's mind. But at the same time, they may still have been thinking of gaining merit. That is always rejected in Zen. If you have anything in your mind that you want to make a show of, you are criticized. In Zen, you are supposed to act innocently, in other words, not to deviate from ordinary mind. If you keep to ordinary mind, you will not be affected by any criticism you may encounter. This case is similar to the story of Jōshū visiting the two hermits (Case 11).

• *Who gained and who lost?* This is again Mumon's trick of putting you on the horns of a dilemma.

• *The secret.* There is no gain and no loss. Those who come arguing about right and wrong are those who are enslaved by right and wrong.

• *Seiryō Kokushi failed.* If you are not moved by Hōgen's criticism, it is Hōgen who has failed. Kokushi, meaning "National Teacher," was a title given to Hōgen by the emperor.

• *I warn you strongly against discussing gain and loss.* This line is now self-explanatory.

• *Rolling up the blinds, the great sky is open.* Attaining realization is rolling up the blinds of your delusion; then you emerge under the open sky.

• *But the great sky does not come up to Zen.* When you have made a certain progress in your practice of Zen, you are advised to forget whatever realization you may have attained.

• *Keep your practice so close that no air can escape.* Do not let the left hand know what the right hand is doing.

Case 27 Nansen's "Not Mind, Not Buddha, Not Things"

A monk asked Nansen, "Is there any Dharma that has not been preached to the people?" Nansen answered, "There is." "What is the truth that has not been taught?" asked the monk. Nansen said, "It is not mind; it is not Buddha; it is not things."

MUMON'S COMMENT   At this question, Nansen used up all his treasure and was not a little confused.

MUMON'S VERSE
  Talking too much spoils your virtue;
  Silence is truly unequaled.
  Let the mountains become the sea;
  I'll give you no comment.

NOTES   *Dharma that has not been preached.* The ultimate truth, or Dharma, has not been taught because it cannot be taught. It can only be learned. Even the great philosophers cannot make their philosophies clear to us unless we ourselves philosophize. Shakyamuni Buddha delivered about three hundred sermons during his lifetime, but when he was dying he said, "During the forty-nine years of my teaching I did not preach even one word." In this case you can suppose either that the monk knew something of the matter or that he was quite uninitiated. (In Case 28 of *Hekiganroku* the monk is represented as Hyakujō Nehan, the successor to Hyakujō Ekai, who appears in Cases 2 and 40 of *Mumonkan* and in Cases 26, 53, 70, 71, and 72 of *Hekiganroku*.) Either way, it mattered little to Nansen. He had no scruples about simply stating, "There is."

  • *It is not mind; it is not Buddha; it is not things.* It is an old axiom that the mind is Buddha. Nansen, however, denies the mind. Buddha is also denied. Only things (all creatures) remain, but these too are denied. In your samadhi, you are directly exercising that which is not mind, not Buddha, not things. Only then can you say that you exercise your mind, your Buddha, and your things.

  • *Nansen used up all his treasure.* Nansen gave up everything that he had. If you can understand it, then do it yourself.

  • *Not a little confused.* Tremendous treasures are being piled up in front of you in bewildering profusion. This is only to confuse you.

• *Talking too much spoils your virtue.* This can be read in two ways. First, Mumon is saying that too much talking spoils the truth; "virtue" here means Dharma virtue. Second, this can also be read to mean that Nansen himself talked too much in this instance and his own virtue was spoiled.

• *Let the mountains become the sea; | I'll give you no comment.* Once more Mumon is exhorting you to make the effort yourself. You work it out: discover the meaning for yourself. Mumon is not going to spoon-feed you.

Case 28   Ryūtan Blows Out the Candle

Tokusan asked Ryūtan about Zen far into the night. At last Ryūtan said, "The night is late. Why don't you retire?" Tokusan made his bows and lifted the blinds to withdraw, but he was met by darkness. Turning back to Ryūtan, he said, "It is dark outside." Ryūtan lit a paper candle and handed it to him. Tokusan was about to take it when Ryūtan blew it out. At this, all of a sudden, Tokusan went through a deep experience and made bows.

Ryūtan said, "What sort of realization do you have?" "From now on," said Tokusan, "I will not doubt the words of an old oshō who is renowned everywhere under the sun."

The next day Ryūtan ascended the rostrum and said, "I see a fellow among you. His fangs are like the sword tree. His mouth is like a blood bowl. Strike him with a stick, and he won't turn his head to look at you. Someday or other, he will climb the highest of the peaks and establish our Way there."

Tokusan brought his notes on the *Diamond Sutra* to the front of the hall, pointed to them with a torch, and said, "Even though you have exhausted the abstruse doctrines, it is like placing a hair in a vast space. Even though you have learned all the secrets of the world, it is like a drop of water dripped on the great ocean." And he burned all his notes. Then, making bows, he took his leave of his teacher.

MUMON'S COMMENT   Before Tokusan crossed the barrier from his native place, his mind burned and his mouth uttered bitterness. He went southward, intending to stamp out the doctrines of special transmission outside the sutras. When he reached the road to Reishū, he asked an old woman to let him have lunch to "refresh the mind." "Your worship, what sort of literature do you carry in your pack?" the old woman asked. "Commentaries on the *Diamond Sutra*," replied Tokusan. The old woman said, "I hear it is said in that sutra, 'The past mind cannot be held, the present mind cannot be held, the future mind cannot be held.' Now, I would like to ask you, what mind are you going to have refreshed?"

At this question Tokusan was dumbfounded. However, he did not remain inert under her words but asked, "Do you know of any good teacher around here?" The old woman said, "Five miles from here you will find Ryūtan Oshō."

Coming to Ryūtan, Tokusan got the worst of it. His former words were inconsistent with his later ones. As for Ryūtan, he seemed to have lost all sense of shame in his compassion toward his son. Finding a bit of live coal in the other, enough to start a fire, he hurriedly poured on muddy water to annihilate everything at once. A little cool reflection tells us it was all a farce.

MUMON'S VERSE
  Hearing the name cannot surpass seeing the face;
  Seeing the face cannot surpass hearing the name.
  He may have saved his nose,
  But alas! he lost his eyes.

NOTES   *Ryūtan* lived around 850. He succeeded Tennō Dōgo and was the teacher of Tokusan. As a boy he used to take rice cakes to Dōgo of Tennō Temple. This led him to become Dōgo's disciple. Little is recorded of him except the story in the present case.

· *Tokusan* was discussed in Case 13. He was born in a town near Chengtu in Szechwan Province in northwestern China. He became a monk when young and at first studied the Buddhist sutras, especially the *Diamond Sutra*, on which he wrote a commentary. Hearing that the Zen sect talked of a special transmission from mind to mind, independent of words and outside the scriptures, he was indignant and wanted to stamp out this heretical teaching. He went down the Yangtze River, southward to the vicinity of Tungt'ing Lake, and there, coming across an old woman, the keeper of a wayside tea booth, he met with a reverse in a conversation with her, as Mumon records. Following her words, he went to Ryūtan, and at the beginning of the interview, he said, "Ryūtan [*ryū*, dragon; *tan*, abyss] is well known, but when I am here, I see neither dragon nor abyss." Ryūtan said, "You see Ryūtan with your own eyes." Tokusan was impressed, and talking with Ryūtan, he was converted. He asked Ryūtan earnestly about Zen far into the night, and on leaving the teacher's room, he suddenly went through a deep experience, as described in this case.

This sort of experience is found in Christianity, too—for example, in the conversion of Saint Paul. But Paul's understanding and demonstration of his experience were different from those of Shakyamuni and other Zen masters. The activity of consciousness is subtle; it comes to be mingled with the experience itself and even determines the course of the experience according to its preconceived ideas. Even among Zen people, subtle differences of understanding appear, depending on their personal histories. Long and scrupulous training and meditation after an enlightenment experience is necessary in order to achieve full maturity of realization.

Tokusan's experience was great, but he could not immediately become mature in his understanding. His saying, "Even though you have exhausted the abstruse doctrines, it is like placing a hair in a vast space," was right; but his action in immediately taking leave of his teacher was premature and too hurried. (See *Hekiganroku*, Case 4.)

Ryūtan, too, was not without blame. His eulogy was an invitation to Tokusan to do what he did. But it is recorded that Tokusan later returned to Ryūtan and stayed with him for thirty years. A prudent mind never fails to reflect upon its faults. Tokusan came to be a great Zen master in his later years. The text of the present case is self-explanatory.

• *Ryūtan blew it out.* Ryūtan's was an intuitive action, not a conceptual one. Sensation (the first nen) plays an important part in realization, and Ryūtan intuitively knew this. The sudden change from light to darkness had a great effect on Tokusan. But if the action had been done intentionally, all would have been spoiled.

• *I will not doubt the words of an old oshō.* "An old oshō" means Ryūtan, and at the same time means the true Dharma.

• *Someday or other, he will climb the highest of the peaks and establish our Way there.* Someday when he has reached maturity (which he has not yet attained) he will become a great Zen master. Ryūtan had not yet given Tokusan his full approval, but Tokusan was still unaware of this.

• *He hurriedly poured on muddy water to annihilate everything at once.* Mumon's language here is peculiar. He means that Ryūtan annihilated all delusive thought in Tokusan and at the same time blew the bit of live coal in him to make it burn brighter.

• *It was all a farce.* As usual Mumon is being satirical. Here he means that to make a fuss about Tokusan's poor experience was a farce.

• *Hearing the name cannot surpass seeing the face.* Before you attain realization, realization is of the greatest importance.

• *Seeing the face cannot surpass hearing the name.* When realization is attained, it is to be regarded as if it were of no value.

• *He may have saved his nose.* He may have attained realization. That would be a gain.

• *But alas! he lost his eyes.* He is still short of maturity. That is a loss.

Case 29   The Sixth Patriarch's "Your Mind Moves"

The wind was flapping a temple flag, and two monks started an argument. One said the flag moved, the other said the wind moved; they argued back and forth but could not reach a conclusion. The Sixth Patriarch said, "It is not the wind that moves, it is not the flag that moves; it is your mind that moves." The two monks were awe-struck.

MUMON'S COMMENT   It is not the wind that moves; it is not the flag that moves; it is not the mind that moves. How do you see the patriarch? If you come to understand this matter deeply, you will see that the two monks got gold when buying iron. The patriarch could not withhold his compassion and courted disgrace.

MUMON'S VERSE

Wind, flag, mind moving,
All equally to blame.
Only knowing how to open his mouth,
Unaware of his fault in talking.

NOTES *The wind was flapping a temple flag.* When a master delivered a sermon at a temple, a flag was hoisted at the gate to announce it to the public. Two monks started an argument; one said the wind was moving, while the other said the flag was moving. It was true that the wind was moving the flag, but it was also true that the flag was moving. At first they may have enjoyed their argument, but presently it became heated. They became excited, each bent on defeating the other. In short, their minds lost their anchors and started drifting. But the monks were unaware of the disturbed condition of their minds. That was what the Sixth Patriarch, Enō, pointed out. They were led to introspect into their own minds. Perhaps it was rare for the people of those days to reflect upon the condition of their own minds. Enō's words took them by surprise.

• *It is not the mind that moves.* Mumon seems to contradict Enō's words. But again, this is Mumon's peculiar way of talking. Actually, Mumon has borrowed these words. They were first said by a nun who lived in a detached temple belonging to Kyōzan's monastery. Some monks from a distant district who wanted to have interviews with Kyōzan stopped at the nun's temple. In the course of the evening's conversation, they discussed the Sixth Patriarch's words in the present·case. The nun, hearing them, rejected their words and said, "It is not the wind that moves, it is not the flag that moves, it is not the mind that moves." The enlightened mind does not move. And that was what the Sixth Patriarch really meant: Your mind is moving; don't let it move. This is not only Mumon's warning; it is the warning of all Zen.

• *Courted disgrace.* It is a Zen master's way to employ illogical language, indifferent to his own inconsistencies.

• *Unaware of his fault in talking.* He is fully aware but takes no notice of his error.

Case 30 Baso's "This Very Mind Is the Buddha"

Daibai asked Baso, "What is the Buddha?" Baso answered, "This very mind is the Buddha."

MUMON'S COMMENT If you directly grasp Baso's meaning, you wear the Buddha's clothes, eat the Buddha's food, speak the Buddha's words, do the Buddha's deeds—that is, you are the Buddha himself. However, alas! Daibai misled not a few people into taking the mark on the balance for the weight itself. How could he realize that even mentioning the word "Buddha" should make us rinse out our mouths for three days? If a man of understanding hears anyone say, "This very mind is the Buddha," he will cover his ears and rush away.

MUMON'S VERSE
  The blue sky and bright day,
  No more searching around!
  "What is the Buddha?" you ask:
  With loot in your pocket, you declare yourself innocent.

NOTES Daibai (752–839) was a distinguished disciple of Baso. As related in the present case, he was enlightened at Baso's words, "This very mind is the Buddha." The Dharma Seal having been transmitted to him, he retired to a mountain called Shimei, where he lived a hermit's life. A monk happened to visit him and asked, "How long have you been here?" "I have many times seen the mountains change their tints from green to yellow." "Where can I find the way down from this mountain?" asked the monk. "Follow the stream," replied Daibai. And he composed a verse:

  A dead tree in a mountain recess
  Passed many a spring, and had no mind to change.
  The woodcutters would ignore it,
  People found no way to approach it.

The lotus leaves of the marsh were enough for clothes;
The seeds of the pine trees, sufficient for food.
Now that they have found out my dwelling place,
I want to move farther into the hills.

However, in the later years of his life, people gathered around him and built Daibai Monastery for him to teach in.

• *Baso* (709–88) was a peak in ancient Zen history. A total of 139 distinguished Zen teachers were disciples of his. He had an imposing appearance, with piercing eyes, and is said to have looked like a tiger and walked like a bull. He could stretch out his tongue so far that it covered his nose. His way of discipline was ever changing: using the stick, shouting, seizing, pushing, knocking down. What is called "using Zen spirit" is said to have originated with him.

Case 53 in *Hekiganroku* relates a famous episode in which Hyakujō came to enlightenment when Baso pinched his nose. Many years after that, when Hyakujō was about to go out into the world as a Zen master, he went up to Baso. Seeing Hyakujō coming, Baso looked at a *hossu* (a baton with a tuft of white horsehair at one end) which was hanging at the corner of his seat. He took up the hossu and set it upright. Hyakujō said, "Are you in the use of it or apart from the use of it?" Baso hung the hossu as it was before. After a little while, Baso asked Hyakujō, "Henceforth, how do you use those two lips of yours for others' sake?" Hyakujō took up the hossu and set it upright. Baso asked, "Are you in the use of it or apart from the use of it?" Hyakujō hung the hossu as it was before. That very moment, Baso, gathering all his majestic power, gave a loud shout, "Katsu!" And Hyakujō came to a great enlightenment. In his later years, Hyakujō told Ōbaku of this great shout, saying, "My ears were deafened for three days by this great shout of Baso's." When Baso was dying, he said, "Sun-faced Buddha, Moon-faced Buddha." (See *Hekiganroku*, Case 3.)

• *Daibai misled not a few people.* Mumon is cautioning his disciples not to fall into a shallow understanding of Baso's words.

• *Mentioning the word "Buddha."* While you make a fuss about the Buddha, you are under the Buddha's influence. You have to trample on the head of the Buddha in order to go ahead.

• *He will cover his ears and rush away.* Mumon is exaggerating somewhat to emphasize the importance of transcending the Buddha.

• *The blue sky and bright day, | No more searching around!* It is as clear as day. There is no need to search around for the Buddha.

• *With loot in your pocket.* You have your treasure within you and are not aware of it.

Case 31   Jōshū Investigates an Old Woman

A monk asked an old woman, "What is the way to Taisan?" The old woman said, "Go straight on." When the monk had proceeded a few steps, she said, "A good, respectable monk, but he too goes that way."

Afterward someone told Jōshū about this. Jōshū said, "Wait a bit, I will go and investigate the old woman for you." The next day he went and asked the same question, and the old woman gave the same answer. On returning, Jōshū said to his disciples, "I have investigated the old woman of Taisan for you."

MUMON'S COMMENT   The old woman only knew how to sit still in her tent and plan the campaign; she did not know when she was shadowed by a spy. Though old Jōshū showed himself clever enough to take a camp and overwhelm a fortress, he displayed no trace of being a great commander. If we look at them, they both have their faults. But tell me, what did Jōshū see in the old woman?

MUMON'S VERSE
  The question was like the others,
  The answer was the same.
  Sand in the rice,
  Thorns in the mud.

NOTES   *Taisan.* From early times this was a sacred mountain, being long dedicated to the Bodhisattva Manjusri. It is located in Shansi Province in northern China. It has five peaks—east, west, north, south, and central —each of which is topped by a plateau, and many temples were built there. Even now about twenty Zen temples and nearly thirty lamaseries are said to be flourishing there. Many learned and virtuous priests lived on this mountain, and many people made pilgrimages there. At the foot of the mountain there was a tea booth where an old woman lived and served visitors. She seems to have attained something of Zen, like the old woman who puzzled Tokusan (Case 28).

• *What is the way to Taisan?* Many monks who rested at the tea booth asked this question of the old woman. They may have been simply asking the way to the mountain, but the old woman's answer implied something more.

• *Go straight on.* Zen teachers used these words to their disciples, exhorting them to go directly foward with their practice of Zen.

• *A good, respectable monk, but he too goes that way.* The old woman deplored the fact that despite the monks' apparent respectability and zeal, she found them in fact mediocre, willing to follow others shiftlessly.

• *Someone told Jōshū about this.* The old woman's remark embarrassed the monks, and someone told Jōshū about this.

• *I will go and investigate the old woman.* Jōshū had something in mind.

• *I have investigated the old woman.* He could see through the old woman with half an eye.

• *For you.* I went and saw through her, Jōshū is saying; if you want to do so, you must do it for yourself.

• *The old woman only knew . . .* To understand Zen is one thing; to demonstrate it in actual life is another.

• *Though old Jōshū showed himself clever enough to take a camp.* When taking a camp, he is taking a camp.

• *He displayed no trace of being a great commander.* When acting as a commander, he acts as a commander.

• *Both have their faults.* Everything has two phases. When one gains, one gains; when one loses, one loses.

• *What did Jōshū see in the old woman?* What do you see in the old woman? Was her action met with appreciation or thanklessness? Can you go straight on, following her advice? Can you tell the difference between the monks and Jōshū, and between the old woman and Jōshū?

• *The question was like the others.* Jōshū's question was the same one that everyone else asked, but was it really the same?

• *The answer was the same.* Did the old woman give just the same answer to both the monks and Jōshū?
• *Sand in the rice, / Thorns in the mud.* Be careful; some unexpected thorns may be lying in wait for you.

Case 32   A Non-Buddhist Philosopher Questions the Buddha

A non-Buddhist philosopher said to the Buddha, "I do not ask for words; I do not ask for non-words." The Buddha just sat there. The philosopher said admiringly, "The World-honored One, with his great mercy, has blown away the clouds of my illusion and enabled me to enter the Way." And after making bows, he took his leave.

Then Ananda asked the Buddha, "What did he realize, to admire you so much?" The World-honored One replied, "A fine horse runs even at the shadow of the whip."

MUMON'S COMMENT   Ananda was the Buddha's disciple, but his understanding was not equal to that of the non-Buddhist. I want to ask you, what difference is there between the Buddha's disciple and the non-Buddhist?

MUMON'S VERSE
  On the edge of a sword,
  Over the ridge of an iceberg,
  With no steps, no ladders,
  Climbing the cliffs without hands.

NOTES   *A non-Buddhist philosopher.* This case also occurs in *Heki-*

ganroku (Case 65). See the notes to that case. There were said to be ninety-six schools of philosophers in ancient India.

• *I do not ask for words; I do not ask for non-words.* Words represent affirmative theories, non-words negative ones. The affirmative theories expounded the doctrine of the immortality of the soul, while the negative ones denied it. The philosopher who questioned the Buddha in the present case was satisfied with neither the affirmative nor the negative theories but could not himself reach a satisfactory answer. Alternatively, we might say that the philosopher did not want to remain in either positive samadhi or absolute samadhi.

• *The Buddha just sat there.* True samadhi combines in itself both absolute and positive samadhi.

• *The World-honored One . . . has blown away the clouds of my illusion and enabled me to enter the Way.* The non-Buddhist had experienced both absolute and positive samadhi but was still in doubt about his attainment. At the Buddha's demonstration his doubts vanished.

• *Ananda asked the Buddha.* Ananda did not experience realization while the Buddha was alive. He attained it while studying under Maha-kashyapa (see Case 22). At the time of the incident related in the present case he did not understand the philosopher's words, hence this question.

• *What difference is there between the Buddha's disciple and the non-Buddhist?* There is no difference; at the same time, there is a great difference. Zen is attained by individual effort. But the attainment is accomplished by transmission from mind to mind.

• *On the edge of a sword, / Over the ridge of an iceberg.* The slightest deviation from the path can cause a fatal slip.

• *With no steps, no ladders.* You can attain realization suddenly, absolutely, with no steps or gradations.

• *Climbing the cliffs without hands.* Once throw away your life and everything else, and you will regain them in a purified condition.

Case 33   Baso's "No Mind, No Buddha"

A monk asked Baso, "What is the Buddha?" Baso answered, "No mind, no Buddha."

MUMON'S COMMENT   If you understand this, you have finished studying Zen.

MUMON'S VERSE
  Present a sword if you meet a swordsman;
  Don't offer a poem unless you meet a poet.
  When talking, tell one-third of it;
  Don't divulge the whole at once.

NOTES   *What is the Buddha?* This question is constantly asked by struggling Zen monks. And no two masters offer the same answer.
• *No mind, no Buddha.* Earlier Baso had said, "This very mind is the Buddha," and Daibai reached an understanding (Case 30). But now Baso is denying his former words. Many elaborate explanations have been given of this problem. But to put it briefly, "This very mind is the Buddha" is the thesis, and "No mind, no Buddha" is the antithesis. Then what is the synthesis? Baso himself answered this question. He once said, "To say 'This very mind is the Buddha' is to stop a baby from crying." "Then what do you say when the baby stops crying?" asked a monk. "No mind, no Buddha." "What do you say when a man comes who has finished these two?" "I would say to him, 'No things.'" "How about when a man comes who has finished all these?" "I would make him understand the Great Way."
  Then what is the Great Way? "This very mind is the Buddha," and again on to "No mind, no Buddha." This circuit was also stopped by Baso. He sent a monk to ask Daibai, who had now retired to live the life of a hermit, "What did you get under Baso, and what makes you live on this mountain?" Daibai answered, "Baso said to me, 'This very mind is the Buddha,' and that made me live a life of seclusion on this moun-

tain." "But lately Baso's Buddhism is different." "Different how?" "He says, 'No mind, no Buddha.' " "The old dotard bewilders others. Let him say what he likes: I say nothing but 'This very mind is the Buddha.' "

The monk returned and informed Baso of this, and Baso said, "The plum is ripened." (The ideographs of Daibai's name are *dai*, great, and *bai*, plum.)

• *If you understand this, you have finished studying Zen.* First you have to understand "This very mind is the Buddha," then you understand "No mind, no Buddha."

• *Present a sword if you meet a swordsman.* Suit your sermon to your audience.

• *Don't offer a poem unless you meet a poet.* Don't cast pearls before swine.

Case 34   Nansen's "Reason Is Not the Way"

Nansen said, "Mind is not the Buddha; reason is not the Way."

MUMON'S COMMENT   Nansen, growing old, had no shame. Just opening his stinking mouth, he let slip the family secrets. Yet there are very few who are grateful for his kindness.

MUMON'S VERSE
The sky clears, the sun shines bright,
The rain comes, the earth gets wet.
He opens his heart and expounds the whole secret,
But I fear he is little appreciated.

NOTES   *Mind is not the Buddha.* Nansen means that mind is not what you think it is; the Buddha is not as you think him to be. This is another version of Baso's "No mind, no Buddha." Baso was Nansen's teacher, and they developed a similar way of thinking. Nansen elsewhere says that when a Buddha appears, words come into existence, and consequently we become attached to them.

• *Reason is not the Way.* The Chinese character translated "reason" is *chi*, which means wisdom, knowledge, and reason. Nansen once said, "The Great Way knows no wise or foolish man, no saint or sinner." Therefore wisdom cannot cover the Way, and knowledge and reason fall short of the Way.

• *Nansen, growing old, had no shame.* When one grows old, one becomes shamelessly talkative.

• *The family secrets.* The truth of Zen is a secret to those who do not understand it.

• *The sky clears, the sun shines bright.* Truth is clear, and it shines brightly.

• *The rain comes, the earth gets wet.* The world is full of blessings.

Case 35   Seijo's Soul Separated

Goso said to his monks, "Seijo's soul separated from her being. Which was the real Seijo?"

MUMON'S COMMENT   When you realize what the real is, you will see that we pass from one husk to another like travelers stopping for a night's lodging. But if you do not realize it yet, I earnestly advise you not to rush about wildly. When earth, water, fire, and air suddenly separate, you will be like a crab struggling in boiling water with its seven or eight arms and legs. When that happens, don't say I didn't warn you!

MUMON'S VERSE
   The moon above the clouds is ever the same;
   Valleys and mountains are separate from each other.

All are blessed, all are blessed;
Are they one or are they two?

Notes   *Goso* (d. 1104) became a priest when he was thirty-five. At first he studied sutras under lecture-masters but could not achieve peace of mind. He visited several Zen teachers and finally stayed with Hakuun Shutan. One day when he heard Hakuun instruct a monk on Jōshū's "Mu," he suddenly became enlightened. His poem on that occasion is as follows:

A piece of land in front of the hill,
Which I asked the old man, my teacher, about;
And I sold and bought it many a time.
Now, how I enjoy the cool breeze that blows through
The pines and bamboo that I've carefully tended.

"Land" means the mind and is often used to mean the land of the mind. "I sold and bought it" means he dealt with his mind in every possible way—subjectively, objectively, and so forth.

Of the twenty-four divisions of the Zen sect now existing in Japan, twenty are related to Goso by lineage, the four remaining ones being the three divisions of the Sōtō sect and the Ōryū division. Engo, the compiler of *Hekiganroku*, was Goso's disciple. Further details of Goso's life are given in the notes to Case 36.

• *Seijo*. The story of Seijo's two souls comes from a Chinese book of ghost stories. When a baby, Seijo was betrothed to her cousin Ōchū. However, when she grew up, her father wanted to give her in marriage to another young man. Ōchū left home in indignation and went up the Yangtze River by boat. At midnight someone came running along the bank eagerly calling Ōchū's name. It was Seijo. They journeyed together to a distant place, and there they lived and had two children. Five years went by, and they became homesick; they yearned to see their parents again. So they decided to visit their birthplace. Coming down the river, Ōchū left Seijo in the boat and went alone to her father to make an apology for their having run away. But to his astonishment, he was told that Seijo had been in bed unconscious ever since he left home. There were found to be two Seijos, one in the boat and the other sick in bed. But when the one in the boat came into the house, the other one got out of bed, whereupon the two met and melted together into one Seijo.

• *Which was the real Seijo?* First discover your own real self, then you can see which is the real Seijo.

• *When you realize what the real is.* Buddhism asserts that there is no man, but causation alone: no constant ego, and no entity called the soul. Everything mutates in the stream of cause and effect. What has appeared is vividly there. When it has gone, it is gone. Moment after moment, it streams along. Beyond this appearing and going, there is essentially nothing else. Phenomena themselves are the real. When you ask what is real, you have already missed it. The real is realized in your samadhi.

• *We pass from one husk to another.* This line can easily be misleading. "Husk" here means nothing solid, but only a temporary state of mind.

• *I earnestly advise you not to rush about wildly.* Quietly and earnestly practice zazen, then everything will become clear.

• *Earth, water, fire, and air.* According to ancient philosophy, one's body and mind consist of earth, water, fire, and air.

• *Don't say I didn't warn you!* I have long advised you to practice zazen, to come to experience reality, and to achieve enlightenment.

• *The moon above the clouds is ever the same.* A clear moon and a veiled moon, a full moon and a crescent, are ever one and the same moon.

• *Valleys and mountains are separate from each other.* Valleys and mountains are one land, but they are separated into valleys and mountains.

• *All are blessed.* Everything is all right.

• *Are they one or are they two?* They are one and they are two.

Case 36　When You Meet a Man of the Way

Goso said, "When you meet a man of the Way on the path, do not meet him with words or with silence. Tell me, how will you meet him?"

MUMON'S COMMENT　In such a case, if you can manage an intimate meeting with him it will certainly be gratifying. But if you cannot, you must be watchful in every way.

MUMON'S VERSE
Meeting a man of the Way on the road,
Meet him with neither words nor silence.
A punch on the jaw:
Understand, if you can directly understand.

NOTES   *Goso* appears four times in *Mumonkan*, of which this is the second. He first studied Buddhist philosophy of the Consciousness Only school at Chengtu, Szechwan Province, his native place. When he came across Genjō's words about experiencing realization—"It is just like a man who drinks water and nods to himself, knowing whether it is warm or cold"—he said to himself, "Knowing whether the water is warm or cold is easy, but what makes him nod to himself?" In order to solve this question he went south to study Zen and stayed with Hakuun, whom he later succeeded. (Genjō was a great Buddhist scholar and translator. He went to India in 633 and returned to China in 645, bringing with him 657 Buddhist sutras. He also wrote the famous *Record of Western Countries*.)

• *Do not meet him with words or with silence.* Remember Shōgen's proposition in Case 20, "It is not the tongue he speaks with." If you have no plot or scheme, you can act freely and innocently. In other words, if you do not deviate from ordinary mind, you can meet a man of the Way with either words or silence. But I must remind you that this is only a conceptual explanation.

• *Tell me, how will you meet him?* Tell me, how do you meet yourself? Goso asked himself, "What makes him nod to himself?" This "what" is the problem. Catch hold of this "what" directly, but not through conceptual understanding.

• *If you can manage an intimate meeting with him.* First meet yourself and be intimate with yourself. You were born with a silver spoon in your mouth.

• *You must be watchful in every way.* Do not deviate from your samadhi in any way.

• *Meeting a man of the Way.* You yourself are the man of the Way.

• *Meet him with neither words nor silence.* Meet him with either words or silence. Nothing restricts you but you yourself.

• *A punch on the jaw.* Mumon is not recommending the use of vio-

lence; he simply uses these words as an image of direct, intimate contact.
• *Understand, if you can directly understand.* This is an emphatic way of saying, "Understand it directly."

Case 37   Jōshū's Oak Tree

A monk asked Jōshū, "What is the meaning of Bodhidharma's coming to China?" Jōshū said, "The oak tree in the garden."

MUMON'S COMMENT   If you understand Jōshū's answer intimately, there is no Shakya before you, no Maitreya to come.

MUMON'S VERSE
  Words cannot express things;
  Speech does not convey the spirit.
  Swayed by words, one is lost;
  Blocked by phrases, one is bewildered.

NOTES   *What is the meaning of Bodhidharma's coming to China?* This was a popular question among ancient Zen monks. It was equivalent to asking, "What is the essence of Buddhism?"
• *The oak tree in the garden.* There were many giant oaks in the garden of Jōshū's temple. We can well imagine that Jōshū himself was personally familiar with every tree, stone, flower, weed, and clump of moss in the precincts of his temple—as intimately acquainted with them as if they were his own relatives. I once saw an example of such intimacy in an old priest who lived by himself in his temple. He had been ill, and when I visited him he was sitting quietly at the window basking in the sun. A few books of haiku and a notebook were beside him. He had been composing haiku. It was a calm winter day. In the course of our conversation, he pointed to a pine grove in front of the temple and said, "You

know the Zen question, 'The Bodhisattva of Great Mercy [Avalokites-vara, or Kannon] has a thousand hands and a thousand eyes; which is the true eye?' I could not understand this for a long time. But the other day, when I looked at the pine trees bending before the cold blasts from the mountain, I suddenly realized the meaning. You see, all the boughs, branches, twigs, and leaves simultaneously bend to the wind with tre-mendous vigor." He said this with a quiet but earnest gesture. I could feel his close intimacy with the pine trees. He had to convey his experience to somebody else. It was the evening glow of his life. He died a few weeks after our meeting.

• *If you understand Jōshū's answer intimately.* In *Hekiganroku*, Case 50, Ummon says, "Rice in the bowl, water in the pail," in answer to a monk's question, "What is the particle after particle's [moment by moment's] samadhi?" This is just like saying, "Rose in the vase, apple on the table." Look at them with a painter's eye.

• *There is no Shakya before you, no Maitreya to come.* Shakya (Shakya-muni) was a past Buddha; Maitreya is a Buddha who is to come in the future. No past or future Buddha can surpass you. You are your own lord throughout heaven and earth.

• *Words cannot express things.* The mind is enriched and develops it-self through the use of words. But the pure cognition of the mind thus enriched by words is intuitive, while the word itself remains a con-ception. A conception is a duplicate copy of pure cognition and cannot express things directly. However, in language samadhi you can achieve pure intuitive cognition through words. You must have had that experi-ence when reading your favorite poems or perusing the Bible. "Words cannot express things" is an admonition not to be merely conceptual in your understanding but to achieve pure cognition—in this case, of the oak tree.

• *Speech does not convey the spirit.* This line is concerned with the spiritual domain, while the first line is concerned with the external world. In both cases, conceptual understanding is of no use, as far as pure cogni-tion is concerned. The full text of this case from *Jōshū's Words* is as follows: "A monk asked Jōshū, 'What is the meaning of Bodhidharma's coming to China?' Jōshū said, 'The oak tree in the garden.' 'Don't answer me with the things of the external world,' said the monk. 'No, I do not,' answered Jōshū. 'What is the meaning of Bodhidharma's coming to China?' 'The oak tree in the garden.'"

• *Swayed by words, one is lost; / Blocked by phrases, one is bewildered.* While you are enslaved to words and depend solely on conceptual understanding, heedless of the pure cognition of the first nen, you will be lost and bewildered.

Case 38   A Buffalo Passes the Window

Goso said, "A buffalo passes by the window. His head, horns, and four legs all go past. But why can't the tail pass too?"

MUMON'S COMMENT   If you make a complete about-face, open your eye, and give a turning word on this point, you will be able to repay the four kinds of love that have favored you and help the sentient beings in the three realms who follow you. If you are still unable to do this, return to this tail and reflect upon it, and then for the first time you will realize something.

MUMON'S VERSE
  Passing by, it falls into a ditch;
  Coming back, all the worse, it is lost.
  This tiny little tail,
  What a strange thing it is!

NOTES   *A buffalo passes by the window.* In the practice of zazen you must experience the Great Death. The activity of consciousness dies away in absolute samadhi. First sensation drops away, then body and mind fall away.
• *His head, horns, and four legs all go past.* His body goes past. That is, observing ego (the first nen), reflecting ego (the second nen), and integrating ego (the third nen) all go past.
• *Why can't the tail pass too?* Samadhi itself never passes away. But what

is found in samadhi? Jishu-zammai, or self-mastery, is what is discovered. But how can you notice it while the activity of your consciousness has ceased? Retention (the direct past) is reflected upon and perceived, and you become aware of it. This topic has been regarded as the most difficult of Hakuin's "eight difficult cases," but I seem to have given it an easy interpretation. However, have I not simply replaced the tail, which sounds mysterious, with jishu-zammai, which sounds reasonable? Here is an instance of the sophistry of words. Unless you really master jishu-zammai, you have reached no real solution to the problem. However you look at it, this tail is a monster.

• *If you make a complete about-face.* If you make a turn of 180 degrees in your thoughts, desires, and attachments . . .

• *Open your eye.* . . . and become enlightened . . .

• *And give a turning word.* . . . and can demonstrate your enlightenment . . .

• *You will be able to repay the four kinds of love.* . . . then you can repay the favor of (1) your parents, (2) your country, (3) all beings in the world, and (4) all teachers, teachings, and the Sangha (the Buddhist monastic order).

• *The three realms.* The three realms are also called the three existences: (1) the world of desire (hell, hungry ghosts, animals, asuras, and human beings), (2) the world of form, and (3) the world of non-form —in effect, all living creatures.

• *Passing by, it falls into a ditch.* If you deviate from samadhi, you will fall into delusive thinking.

• *Coming back, all the worse, it is lost.* Coming back to the old condition—that is, to the world of delusion—you will be lost.

• *This tiny little tail, / What a strange thing it is!* Why don't you catch hold of it directly?

Case 39   A Mistake in Speaking

A monk said to Ummon, "The brilliance of the Buddha silently illuminates the whole universe . . ." But before he could finish the verse,

Ummon said, "Aren't those the words of Chōsetsu the Genius?" "Yes, they are," answered the monk. "You have slipped up in your speaking," Ummon said.

Afterward, Shishin Zenji brought up the matter and said, "Tell me, at what point did the monk err in his speaking?"

MUMON'S COMMENT   If you clearly understand this and realize how exacting Ummon was in his method, and what made the monk err in his speaking, you are qualified to be a teacher of heaven and earth. If you are not yet clear about it, you are far from saving yourself.

MUMON'S VERSE
A line is cast in the rapids,
The greedy will be caught.
Before you start to open your mouth,
Your life is already lost!

NOTES   *Chōsetsu* was called "Chōsetsu the Genius," Genius being the honorific title given to an official who had passed the civil service examinations (the "Dragon Gate"; see *Hekiganroku*, Case 7), which were the only opening to eminence. When he first met Sekisō Keisho, who was famed for his assiduous practice of zazen, Sekisō asked him, "What is your name?" Chōsetsu answered, "My family name is Chō, and my own name is Setsu." The word *setsu* happened to mean "unskilled," and Sekisō said, "To seek after skill is of no avail. Tell me, where does your 'setsu' come from?" At this, Chōsetsu experienced sudden realization and composed the following poem:

The brilliance of the Buddha silently illuminates the whole universe.
Wise and ignorant, sentient and nonsentient form one family.
No nen-action appearing, the whole is manifested.
The slightest stir of the six roots makes it overcast.
Cutting off delusion increases evils,
Seeking after the absolute invites a curse,
Looking after worldly affairs does no harm,
Nirvana and *samsara* are like flowers in a fantasy.

Here "samsara" means existence in the world—the unceasing round of becoming and passing away, of birth and death. It is the antithesis of Nirvana, the state of supreme enlightenment.

• *You have slipped up in your speaking.* What is the use of borrowing others' words?

• *Tell me, at what point did the monk err in his speaking?* Sometimes you can use others' words as much as you like, without fault, and sometimes you cannot. When can you and when can you not? That is Shishin's question.

• *How exacting Ummon was in his method.* In the original, the word for "exacting" is *koki* (*ko*, unapproachable; *ki*, steep). But this "unapproachably steep" also implies something of the unwearying exploitation of a usurer. Ummon deprives his disciple of his treasured understanding, of the beautiful statement, "The brilliance of the Buddha silently illuminates the whole universe," which must have fascinated the monk.

• *You are qualified to be a teacher of heaven and earth.* Mumon expresses his admiration for Ummon's words and deeds, while at the same time saying that anyone can be a teacher of heaven and earth if he is as mature as Ummon.

• *A line is cast in the rapids, / The greedy will be caught.* A Zen story is your own story. A line is always cast before you; if you are greedy, you will be caught.

• *Before you start to open your mouth.* There may be political, economic, or social freedom. Freedom of that sort is inevitably controlled by outward circumstances. But genuine freedom is solely concerned with your own mind. That is to say, being free from your greedy desires is genuine freedom. You are tempted not by external circumstances but by your own desires. Before you start to open your mouth, your freedom is restricted. You have no one to blame for it but yourself.

• *Your life is already lost!* We have all experienced this "lost" thousands of times and forgotten about it, as if nothing had happened.

Case 40   Tipping Over a Water Bottle

When Isan Oshō was with Hyakujō, he was *tenzo*, or head cook, of the monastery. Hyakujō wanted to choose a master for Mount Tai-i, so he called together all the monks and told them that anyone who could answer his question in an outstanding manner would be chosen. Then he took a water bottle and stood it on the floor, and said, "You may not call this a water bottle. What do you call it?" The head monk said, "It cannot be called a stump."

Hyakujō asked Isan his opinion. Isan tipped over the water bottle with his feet and went out. Hyakujō laughed and said, "The head monk loses." And Isan was named as the founder of the new monastery.

MUMON'S COMMENT   Isan displayed great spirit in his action, but he could not cut himself free from Hyakujō's apron strings. He preferred the heavier task to the lighter one. Why was he like that, eh? He took off his headband to bear the iron yoke.

MUMON'S VERSE
    Tossing bamboo baskets and ladles away,
    He made a glorious dash and swept all before him.
    Hyakujō's barrier cannot stop his advance;
    Thousands of Buddhas come forth from the tips of his feet.

NOTES   *Isan Oshō*, or Isan Reiyū (771–853), became a monk when he was fifteen. At first he studied under lecture-masters. When twenty-two, he went to Hyakujō (see Case 2) and studied Zen with him. One night he was in attendance on Hyakujō, sitting till late in the quietness of the mountain temple. "Who are you?" Hyakujō asked. "Reiyū," replied Isan. "Rake in the fireplace." Isan did as he was told and said, "I find no embers left." Hyakujō took up the tongs and, raking deep down, brought up a tiny burning ember, which he showed to Isan, and said, "Just this, you see!" Isan was suddenly enlightened. He made deep bows and presented his views to Hyakujō, who said, "You have reached a crossroads on the journey. It is said in the sutra, 'If you want to see Buddha Nature, you should observe time and causation.' When the time comes, you will realize it, just like remembering something you have forgotten. It is not obtained from others. Therefore, when you are enlightened it is just like when you were not enlightened. No mind, no Dharma. If only you have no delusions, and no discrimination between the Buddha and the unenlightened, your original nature manifests itself. Now you have attained it. Mindfully cultivate it."

Isan stayed with Hyakujō for twenty years. He was forty-three when Hyakujō died at the age of ninety-four. Then Isan went to Mount Tai-i, where he lived the life of a hermit, cultivating Holy Buddhahood. In the course of seven or eight years monks assembled around him, and eventually a great monastery grew up. Many distinguished Zen masters developed under his instruction, such as Kyōgen (Case 5) and Kyōzan (Case 25).

• *Hyakujō wanted to choose a master for Mount Tai-i.* A certain traveler, a discerning observer of scenery, returned from his journeyings and told Hyakujō about a beautiful mountain called Tai-i, which he recommended as a fine site for a monastery. Hyakujō wanted to nominate Isan as the master of it. But the head monk protested, saying that he should be the first man to be considered for the post. Then the test was made.

• *You may not call this a water bottle.* This is the question of objective fact and idea. When the bottle is broken, it is a bottle no longer. If you call it a water bottle, you go against the truth; if you do not call it a water bottle, you go against the fact. What do you call it? This is Hyakujō's question.

• *It cannot be called a stump.* The head monk's answer was not so bad. But he was evading the frontal attack.

• *Isan tipped over the water bottle.* Isan disposed of the nonsensical question in a striking manner. But can you really call Hyakujō's question nonsensical?

• *Isan was named as the founder of the new monastery.* The monastery was to be started from scratch. Isan sat in his cottage in a primeval wood with a miniature iron pagoda on his head. When he was sleepy and his posture collapsed, the pagoda would fall from his head. What is done by night appears by day. Buddhism recognizes thankless deeds done by stealth. As we have said, in seven or eight years monks gradually gathered around Isan, and eventually a great Zen monastery came into being.

• *Isan displayed great spirit.* He simply displayed his ordinary mind. He was disinterested in whether he became the master of a new monastery or not, and even in the special contest. This is why he could perform the daring feat.

• *He could not cut himself free from Hyakujō's apron strings.* You are advised to trample on your teacher's head, and at the same time, you are supposed to follow your teacher's instructions.

• *He preferred the heavier task to the lighter one.* He left the post of head cook to go through the hardship of starting the monastery, teaching disciples, and keeping the Lamp of the Dharma for transmission.

• *He took off his headband.* When cooking, the monk wears a headband.

• *To bear the iron yoke.* Both teacher and disciple underwent great hardships to secure the transmission of the Dharma; it was regarded as an inevitable burden.

• *Bamboo baskets and ladles.* These are kitchen utensils.

• *Thousands of Buddhas came forth from the tips of his feet.* He produced many distinguished Zen teachers.

Case 41   Bodhidharma's Mind-Pacifying

Bodhidharma sat facing the wall. The Second Patriarch stood in the snow. He cut off his arm and presented it to Bodhidharma, crying, "My mind has no peace as yet! I beg you, master, please pacify my mind!" "Bring your mind here and I will pacify it for you," replied Bodhidharma. "I have searched for my mind, and I cannot take hold of it," said the Second Patriarch. "Now your mind is pacified," said Bodhidharma.

MUMON'S COMMENT   That broken-toothed old Hindu came so importantly, thousands of miles over the sea. This was raising waves where there was no wind. In his last years he induced enlightenment in his disciple, who, to make matters worse, was defective in the six roots. Why, Shasanro did not know four ideographs.

MUMON'S VERSE
Coming east, directly pointing,
You entrusted the Dharma, and trouble arose;
The clamor of the monasteries
Is all because of you.

NOTES   *Bodhidharma* went by boat from India to South China around
A.D. 520. He was already an old man, and the voyage took three years.
He wandered northward, finally reaching the kingdom of Wei, and
established himself not far from the capital city, Lo-yang, in Shōrin
Temple on Mount Su, where he sat for nine years in silent meditation
facing the wall of his room. From this derives the term "wall-gazing."
The author of *The History of the Buddhist Temples of Lo-yang*, written
in 547, states that when he was visiting Einei Temple, one of the famous
temples of Lo-yang, he came upon Bodhidharma sitting in quiet admiration before the beauties of the shrines and pagodas; the old monk said he
was one hundred fifty years old. The date of his death is not known.

• *The Second Patriarch* was named Eka. (He is also known as Shinkō;
see *Hekiganroku*, Case 47.) From childhood he was different from others
in the spiritual quality of his nature. He read widely in the Chinese classics
and poetry. He paid little attention to worldly affairs but loved to roam
among the beauties of nature. Later he read Buddhist scriptures and became a monk. He visited many lecture-masters and became learned in
the teachings of both Hinayana and Mahayana Buddhism. When
twenty-three years old he started zazen practice and sat assiduously in
silent meditation for eight years. Then he suddenly underwent a spiritual
conversion in which a deity appeared and instructed him to go southward. Following the instruction, he journeyed to Shōrin Temple to visit
Bodhidharma. Bodhidharma at first refused to teach him, saying, "The
subtle and supreme teachings of the Buddhas can be pursued only by endless assiduity, doing what is hard to do and bearing what is hard to bear,
continuing the practice even for kalpas; how can a man of little virtue
and much self-conceit dream of achieving it? It will end only in fruitless
labor."
One night it snowed heavily. Eka stood in the snow. At dawn the
snow was up to his knees. Bodhidharma said, "What are you doing
there?" Eka replied, "I beg you to teach me."

A legend says that Eka cut off his arm and laid it before Bodhidharma to show his strong determination. Many Zen stories are symbolic in this way. At length, Bodhidharma admitted him to his room, and the questions and answers followed as described in the present case.

• *My mind has no peace.* Only when he has emptied himself has he peace of mind.

• *I beg you.* There is no point in begging for one's peace of mind, but one cannot help doing it all the same.

• *Please pacify my mind.* You cannot pacify your mind while you are asking others to do it for you.

• *Bring your mind here.* You cannot find your mind, much less bring it forth.

• *I will pacify it for you.* Peace of mind is spontaneously brought about.

• *I have searched for my mind.* Human beings have long searched for the mind.

• *I cannot take hold of it.* You can take hold of it, but not in the way you expected.

• *Now your mind is pacified.* Your mind is pacified spontaneously, not by others. The literal translation of the original text is "I have pacified the mind for you." But this "for you" is the same figure of speech as in Jō-shū's "I have investigated the old woman of Taisan for you" (Case 31).

• *The broken-toothed old Hindu.* Bodhidharma was old, and it seems he was called a toothless Hindu. This may also refer to a legend which says that he was poisoned by envious priests and had his teeth broken.

• *This was raising waves where there was no wind.* When one keeps to ordinary mind, there is no problem about life. But Bodhidharma introduced a troublesome theme and started a struggle in Eka to attain enlightenment. In fact, when the struggle is over and the ordinary condition of mind is restored, one finds that everything is all right. What is all this fuss about nothing?

• *Defective in the six roots.* The six roots are the trunk, the four limbs, and consciousness. The Second Patriarch is accused of being defective as an allusion to the purging of his mind of all disturbing elements. This is Mumon's usual praise in the guise of deprecation.

• *Shasanro did not know four ideographs.* Shasanro was the nickname of Gensha, who was an outstanding Zen master and a Dharma brother of Ummon. He was a fisherman until he was thirty years old and is said to have been illiterate, not even knowing the four ideographs written on a

Chinese coin. Knowing little but knowing everything is the characteristic of Zen masters. Mumon also had another reason for mentioning Gensha. Gensha once went on a pilgrimage, visiting Zen teachers. On the way he stumbled over a stone and stubbed his toes. "Ouch!" he cried. At that moment he felt the pain penetrating throughout his entire being and suddenly was enlightened. He stopped his pilgrimage, saying, "Bodhidharma did not come to China, the Second Patriarch did not go to India." This saying is much appreciated by Zen students and has a close connection with both the present case and Case 37. Gensha also appears in Cases 22, 56, and 88 of *Hekiganroku*.

• *Coming east, directly pointing, / You entrusted the Dharma, and trouble arose.* Chinese Zen was started by Bodhidharma.

• *The clamor of the monasteries / Is all because of you.* This is again Mumon disguising praise as blame.

Case 42   The Girl Comes out of Samadhi

Once, in the old days, in the time of the World-honored One, Manjusri went to the assembly of the Buddhas and found that everyone had departed to his original dwelling place. Only a girl remained, sitting in samadhi close to the Buddha's throne. Manjusri asked Shakyamuni Buddha, "Why can the girl get near the Buddha's throne, while I cannot?" Shakyamuni Buddha said, "Bring her out of her samadhi and ask her yourself." Manjusri walked around the girl three times, snapped his fingers once, took her to the Brahma heaven, and exerted all his miraculous powers to bring her out of her meditation, but in vain.

The World-honored One said, "Even a hundred thousand Manjusris cannot make her wake up. But down below, past twelve hundred million lands as innumerable as the sands of the Ganges, there is the Bodhisattva Mōmyō. He will be able to arouse her from her samadhi." Instantly the Bodhisattva Mōmyō emerged from the earth and made a bow to the World-honored One, who gave him his imperial order. The Bodhisattva went over to the girl and snapped his fingers once. At this she came out of her samadhi.

MUMON'S COMMENT Old Shakyamuni put a petty drama on the stage and failed to enlighten the masses. I want to ask you: Manjusri is the teacher of the Seven Buddhas; why couldn't he arouse the girl from her samadhi? How was it that Mōmyō, a Bodhisattva at the beginner's stage, could do it? If you understand this intimately, you will enjoy Nagya's grand samadhi in the busiest activity of consciousness.

MUMON'S VERSE
One was successful, the other was not;
Both secured freedom of mind.
One in a god-mask, the other in a devil-mask;
Even in defeat, a beautiful performance.

NOTES *Manjusri* is the Bodhisattva who represents wisdom. He is often shown standing on Shakyamuni's left, with Samantabhadra, who represents virtue, standing to the right of the Buddha. Manjusri holds a sutra in one hand and in the other the sword of wisdom, which cuts off all delusions. He rides upon a lion, the symbol of power and majesty.

• *Assembly of the Buddhas.* The Buddhas assembled and consulted about how to make unenlightened beings enter the Supreme Way and achieve Holy Buddhahood.

• *A girl remained, sitting in samadhi.* The girl represents your mind, and now she is sitting in samadhi.

• *Why can the girl get near the Buddha's throne, while I cannot?* The Buddha's throne symbolizes the center of samadhi. The girl's samadhi is hers alone. Even Manjusri cannot see into it, much less get near it.

• *Bring her out of her samadhi and ask her yourself.* Shakyamuni asks the impossible, to prove it is impossible.

• *Took her to the Brahma heaven.* Manjusri exercised miraculous powers and performed superhuman feats, but in vain.

• *Down below, past twelve hundred million lands.* One's absolute samadhi goes deep down below the twelve hundred million lands of the mind's realm.

• *Instantly the Bodhisattva Mōmyō emerged.* Mōmyō is a Bodhisattva at the beginner's stage, and when he wants to return to the level of the ordinary activity of consciousness, he can do so in an instant.

• *She came out of her samadhi.* The girl is the counterpart of Mōmyō.

• *Shakyamuni put a petty drama on the stage.* In the middle of the stage the Buddha's throne is set up. Near the throne a girl is sitting in meditation. Manjusri approaches, and his question and the Buddha's answer, the demonstration of Manjusri's miraculous powers of taking the girl up to the Brahma heaven, the emergence of the Bodhisattva Mōmyō, and the girl's coming out of her samadhi are all parts of the performance.

• *Failed to enlighten the masses.* The masses did not understand the drama.

• *Why couldn't he arouse the girl?* No one can arouse the girl from absolute samadhi except the girl herself.

• *How was it that Mōmyō, a Bodhisattva at the beginner's stage, could do it?* There are four wisdoms: Great Perfect Mirror Wisdom, Universal Nature Wisdom, Marvelous Observing Wisdom, and Perfecting of Action Wisdom. The former two are the fundamental wisdoms; the latter two are wisdoms achieved on the level of the ordinary activity of consciousness and belong to positive samadhi. One who has mastered these four wisdoms is at the stage of a Buddha. Mōmyō still has to achieve the latter two wisdoms and has to train himself in positive samadhi. So for this reason he makes the girl, his counterpart, come out into the realm of positive samadhi—the realm of the ordinary activity of consciousness.

• *If you understand this intimately.* If you understand this point and achieve perfect freedom in positive samadhi, then you will enjoy Nagya's grand samadhi even in the busiest activity of consciousness.

• *Nagya's grand samadhi.* "Nagya's grand samadhi" means the Buddha's profound samadhi. Nagya is a dragon, here used to symbolize the great power of the Buddha.

• *In the busiest activity of consciousness.* Samadhi in the busiest activity of consciousness is positive samadhi. The free command of positive samadhi is the aim of Zen practice. In *Hekiganroku*, Case 15, Setchō says, "How turbulent— / The moon reflected on the waves."

• *One was successful.* Whether you will be successful or not, I don't know. Simply play your part as well as a great actor on the stage plays his: with complete immersion in all he does.

• *The other was not.* In Nagya's samadhi, there is no discrimination between being successful and unsuccessful.

• *Both secured freedom of mind. / One in a god-mask, the other in a devil-mask; / Even in defeat, a beautiful performance.* In playful samadhi everything is all right, everything is beautiful.

Case 43   Shuzan's Shippei

Shuzan Oshō held up a *shippei* [staff of office] before his disciples and said, "You monks! If you call this a shippei, you oppose its reality. If you do not call it a shippei, you ignore the fact. Tell me, you monks, what will you call it?"

MUMON'S COMMENT   If you call it a shippei, you oppose its reality. If you do not call it a shippei, you ignore the fact. Words are not available; silence is not available. Now, tell me quickly, what is it?

MUMON'S VERSE
  Holding up the shippei,
  He takes life, he gives life.
  Opposing and ignoring interweave.
  Even Buddhas and patriarchs beg for their lives.

NOTES   *Shuzan* (926–93) became a monk when he was young. Because he liked to recite the *Lotus Sutra*, he was called "Nen-hokke" (*nen*, reciter; *Hokke*, the *Lotus Sutra*). In his prime he set out to visit Zen masters and studied with Fuketsu (see Case 24), whom he succeeded, thus being in the lineage of the Rinzai sect.

• *Shippei.* This is a staff of office made of a piece of bamboo about three feet long, the head of which is bound around with wisteria vine. Another name for it is "broken bow," from its shape. It is used by a master when he appears at a Dharma battle.

• *If you call this a shippei, you oppose its reality. If you do not call it a shippei, you ignore the fact.* If you try to answer this question, you will find yourself involved in the problem of reality and fact, mental idea and objective phenomenon.

• *What will you call it?* A child will be able to name it properly without much trouble.

• *Words are not available.* Words come from conceptions. You cannot answer this question while you are relying upon conceptual manipulation.

• *Silence is not available.* Silence, meaning the opposite of words, is also not available. While you think in a relative way, you cannot answer.

• *Now, tell me quickly.* What is the use of being in a hurry? You can say it calmly.

• *What is it?* Call it what you like.

• *He takes life, he gives life.* What's the use of being under his sway? You have nothing to do with him.

• *Opposing and ignoring interweave.* Simply watch the shippei or anything else in your samadhi, and what a different world appears! Everything is simplified and beautiful, and everything is all right. Call it by whatever name you like and you are right.

• *Even Buddhas and patriarchs beg for their lives.* Begging or not begging, they enjoy their playful samadhi.

Case 44   Bashō's Staff

Bashō Oshō said to his disciples, "If you have a staff, I will give you a staff. If you have no staff, I will take it from you."

MUMON'S COMMENT   It helps me wade across a river when the bridge is down. It accompanies me to the village on a moonless night. If you call it a staff, you will enter hell like an arrow.

MUMON'S VERSE
   The depths and shallows of the world
   Are all in its grasp.
   It supports the heavens and sustains the earth.
   Everywhere, it enhances the doctrine.

NOTES *Bashō Oshō* was a Korean monk who went to China, visiting Zen masters, and succeeded Nantō. He lived on Mount Bashō, from which his name was derived. Seijō Oshō of Case 9 was his disciple. The dates of his birth and death are not known. He seems to have been more or less a contemporary of Fuketsu (Case 24).

• *If you have a staff, I will give you a staff. If you have no staff, I will take it from you.* A staff about seven feet long was used by a monk when he went on his travels, visiting teachers or seeking a quiet hermitage. It naturally developed a symbolic meaning, representing a guide to and eventually the essence of Zen itself, just as the cross does in Christianity. Ummon once showed his staff to his assembled disciples and said, "This staff has transformed itself into a dragon and swallowed up the universe. Where are the mountains, the rivers, and the great world?" In the present case, Bashō is saying: Even if you have already attained something of enlightenment, you have not yet fully secured it. So I must give you a helping hand to lead you to a mature enlightenment. (If you have a staff, I will give you a staff.) And when you are mature in your enlightenment, you must not remain there; you must go a step further to transcend it, and forget your own enlightenment. This forgetting is called "leaving no trace behind," and it is a most exacting piece of practice. The effacement of the trace of enlightenment is emphatically and repeatedly advocated by Zen masters, as well as in the Zen literature. Bashō is emphasizing this point: If you have the slightest idea that you already have no staff, you must be deprived of that "no staff." (If you have no staff, I will take it from you.)

• *It helps me.* The genuine staff helps you in every way.

• *Wade across a river.* In your playful samadhi, you enjoy even hardship, pain, adversity, defeat, and suffering. How poetic is the broken bridge, how quiet the moonless night!

• *If you call it a staff, you will enter hell like an arrow.* Even merely mentioning the word "Buddha" makes us rinse out our mouths for three days (see Case 30).

Case 45 Hōen's "Who Is He?"

Hōen of Tōzan said, "Even Shakya and Maitreya are servants of another. I want to ask you, who is he?"

MUMON'S COMMENT If you can really see this "another" with perfect clarity, it is like encountering your own father at a crossroads. Why should you ask whether you recognize him or not?

MUMON'S VERSE
   Don't draw another's bow,
   Don't ride another's horse,
   Don't discuss another's faults,
   Don't explore another's affairs.

NOTES *Hōen of Tōzan.* Tōzan was another name for Mount Goso, from which Goso (who appears in Cases 35, 36, and 38) derived his name. Hōen was Goso's personal name.

• *Even Shakya and Maitreya are servants of another.* How great that "another" must be!

• *I want to ask you, who is he?* It is easy to answer this question, but to identify yourself as "he" is most difficult.

• *Don't draw another's bow.* Hōen's "another" developed into your father in Mumon's comment and turned into yet another person in his verse. "Bow" represents knowledge or wisdom, and "Don't draw another's bow" is interpreted as meaning, "Don't borrow from other authorities."

• *Don't ride another's horse.* "Horse" represents achievement, and this line is telling you not to play an ass in a lion's skin.

• *Don't discuss another's faults.* Don't speak ill of another.

• *Don't explore another's affairs.* Don't meddle in another's business. The first and second lines of Mumon's verse advise you to behave prudently; the third and fourth lines, to refrain from interfering in another's concerns.

The problem of unity and difference is an important topic in Zen. In absolute samadhi, absolute unity appears and Universal Nature Wisdom develops. When emerging from absolute samadhi into the world of the ordinary activity of consciousness, differentiation necessarily appears, and how to behave yourself in relation to other people then becomes a problem. Zen develops Marvelous Observing Wisdom and Perfecting of Action Wisdom to solve this problem. Dōgen Zenji says, "Learning Buddhism is studying yourself." Your self develops from universal nature to differentiated nature. Therefore it is said, "Equality without difference is a bad equality; difference without equality is a bad difference." How to master equality and difference is the theme of the cultivation of Holy Buddhahood after realization. (See chapter 17 of *Zen Training* for a discussion of this question.)

Case 46   Proceed On from the Top of the Pole

Sekisō Oshō asked, "How can you proceed on further from the top of a hundred-foot pole?" Another eminent teacher of old said, "You, who sit on the top of a hundred-foot pole, although you have entered the Way you are not yet genuine. Proceed on from the top of the pole, and you will show your whole body in the ten directions."

MUMON'S COMMENT   If you go on further and turn your body about, no place is left where you are not the master. But even so, tell me, how will you go on further from the top of a hundred-foot pole? Eh?

MUMON'S VERSE
He darkens the third eye of insight
And clings to the first mark on the scale.
Even though he may sacrifice his life,
He is only a blind man leading the blind.

NOTES   *Sekisō Oshō.* This is Sekisō Soen (986–1039), who was a spiritual grandson of Shuzan and great-grandfather of Goso. He became a monk at the age of twenty-two, visited famous teachers of the time, and succeeded Funyō Zenshō. His life was rather short, but he left a notable imprint on the history of Zen. This Sekisō is not the same person as Sekisō Keisho, who appears in Cases 55 and 91 of *Hekiganroku*.

• *How can you proceed on further from the top of a hundred-foot pole?* This saying has long been popular among Zen students, and its spirit has become part of the cultural background of the East. It is a common saying even on the lips of ordinary lay people.

When you have made considerable progress in your zazen practice, you come to a sort of extremity, where you find yourself on the brink of an abyss which is veiled in complete darkness. Suddenly you are scared. You feel that there is no knowing what calamity may follow if you proceed a step further into the darkness. Some psychotic people are said to be thrown into a panic the moment they find sleep starting to blur their consciousness because they feel their activity of consciousness may never return. In zazen practice, consciousness does not sleep, but it does come nearly to a stop, and when a Zen student first experiences this, he often becomes panic-stricken. It is just as if he were trembling on the top of a pole. But Zen masters require you to let your hands go and proceed further. What follows? The Great Death occurs: the activity of consciousness stops. You jump into the abyss. But don't worry, no calamity ensues.

In order to make a clean sweep of the habitual deluded way of consciousness, one must repeatedly go through this condition of the Great Death. Up to now, I have been speaking in the context of absolute samadhi. How will it be in positive samadhi, in the busiest activity of consciousness? Climbing the cliff face, let your hands go. Throw away your enlightenment. In other words, throw away all that you have achieved. Throw away your enlightenment, original nature, Buddhahood, Dharma, ordinary mind, everything. Be reduced to emptiness. Cast away even the emptiness. This is proceeding on further from the top of a hundred-foot pole.

But Sekisō asks, "How can you proceed on further?" How to do this in practice is the constant problem, ever to be returned to with all the earnestness we are capable of.

• *Another eminent teacher of old.* The eminent teacher referred to here is Chōsa Keishin (see *Hekiganroku,* Case 36), who was a disciple of Nansen and a spiritual brother of Jōshū. Once a monk asked Nansen, "How can I proceed on further from the top of a hundred-foot pole?" "Walk on a step further" was Nansen's answer.

Chōsa put this injunction into a fine verse of four lines, which is quoted in the present case.

• *You, who sit on the top of a hundred-foot pole.* This is the first line of Chōsa's verse. Many Zen students stick to their *satori* (enlightenment) and are satisfied with it. They never think to proceed further. They do not know that if they stand still for one day, one day's stagnation necessarily appears.

• *Although you have entered the Way, you are not yet genuine.* If you want your enlightened condition to be truly genuine, you must empty yourself of everything, and then again cast away what you have emptied.

• *You will show your whole body in the ten directions.* The ten directions are all directions in which you do not experience any restriction. You enjoy perfect freedom.

• *Turn your body about.* It is important to know how to turn about.

• *Tell me, how will you go on further from the top of a hundred-foot pole?* Why is this question asked over and over again? Because it expresses a very important Zen truth, which requires the strongest emphasis. Climbing to the top of the pole is attaining your own enlightenment. But once you have attained it, you must come down to help others to attain their enlightenment. Rising is for your own benefit; coming down is for others' profit. Benefiting yourself and profiting others are the two pillars of Zen practice. But really, what sort of thing is the coming down? It is returning to the world to admit and embrace people of all types. Unless you achieve that capacious sort of mind, your practice cannot be said to be successful.

• *He darkens the third eye of insight.* He who sits on the top of a hundred-foot pole and does not know how to proceed further darkens the third eye of insight. (Although he has entered the Way, he is not yet genuine.)

• *And clings to the first mark on the scale.* It is as if he clings to the first mark on the scale when weighing something, not knowing how to change the position of the weight along the scale of the balance.

• *Even though he may sacrifice his life.* Even if he goes so far as to sacrifice his life in his practice of Zen, if he sticks to anything he is going the wrong way. He is still blind to the genuine truth of Zen.

• *He is only a blind man leading the blind.* If he, being blind to Zen truth, tries to lead others it will end in the blind leading the blind.

Case 47   Tosotsu's Three Barriers

Tosotsu Etsu Oshō set up three barriers for his disciples:

1. You leave no stone unturned to explore profundity, simply to see into your true nature. Now, I want to ask you, just at this moment, where is your true nature?
2. If you realize your true nature, you are free from life and death. Tell me, when your eyesight deserts you at the last moment, how can you be free from life and death?
3. When you set yourself free from life and death, you should know your ultimate destination. So when the four elements separate, where will you go?

MUMON'S COMMENT   If you can put turning words to these three questions, you are the master wherever you may stand and command Zen whatever circumstances you may be in. If otherwise, listen: gulping down your meal will fill you easily, but chewing it well can sustain you.

MUMON'S VERSE
   This moment's thought sees through eternal time;
   Eternal time is just this moment.
   If you see.through this moment's thought,
   You see through the man who sees through this moment.

NOTES   *Tosotsu Etsu Oshō* (1044–91) became a monk in his early years, studied both Hinayana and Mahayana Buddhism, and traveled about the country to visit Zen masters. He succeeded Hōhō Kokubun. He set up the three barriers to teach his disciples.

• *You leave no stone unturned to explore profundity.* You cannot help doing so, because you are impelled to solve the problem of your mind.

• *Simply to see into your true nature.* Look into your own samadhi.

• *Just at this moment, where is your true nature?* Look into your own samadhi.

• *You are free from life and death.* You do not worry about them.

• *When your eyesight deserts you.* When it has appeared, it is there before you. When it has gone, it is gone.

• *How can you be free from life and death?* It is very simple: you can be free from life and death in your samadhi.

• *You should know your ultimate destination.* Bodhidharma did not come to China, and the Second Patriarch did not go to India.

• *When the four elements separate.* The four elements are earth, water, fire, and air; it is from these, according to ancient theory, that man is made.

• *Where will you go?* What will you become?

• *If you can put turning words to these three questions.* For "turning words" see the notes to Case 2. You may say first samadhi, second samadhi, and third samadhi.

• *You are the master wherever you may stand.* You can benefit yourself.

• *And command Zen whatever circumstances you may be in.* And you help others.

• *Gulping down your meal will fill you easily.* Many are easily satisfied with petty experiences.

• *Chewing it well can sustain you.* A certain celebrated Zen master spent fifteen years before he had his great experience. But once he hit on it, he made such rapid progress that he soon outdistanced his comrades, who had been ahead of him.

• *This moment's thought sees through eternal time.* The first nen looks on outward things. The second nen reflects upon the immediately preceding first nen. The third nen reflects upon the preceding first nen and second nen and synthesizes them into one thought, and there self-consciousness appears. No nen-thought reflects upon itself. (Subjectivity cannot objectify itself. When objectified by the reflecting action, it is already turned into an object.) Therefore, every action of consciousness is unconscious of itself. Illogical as it may sound, consciousness works unconsciously.

The first nen is the first ego, which looks on outward things. The second nen is the second ego, which reflects on the action of the immediately preceding first ego. The third nen is the third ego, which reflects on the preceding first and second egos, recognizes them as oneself, and produces self-consciousness. None of the three egos recognizes itself, so that each ego acts unconsciously of itself. To ask which is the fundamental ego is nonsense. Each appears in succession to the others, and while each is playing its role it is the master of the mind. Each ego is unique. The third ego is reflected upon and recognized by the next-coming ego (which may be the first, second, or third ego). Any ego that is not reflected upon (not recognized) is not remembered and passes into oblivion. Each ego is pure and original; it is different from the so-called empirical self.

The third ego synthesizes all the preceding egos into one self, but the synthesized self has already lost its originality. It is not direct. It is an artificial and empirical self, or a remembered ego. However, this synthesized self claims, in its delusion, to regard itself as a constant self: this is the origin of the deluded way of thinking of consciousness. It must be stressed that there is no constant ego, only moment after moment's ego appearing in succession. Your identification of yourself comes from the warm, direct feeling that pervades each ego.

Now one can see the truth of the saying that this moment's thought sees through eternal time: it is because this moment is the eternal present. You can realize this eternity in your samadhi.

• *Eternal time is just this moment.* What really exists is this present moment. In your samadhi this present is sustained as long as your samadhi continues, and there eternity is demonstrated.

• *If you see through this moment's thought.* This moment's thought can be the first, second, or third nen, or the first, second, or third ego, which plays its role at that moment.

• *You see through the man who sees through this moment.* The man who sees through this moment is the ego that plays its role at this moment. It can be the first, the second, or the third ego. You, who see through the man, who see this moment's thought, are the reflecting action of the third nen, which recognizes all the preceding egos and synthesizes them into one ego. Thus self-consciousness is established, and seeing into one's original nature (pure ego) is accomplished. Nothing can be more fundamental than the recognition of one's own pure ego. That is realization. (For a further discussion see *Zen Training*, chapter 10.)

Case 48   Kempō's One Road

A monk said to Kempō Oshō, "It is written, 'Bhagavats in the ten directions. One straight road to Nirvana.' I still wonder where the road can be." Kempō lifted his staff, drew a line, and said, "Here it is."

Later the monks asked the same question of Ummon, who held up his fan and said, "This fan jumps up to the thirty-third heaven and hits the nose of the deity Sakra Devanam Indra. When you strike the carp of the eastern sea, the rain comes down in torrents."

MUMON'S COMMENT   One, going to the bottom of the sea, lifts up clouds of dust; the other, on top of the highest mountain, raises towering waves to wash the sky. One holding fast, the other letting go, each stretches out his hand to support the profound teaching. They are just like two riders starting from opposite ends of the course and meeting in the middle. But none on earth can be absolutely direct. When examined with a true eye, neither of these two great masters knows the road.

MUMON'S VERSE
　　Before a step is taken, the goal is reached;
　　Before the tongue is moved, the speech is finished.
　　Though each move is ahead of the next,
　　There is still a transcendent secret.

NOTES   *Kempō Oshō.* Little is known of Kempō except that he was a disciple of Tōzan, the founder of the Sōtō sect.

• *Bhagavats in the ten directions.* Buddhas (Bhagavats) are found everywhere (in the ten directions). There is nothing but Buddhas.

• *One straight road to Nirvana.* A broad, level highway leads to Nirvana. The monk quoted these two lines from the *Surangama Sutra*.

• *I still wonder where the road can be.* "Swayed by words, one is lost; / Blocked by phrases, one is bewildered" (Case 37). This monk was trying to find truth in the lines of the sutra, and was blocked and bewildered by them. Words and phrases are not to blame. But first you must practice; then you will find that words and phrases are very helpful.

• *Kempō lifted his staff, drew a line, and said, "Here it is."* Kempō drew a line in the air, or perhaps on the ground. Anyway, he showed that the road was not far away but here before the monk.

• *Ummon . . . held up his fan.* Kempō used his staff, Ummon his fan. Both used the article at hand as an immediate and spontaneous symbol of Bhagavat, Nirvana, and the road. Kempō's illustration was simple, but Ummon's was elaborate. His fan jumped up to heaven. The thirty-third heaven is the highest part of the universe, and the deity Sakra Devanam Indra presides there. These mythological figures were familiar to Zen students, just as Greek mythology is familiar to Westerners. Ummon's fan rose to the highest place in the universe and performed a conspicuous action in striking the supreme deity. But these words of Ummon's are a little more elaborate than his usual acute, pithy utterances. He must have been in a relaxed mood, in a state of playful samadhi. He did not stop here but went further.

• *When you strike the carp of the eastern sea, the rain comes down in torrents.* The carp of the eastern sea is also a mysterious being. When the time comes, it becomes a dragon and ascends to heaven, accompanied by a stormy wind and black clouds of torrential rain. This is a metaphorical description of a monk's attaining enlightenment.

• *One holding fast, the other letting go.* There are two phases in Zen activity, which we may call holding fast, or grasping, and letting go, or releasing. In the former a Zen master is negative, close, severe, and exacting; in the latter he is positive, open, relaxed, and generous. (See the notes to Case 4 of *Hekiganroku* for a more extensive discussion of this point.)

• *One, going to the bottom of the sea, lifts up clouds of dust.* Going to the bottom of the sea is "close," but he lifts up clouds of dust, which is "open."

• *The other, on top of the highest mountain, raises towering waves to wash the sky.* Standing on the top of the highest mountain is "open," but raising towering waves to wash the sky is unapproachable.

• *Each stretches out his hand to support the profound teaching.* One drew a line; that seems unapproachable. The other played with his fan, as if relaxed. Each represents one of the two phases and stretches out a helping hand. But are they simply unapproachable or simply relaxed?

• *They are just like two riders starting from opposite ends of the course and meeting in the middle.* Two riders started from opposite ends of a racecourse—the two ends representing the two phases, holding fast and letting go—and, meeting in the middle of the course, thus covered the whole length of it.

• *But none on earth can be absolutely direct.* Why don't you reveal the secret of Zen directly instead of resorting to the roundabout way of drawing a line or playing with a fan?

• *Neither of these two great masters knows the road.* Here again Mumon's idiosyncratic way of talking is not really about the two masters but is an exhortation to you to do the job yourself.

• *Before a step is taken, the goal is reached.* Bodhidharma did not come to China. Zen is not a matter of coming and going. Truth is in front of your nose.

• *Before the tongue is moved, the speech is finished.* It is not the tongue that you speak with.

• *Though each move is ahead of the next.* However shrewd you may be . . .

• *There is still a transcendent secret.* . . . . Zen's secret transcends your conceptual understanding.

Mumon's Postscript

THE SAYINGS AND DOINGS of the Buddha and the patriarchs have been set down in their original form. Nothing superfluous has been added by the author, who has taken the lid off his head and exposed his eyeballs. Your direct realization is demanded; it should not be sought through others.

If you are a man of realization, you will immediately grasp the point at the slightest mention of it. There is no gate for you to go through; there are no stairs for you to ascend. You pass the checkpoint, squaring your shoulders, without asking permission of the keeper.

Remember Gensha's saying, "No-gate is the gate of emancipation; no-meaning is the meaning of the man of the Way." And Hakuun says, "Clearly you know how to talk of it, but why can't you pass this simple, specific thing?"

However, all this kind of talk is like making a mud pie with milk and butter. If you have passed the Mumonkan, you can make a fool of Mumon. If not, you are betraying yourself. It is easy to know the Nirvana mind but difficult to attain the wisdom of differentiation. When you have realized this wisdom, peace and order will reign over your land.

The change of era to Jōtei [1228], five days before the end of the summer session

Respectfully inscribed by Mumon Ekai Bhikkhu, eighth in succession from Yōgi

NOTES *Gensha.* See the notes to Case 41.
• *Hakuun* was Goso's teacher.
• *Why can't you pass this simple, specific thing?* Why can't you pass through to the ultimate truth?
• *Yōgi* was descended from Rinzai and was the founder of a new division within the Rinzai sect called the Yōgi school.

The four pieces that follow are traditionally printed with *Mumonkan*, though they do not form part of the original text.

Mumon's Zen Warnings

To stick to rules and regulations is to tie yourself without a rope. Arbitrary self-indulgence is heresy and devilry. Clinging to silence is *mokushō*, false Zen. Selfish neglect of your surroundings is falling into a deep pit. Perfectionist watchfulness is wearing the yoke and chains. Thinking good and evil is attachment to heaven and hell. Addiction to Buddha and Dharma invites banishment beyond the two iron Cakravala.

Alternately daydreaming and awakening is playing with your own spirit. Practicing zazen of the dead is the devil's project. Proceeding, you fall into delusion; withdrawing, you go against the truth. When neither proceeding nor withdrawing, you are a breathing corpse. Tell me, how will you do it? Finish it in this life. Don't let yourself suffer an eternal karmic debt.

NOTES   *Clinging to silence is mokushō, false Zen.* Blank sitting in idle quietism is denounced (*moku*, silent; *shō*, illumination). The form of zazen practice called *shikantaza* is often called mokushō Zen, but this is not the mokushō referred to here.

• *Banishment beyond the two iron Cakravala.* There are nine Cakravala, which are mountain ranges around Mount Sumeru, the center of the universe. The outermost range, the ninth, of which Mumon speaks here, is of iron. The idea of "two" may have come from thinking of the outside and inside of the wall. Banishment beyond this mountain range means banishment from the universe, the greatest punishment. There is a Zen saying, "Last night Manjusri entertained the idea of being a Buddha and was immediately banished beyond the iron Cakravala." Addiction to Buddha is emphatically condemned.

• *Zazen of the dead.* Sitting in idle blankness is called "dead man's zazen."

• *Proceeding, you fall into delusion.* Conceptual research into enlightenment will lead only to bewilderment.

• *Withdrawing, you go against the truth.* If you return to your old delusive condition, having known the truth, then you will be lost. "Passing by, it falls into a ditch; / Coming back, all the worse, it is lost" (Case 38).

• *When neither proceeding nor withdrawing, you are a breathing corpse.*
He who lacks force and determination is a hopeless waverer.

• *Karmic debt.* Your present thoughts and actions are the product of your past thoughts and actions. Likewise, your present thoughts and actions will produce your future karma. What can give a new direction to the mind and its karma is your present thoughts and actions. Through the repeated practice of samadhi, the old trend of the mind is slowly changed. This is redeeming one's karmic debt.

Sōju's Verses on Ōryū's Three Barriers

HOW ARE MY HANDS LIKE THE BUDDHA'S HANDS?
Feeling for the pillow at the back of my head,
I gave, involuntarily, a loud laugh
To find my entire body all originally hand.

HOW ARE MY LEGS LIKE A DONKEY'S LEGS?
Before stepping out, I am already moving on,
Stalking freely all over the four seas,
Facing backward astride Yōgi's three-legged creature.

EVERYBODY HAS HIS KARMA RELATION.
Each expresses his original nature before his thoughts arise.
Nada broke his own bones and gave them back to his father.
Did the Fifth Patriarch have a father?

The Buddha's hands, the donkey's legs, the karma relation:
Not the Buddha, not the Way, not Zen;
No wonder the Mumonkan is so steep.
It elicits the deepest animosity among Zen monks.

Mumon recently at Zuigan Temple
Gave his lectures and judged ancient and modern masters.

He cut off all thought of people and sages,
And dragons arose roaring from their hibernation.

> *Presented as poor verses to express deep gratitude to Head Monk
> Mumon for coming and guiding the monks in compliance with our
> invitation*
> *Late spring of the third year of Jōtei [1230]*
> *Written by Muryō Sōju*

NOTES *Sōju*. Little is known of Muryō Sōju except that he was descended from Rinzai. He invited Mumon to deliver lectures on the forty-eight cases of *Mumonkan* and presented these verses in gratitude. The lines printed in small capitals are by Ōryū, the rest by Sōju.

· *Ōryū*. Ōryū Enan (1002–69) was the eighth in succession from Rinzai and initiated the so-called Ōryū school, one of two new schools within the Rinzai sect. In his interviews he would pose his disciples these three problems. Many gave their individual answers. Ōryū would listen to them, but said nothing by way of giving judgment. Some asked why he gave no judgment. He answered, "A guilty conscience needs no judge."

· *How are my hands like the Buddha's hands?* How like my hand is the watch in my hand!

· *Feeling for the pillow at the back of my head*. Ungan, the teacher of Tōzan, once asked Dōgo, his Dharma brother, "What use does the Great Bodhisattva of Mercy [Avalokitesvara] make of all those hands and eyes of his?" Dōgo said, "It is just like feeling for one's pillow at the back of one's head at dead of night." Ungan said, "I understand; his entire body is hand and eye."

· *How are my legs like a donkey's legs?* No man on the saddle, no horse under the saddle; man and horse make one body, and the circus performance is beautifully accomplished.

· *Before stepping out, I am already moving on.* Before the thought flashes, it is already done.

· *Stalking freely all over the four seas.* While walking, I do not know that I am walking.

· *Facing backward astride Yōgi's three-legged creature.* Yōgi, like Ōryū, was a disciple of Sekisō, and was the founder of the Yōgi school within the Rinzai sect. Once a monk asked Yōgi, "What is the Buddha?" Yōgi said, "A three-legged donkey goes moving its hooves." The "three-legged creature" refers to the Buddha's three bodies: Dharmakaya, Sambhogakaya, and Nirmanakaya.

• *Everybody has his karma relation.* Everybody has his parents and family relationships.

• *Each expresses his original nature before his thoughts arise.* Even a newborn baby, who has no activity of consciousness, acts according to his original nature.

• *Nada broke his own bones and gave them back to his father.* According to legend, Prince Nada cut off his flesh, giving it to his mother, broke his bones, giving them to his father, and then, manifesting his original nature, delivered a sermon for the sake of his father and mother.

• *Did the Fifth Patriarch have a father?* The Fifth Patriarch was said to have been born of a virgin.

Mōkyō's Epilogue

BODHIDHARMA COMING from the West, unattached to words, pointing directly to the mind of man, advocated seeing into one's nature and becoming Buddha.

To say "pointing directly" is already meandering. "Becoming Buddha" is not a little confusing. From the beginning it has been gateless; how can there be a checkpoint? Grandmotherly kindness caused much criticism. Muan is adding an extra one to make Case 49. There we have a little complication. See through it with your eyes open.

Summer of the fifth year of Junyū [1245]
The second edition
Written by Mōkyō

NOTE *Mōkyō* was a warrior who spent much of his time on the battlefield. But he is said to have been learned in Buddhism. He called himself Muan (*Mu*, Mu; *an*, hermitage; hence, the master of a hermitage of Mu).

Amban's Forty-ninth Case

OLD MASTER MUMON DRAFTED forty-eight cases and judged the koans of ancient teachers. He is like a fried-bean-cake seller who wants to open the customer's mouth and stuff it with his cakes until the customer can neither swallow nor disgorge them. Be that as it may, now Amban wants to cook an extra one on Mumon's hot oven and add it to the forty-eight, and offer it to you in Mumon's manner. I wonder where the master would put his teeth into it? If anyone can swallow it at once, he will emit the Buddha-light and make the earth shake. If he cannot, the present forty-eight plus this one will turn into the red-hot sands of hell. Say quickly! Say quickly!

THE CASE   The sutra says, "Stop! Stop! Don't try to expound it. The Dharma mysteriously transcends thinking!"

AMBAN'S COMMENT   Where does the Dharma come from? How could it be mysterious? What about when it is expounded? Not only Bukan was talkative; Shakyamuni himself was the original chatterbox. That old fellow created a lot of phantoms and made a thousand generations tumble about in entanglements, unable to stick their heads out. As for the present fine cases of Mumon, you cannot scoop them up or steam them. Some puzzled people may ask, "After all, what is the conclusion of all this?"

Amban puts his ten fingernails together and says, "Stop! Stop! Don't try to expound it; the Dharma mysteriously transcends thinking!" And in a flash he draws a small circle over the two words "transcends thinking" and shows it, saying, "The five thousand volumes of the sutras and Vimalakirti's 'One Gate Only' are all here."

AMBAN'S VERSE
If anyone tells you, "Light is fire,"
Move your head and make no answer.

One devil knows the way of another;
At one question all is clear.
    Summer of the sixth year of Junyū [1246]
    Written by Amban at the Fishing Villa of West Lake

NOTES   *Amban* was a civil official and literary man. It seems he did not know about Mōkyō's epilogue and wrote his a year later than Mōkyō's, making two forty-ninth cases.

• *Amban puts his ten fingernails together.* He joins his hands and recites the sutra. He is not explaining it, he is simply reciting it.

• *Vimalakirti's "One Gate Only."* See *Hekiganroku*, Case 84.

• *Light is fire.* Truth is directly manifested, just as fire is fire. Don't seek after it elsewhere.

• *Move your head and make no answer.* There is no need to make any answer.

• *One devil knows the way of another.* Like knows like.

• *At one question all is clear.* The moment you open your mouth, you are seen through.

HEKIGANROKU

Case 1 Emperor Wu Asks Bodhidharma

ENGO'S INTRODUCTION Smoke over the hill indicates fire, horns over the fence indicate an ox. Given one corner, you grasp the other three; one glance, and you discern the smallest difference. Such quickness, however, is only too common among robed monks. When you have stopped the deluded activity of consciousness, then, whatever situation you may find yourself in, you enjoy perfect freedom, in adversity and prosperity, in taking and giving. Now tell me, how in fact will this sort of person behave? See Setchō's complications.

MAIN SUBJECT Emperor Wu of Liang asked Bodhidharma, "What is the first principle of the holy teachings?" Bodhidharma said, "Emptiness, no holiness." "Who is this standing before me?" "No knowing." The emperor did not grasp his meaning. Thereupon Bodhidharma crossed the river and went to the land of Wei.

The emperor later spoke of this to Shikō, who said, "Do you in fact know who this person is?" The emperor said, "No knowing." Shikō said, "This is the Bodhisattva Kannon, the bearer of the Buddha's Heart Seal." The emperor was full of regret and wanted to send for Bodhidharma, but Shikō said, "It is no good sending a messsenger to fetch him back. Even if all the people went, he would not turn back."

SETCHŌ'S VERSE
The holy teaching? "Emptiness!"
What is the secret here?
Again, "Who stands before me?"
"No knowing!"

Inevitable, the thorns and briars springing up;
Secretly, by night, he crossed the river.

All the people could not bring him back.
Now, so many years gone by,
Still Bodhidharma fills your mind—in vain.
Stop thinking of him!
A gentle breeze pervades the universe.

The master looks around:
"Is the patriarch there?
—Yes! Bring him to me,
And he can wash my feet."

NOTES *Given one corner, you grasp the other three.* This is a reference to the *Analects* of Confucius, book 7, chapter 8, where it is said, "When I have presented one corner of a subject to anyone and he cannot learn from it the other three, I do not repeat my lesson."

• *Complications.* The literal translation here is "vines and creepers," referring to the tangled growths that had to be cleared away from the sites of monks' hermitages. The word came to mean koans, which entangle students in difficulties.

• *Emperor Wu* (502–50), founder of the Liang dynasty in southern China, was one of the early Buddhist emperors of China. He built many temples, translated sutras, and himself gave lectures on Buddhism. He appears again in Case 67.

• *Bodhidharma* came to China in 520. (See *Mumonkan*, Case 41.)

• *Emptiness.* The characters used in the original text are *kakunen* (*kaku*, empty and boundless as outer space; *nen*, -ness). Hence, the literal translation would be "emptiness and boundlessness."

• *Who is this standing before me?* This was prompted by "No holiness."

• *No knowing.* The original text has *fushiki* (*fu*, no; *shiki*, knowing), which is generally, but inadequately, translated as "I don't know."

• *Shikō* (d. 514) was the priest most trusted by the emperor.

• *The holy teaching? "Emptiness!"* Setchō always summarizes the gist of the case at the beginning of his verse.

• *Inevitable, the thorns and briars springing up.* Despite himself, Bodhidharma introduced many complications, such as emptiness, no holiness, and no knowing. These were all thorns and briars.

• *A gentle breeze pervades the universe.* Feel this cool breeze and your troubled mind will be pacified.

• *He can wash my feet.* Christ washed his disciples' feet. What difference is there? When it comes to service, everyone is the servant of others. When it comes to independence, everyone is his own master throughout heaven and earth.

Case 2 Jōshū's "The Real Way Is Not Difficult"

ENGO'S INTRODUCTION   The universe is too narrow; the sun, moon, and stars are all at once darkened. Even if blows from the stick fall like raindrops and the "katsu" shouts sound like thunder, you are still far short of the truth of Buddhism. Even the Buddhas of the three worlds can only nod to themselves, and the patriarchs of all ages do not exhaustively demonstrate its profundity. The whole treasury of sutras is inadequate to expound its deep meaning. Even the clearest-eyed monks fail to save themselves. At this point, how do you conduct yourself? Mentioning the name of the Buddha is like trudging through the mire. To utter the word "Zen" is to cover your face with shame. Not only those who have long practiced Zen but beginners, too, should exert themselves to attain directly to the secret.

MAIN SUBJECT   Jōshū spoke to the assembly and said, "The real Way is not difficult. It only abhors choice and attachment. With but a single word there may arise choice and attachment or there may arise clarity. This old monk does not have that clarity. Do you appreciate the meaning of this or not?" Then a monk asked, "If you do not have that clarity, what do you appreciate?" Jōshū said, "I do not know that, either." The monk said, "If you do not know, how can you say you do not have that clarity?" Jōshū said, "Asking the question is good enough. Now make your bows and retire."

SETCHŌ'S VERSE
The real Way is not difficult.
Direct word! Direct speech!

One with many phases,
Two with one.

Far away in the heavens the sun rises, the moon sets;
Beyond the hills the high mountains, the cold waters.

The skull has no consciousness, no delight;
The dead tree sings in the wind, not yet rotten.

Difficult, difficult!
Attachment and clarity; watch, and penetrate the secret!

NOTES   *The universe is too narrow* . . . Compared with the limitless extent of the real Way, the universe seems restricted, and beside the brilliance of the Way, the sun, the moon, and all the other heavenly bodies look dim.
   • *Even if blows from the stick fall like raindrops* . . . Blows and "katsu" shouts are used to inspire the monks, but even with such help you are still far from reaching the Way.
   • *The Buddhas of the three worlds.* The Buddhas of the past, present, and future.
   • *Mentioning the name of the Buddha.* In Case 30 of *Mumonkan*, Mumon says, "Even mentioning the word 'Buddha' should make us rinse out our mouths for three days. If a man of understanding hears anyone say, 'This very mind is the Buddha,' he will cover his ears and rush away."
   • *Jōshū.* See *Mumonkan*, Case 1. Jōshū appears in seven cases in *Mumonkan* and twelve in *Hekiganroku*.
   • *The real Way is not difficult. It only abhors choice and attachment.* This is a quotation from *A Poetical Manuscript on Belief in the Mind* by the Third Patriarch, Sōsan. The opening lines of the poem run, "The real Way is not difficult. It only abhors choice and attachment. If you have no attachments, you have positively attained clarity." Here "clarity" means

enlightenment. In other words, if you have no attachments you are enlightened—a simple precept which forms the theme of the poem and pithily expresses the principle of Buddhism. Jōshū admired these lines but gave them a characteristic twist when he quoted them.

• *With but a single word there may arise choice and attachment or there may arise clarity.* If you come out into the world of the activity of consciousness (if you say but a single word), there may arise either delusion or enlightenment.

• *This old monk does not have that clarity.* I have no attachment, even to enlightenment. Enlightenment is valued, but if you are content with it and stick to it, then a new trouble will arise, namely, Dharma-sticking blindness (see Case 10). Jōshū has no attachment, not even to enlightenment, which he has outgrown. Zen students are supposed to throw away whatever they achieve as it is achieved. This is called "leaving no trace behind."

• *Do you appreciate the meaning of this or not?* Do you value the attitude of mind that does not stick to anything? But valuing this attitude is itself open to criticism, since it implies attachment to that state of mind. Jōshū, of course, knew perfectly well that he was exposing himself to criticism here. Zen masters are willing to risk ridicule and even shame for the sake of teaching their students. This is called "trudging through the mire."

• *If you do not have that clarity, what do you appreciate?* In point of fact, a monk came forward and pointed out Jōshū's weakness.

• *I do not know that, either.* Jōshū's answer came quite calmly.

• *Asking the question is good enough. Now make your bows and retire.* You were successful in chopping logic. Now it is finished. Retire!

• *Direct word!* In language samadhi, words make direct connection with reality.

• *One with many phases, / Two with one.* Differentiation in equality.

• *The sun rises, the moon sets.* They are demonstrating absolute truth.

• *The high mountains, the cold waters.* The aspect of nature is itself the Way.

• *The skull has no consciousness, no delight; / The dead tree sings in the wind.* Absolute samadhi and positive samadhi.

• *Difficult, difficult! / Attachment and clarity; watch, and penetrate the secret!* Of course there is enlightenment. However, when it is outgrown, attachment itself is enlightenment.

Case 3 Baso's "Sun-faced Buddha, Moon-faced Buddha"

ENGO'S INTRODUCTION Each *ki* and every *kyo*, every word and phrase, is a means, for the moment, of leading students to realization. But every such manipulation is like performing an operation on a healthy body and will give rise to complication upon complication. The Great Way manifests itself naturally. It is limited by no fixed rules. But I must tell you that there is an advanced theme that you will have to learn. It presides over heaven and earth. However, if you try to guess at it you will be confused. This can be right, and that also can be right. It is so delicate. This cannot be right, and that also cannot be right. An unapproachable cliff face! How could you manage without stumbling here or there? Study the following.

MAIN SUBJECT The great master Baso was seriously ill. The chief priest of the temple came to pay his respects. He asked, "How do you feel these days?" The master said, "Sun-faced Buddha, Moon-faced Buddha."

SETCHŌ'S VERSE
Sun-faced Buddha! Moon-faced Buddha! Compared with them,
How pale the Three Sacred Sovereigns, the Five Ancestral Emperors!

For twenty years I have had fierce struggles,
Descending into the dragon's cave for you.

The hardship defies description.
You clear-eyed monks—don't make light of it.

NOTES *Each ki and every kyo.* When a bow is fully drawn—"in the form of a full moon," as it is called—it contains a certain potential energy. There is a state of strain before the arrow is discharged. In mental activity, too, a certain strain or tension arises before an action is performed. This mental strain is called *ki*, and the act of discharging it is called *kyo*. Ki and kyo are important terms in Zen. They refer to the realm of positive samadhi. Ki is used here in the sense of Zen-ki, which is a keen, spontaneous action of the Zen spirit. Kyo refers to an action or gesture manifesting Zen-ki, such as raising a finger, lifting a fist, nodding the head, and so on. Baso once said, "I move my eyebrows to demonstrate the Zen spirit."

• *The Great Way.* The literal translation of the Chinese is "the Great Use." "Use" is the way of activity of the absolute.

• *Baso.* See *Mumonkan*, Case 30. His methods of handling his disciples were kaleidoscopic: using the stick, shouting, grasping, slapping, knocking, pushing, and so on. He set many precedents in the exercise of Zen-ki.

• *The chief priest.* This was the priest responsible for managing the temple.

• *Sun-faced Buddha, Moon-faced Buddha.* A scripture called *Butsumyō-kyō* (*butsu*, Buddhas; *myō*, names; *kyō*, sutra) gives the names of 1,193 Buddhas and Bodhisattvas. Among them are the Sun-faced Buddha, said to live for eighteen hundred years, and the Moon-faced Buddha, said to live for a day and a night. This saying of Baso's, "Sun-faced Buddha, Moon-faced Buddha," stands out conspicuously among notable Zen sayings. Imagine you are watching the glorious setting sun at the far end of the ocean. Moment by moment, the golden-faced Buddha sinks below the horizon. No words can describe the glory and radiance of his face. Everything is condensed into this present moment. It is eternal. And again, imagine that, at midnight, you are watching the moon's mirrorlike face, inclined a little in her musing, poised over the mountains. Everything is silent. Her life may be only one day and one night, but this moment after moment's being truly represents real existence.

• *The Three Sacred Sovereigns.* In mythological times there were three sages who established the ancient states around the Yellow River and taught the people how to live. They are regarded by the Chinese people as their ancestral divinities.

• *The Five Ancestral Emperors.* Following the Three Sacred Sovereigns came the Five Emperors, who also developed prehistoric states in which people lived blissfully through long ages. They are regarded as ideal figures and have been worshiped throughout history by the Chinese people.

• *I have had fierce struggles.* Zen students train themselves for many years and undergo bitter struggles.

• *The dragon's cave.* A legend tells of the jewels of many colors hidden in a cave guarded by a dragon in the depths of the sea. Anyone who wants to obtain the treasure must dive into the depths, enter the cave, and wrest the treasure from the dragon. Setchō associates this old legend with the hardships of Zen training.

• *For you.* These words can be read to mean both "in order to attain to you, Sun-faced Buddha, Moon-faced Buddha" and "in order to attain to these for you, for me, and for all others."

Case 4   Tokusan Visits Isan

ENGO'S INTRODUCTION   The blue sky, the bright sun; there is no distinguishing east and west. Time and causation; medicine must be given to the sick. Tell me, is it best to let go or to hold fast? See the following.

MAIN SUBJECT   Tokusan came to Isan's temple. Carrying his pilgrim's bundle under his arm, he crossed the lecture hall, from east to west and from west to east; then, staring around, he said, "Mu, Mu," and went out. [Setchō says, "It is seen through."] Tokusan reached the gate but then said to himself, "I should not be in a hurry." So he dressed formally and entered a second time to have an interview. Isan was sitting in his place. Tokusan, holding up his kneeling cloth, said, "Oshō!" Isan made as if to take up his hossu. Then Tokusan gave a "katsu" shout, swung his sleeves, and went out. [Setchō says, "It is seen through."] Tokusan, with his back turned on the lecture hall, put on his straw sandals and went off. In the evening Isan asked the chief monk, "The new arrival, where is he?" The chief monk said, "When he went out he turned his back on the lecture hall, put on his sandals, and went away." Isan said, "Someday that fellow will go to an isolated mountaintop, establish a hermitage, and scold the Buddhas and abuse the patriarchs." [Setchō says, "Frost on top of snow!"]

SETCHŌ'S VERSE
The first seeing through,
The second seeing through,
Frost on top of snow:
Great risk of slipping.

Like General Hiki, he entered the enemy camp
And narrowly escaped.
He made a dash for it,
But was not let alone.

Alas! He is seated among the weeds
On the isolated mountaintop.

NOTES   *The blue sky, the bright sun.* These symbolize absolute reality, which is boundless and indescribable.
• *No distinguishing east and west.* In absolute reality, and in absolute samadhi, there are no east and west, no relative and absolute, no enlightenment and non-enlightenment, no good and evil, no sage and sinner, and so on.
• *Time and causation.* When you come out into the world of the ordinary activity of consciousness, there appear time and causation, east and west, good and evil, success and failure, and health and disease—and medicine has to be administered to the sick.
• *To let go or to hold fast.* These two terms, which recur frequently in *Hekiganroku*, represent fundamental, complementary aspects of Zen activity. "To let go" (or "release") denotes a relaxation of one's grip or discipline. It relates to the world of positive samadhi, to the ordinary, busy activity of consciousness, in which we are aware of cause and effect, right and wrong, and so on. It relates to what is constructive, adaptable, and life-giving in our activities or those of a Zen master teaching his disciples. "To hold fast" (or "grasp"), on the other hand, relates to absolute samadhi, to a realm in which there are no cause and effect, no right and wrong, and so on. It also denotes that aspect of a Zen master's actions in which he denies and deprives—rejecting his students' answers, taking away their achievements in order to spur them to still further advances. Engo is urging you to study most carefully the question of holding fast and letting go in the present case.

• *Tokusan* (780–865) attained his great experience under Ryūtan (see *Mumonkan*, Case 28). He came to visit Isan full of self-confidence and vigor, and was inclined to behave as if he were invincible.

• *Isan.* See *Mumonkan*, Case 40.

• *Carrying his pilgrim's bundle.* The regulations governing monastic life were laid down by Hyakujō, Isan's teacher, and covered all activities. The attire of a monk visiting a teacher for an interview was formally specified. But Tokusan disregarded the regulation and, carrying his bundle under his arm, intruded into the lecture hall, passing to and fro as if he enjoyed perfect freedom to do as he pleased.

• *Mu, Mu.* Mu is "nothing" (see *Mumonkan*, Case 1). Tokusan came to know this "nothing" when he had his great experience. When one has this experience for the first time, one is overwhelmed by its magnificence and thinks one has attained to the ultimate truth. It is true that one has had a glimpse of ultimate truth, but this is, all the same, a one-sided realization. One has come to understand only one of the two pillars of Zen. After such an experience one must once again return to the world of the ordinary activity of consciousness and become versed in positive samadhi. This is called "the cultivation of Holy Buddhahood after enlightenment." In other words, Tokusan had experienced negation but had as yet hardly dreamed of the constructive activity of positive samadhi. Nevertheless, Tokusan's experience was a genuine one and not to be belittled. His "Mu, Mu" was much appreciated by Setchō.

• *It is seen through.* This saying of Setchō's is subtle and delicate. What was seen through? Is he saying that Tokusan saw through Isan's Zen, or that Isan saw through Tokusan, or that he himself has seen through both of them? If the last, how has he seen through them? Engo puts in a comment on Setchō's words, saying, "No, no; hear, hear; marked!" "No, no" is negative; "hear, hear" is affirmative; "marked" means taking note of merits and demerits. But of whose merits and demerits is he taking note?

• *I should not be in a hurry.* Tokusan, high-spirited as he was, retained some sense of discretion and, on further thought, turned back.

• *Isan was sitting in his place.* Isan was mature and knew everything. He had seen through Tokusan and remained quietly sitting in his place.

• *Tokusan, holding up his kneeling cloth, said, "Oshō!"* Tokusan retained his severe look. He was on the offensive. The kneeling cloth is a folded cloth which a monk carries on his left arm on formal occasions. When he makes his bows, he first spreads it on the floor where he is to bow. Oshō is a term of respect applied to a teacher.

• *Isan made as if to take up his hossu.* Isan's camp was as quiet as the forest. The hossu is a stick or baton, on the tip of which is fixed a tassel of long white horsehair. It is a symbol of the teacher's authority and is sometimes used by him when he is lecturing.

• *Tokusan gave a "katsu" shout.* This was a demonstration of Zen spirit (Zen-ki; see Case 3).

• *Setchō says, "It is seen through."* This second "seen through" expresses admiration of Tokusan's Zen-ki and, of course, of Isan's maturity. Engo once again adds his comment: "No, no; hear, hear; marked!" The words of these two Zen masters call for your careful study.

• *Tokusan, with his back turned on the lecture hall, put on his straw sandals and went off.*

> The storm is passed,
> Dewdrops and snails in the hedge.
> Good morning, doggie!

• *Isan asked the chief monk.* There are several kinds of questions: a beginner's question, a demonstrative question, an interrogatory question, a question echoed by a harmonious answer, and so on. What sort of question was Isan's?

• *Someday that fellow will go to an isolated mountaintop . . . and scold the Buddhas and abuse the patriarchs.* Scolding the Buddhas and abusing the patriarchs are examples of "holding fast." But this is only one side of Zen, as we noted above. "The isolated mountaintop" means the summit of Mount Sumeru (the supposed central mountain of the universe), a symbol of the absolute condition of being. But if a student remains there, his Zen is one-sided. He is like a man sitting on top of a hundred-foot pole, unable to stir an inch. With this comment Isan showed his grasp of Tokusan.

• *Frost on top of snow!* This can have two meanings: "superfluous" or "severe." Here, for the third time, Engo puts in his comment: "No, no; hear, hear; marked!"

• *The first seeing through, / The second seeing through, / Frost on top of snow*. Engo's comment here is "The three phrases are not the same," which is an important clue to understanding this case.

• *Great risk of slipping*. Every situation in this episode is steepness itself. Tokusan's action was as dangerous as entering the enemy camp. The least false step would have proved fatal.

• *General Hiki* was a Chinese general who was captured by the enemy but escaped by a strategem.

• *He made a dash for it*. Tokusan dashed away.

• *But was not let alone*. Isan did not completely acknowledge Tokusan's achievement. He was not content to leave him alone. He demonstrated holding fast and letting go at the same time.

• *Alas!* One might translate this as "tut, tut." The more one talks, the more one falls into error.

• *He is seated among the weeds*. Weeds are a symbol of the busy world. The word also implies a sordid, shabby condition, and at the same time it refers to the constructive way of "letting go" and the playful samadhi of Hotei Oshō in the tenth stage of the Search for the Missing Ox (see *Zen Training*, chapter 17). The master goes out into the world and does not mind trudging through the mire (shame and shabbiness) for the sake of a lost soul. But who is in the weeds—Tokusan or Isan? The variety of interpretations that Zen koans permit is one source of their profundity.

• *On the isolated mountaintop*. This is the state of absolute independence. But if you try to settle down there, you will find yourself thrown into a filthy, weed-filled plot. The last two lines of Setchō's verse can be applied to both Isan and Tokusan, but in different senses. Isan was both holding fast and letting go.

Case 5 Seppō's "A Grain of Rice"

ENGO'S INTRODUCTION To guard and maintain the essential teachings of Buddhism must be the vocation of the noble soul. He does not blink when killing a man, and then the man may be instantly enlightened. Hence he observes and acts simultaneously, and holds fast and lets go without restraint. He sees that essence and phenomenon are not two, that experience and reality run parallel. He often rejects the first principle and adopts the second. This is because to cut through the complications too abruptly causes the beginner to lose his footing. A day like yesterday—that could not be avoided. Again, a day like today—his transgressions fill the heavens. If you are clear-sighted, however, you cannot blame him. If otherwise, you put yourself in the tiger's mouth. You will lose your life instantly. Now see the following.

MAIN SUBJECT Seppō addressed the assembly and said, "All the great world, if I pick it up with my fingertips, is found to be like a grain of rice. I throw it in front of your face, but you do not see it. Beat the drum, telling the monks to come out to work, and search for it."

SETCHŌ'S VERSE
The ox-head disappearing, the horse-head appears;
No dust on the mirror of the Patriarch Sōkei.
You beat the drum and search for it in vain.
For whom do the spring flowers bloom?

NOTES Seppō (822–908). See Mumonkan, Case 13. He was a conscientious, dedicated man and a person of great spiritual power. He seems to have been rather slow in achieving enlightenment, but in the end he became a great Zen master, with fifteen hundred students, whom he taught with great care and thoroughness. He was the noble soul to whom Engo refers, one worthy to pass on the Buddha's teachings.
• He does not blink. He does not hesitate.
• When killing a man. Not literally, of course, but when wielding the death-dealing blade, which is also the life-giving sword.
• Essence and phenomenon are not two. From the Zen point of view there is no distinction between the two.
• To cut through the complications too abruptly causes the beginner to lose his footing. "Complications" are such entanglements as koans, sophisti-

cated formulations of doctrine, teachings, the student's attachments, and so on. To sweep them all away too quickly may leave the beginner in a state which he is not yet ready to deal with.

• *A day like yesterday.* Yesterday was not a satisfactory day, but it could not have been otherwise. That today is like this is also inevitable. This is because the teacher has to adapt himself to the level of the novice.

• *The ox-head disappearing, the horse-head appears.* "Ox-head" and "horse-head" represent the momentary nen-thoughts of consciousness. "Ox" and "horse" are not important, but the heads' appearing and disappearing are. In your daily life you experience the instantaneous appearance and disappearance of nen-thoughts, flickering and dancing like flames. They are fractions of mental activity, often not forming a complete idea. In our ordinary life they are often ignored, but they are nonetheless there. In positive samadhi they are refined and constitute the stream of the mind. If the wisdom mirror of the mind is clear and the mind is enlightened, the nen-thoughts which pass momentarily across the mind are reflected by the mirror as they are, not deformed or distorted by illusory thinking.

The origin of the strange-sounding names ox-head and horse-head is to be found in the *Surangama Sutra*, in which there is a passage that runs, "When a man is dying, he first sees great mountains come pressing upon him from the four directions. There is no way to escape from them. And he sees, in his illusion, a great iron castle appear. Fire serpents, fire bulls, tigers, wolves, lions, ox-head fiends, and horse-head ogres, carrying spears and halberds, rush into the castle." Setchō, in using these names in his verse, is simply alluding to their ever changing, phantasmagoric movements, making them represent the nen-thoughts momentarily appearing and disappearing.

• *The mirror of the Patriarch Sōkei.* Sōkei was the Sixth Patriarch, this name deriving from the place where he lived. He was originally called Enō (see *Mumonkan*, Case 23). When still a layman, Enō studied Zen with the Fifth Patriarch, Ōbai. The latter, growing old, wished to nominate his successor, to whom he could transmit the Dharma Seal of the Buddha. The head monk, Shinshū, presented a poem demonstrating his degree of attainment. It ran:

> The body is the Bodhi tree,
> The mind is like a mirror.

Every now and then dust and polish it,
And let no dust settle on it.

Enō's poem was:

Bodhi by nature is no tree,
The mirror is inherently formless,
There is originally nothing.
On what, then, can the dust settle?

This poem made Enō the Sixth Patriarch. Shinshū's Zen was a method of gradual enlightenment which flourished in North China and was called the Northern school. Enō's was a way of sudden enlightenment and was called the Southern school. It has survived until now, while Shinshū's died out.

• *You beat the drum and search for it in vain.* If you once obtain the clear mirror of the mind, you will not search for it outside yourself. The clear mirror itself is what you are seeking.

• *For whom do the spring flowers bloom?* The countless spring flowers are a manifestation of truth. They are for themselves, by themselves, of themselves; but if you really have the eye of enlightenment, you will find they are there for you to appreciate.

Case 6   Ummon's "Every Day Is a Good Day"

MAIN SUBJECT   Ummon addressed the assembly and said, "I am not asking you about the days before the fifteenth of the month. But what about after the fifteenth? Come and give me a word about those days." And he himself gave the answer for them: "Every day is a good day."

SETCHŌ'S VERSE
 Setting aside one, you gained seven;
 No one can rival you—above, below, or in the four directions.

Quietly wading the rapids, you extinguish the sound of the waters.
Watching at leisure, you retain the tracks of flying birds.
Grass grows rampant, mist lies thick.

Famed for emptiness in zazen,
Yet flowers rain down on you; for shame!
Snapping my fingers, I scold you, Sunyata.
Don't be confused!
Or else—thirty blows!

NOTES *Ummon.* See *Mumonkan*, Case 15. Ummon appears eighteen times in *Hekiganroku*.

• *The days before the fifteenth of the month.* These, you might say, are (1) the days before today, (2) the days before you were born, (3) the days before your enlightenment, and (4) the days before your coming out of absolute samadhi. In short, Ummon is saying that he is not asking you about what has already happened but about the things of this moment and to come.

• *What about after the fifteenth?* What is the nature of the busy activity of your consciousness at this moment and in the future?

• *He himself gave the answer for them.* No one could answer Ummon, so he gave the answer himself. This answering for others seems to have been started by Ummon.

• *Every day is a good day.* Children have faith in life, and enjoy life, because they are in positive samadhi every moment. They do not say, as the adult does, "I was given my life without being asked if I wished to be born." When you are in positive samadhi, as children are, everything is all right, and every day is a good day. In Christ's words, "Sufficient unto the day is the evil thereof."

• *Setting aside one, you gained seven.* You put the past aside, you ignore even enlightenment; that is "setting aside one." And penetrating into the present moment's activity of consciousness, you meet with many things; that is how you "gained seven," "seven" here meaning "many." In positive samadhi, pure consciousness appears; it deals with numerous affairs, and each of them is all right—a wonderful thing!

• *No one can rival you.* You, like Ummon or any other person who enjoys positive samadhi, sit on the throne of existence. No one can rival you, above in heaven, below in hell, or in any part of the world.

• *Quietly wading the rapids, you extinguish the sound of the waters.* In your positive samadhi, even the noisiest sounds and the busiest activities are brought to an all-pervading stillness.

> Silence reigning all around,
> The song of the cicadas
> Penetrates the rocks.

This is the silent side of positive samadhi in the keen activity of consciousness.

• *Watching at leisure, you retain the tracks of flying birds.* Flying birds leave no tracks. Yet in positive samadhi you see them clearly, as if you were watching a slow-motion film. In other words, when the first nen recovers its inherently clear and vivid activity, the present moment becomes rich in content, just as a dying man in his last moments sees scenes of his whole life, or as a musician, who hears far more in a piece of music than an ordinary listener, virtually catches hold of the traces of the flying notes. I have discussed this question at length elsewhere (see *Zen Training*).

Reason can make contact with the outside world only indirectly. Direct cognition of the world is achieved through the intuitive action of the first nen. Putting it in more abstract terms, we may say that the first nen represents our intuitive, sensory, and perceptive activity, which receives impressions directly from external objects. The second nen reflects upon the first nen and recognizes it as one's own thought, thus producing self-consciousness and the recognition of one's ego. The ego stems from this recognition of one's self. Animals are thought to have the first nen but no second, and hence no self-consciousness or ego.

If the first nen is not reflected upon by the second nen, it is not recognized and not retained in the memory. Our daily life is full of actions—eating, smoking, walking, even talking and thinking—which are carelessly or casually done and forgotten. The second nen, too, does not reflect upon itself, and again, if it is not reflected upon by another, ensuing reflecting action of the mind, it is not recognized. This next-coming action may be called the secondary reflecting action. This, too, does not reflect upon itself, but it can be repeated, so that, for instance, we think, "I recognize that I was reflecting upon my thought that had been thinking, 'What a detestable fellow he is!' " This secondary reflecting action constitutes the reasoning and synthesizing function of the mind which we call the third nen. This embraces the preceding actions of the first and second nen and also other third-nen actions, and it integrates them into a line of thought. The materials originally obtained as impressions by the first nen are thus synthesized by the third nen, and complete cognition is effected.

The third nen does not itself come into direct contact with external objects; it does so only indirectly, through the medium of the first nen. The latter therefore plays a vital role in cognition. The third nen in most people develops an egocentric pattern of activity, which leads to a delusive way of thinking and affects the first nen, distorting its activity. The experience of samadhi in zazen leads to the realization of no-ego (self-nature is no-nature), thus eliminating the source of delusive thinking.

It is important to note that every nen-thought, even if is not recognized, is necessarily accompanied by its own internal pressure, which is retained in the mind. There it contributes to what in Buddhist terminology is called the accumulations of the mind. Some internal pressures enrich your mind, while others create the traumas on which the psychoanalysts elaborate so much. The accumulations make up your mood, your personality, and your identification of yourself. I have described the three nen-actions as if they were quite separate and distinct, but in reality they blend with each other and are more like one thread dyed differently, now working as the first nen, now the second, and now the third, each as an extension of the others.

To illustrate the above way of analyzing mental events, I wish to return to the example of the musician. He first catches the sound of the music by the first nen. The changes in the sound—the tune or melody—constitute the stream of music, and the first nen, following the stream, also changes its stream of impressions. An impression is the content of the first nen; indeed, it is the first nen itself. The first nen changes moment by moment, first nen 1 being followed by first nen 2, 3, and so on, each representing a new impression of the changing music. This succession of first nen is followed by second and third nen, each itself in the succession 1, 2, 3, and so on, corresponding to that of the first nen.

Each third nen receives the impression of all the first and second nen, as well as the understanding of all the third nen that precede it, and it retains and integrates them into one stream of music. Thus, the whole course of the music is understood. The third nen, it will be seen, is the final agent that realizes the music. Final and complete cognition of the music is effected by the third nen. But the third nen does not itself come into direct contact with the music: it works on material provided by the first nen, which it integrates and synthesizes. The first nen engages in sensory perception and habituated conceptions; the third nen produces new conceptions and works in the mode of reasoning. It is the basis, in fact, of reason, which we regard as the master of the mind.

In understanding music there is no place for egocentric thought. The same is true of pure philosophizing and pure reasoning. In our ordinary daily life, however, there operates what we call the habitual way of consciousness, the first consideration of which is to make use of things and other people for our own ends. Egocentric thinking necessarily arises here. The activity of the third nen in our ordinary life is permeated through and through with this self-centered thinking. Such thinking affects adversely the action of the first nen, so that cognition is distorted. Zazen brings about samadhi, in which this distortion of the first and third nen dies away. In a mature state of Zen practice we achieve a complete elimination of self-centered thinking. Our cognition of objects is then perfect, just as is the musician's understanding of music.

• *Grass grows rampant, mist lies thick.* The activity of consciousness often becomes entangled in junglelike complications, which bring worries and suffering. In positive samadhi, however, you penetrate into the complications, and this brings serenity of mind, just as the shrill singing of the cicadas penetrates into the rocks and, by contrast, creates serenity all around. "Grass grows rampant" represents the busy activity of consciousness in active, positive samadhi. By contrast, "mist lies thick" represents the absolute aspect of samadhi, where all phenomena retire into the background of consciousness.

• *Famed for emptiness in zazen, / Yet flowers rain down on you; for shame!* Sunyata was famous for his practice of emptiness in his meditation. Once when he was practicing, and doing well, the heavenly deities came to admire him. They sent flowers raining down on him in praise of his merit. Sunyata said, "How could you discover me and cast flowers on me while I am in emptiness?" The deities said, "We admire your practice of emptiness," and rained down flowers all the more. Had Sunyata been truly in a state of profound emptiness, they would not have been able to find any trace of him. (See also Case 97.)

• *Snapping my fingers, I scold you, Sunyata.* Setchō deplores Sunyata's poor practice of emptiness. Setchō requires both absolute and positive samadhi. He is criticizing one-sided practice. You can find true emptiness in positive samadhi, in the busiest activity of consciousness, as well as in absolute samadhi, in which the activity of consciousness is not noticed.

• *Don't be confused!* Setchō has introduced a lot of subtle matters: before and after, removing and obtaining, extinguishing and retaining, grass and mist, Sunyata and scolding. If you are clear-eyed, you will not be thrown into confusion by all this talk about different topics.

Case 7 Hōgen's "You Are Echō"

ENGO'S INTRODUCTION As to what stands prior to the Word, not one phrase has been handed down, even by the thousand holy ones. If you are not yet intimate with it, you are separated from it by the three thousand worlds. Even if you have attained some understanding of it, and could stop the mouths of people living in the world, you are not yet worthy to be called clear-eyed. That is why it is said that heaven cannot cover it, earth cannot hold it, space cannot accommodate it, sun and moon cannot shine on it. When there is no Buddha and when you alone are the master, then for the first time you are worthy of being talked about a little.

Now, if you are not yet like that, you have to become enlightened in relation to the slightest object and give out illumination yourself. Then you can go anywhere and enjoy perfect freedom in your Dharma activity. Whatever you take up, you act rightly. Tell me, how could you achieve such freedom?

Once again I ask you, do you understand this?

"None hitherto had noticed the sweat of his steed,
But his merits must be recognized."

Now, what is Setchō's koan? See below.

MAIN SUBJECT A monk said to Hōgen, "My name is Echō. I ask you, what is the Buddha?" Hōgen said, "You are Echō."

SETCHŌ'S VERSE
In the land of the river,
Faintly stirring, the gentle breeze of spring.
Far away, deep among blossoms,
The partridge sings.

Ascending the falls,
The carp became a dragon,
Yet still, by night,
Fools fish for him below.

NOTES   *Hōgen.* See *Mumonkan*, Case 26.

• *As to what stands prior to the Word . . .* This is a free translation. A closer rendering would be that suggested by R. D. M. Shaw: "One phrase of the Pre-Voice, ten thousand holy ones have not handed down." "The Pre-Voice" is absolute reality, or, as Shaw puts it, "that which is behind or beyond the Voice or expression of ultimate Truth."

• *You have to become enlightened in relation to the slightest object.* "The slightest object" is a blade of grass, a drop of water, a stone by the roadside, a dog's droppings on the path in the park.

• *None hitherto had noticed the sweat of his steed, / But his merits must be recognized.* These lines are quoted from Tōzan Zenku Oshō:

In a moment, peace was restored throughout the land;
All directions lay open to the master of the mind.
None hitherto had noticed the sweat of his steed,
But his merits must be recognized.

Here the third line compares a monk's hard training to a warrior's desperate fighting against heavy odds; his horse is covered with sweat, not to mention himself.

• *You are Echō.* "Echō" came echoing back to the question. (The pun is, of course, pure chance.) Pure cognition consists of the immediate echoing by the first nen; it is not a matter of reasoning by the third nen. This echoing connects the absolute and the phenomenal worlds, and it forms the subject of the present case.

• *The land of the river.* The provinces around the Yangtze River were famed for their beautiful scenery.

• *Faintly stirring, the gentle breeze of spring.* A literal rendering of this line would be "The spring breeze hardly arises." It is said that the phrase "hardly arises" was used deliberately by Setchō to allude to the two spheres of the mind: the sphere of the absolute, which transcends the activity of consciousness, and the sphere of the positive activity of consciousness. (There are technical terms in Buddhist philosophy for these: "dark" for the one, "light" for the other.) You are intended to feel the two worlds in the soft, scarcely felt breath of spring.

• *Far away, deep among blossoms, / The partridge sings.* These lines again suggest the two worlds. The distant voice of the singing bird, deep among blossoms, is faintly heard.

• *Ascending the falls, / The carp became a dragon.* The original text may be literally rendered as "The waters of the three-terraced falls were high, and the carp became a dragon." An old legend refers to Emperor Gyō, who harnessed the Yellow River. When he cut into the high cliffs to let the river through, the three-terraced falls called the Dragon Gate were made. When spring came, thousands of carp gathered below the falls, but only the strongest were able to ascend the falls and become dragons, rising to heaven. The ascent of the carp was used as a metaphor to describe passing the very severe government examinations. Setchō applied this metaphor to Echō, who attained enlightenment at Hōgen's words.

• *Yet still, by night, / Fools fish for him below.* Fools go fishing for the carp even though it has already ascended to heaven as a dragon. The fools are those who loiter on this side of the gate, while others have climbed the falls and attained enlightenment. "By night" refers to the practice of fishing by torchlight and also to the darkness of the unenlightened mind.

Case 8 Suigan's Eyebrows

ENGO'S INTRODUCTION The enlightened man enjoys perfect freedom in active life. He is like a dragon supported by deep waters or like a tiger that commands its mountain retreat. The man who is not enlightened drifts about in the affairs of the world. He is like a ram that gets its horns caught in a fence or like a man who waits for a hare to run against a tree stump and stun itself.

The enlightened man's words are sometimes like a lion crouched to spring, sometimes like the Diamond King's treasure sword. Sometimes their effect is to shut the mouths of the world-famed ones, sometimes it is as if they simply follow the waves coming one after another. When the enlightened man meets others who are enlightened, then friend meets friend. He values them, and they encourage each other. When he meets those who are adrift in the world, then teacher meets disciple. His way of dealing with such people is farsighted. He stands firm before them, like a thousand-fathom cliff.

Therefore it is said that the Way of the absolute is manifest everywhere: it has no fixed rules and regulations. The teacher sometimes makes a blade of grass stand for the golden-faced Buddha, sixteen feet high, and sometimes makes the golden-faced Buddha, sixteen feet high, stand for a blade of grass. Tell me, on what principle is all this based? Do you understand? See the following.

MAIN SUBJECT Suigan, at the end of the summer session, spoke to the assembly and said, "During the summer session I have talked to you a great deal. Now, look! Has Suigan any eyebrows?" Hofuku said, "He who commits theft has a guilty conscience." Chōkei said, "They have grown." Ummon said, "Kan!"

SETCHŌ'S VERSE
Suigan's words! Unanswerable in thousands of years.
Ummon's "Kan!" Losing his money, committing a crime.
Dotard Hofuku! Was he nimble or did he mumble?
Long-tongued Suigan! Definitely a thief.
Flawless is the jewel! Who can appraise the priceless?
Chōkei knew well! He said, "They have grown."

NOTES *Like a dragon supported by deep waters.* When a dragon gains the water it can exercise its full power, causing clouds to gather, commanding the winds, and creating the storm by which it ascends to heaven.

• *Like a tiger that commands its mountain retreat.* When a tiger takes to the mountains, it acquires formidable strength. It becomes a majestic, unapproachable creature.

• *Like a man who waits for a hare* . . . This alludes to an incident in an old Chinese story. A peasant once caught a hare that happened to run against a tree stump and stun itself. After that he stayed watching the stump, hoping to catch another hare running into it.

• *The Diamond King's treasure sword.* The diamond cuts supremely well, the king is strong, treasure is precious. The Zen master's words cut through the complications once and for all.

• *As if they simply follow the waves coming one after another.* The teacher does not necessarily reject his student's ideas or cut through the complications all at once. Sometimes he adapts himself to the condition of the student and follows his steps as a mother follows her baby's. (See the notes to Case 27.)

• *The golden-faced Buddha, sixteen feet high.* This means an image of the Buddha, but at the same time it stands for the Buddha himself. The enlightened man finds a Buddha in a blade of grass.

• *Has Suigan any eyebrows?* It was said proverbially that if one spoke faultily on Buddhism one's eyebrows would fall off. Suigan's question referred to this proverb, but his real intention, of course, was to test his audience. Here Engo comments, "Your eyes, too, have fallen to the ground," and again, "Your nose, too," and again, "You go to hell as fast as an arrow." Bodhidharma had no beard, no eyes, no nose, no face (see *Mumonkan,* Case 4). Hyakujō said, "Don't mind going to hell" (see *Mumonkan,* Case 2).

The four great Zen masters who appear in this case were all disciples of Seppō.

• *He who commits theft has a guilty conscience.* Engo's comments on this are "Hear!" and "One devil knows another." Zen masters are all robbers.

• *They have grown.* Chōkei is saying the opposite of Engo, whose comment was "Your eyes, too, have fallen to the ground." Are they contradicting each other? Remember Setchō's words in Case 6, "Grass grows rampant." Here Engo says again, "Hear!"

• *Kan.* This word means "barrier." Ummon's "Kan" is significant and highly regarded by Zen students. Ummon is saying, "I do not readily allow all of you to pass through this barrier." There is a famous story of how Kanzan Zenji, the founder of the Myōshinji school of the Rinzai sect, broke through this barrier after a hard struggle and attained great enlightenment. (Kanzan, indeed, gained his name from this, *zan* meaning mountain.) Are the words of these masters like a lion crouched to spring or like the Diamond King's treasure sword? Are they like the waves following one after another or like a thousand-fathom cliff? They may prove to be any of these, depending on your degree of attainment.

• *Ummon's "Kan!"* On this Engo's comments are "Wonderful!" and "This is the man who can say this."

• *Losing his money, committing a crime.* Under the criminal law of that time, one who lost his money was punished. Ummon's saying "Kan!" was like losing his money and, to compound the misery, being punished. What does this mean? Zen masters do not spare themselves. They undergo all sorts of humiliations in order to lead others to enlightenment. Ummon himself was losing his eyebrows by mentioning this word (for the Zen proverb says, "Silence is best"), but he could not help doing so. In Setchō's estimation, that "barrier" was irresistibly exquisite. Engo says, "I lost my breath and my voice at this."

• *Was he nimble or did he mumble?* Engo's comments here are "Was he holding fast or letting go?" (see Case 4) and again, "Living on the same floor, dying in the same bed," which means one devil (Setchō) knows another (Hofuku).

• *Flawless is the jewel!* Suigan is flawless.

Case 9   Jōshū's Four Gates

ENGO'S INTRODUCTION   In the bright mirror on its stand, beauty and ugliness are revealed. With the Bakuya sword in hand, killing and sparing are brought under control. A handsome fellow disappearing, an ugly one comes; an ugly fellow disappearing, a handsome one comes. Life is found in death, death in life. If you have no eye to penetrate the barrier, no freedom to turn about, you will be lost on the way. Tell me, what is the eye that penetrates the barrier, what is the freedom to turn about? See the following.

MAIN SUBJECT   A monk asked Jōshū, "What is Jōshū?" Jōshū said, "The East Gate, the West Gate, the North Gate, the South Gate."

SETCHŌ'S VERSE
  Its intention concealed, the question came;
  The Diamond King's eye was as clear as a jewel.
  There stood the gates, north, south, east, and west,
  But the heaviest hammer blow could not open them.

NOTES   *The bright mirror.* This is the mirror of Zen wisdom. It is clear. It reflects things as they are, a gentleman as a gentleman, a boor as a boor. But who is gentleman, who is boor?
  • *The Bakuya sword.* This is a highly celebrated sword in Chinese literature, and many legends are related in connection with it. The mirror represents the Zen master's Marvelous Observing Wisdom, the sword his Perfecting of Action Wisdom.
  • *Killing and sparing.* On the way to enlightenment the deluded ego must necessarily be killed. However, it is difficult for Zen students to do this by themselves, and the teacher comes to their aid. He wields the death-dealing blade, which proves ultimately to be the life-giving sword.
  • *No eye to penetrate the barrier.* The Zen master's eye sees not only through the barrier but through every person's mind. Jōshū could see through the monk's plot.
  • *No freedom to turn about.* When you are driven against a wall or stranded, how can you extricate yourself from the situation? You can do so only by being free from yourself. If you are not truly independent of your own ego, you cannot attain freedom. True freedom can be achieved only by achieving maturity like Jōshū's.
  • *What is Jōshū?* Jōshū's name derived from the place where he was living, the town of Jōshū. The monk's question therefore had alternative meanings. If Jōshū had answered concerning himself, the monk would have answered, "No, I did not ask about you but about the town of

Jōshū," and vice versa. Engo's comment on this is "Thorns in the mud."

• *The East Gate, the West Gate, the North Gate, the South Gate.* The town of Jōshū was surrounded by walls and had four gates. These were open to anyone who wanted to go in or out. Men and women, young and old, officials and criminals, dogs and cattle, coaches and wagons—all could pass through them. Now, Jōshū himself also had gates: conversion, training, enlightenment, and Nirvana (or holding fast, letting go, being constructive, and sweeping away; or emptiness, reality, phenomenon, and essence; and so forth). They were open to anyone who wanted to visit him and learn from him. But unless you have made progress in your training, you cannot pass through the gates. It is not Jōshū who blocks you, but you yourself.

• *The Diamond King's eye.* The Zen master's Marvelous Observing Wisdom.

• *There stood the gates.* The gates were open, but hard to pass through.

• *But the heaviest hammer blow could not open them.* In truth, there were no gates to open. What is the use, then, of wielding a hammer? Jōshū was open-armed, saying, "Come bumping against me." But no bumping could penetrate him. He also said, "Abuse me; I let you do it with your mouth touching me!" and "Spit upon me; I let you do it as if you were pouring water on me!"

Case 10   Bokushū's "Empty-headed Fool"

ENGO'S INTRODUCTION   Yes is yes, no is no. In the Dharma battle, each stands on his own ground. Therefore it is said, when one's activity is upward, even Shakyamuni, Maitreya, Manjusri, Samantabhadra, the thousand holy ones, and the religious teachers of the whole world become spiritless and silent. When one's activity is downward, even maggots, gnats, and all creatures become brilliantly illuminating and as independent as a ten-thousand-fathom cliff. However, how is it when one's activity is neither upward nor downward? If there is any rule, rely on the rule; if there is no rule, follow a precedent. See the following.

MAIN SUBJECT Bokushū asked a monk, "Where are you from?" The monk gave a "katsu" shout. Bokushū said, "This old monk is shouted down by you." The monk shouted again. Bokushū said, "What about after the third and fourth shouts?" The monk stayed silent. Bokushū hit the monk and said, "You empty-headed fool!"

SETCHŌ'S VERSE
Two shouts, three shouts;
The knowing one knows well;
If going hell-bent,
Both are blind.
Who is blind? Fetch him!
Expose him to the world!

NOTES *Bokushū* (780–877) was a disciple of Ōbaku and in Dharma relation the elder brother of Rinzai.

• *Yes is yes, no is no.* This is a tentative translation. In the original text what we have translated as "yes" is *inmo*, which means "like this," and "no" is *fu-inmo*, which means "not like this." "Yes" takes a thing as it is. "No" suggests that a thing is not as it appears. "Yes" represents a positive, affirmative, constructive attitude and belongs to the domain of positive samadhi. "No" represents a negative, destructive, annihilating attitude and belongs to the domain of absolute samadhi. Affected by our subjective distortion of things, we often do not admit yes to be yes and no to be no. In consequence, we suffer misery of our own causing.

• *In the Dharma battle, each stands on his own ground.* These are Gantō's words. They mean that everyone is independent.

• *When one's activity is upward.* Going to the top of a pole is upward activity (see *Mumonkan*, Case 46). It is the route to enlightenment and is for one's own benefit. Absolute samadhi is the practice of going to the top of the pole. There you find no Buddha, no Manjusri, no people, no creatures of any kind. You are seated on an isolated mountaintop.

• *When one's activity is downward.* If you remain at the top of the pole, you will be like a snail that climbs up a wall and, not knowing about coming down, dries up and perishes there. Enlightenment is necessary in order to attain peace of mind, but if you stay there long, stagnation will set in and you will become dried up. Once you have attained enlightenment, you must come down the pole and return to the world of the ordinary activity of consciousness, in which you enjoy positive samadhi. In this you find that maggots, dogs, cattle, even your enemies shine with the brilliant light of existence. Downward movement is an activity benefiting others as well as yourself. In Zen terminology this is called the "constructive gate," while the upward movement is called the "sweeping-away gate."

• *Independent.* Individuality and the dignity of the personality are to be respected.

• *Neither upward nor downward.* The present case is an instance of this.

• *The monk gave a "katsu" shout.* "Katsu" is an onomatopoeic word for Zen shouting, which was originally used by the teacher when he wanted to sweep from the student's mind all kinds of complications, delusive thinking, and so on. Later it came to have several uses. In the present case the monk used it to express his condition. "Katsu" was first used by Baso, who discharged it in a thunderous voice upon Hyakujō, whose ears were deafened for three days.

• *This old monk is shouted down by you.* Bokushū's reply did away with the monk's shout as if it had been absorbed by empty space. It is also said that it was like beating a cloth drum (see Case 57). Engo's comment on this is "The spirit to hit the tiger."

• *The monk shouted again.* Is he a true dragon or a common snake?

• *What about after the third and fourth shouts?* The lion was staying crouched. However, Engo puts in a pithy comment: "Choppy waters."

• *The monk stayed silent.* The monk's silence is appreciated by Setchō, who says, "If going hell-bent, both are blind" (see below).

• *Bokushū hit the monk.* Tokusan used to say, "I hit you if you answer, and I hit you if you do not answer." Rinzai often used hitting to express approval.

• *You empty-headed fool!* This is an instance of approving while seeming to denigrate.

• *The knowing one knows well.* He knows when to advance, when to retreat.

• *If going hell-bent.* A literal translation of what is rendered here as "hell-bent" is "sitting astride the tiger's head." It means doing something by sheer force of circumstances. The tiger is often thought to dash forward blindly, not knowing how to turn aside.

• *Both are blind.* Zen recognizes five kinds of blindness:

1. The blindness of the general run of ignorant people.
2. The evil blindness of the heretic.
3. The true blindness of the enlightened student. The worldly eye of such a person has become blind.
4. The blindness of those who stick to their realization and make much of being enlightened.
5. The transcendent, or genuine, blindness that is the condition of Buddhas. This appears when one outgrows true blindness—that is, when one achieves maturity in Zen practice.

• *Who is blind?* What sort of blindness did the monk display?
• *Fetch him! | Expose him to the world!* A Zen story is about yourself. You have first to understand this monk and Bokushū as they refer to yourself before exposing them to the world. Attain genuine blindness for yourself and expose yourself to the world.

Case 11   Ōbaku's "Partakers of Brewer's Grain"

ENGO'S INTRODUCTION   The Buddha's supreme power is wholly within his grasp. All the souls and all the spirits of heaven and earth are under his command. Even his casual words and sayings amaze the masses and arouse the crowds. His every gesture and action remove the sufferers' chains and knock off their cangues. If a transcendent man appears, the Buddha meets him with the transcendent principle. Who can ever be so wonderful? If you want to understand the secret, see the following.

MAIN SUBJECT   Ōbaku addressed the assembly and said, "You are all partakers of brewer's grain. If you go on studying Zen like that, you will never finish it. Do you know that in all the land of T'ang there is no

Zen teacher?" Then a monk came forward and said, "But surely there are those who teach disciples and preside over the assemblies. What about that?" Ōbaku said, "I do not say that there is no Zen, but that there is no Zen teacher."

SETCHŌ'S VERSE

Commanding his way of teaching;
But he made it no point of merit.
Seated majestically over the whole land,
He distinguished the dragon from the snake.
Emperor Taichū once encountered him
And thrice fell into his clutches.

NOTES   *Ōbaku* (d. 850) succeeded Hyakujō and was the teacher of Rinzai. Engo, in his comment on this case, says that Ōbaku stood seven feet tall and had a round, gemlike boss in the middle of his forehead. He knew Zen intuitively. When he first went to see Hyakujō, Hyakujō asked him, "Where have you come from in that stately way?" Ōbaku answered, "In this stately way I have come from Richū." "What did you come for?" "For nothing but this thing." Hyakujō was greatly interested in him. Ōbaku wanted to visit Baso, but being told of Baso's death, he asked about him. Hyakujō then related the story (contained in the notes to *Mumonkan*, Case 30) of how he went to see Baso before going out into the world as a Zen master.

After becoming the master of his monastery, Ōbaku was famous for his keen spirit in guiding his monks, one of whom was Rinzai. Bokushū (see Case 10), the head monk, said to Rinzai, "You have been here a long time. Why don't you go to the master to ask about Zen?" Rinzai said, "What should I ask him?" "Ask him what is the general principle of Buddhism." Rinzai went to Ōbaku, asked the question, and was driven away with blows. This was repeated three times. Rinzai wanted to leave the monastery. Bokushū told him to take leave of Ōbaku and, before Rinzai did so, went himself to Ōbaku and said that Rinzai was of rare promise and should be given a helping hand so that he might grow to be a large tree that would give friendly shade to people. Ōbaku said that he had realized this.

When Rinzai went to see him, Ōbaku told him to go to Taigu. Rinzai went to Taigu, related his story, and asked, "Where is my fault?" Taigu said, "Ōbaku has been striving for you with such grandmotherly kindness. How can you ask where your fault is?" At this, Rinzai suddenly reached great enlightenment. He exclaimed, "Now I know that Ōbaku's Zen is not much to speak of." Taigu caught hold of him and said, "A moment ago you asked where your fault was, and now you say that Ōbaku's Zen is not much to speak of." Rinzai gave Taigu three pushes under his arm. Taigu pushed Rinzai away and said, "Your teacher is Ōbaku."

• *You are all partakers of brewer's grain.* These words of Ōbaku's are now a popular saying used to belittle those who imitate old Zen masters. The literal meaning is that you eat the grain left over by the brewers after they have removed the wine and then think that you have had a taste of the real thing.

• *There is no Zen teacher.* It is an iron rule that Zen cannot be taught. You must attain it by your own practice, study, and research. No doubt when Ōbaku first said this it must have sounded astonishing to his students. His words have been handed down to the present day. The Buddha said, "In my forty-nine years of Dharma activity I did not preach a word."

• *Emperor Taichū once encountered him / And thrice fell into his clutches.* Emperor Taichū's personal name was Sensō, and his reign (847–59) was called Taichū. When he was still a prince he lived in Enkan Zenji's monastery, where Ōbaku was at that time head monk. Ōbaku was famous for bowing many times before the Buddha's image. Sensō said, "It is said, 'Don't seek after it in the Buddha, don't seek after it in the Dharma, don't seek after it in the Sangha.' Why do you make so many bows?" Ōbaku said, "I do not seek after it in the Buddha, I do not seek after it in the Dharma, I do not seek after it in the Sangha, and I make my bows like this." Sensō said, "What is the use of making bows, then?" Ōbaku slapped his cheek. Sensō said, "You are a rough fellow!" Ōbaku replied, "At this moment of dealing with you, there is no talk of rough or gentle!" and he gave Sensō another slap. The retort and the two slaps are what Setchō means when he says, "And thrice fell into his clutches."

Case 12   Tōzan's "Masagin"

ENGO'S INTRODUCTION   The death-dealing blade, the life-giving sword: they were the custom in ancient days and are still today the touchstone. In death-dealing, not a hair is harmed; in life-giving, the body is denied and life is neglected. It is said that the thousand holy ones have not preached a word on the upward route. Scholars labor at their formulas like monkeys struggling to catch the moon reflected on the waves. But say! If there is no preaching, how is it that there are so many complications, so many koans? If you have an eye to see, see the following.

MAIN SUBJECT   A monk asked Tōzan, "What is Buddha?" Tōzan said, "Masagin!" [three pounds of flax].

SETCHŌ'S VERSE
  The golden crow swoops, the silver hare bounds;
  The echo comes back, direct and free.
  Who judges Tōzan by his word or phrase
  Is a blind tortoise, lost in a lonely vale.

  The abundant blossoms, the luxuriant flowers,
  The southern bamboo, the northern trees.
  One recalls Riku Taifu and Chōkei:
  "You should not cry, but laugh!" Eh!

NOTES   *The death-dealing blade.* The *Heart Sutra* says, "Form is emptiness." This is the "sweeping-away gate" (see the notes to Case 10).
• *The life-giving sword.* The sutra also says, "Emptiness is form." This is the "constructive gate" (see the notes to Case 10).
• *In death-dealing.* Death-dealing is life-giving, so not a hair is harmed.
• *In life-giving.* Zen practice is like constructing a new building: first you have to demolish the old house.
• *Have not preached a word on the upward route.* The upward route is

the way to enlightenment. It must be understood that there is no end to the process of enlightenment. It goes on endlessly, and that is what is meant by the cultivation of Holy Buddhahood. You must not stop at the top of the hundred-foot pole (see *Mumonkan*, Case 46). It is a subtle and profound process. Sometimes you must come down from the pole and reenter the busy world of the ordinary activity of consciousness. Sometimes you must proceed a step further upward. It is not an easy matter. There are no rules: you have to establish your own practices. No one can teach you the way upward. Everything must come from within yourself. For this reason, no two masters have ever given the same answer to the question, "What is Buddha?" They have said, "The bamboo root on the back mountain," or "Fire boys come asking for fire," or "What is the price of wheat at the market?" or "The three-legged donkey goes moving its hooves."

• *Scholars labor at their formulas.* Scholars define their ideas elaborately and carefully, and build up great structures of argument and analysis. If we follow them, they lead us deep into their discussions, which may seem very logical and correct. But when we reflect on the matter, we find we have been given nothing that we really want—that is, true peace and freedom of mind. Scholars seem to attach first importance to their knowledge of other people's work; they are erudite, but they do not try to think their own original thoughts.

• *Like monkeys struggling to catch the moon reflected on the waves.* There is an allegorical story about monkeys trying to catch the reflection of the moon, alluding to scholars who think they are looking for the truth but who in fact are not dealing directly with truth itself. This story is a favorite subject of Chinese and Japanese painting.

• *Complications.* Complicated problems; a synonym for koans.

• *Masagin!* "Masagin" (three pounds of flax) came shooting out, an unpremeditated, instantaneous answer to the monk's question. This direct echoing back is greatly admired, as we see in Setchō's verse. This story is the same as that in Case 18 of *Mumonkan*.

• *The golden crow swoops, the silver hare bounds.* In ancient times people noticed a spot on the sun and thought a certain mysterious three-legged spiritual crow lived there. "Golden" is a poetic embellishment. They also conceived of a hare living on the moon. These two spiritual beings came to be used to represent the sun and moon, respectively, and eventually even to represent light. "Swoops" and "bounds" are used to convey the way "Masagin" came shooting out, with the speed of light, in answer to the monk's question.

• *The echo comes back, direct and free.* Out came Tōzan's reply, as the hill echoes the sound of the bell from the moonlit temple tower (see *Mumonkan*, Cases 17, 18, 21, and 22).

• *Who judges Tōzan by his word or phrase | Is a blind tortoise, lost in a lonely vale.* If a Westerner not knowing the meaning of the word had heard Tōzan say "Masagin" he would probably have been impressed by the action and the situation in which it took place: by the vigor of Tō-zan's speech, the immediacy of his response, the stress placed on the word, and, most important, the image received of Tōzan himself. And all this might have produced a strong effect. But people who understand the meaning of the word—three pounds of flax—when they study this case will get caught by the idea the word conveys to them and be too preoccupied by it to see the action as it is. Their understanding of Tōzan will be destroyed, and they will be like a blind tortoise, bewildered and lost. "A lame turtle and a blind tortoise" is a Zen phrase applied to the mentally blind.

• *The abundant blossoms, . . . the northern trees.* A monk asked Chi-mon, Setchō's teacher, "What is the meaning of Tōzan's 'Masagin'?" Chimon answered, "The abundant blossoms, the luxuriant flowers." The monk said, "I don't follow you." Chimon said, "The southern bamboo, the northern trees." Bamboo is abundant in the south of China, and trees are luxuriant in the north. Blossoms are gorgeous, flowers are beautiful, bamboo is crisp and clean, trees and woods are gigantic, and all this rich-ness and abundance and beauty is to be found in Tōzan's "Masagin." That is the meaning of these two lines.

• *One recalls Riku Taifu and Chōkei: | "You should not cry, but laugh!"* When Nansen died, Riku Taifu, one of his disciples, stood in front of his master's coffin and gave a loud laugh. A priest reproached him, saying, "Wasn't he your teacher? Why do you laugh, when you should lament for him?" Riku Taifu said, "Say a word, and if it fulfills the Buddha's teaching I will lament." But the priest could not utter a word. Deploring this, Riku Taifu said, "Alas! Our teacher has long gone!" And he wept aloud. Later Chōkei, hearing of this, said, "You should not cry, you should laugh!" What relation has this laughter to Tōzan's "Masagin"?

One might say that both stand outside all forms of conceptual manipulation. But perhaps a better answer would be to say, "I don't know; ask the moon in the sky."

Case 13   Haryō's "Snow in the Silver Bowl"

ENGO'S INTRODUCTION   Clouds gather over the great plain, but the universe can still be discerned. Snow covers the flowering reeds and it is difficult to distinguish them. Speaking of the coldness of it, it is colder than frozen snow; as for the fineness, it is finer than powdered rice. With regard to the deepness, even the Buddha's eyes cannot penetrate it, while as for the way it is hidden, devils would be unable to spy it out. I allow you are clever enough to know three corners from one, but how would you speak to shut the mouths of the people of the world? Who has the capacity to do that? See the following.

MAIN SUBJECT   A monk asked Haryō, "What is the Daiba school?" Haryō said, "Snow in the silver bowl."

SETCHŌ'S VERSE
Remarkable, the old man of Shinkai Temple;
It was well said, that "Snow in the silver bowl."

The ninety-six can learn for themselves what it means;
If they cannot, let them ask the moon in the sky.

Daiba school! Daiba school!
Scarlet banners flapping, the wind is cool!

NOTES   *Clouds gather over the great plain, but the universe can still be discerned.* Although when clouds cover the plain it is misty and things are obscure, you can still find the universe right there. This is to say, "Emptiness is form."

• Snow covers the flowering reeds and it is difficult to distinguish them. Snow is white, and so are the reed flowers; it is hard to distinguish them when they are covered with snow. This is to say, "Form is emptiness." The analogy of reeds and snow is popular in Zen literature.

• Speaking of the coldness . . . The absolute is unapproachable. When it is cold, it is infinitely colder than frozen snow. And so, too, with its other attributes: they are beyond human measure.

• Haryō was a disciple of Ummon and a Dharma brother of Tōzan of Case 12. The dates of his birth and death are not known. His personal name was Kōkan. "Haryō" derived from the name of the place where he lived, on the east side of Tungt'ing Lake, which was famous for its beautiful scenery. That may explain why his words were often poetic. Zen masters' words are often succinct and pithy: for example, Tōzan's "Masagin," Ummon's "Kanshiketsu," and Jōshū's "Mu." But every master has his own individuality, and Haryō was often wordy. He was called "talkative Kan" (Kan being an abbreviation of Kōkan). His wordiness gave rise to criticisms among Zen monks. But what blame can be ascribed to words?

• What is the Daiba school? Daiba is Kanadaiba (Kanadeva), the Fifteenth Patriarch in India. He was a disciple of Nagarjuna (c. 150–c. 250), who brought Buddhist philosophy to completion. Daiba himself was also a philosopher. He spoke fluently and was strong in argument, in which he is said to have defeated many non-Buddhist philosophers. This inevitably gave rise to questioning among Zen monks, who used to say that Zen could not be understood by logic, that it could not be explained in words and writing, that it could not be measured by reason. Hence, why was Daiba so argumentative? Knowing that this question must be answered, Setchō seems to have selected the present topic to place next to Tōzan's "Masagin," which transcends words.

• Snow in the silver bowl. Clouds gather over the great plain, but you can still discern the universe; snow covers the reeds and you cannot make them out. The Great Way naturally manifests itself. There are no laws. Words are all right; silence is also all right. This can be right, and so can that. It is so subtle. This cannot be right, and that also cannot be right. Then what should we do? It must be pointed out that "snow" can stand for the Daiba school and "the silver bowl" for Buddhism.

• *Remarkable, the old man of Shinkai Temple.* Shinkai Temple was Haryō's temple, and the old man is Haryō himself. "Old" is expressive of an intimate feeling.

• *The ninety-six can learn for themselves what it means.* There were ninety-six schools of non-Buddhist philosophers in ancient India. Heated arguments took place between them and the Buddhists. It was the custom in those days for the winner of a debate to put up red banners and to make disciples of the defeated. Setchō says that the ninety-six non-Buddhists must learn by themselves the subtle teachings of the Buddha, because he is sick of making a picture book of Zen.

• *If they cannot, let them ask the moon in the sky.* If they cannot understand, there is no remedy but to ask the moon.

• *Daiba school! Daiba school!* Hurrah for the Daiba school! Baso once said, "If there are ever words going on, it is the Daiba school." Here the Daiba school represents Haryō.

• *Scarlet banners flapping, the wind is cool!* The wind of victory is cool and refreshing.

Case 14 Ummon's "Preaching Facing Oneness"

MAIN SUBJECT   A monk asked Ummon, "What is the teaching of the Buddha's lifetime?" Ummon said, "Preaching facing oneness."

SETCHŌ'S VERSE
Facing oneness! There is no parallel!
He fitted the holeless hammer with a handle.

From under the Jambu tree, laughter rings out: Ha! Ha! Ha!
Last night the dragon got his horns broken.

Remarkable, the old man of Shōyō;
He has one tally here.

NOTES *Preaching facing oneness.* "Oneness" means absolute truth. "Facing" is a reference to the fact that Zen masters deliver their lectures facing the Buddha's image. But the meaning can be extended. For instance, when you talk to children, you talk like a child; when you talk to a youth or an old man, to men or women, to scholars or fools, you talk like them in each case. In other words, you adapt yourself to them. Here we are operating in the way of the "constructive gate," or following the waves as they come one after another. This is an instance of downward movement—downward from the top of the hundred-foot pole (see Cases 10 and 11). "Facing" is the most important word here: Ummon preaches facing oneness, facing the world, facing every being and every thing.

• *He fitted the holeless hammer with a handle.* The teachings of the Buddha's lifetime have been classified into three groups: sutras, philosophical discourses, and precepts (commandments). They have also been divided into manifest, mysterious, Zen, and Pure Land teachings, and have been further classified into Hinayana, Mahayana, and so on. All the texts are accompanied by elaborate interpretations and commentaries. This all goes to make the Buddha's teachings a very complicated matter. They are, in fact, a difficult problem, just as is a holeless hammer. But Ummon, when he answered the monk, deftly fitted this holeless hammer with a handle.

• *From under the Jambu tree, laughter rings out: Ha! Ha! Ha!* The Jambu tree is a gigantic mythological tree growing in and covering Jambudvipa, which is this universe of ours. From under this tree there comes the sound of loud laughter, which ripples out and reaches to the ends of the world. Whoever laughs like that must be a giant. But how and why does that laughter come? Many interpreters take it to be Setchō's. But it can also be taken as yours, or Ummon's, or the monk's. A Zen koan allows a variety of interpretations.

• *Last night the dragon got his horns broken.* Out came the question, with all the ferocity of a dragon accompanied by rain and wind. But it was met with an irresistible counterattack and got its horns broken. And then the laughter arose. But really, whose laughter is this? If you understand this case, your own laughter will eclipse that of everyone else.

• *Shōyō.* Another name for Ummon, derived from the place where he lived.

• *One tally.* The word is used here in the sense of one of the two corresponding or complementary halves or parts of something, referring to the fact that the following case is complementary to this one. In traditional commentaries the word which we have translated as "tally" is taken to mean "horn," and it is asked where Ummon's other horn has gone. Either interpretation amounts to the same thing: Cases 14 and 15 are two halves of a whole.

Case 15   Ummon's "No Preaching on Oneness"

ENGO'S INTRODUCTION   The death-dealing blade, the life-giving sword: they were the custom in ancient days and are still today the touchstone. Tell me, at this moment, what is the death-dealing blade, what is the life-giving sword? See the following.

MAIN SUBJECT   A monk asked Ummon, "What is it when no thought is stirring and nothing presents itself?" Ummon said, "No preaching on oneness."

SETCHŌ'S VERSE
No oneness! Each holds one tally.
He lives and dies with you, all the same.

The eighty-four thousand did not respond quickly;
The thirty-three entered the tiger's cave.

Remarkable: see how turbulent—
The moon reflected on the waves.

NOTES   *No thought is stirring and nothing presents itself.* This is the condition of absolute samadhi. But in positive samadhi, too, even in the midst of the most turbulent activity of consciousness, you may enjoy a serene mental condition in which no confusion or commotion troubles your mind. The present case is concerned with this problem.

• *No preaching on oneness.* This is stepping off from the top of the hundred-foot pole (see *Mumonkan*, Case 46). But there are many sorts of stepping off, depending on the degree of your attainment. This stepping off is a matter of the upward route. But "upward" eventually proves to be "downward." It may sound contradictory, but the ultimate embraces all contradictions and inconsistencies because the ultimate absorbs all.

• *Each holds one tally.* No preaching on oneness and preaching facing oneness (Case 14) together make the two halves of one whole. At the same time, the questioning monk and the answering Ummon hold one tally each.

• *He lives and dies with you.* The Zen teacher goes hand in hand with his disciple, sharing all sorts of hardships in the latter's struggle for enlightenment.

• *The eighty-four thousand did not respond quickly.* "Eighty-four thousand" denotes the Buddha's innumerable followers. When the Buddha was at Mount Grdhrakuta he held out a flower to his listeners. Everyone was silent. Only Mahakashyapa broke into a broad smile, because he understood the Buddha's samadhi. The others did not understand and remained silent. They did not respond quickly. (See *Mumonkan*, Case 6.)

• *The thirty-three entered the tiger's cave.* The thirty-three are the thirty-three patriarchs: twenty-eight in India, of whom the last, Bodhidharma, became the first of the six in China. They put their heads into the tiger's mouth and attained enlightenment. If you wish to master the profound secret of "No preaching on oneness" you have to go through the same experience that they did.

• *Remarkable.* Here is something special I want to tell you. The secret of the present case is summed up in what follows.

• *See how turbulent— / The moon reflected on the waves.* The moon's reflection on the waves is shaken, swayed, and broken to pieces, and never ceases its agitated movement. This is analogous to the seething activity of ordinary consciousness. But when we watch carefully, we see that the moon is not really disturbed at all. It is simply dancing and swaying, and seems to enjoy it. One moment it is dashed to pieces, the next it collects itself together again. In the midst of seeming turbulence, it preserves its integrity. This is the condition of a mature Zen master's mind. Stepping off from the top of the hundred-foot pole belongs to the upward route, but it is really nothing but coming down to the busiest activity of consciousness and retaining the peaceful condition of mind that we enjoy in absolute samadhi.

Case 16 Kyōsei's Instruction on Pecking and Tapping

ENGO'S INTRODUCTION There is no byroad to the Way. There one stands absolutely firm. The Dharma transcends seeing and hearing. There one is independent of words and thoughts. If you make your way through all the thorny entanglements, break down the barriers of the Buddha and the patriarchs, and attain the quiet and secret land, there heaven will find no way to send down flowers to you, and the devil no way to spy you out. All day long you act without acting, preach without preaching. Then you have learned to tap the eggshell at the moment the chick is emerging, to wield the death-dealing sword that also gives life. However, going still further, when you realize in your activity along the constructive route how to grasp the student on the one hand and release him on the other, you will deserve to be called a master. But in the realm of the absolute, things will become different. Now, how will it be with the matter of the absolute? See the following.

MAIN SUBJECT A monk said to Kyōsei, "I want to peck from the inside. Would you please tap from the outside?" Kyōsei said, "Could you attain life or not?" The monk said, "If I could not attain life, I would become a laughingstock." Kyōsei said, "You too are a fellow in the weeds!"

SETCHŌ'S VERSE
Old Buddha had his way of teaching,
The monk's answer won no praise.

Strangers to each other, hen and chick,
Who can peck when the tapping comes?

Outside, the tap was given;
Inside, the chick remained.

Once again the tap was given;
Monks throughout the world attempt the trick in vain.

NOTES   *Kyōsei* (868–937) succeeded Seppō. He also appears in Cases 23 and 46. He taught his disciples by his favorite method of so-called simultaneous pecking and tapping. It is proverbial that when a chick is hatching the mother hen gives a helping tap from outside. If the tap comes too early or too late, the egg is spoiled. The chick's pecking from inside and the mother's tapping from outside are done instinctively and simultaneously. This provides a good analogy to the relation between teacher and disciple at the moment of the latter's attaining realization: if the teacher's helping hand is given too early, the student is spoiled; if it is too late, the chance is missed. The keenest concentration is required of both teacher and student. The subtlety of action necessary at the moment of bringing the student to enlightenment is the subject of the present case.

• *Thorny entanglements.* In the course of life you meet with many entanglements: economic, emotional, illusory, even neurotic. The Zen koan has a close relation to these. Indeed, the koan is another version of the worldly entanglements; and if you pass the koan, you escape those entanglements.

• *The barriers of the Buddha and the patriarchs.* The Buddha's and the patriarchs' words and actions provide many problems in the form of koans. You cannot solve them easily. In other words, they block your way and are therefore called the barriers of the Buddha and the patriarchs. In fact, of course, it is your own deluded thinking that blocks your way. When your mind is open and the deluded way of thinking is overcome, you find that nothing blocks your way.

• *The quiet and secret land.* The peaceful land of the mind.

• *Heaven will find no way to send down flowers to you.* This is a reference to Sunyata (see Case 6).

• *All day long you act without acting, preach without preaching.* You act in emptiness, and no trace of your actions is left behind. You preach, and no trace of your preaching is left behind. It is just like the sun, shining all day long, showing no sign of change in itself and yet producing a great effect on the earth.

• *You have learned to tap the eggshell at the moment the chick is emerging, to wield the death-dealing sword that also gives life.* Such ability comes not from the conceptual manipulation of ideas but from penetrating insight. This insight is attained when the third nen (reason) is purified of its delusive way of thinking and attains unity and harmony with the first nen (intuition). In other words, the intuitive action of pure reason is developed.

• *When you realize in your activity along the constructive route how to grasp the student on the one hand and release him on the other.* See the notes to Case 4. This refers to the Zen master's technique of teaching, which varies according to the Zen school he belongs to, the so-called family customs of the tradition he follows, and his own personal method.

• *But in the realm of the absolute . . .* This and the following sentence can be ignored. The present case is concerned with activity belonging to the constructive route (see the notes to Case 10 for an explanation of this term), and the comment is really finished in what has gone before. But Engo dislikes a one-sided account of things. The constructive route eventually becomes the absolute; the death-dealing blade is the life-giving sword. Rinzai says, "One preaches in the streets but is not outside one's home." Actions in the streets belong to the constructive route, while being at home refers to the absolute route.

• *You too are a fellow in the weeds!* This is a common phrase used to describe a mediocrity. This monk was familiar with Kyōsei's method of teaching and came talking about it. Kyōsei, however, chose to whip the galloping horse by refusing to acknowledge his achievement.

• *Old Buddha had his way of teaching.* A eulogistic description of Kyōsei and his way of instruction.

• *Who can peck when the tapping comes?* The delicate harmony of action between hen and chick is what must be achieved between teacher and disciple. It is a matter of the immediate and intimate communication of mind with mind.

• *Outside, the tap was given.* "Could you attain life or not?" was the first tap.

• *Inside, the chick remained.* It is a tantalizing process. The student often fails to dance to the teacher's piping. But seeming failures may be unexpected assets, contributing to later success.

• *Once again the tap was given.* The first arrow was light; the second went deep. It is not known whether the monk had an experience or not in this encounter, but he must have made some move forward.

• *Monks throughout the world attempt the trick in vain.* The flick by which the chick emerges is a subtle matter. It flaps and flips, and in a moment it is out. So, too, the student struggles before he suddenly finds himself standing outside his broken ego-shell.

Case 17 Kyōrin's "Sitting Long and Getting Tired"

ENGO'S INTRODUCTION Cutting through nails and breaking steel, for the first time one can be called master of the first principle. If you keep away from arrows and evade swords, you will be a failure in Zen. As for the subtle point where no probe can be inserted, that may be set aside for a while; but when the foaming waves wash the sky, what will you do with yourself then? See the following.

MAIN SUBJECT A monk asked Kyōrin, "What is the meaning of Bodhidharma's coming from the West?" Kyōrin said, "Sitting long and getting tired."

SETCHŌ'S VERSE
> One, two, and tens of hundreds of thousands,
> Take off the muzzle and set down the load.
> If you turn left and right, following another's lead,
> I would strike you as Shiko struck Ryūtetsuma.

NOTES   *Kyōrin* (908–87) was one of the four outstanding disciples of Ummon. He followed Ummon for eighteen years as his attendant. Every day Ummon called him, and when he answered, "Yes, sir!" Ummon would say, "What is this?" This was continued for eighteen long years. Then one day Kyōrin exclaimed, "Oh! I understand!" Ummon said, "Why don't you say it in a transcending manner?" And Kyōrin spent another three years with Ummon to attain full maturity. He was a great master but slow to mature. Kyōrin's disciple Chimon (Case 21) was Setchō's teacher. Kyōrin taught his disciples for forty years, and when he was dying, he said, "For forty years I was constantly in one piece." By this he meant that he had maintained his samadhi—both absolute and positive—unbroken throughout that time.

Children enjoy their positive samadhi instinctively, and so do horses and cows, standing peacefully in the evening sun. But there is a special quality about the positive samadhi of a mature master, founded as it is on his laboriously achieved absolute samadhi. It has something of the severity and intensity of the high mountains. However, this is not to say that the master may not sometimes have a pleasant chat with you, just as the Alps occasionally laugh, high up in the clear, serene sky, with the valleys far below, streams running, flowers blooming, bees humming, and wagons rumbling by.

• *Cutting through nails and breaking steel.* Nails and steel stand for the student's attachments and ignorance, and all the difficulties he encounters. The teacher's task is to cut through and break them.

• *The first principle.* The word in the original text is *honbun* (*hon*, prime; *bun*, cause), which means the ultimate truth to be mastered in Zen practice.

• *If you keep away from arrows and evade swords.* The practice and study of Zen is a battle. You must have the determination to overcome all sorts of difficulties and hardships, and not seek to evade them.

• *The subtle point where no probe can be inserted.* The closed condition of absolute samadhi, silent and withdrawn, into which nothing can penetrate.

• *When the foaming waves wash the sky.* The affairs of the world that demand the busiest activity of your consciousness.

• *What is the meaning of Bodhidharma's coming from the West?* Bodhidharma endured three years of hardship on his voyage to China. He must have been possessed of great determination and have had a profoundly serious intention. Yet his first utterance in China, in answer to Emperor Wu's question, "What are the holy teachings of the Buddha?" was "Emptiness" (Case 1). Then he retired to a temple and sat in meditation for nine years, gazing at the wall. This gave rise to the question, "What is the meaning of Bodhidharma's coming from the West?" One answer given to this is "No meaning." In a word, it is labor without reward. The sun shines all day and every day, and it works on endlessly. It is thankless work, yet the sun does not weary of it or wish it had not started. It keeps itself whole and concentrated, always in one piece.

• *Sitting long and getting tired.* This is equivalent to saying, "Sufficient unto the day is the evil thereof." This answer of Kyōrin's is greatly admired by Zen students. When sitting, you are sitting; when you get tired, you get tired. There is no irritation, no regret: you are as you are, all of a piece. This is the central topic of the case. Will you be able to say at the end of your life, "I have sat long and got tired, and am all in one piece"?

• *One, two, and tens of hundreds of thousands.* Innumerable people.

• *Take off the muzzle and set down the load.* When you master Kyōrin's "Sitting long and getting tired," you will be able to set down the burdens that weigh upon your mind.

• *If you turn left and right, following another's lead.* If you busily turn this way and that, imitating others and losing your independence.

• *I would strike you as Shiko struck Ryūtetsuma.* Shiko was a disciple of Nansen and a Dharma brother of Jōshū. He was a master with a sharp Zen spirit. Ryūtetsuma was a nun and a disciple of Isan. She was famous for her shrewdness in Dharma battle. Many monks had mortifying experiences with her. Ryū was her family name; Tetsuma (*tetsu*, iron; *ma*, mill) was a nickname implying that she pounded her opponents in Dharma battle like an iron millstone grinding wheat into flour. One day Ryūtetsuma appeared unexpectedly before Shiko, who said, "Are you not Ryūtetsuma?" "You are warm," answered Ryūtetsuma. "Do you turn right or left?" "You, don't overturn!" Her retort was not bad, but a Dharma contest is an exacting matter. Before she had finished speaking, she was struck by Shiko. It is said that she should have dealt the blow to Shiko herself when he asked, "Do you turn right or left?" The third line of Setchō's verse refers to this story. Ryūtetsuma also appears in Case 24.

Case 18 Emperor Shukusō Asks About the Style of the Pagoda

MAIN SUBJECT Emperor Shukusō asked Chū Kokushi, "When you are a hundred years old, what shall I do for you?" Kokushi answered, "Make a seamless pagoda for this old monk." The emperor said, "I should like to ask you, what style is it to be?" Kokushi remained silent for a while. And then he said, "Do you understand?" "No, I do not," said the emperor. "I have a disciple called Tangen," said Kokushi, "who has the Dharma Seal transmitted by me. He is well versed in this matter. Ask him, please." After Kokushi's death, the emperor sent for Tangen and asked him about it. Tangen said,

"South of Shō and north of Tan,
[Setchō says, "Soundless sound of one hand."]
In between, gold abounds.
[Setchō says, "A staff of a mountain kind."]
The ferryboat under the shadowless tree,
[Setchō says, "Clear is the river, calm is the sea."]
No holy one in the emerald palace you see."
[Setchō says, "All is finished."]

SETCHŌ'S VERSE
A seamless pagoda, it is difficult to describe;
The dragon does not thrive in a placid lake.
Tier after tier, superbly it casts its shadow;
Let it be admired for a thousand ages.

NOTES *Chū Kokushi.* See *Mumonkan*, Case 17. He also appears in Cases 69 and 99. A monk once asked him, "What is the mind of the old [time-honored] Buddha?" Kokushi answered, "Tiles, pebbles, and walls." "Do they understand preaching?" "They preach intensely and unceasingly." Another monk asked him, "What is the true body of the Dharmakaya Buddha?" "Fetch me the water bottle," said Kokushi. When the monk brought it to him, he said, "Put it back where it was." The monk, having done what he was asked to do, repeated his former question. Kokushi said, "Alas! The old Buddha has long gone!"

• *When you are a hundred years old.* After you have passed away.

• *Seamless pagoda.* "Seamless" here means formless. The formless pagoda (the true form of the formless) is nothing but the Dharmakaya Buddha (see the notes to Case 39).

• *What style is it to be?* The emperor may have intended this in an ordinary, worldly sense. However, in the context of a Dharma contest it made an acute question. How could Kokushi answer it? Wasn't it almost impossible? Engo puts in a comment here, saying, "A finger on a sore spot."

• *Kokushi remained silent for a while.* This silence has given rise to many comments. Engo says, "Kept under restraint, you try evasion," and again, "Being shut up, your mouth is like a pole." Monks go through much anguish in dealing with this koan. Ryūge once said, "This question of yours is a real affliction." Baso, in a like situation, said, "Sun-faced Buddha, Moon-faced Buddha" (Case 3). Imagine the glorious sunset and the silvery moonlight in the frosty sky. Kyōgen said in his enlightenment poem, "Spirit, not damp, not dull." Setchō's mention of a "placid lake" in his verse is a reference to this silence (see below).

• *And then he said.* Note that this is not "Kokushi remained silent for a while and then said . . ." but "And then he said . . ."

• *I have a disciple called Tangen. . . . Ask him, please.* Goso commented on this: "You are the National Teacher; why don't you answer directly instead of passing the question on to someone else?" Goso, of course, knew that Kokushi had a special intention in passing the question to his disciple. Tangen's personal name was Ōshin, and he is the hero of Case 17 of *Mumonkan*.

• *South of Shō and north of Tan.* This is equivalent to saying, "South of the North Pole, north of the South Pole." Shō and Tan were the two rivers that formed the boundaries of the area in which Zen was flourishing in those times.

• *Soundless sound of one hand.* One hand does not make a sound. Nevertheless, it makes a tremendous sound, which fills the universe. Hakuin's "The sound of one hand" bears a close relationship to this.

• *In between, gold abounds.* The pure spirit of Zen, like virgin gold, fills the country of the mind. The gold is solid and pure.

• *A staff of a mountain kind.* A staff about seven feet long was used by a monk when he went journeying over hill and dale, visiting teachers or seeking a quiet spot in the mountains for his hermitage. It came to have a symbolic meaning, representing the living spirit of the Zen student and, in turn, the essence of Zen, the truth of the universe, and so on. Ummon, showing his staff to his disciples, once said, "This staff transforms itself into a dragon and swallows up the universe. Where are the mountains, the rivers, and the great world?" "A staff of a mountain kind" means a staff which has not been shaped by human artifice but has simply been made from a tree growing wild in a mountain forest. Hence, it stands for the bare, unadorned truth.

• *The ferryboat under the shadowless tree.* The ferryboat carries people across the water to the opposite shore—that is, to the Pure Land. The shadowless tree symbolizes eternity.

• *Clear is the river, calm is the sea.* The voyage will be quiet and peaceful.

• *No holy one in the emerald palace.* The boat arrives at the opposite shore, where there is a beautiful palace. But in it you find no holy one. "No Buddha, no mind, no thing" is a Buddhist saying. But if you listen intently, you will hear a faint sound of subtle music, which grows louder and louder, and you will come to see the majestic constellation of Buddhas and Bodhisattvas—Shakyamuni, Manjusri, Samantabhadra, and all the others.

• *All is finished.* The building of the seamless pagoda is finished.

• *A seamless pagoda, it is difficult to describe.* But it is far more difficult to build it in yourself.

• *The dragon does not thrive in a placid lake.* Setchō means that Koku-shi's silence was not that of a quiet lake but like the foaming waves that wash the skies. In Zen literature dragons are often used to represent outstanding monks. (See the notes to Case 95.) This line of Setchō's is much admired by Zen students. Goso once said, "Setchō's verses fill a whole volume, of which I like only this line, 'The dragon does not thrive in a placid lake.' "

• *Tier after tier, superbly it casts its shadow.* It commands the ten directions.

• *Let it be admired for a thousand ages.* It stands eternally, through the countless eons of the past and the limitless future to come.

Case 19　Gutei's One-Finger Zen

ENGO'S INTRODUCTION　When even one particle stirs, the whole universe is involved; a blossom opens and the world responds. But what do you see when no particle stirs and a blossom does not open? It is said that it is like cutting the thread on a reel: one cut and you cut it all. Or it is like dyeing the thread on a reel: dye it once and you dye it all. Now, if you eradicate all the complications that affect you and bring out the treasure within you, you will find that everything is all right, above and below, before and behind. If you have not yet done so, see the following.

MAIN SUBJECT　Gutei, whenever he was asked a question, only raised a finger.

SETCHŌ'S VERSE
　Well, now! I like Gutei's way of answering.
　Who could compare with him throughout the whole universe?
　He let down the wooden float into the dark sea,
　Making the blind turtle sink and swim and cling to it.

NOTES　*When even one particle stirs, the whole universe is involved.* When the smallest nen-thought appears in your mind, the whole universe is reflected in it. But you will not be aware of that in the course of your ordinary routine activity. However, if you once enter absolute samadhi and then emerge from it into positive samadhi, you will realize this involvement of the universe in a single nen-thought. This subtle effect is the subject of Engo's introduction.
　• *What do you see when no particle stirs and a blossom does not open?* If you once experience absolute samadhi, you will become aware of a world where no particle stirs and no flower opens.
　• *One cut and you cut it all.* When you once get into absolute samadhi, all the complications of your mind are cut away once and for all.
　• *Like dyeing the thread on a reel.* And if you then come out of absolute samadhi and return to the world of the ordinary activity of conscious-

ness, you will find everything radiant with its own true light. That is positive samadhi.

• *Bring out the treasure within you.* In Gutei's case, the treasure was displayed in the act of raising his finger.

• *Everything is all right.* Everything is found to be all right in Gutei's raising his finger.

• *Above and below, before and behind.* This means everywhere and everything—every event, occasion, and circumstance.

• *Gutei, whenever he was asked a question, only raised a finger.* This case also appears in *Mumonkan* (Case 3). For a commentary on it and an account of Gutei, see the notes to that case.

• *Well, now! I like Gutei's way of answering.* Setchō greatly appreciates Gutei's one-finger Zen.

• *He let down the wooden float into the dark sea, / Making the blind turtle sink and swim and cling to it.* This is an allusion to a story that occurs in the *Parinirvana Sutra* and also in the *Saddharma Pundarika Sutra* (*Lotus Sutra*). There was once a turtle that lived in the deep sea. It had only one eye, and that was in the middle of its belly. One day a log with a hole in it came floating by. The turtle was just able to cling to it from beneath, put its eye to the hole, and look upward to see and worship the sun. The intention of the story is to illustrate how there is but one chance in a million that one can attain human existence, encounter the Buddha, listen to him, and achieve enlightenment. But Gutei made that miraculous feat possible for common people with his one-finger Zen.

Case 20   Ryūge Asks Suibi and Rinzai

ENGO'S INTRODUCTION   Range upon range of mountain peaks, rock faces, and cliffs all deliver their profound sermons. If you stop to think, you will be bewildered. Let a man of great strength appear, overturn the great sea, kick over Mount Sumeru, shout and disperse the white clouds, break up the empty sky, and with each "ki" and every "kyo" shut the mouths of all other men: such a man will be truly incomparable. Has ever a man been so wonderful? See the following.

MAIN SUBJECT   Ryūge asked Suibi, "What is the meaning of Bodhidharma's coming from the West?" Suibi said, "Pass me the board" [chin rest]. Ryūge passed the board to Suibi, who took it and hit Ryūge with it. Ryūge said, "If you strike me, I will let you. But after all, there is no meaning in Bodhidharma's coming from the West."

Ryūge asked Rinzai, too, "What is the meaning of Bodhidharma's coming from the West?" Rinzai said, "Pass me the cushion." Ryūge passed the cushion to Rinzai, who took it and hit Ryūge with it. Ryūge said, "If you strike me, I will let you. But after all, there is no meaning in Bodhidharma's coming from the West."

SETCHŌ'S VERSE
Dragon Mountain, the dragon has no eye.
Still waters don't impart the ancient Way.
If the board and cushion don't benefit you,
Hand them over to me.
(I have not yet exhausted this, hence another verse.)
Even if they are given to me, it's useless.
Not for me to sit like the patriarch.
Beautiful, the evening clouds,
Endless, the distant hills, blue upon blue, peak upon peak!

NOTES   *Range upon range of mountain peaks, rock faces, and cliffs all deliver their profound sermons.* When you emerge from absolute samadhi and are in positive samadhi in the ordinary activity of your consciousness, you will clearly hear mountains and rivers, animals and birds, wayside stones and plants all delivering their sermons. *Shujō seppō* (*shu*, all; *jō*, creatures; *seppō*, [deliver] sermons) is a famous Zen saying. Many outstanding Zen masters, including Tōzan, the founder of the Sōtō sect, attained enlightenment after ruminating long over this saying.

• *If you stop to think, you will be bewildered.* You will never achieve pure cognition of the object by conceptual reasoning, because such conceptual activity of the mind is not directly connected with the object. Direct cognition is achieved only through intuition—that is, by the action of the first nen. (See the notes to Case 6.)

• *The great sea . . . Mount Sumeru . . . white clouds . . . the empty sky.* The great sea represents the wave-tossed condition of the disturbed mind. In zazen these waves are gradually quieted. Mount Sumeru is the mythical mountain supposedly located at the center of the universe; here it represents your stubborn ego, which will eventually drop away in absolute samadhi. The great sea and Mount Sumeru belong to the realm of discrimination. The white clouds and empty sky belong to the realm of universal equality, which is truly realized when the clouds are dispersed and the sky is broken up.

• *Each "ki" and every "kyo."* See the notes to Case 3.

• *Shut the mouths of all other men.* Confronting a man of great strength, people find they have nothing to say.

• *Ryūge* (835–923) succeeded Tōzan, the founder of the Sōtō sect. In his later years he became a distinguished Zen master, but probably when he asked this question he was not so advanced in Zen practice. However, it is obvious from this story that he had a certain understanding of the topic of Bodhidharma's coming from the West.

When one first has a realization experience (kenshō) in Zen practice, one becomes greatly excited and often rather conceited, thinking that one has completely mastered Zen. The phrase used to describe such a student is "He carries with him his bellyful of Zen." Tokusan, in Case 4, was in this state and went to "inspect" Isan. Ryūge, in the same way, came to Suibi to engage in Dharma battle and inspect this old, mature master. In a way, this is to be admired as a display of youthful valor.

• *What is the meaning of Bodhidharma's coming from the West?* The generally acknowledged answer to this question is "No meaning." Nevertheless, the question has been taken up again and again, in generation after generation. Even in Ryūge's time it was a well-worn topic, yet every time it was broached it seemed fresh. What is this "no meaning"? "No meaning" and "no purpose" will sound like nonsense to most people, but this nonsense constitutes the hard nut that Zen students exert all their energies to crack.

• *Pass me the board.* The board, or chin rest, is placed between the chin and the knee to support and rest the body, and even allow a little nap, while sitting in zazen posture. Passing the board is a demonstration of positive samadhi. In the notes to Case 18 we quoted Kokushi's words, "Fetch me the water bottle." Reflect upon similar actions: Gutei raising a finger, the Buddha holding up a flower before his listeners. Suibi was answering Ryūge's question in the most direct way possible, but Ryūge was unaware of it. He was preoccupied with a sort of understanding of the topic that we might call "seeing the sky through a funnel." There is another pithy phrase to describe a man in Ryūge's condition: "a board-shouldering fellow." When you are carrying on your shoulders a board as big as a door, you find it hard to look around or dodge about; you can see in only one direction.

• *Suibi . . . took it and hit Ryūge with it.* In hitting him, Suibi was saying, "Aren't you aware of it?"

• *If you strike me, I will let you.* The conceited young Ryūge was too greatly taken with his own ideas to suppose that he was at fault. And he was ignorant enough to set aside his elder's attempt at instruction.

• *After all, there is no meaning in Bodhidharma's coming from the West.* Ryūge may once have reached an intuitive understanding of this topic; but now he is lingering in the memory of his experience and imagines that he is still the master of that previously attained experience. He is dealing in his experience at second hand, though, full of conceit, he is unaware of this.

• *Ryūge asked Rinzai, too.* Ryūge went to Rinzai intending to test him as he had done Suibi.

• *Rinzai said, "Pass me the cushion."* Was this a coincidence? No, in Zen nothing can be simply a hackneyed repetition. The actions of a Zen master are always fresh and original, springing directly from his innermost reality. Engo interpolates a comment on this, saying, "If the waves of Sōkei [the Sixth Patriarch] are the same as each other, countless people will be drowned on land." Sōkei, which was the place where the Sixth Patriarch lived, was used as his nickname and later became synonymous with Zen because the Sixth Patriarch's influence was so great. "Drowned on land" means "ruined despite the fact that one has a firm foundation." What Engo means to say is that if the actions of Zen masters are no more than conventional repetitions of what has been done before, their students will be led to ruin.

• *Ryūge passed the cushion to Rinzai.* Ryūge knew only too well that he would be hit with the cushion, but he dared pass it. (Ryūge also knew in his encounter with Suibi that he would be hit with the board, but he dared pass it.) Engo's comment here is "Though he was given a fine horse, he did not know how to ride it. Alas!" which means why, when he was given a suitable weapon, did he not hit Rinzai with it? However, we must note here that an outstanding Chinese Zen master, Kidō, from whom the present Japanese Rinzai sect descends, put forward an alternative interpretation of Ryūge's obstinacy. According to him, Ryūge was profoundly enlightened and, knowing everything, did what he did in order to emphasize the "no meaning" of Bodhidharma's coming from the West. In this view, Ryūge's action was beautiful, even though it seemingly caused his own degrading humiliation. Kidō's theory has its advocates today. A Zen story, like a Christian parable, is open to a variety of interpretations, and it may be said that the extent to which this is possible is a measure of the story's depth and subtlety.

• *Dragon Mountain, the dragon has no eye.* "Dragon Mountain" comes from Ryūge's name (*ryū*, dragon; *ge*, fang). "No eye" means blind. In other words, the dragon of Dragon Mountain is blind. Again, we must note that Kidō interprets this line as meaning that, of the five kinds of blindness which Zen recognizes (see the notes to Case 10), Ryūge has attained the final state of genuine, transcendent blindness. We have judged Ryūge to be in the fourth rather than the fifth category, but there is no need to make much of this difference in interpretation. Zen stories are not to be taken as historical fact.

• *Still waters don't impart the ancient Way.* In stagnant water there is no dragon to demonstrate the ancient Way, that is, the Way of Shakyamuni, Bodhidharma, and the Sixth Patriarch.

• *Not for me to sit like the patriarch.* There is no Buddha, no patriarch, no Zen at all. There is also no no-Zen, no no-patriarch, and so forth.

• *Beautiful, the evening clouds, / Endless, the distant hills, blue upon blue, peak upon peak!* The last two lines constitute a famous koan. Recite them for yourself in language samadhi and you will come to appreciate them.

Case 21   Chimon's Lotus Flower and Lotus Leaves

Engo's Introduction   Setting up the Dharma banner and establishing the Dharma teaching is like spreading flowers over brocades. If you take off the muzzle and set down the load, you will enter a time of great peace. If you master the transcendent words, you will be able to know three corners from one. If not, as usual, listen to the following.

MAIN SUBJECT A monk asked Chimon, "What will the lotus flower be when it has not yet come out of the water?" Chimon said, "The lotus flower." "What about when it is out of the water?" "The lotus leaves."

SETCHŌ'S VERSE

The lotus leaves! The lotus flower!
He is so kind to tell you of them!
The flower coming out of the water—
What difference, before or after?
If you wander about, now north of the river,
    now south of the lake,
Questioning Master Wang and the like,
As one doubt is settled others will arise,
And you will puzzle over question after question.

NOTES   *Chimon* was a disciple of Kyōrin (see Case 17) and a Dharma grandson of Ummon. He was Setchō's teacher and thus one of the most recent of the *dramatis personae* appearing in *Hekiganroku*, though the dates of his birth and death are not recorded.

• *Setting up the Dharma banner and establishing the Dharma teaching.* When you are a Zen master you set up your own Dharma banner and establish your own Dharma teaching, although it will still be the banner and the teaching originated by the Buddha and passed on by the patriarchs and the Zen masters of old.

• *Like spreading flowers over brocades.* To spread flowers over brocades adds beauty to beauty but is nevertheless superfluous. To the enlightened eye the Dharma truth is plainly visible. However, for those who cannot see it, instruction is necessary. This is like spreading flowers over brocades.

• *If you take off the muzzle and set down the load.* Like a horse that is muzzled and heavily laden, you are weighed down by your own delusive thoughts. When you cast them off you enjoy great peace.

• *Transcendent words.* Words whose meaning cannot be grasped by ordinary conceptual understanding. Their meaning can be reached only directly and intuitively.

• *To know three corners from one.* See Case 1. If you once attain to realization, all things become clear. It is for this reason that it is said that Zen gives an opening to all the arts. The enlightened mind is very often found to be artistically developed—in drawing and calligraphy, for example, in poetry, and in other artistic activities, such as the tea ceremony, cooking, and garden design.

• *What will the lotus flower be when it has not yet come out of the water?* When it is not out of the water, it is not out of the water.

• *The lotus flower.* This represents absolute reality.

• *When it is out of the water.* When it is out of the water, it is out of the water.

• *The lotus leaves.* While the lotus flower represents absolute reality, the leaves represent its activities. But Buddhism holds that the absolute and its activities are one and the same. When it is not yet out of the water, it is not yet out of the water; when it is out of the water, it is out of the water.

• *He is so kind.* He clearly speaks the truth.

• *Now north of the river, now south of the lake.* The river is the Yangtze; the lake is Tungt'ing Lake. It was principally in the surrounding area that Zen flourished when it was at its peak.

• *Master Wang and the like.* Wang is a common name among the Chinese, rather as Smith or Brown is among the English. If you travel about, visiting this teacher and that, asking first about this question and then about something else, you will simply stir up endless problems and never come to any conclusion. Going on like that is of no avail. What you must do is to catch hold of and achieve a clear understanding of this very moment's thought of yours. Then you will understand the transcendent words and enter the days of great peace.

Case 22 Seppō's Turtle-nosed Snake

ENGO'S INTRODUCTION   The great universe is boundless. As for how small it is, it is like an atom. Grasping and releasing, developing and declining, are not in others' hands; they are all in your own. If you want to get rid of encumbrances and cut through entanglements, you must transcend form and sound and remove all trace of the activity of mind; then you will be in an impregnable position and absolutely independent, like a thousand-fathom cliff. Tell me, who was ever like this? See the following.

MAIN SUBJECT   Seppō, speaking to the assembly, said, "There is a turtle-nosed snake on the South Mountain. You should have a good look at it." Chōkei said, "Today, in this temple, there is obviously one man who has lost his life." Later, a monk related this to Gensha, who said, "Only Brother Ryō [Chōkei Eryō] can answer like that; as for me, I am different." "How are you different?" asked the monk. Gensha said, "What use is there in making use of the South Mountain?" Ummon threw his staff down in front of Seppō and made a gesture as if he were afraid of it.

SETCHŌ'S VERSE
  Mount Seppō was too steep to climb;
  Only the skilled could try it.
  Chōkei and Gensha made nothing of it;
  How many truly lost their lives?

  Ummon knew how to beat the bushes;
  The snake—its nature so—was nowhere to be found.
  The staff, suddenly flung down,
  Opened its mouth right before Seppō.

  It strikes like lightning,
  If you try to look for it, you fail;
  Now it is hidden on this peak of Nyūhō:
  If you want to see it, look at it directly.

[All of a sudden Setchō gave a shout and said, "Look out beneath your feet!"]

NOTES   *Grasping and releasing, developing and declining, are not in others' hands; they are all in your own.* See the notes to Case 4.

• *Encumbrances . . . entanglements.* Complications, attachments, delusive thinking.

• *Form and sound.* These represent external conditions.

• *Remove all trace of the activity of mind.* The key term here is *mushin*, which means "no-mind" (*mu*, no; *shin*, mind). This does not mean a mindless or absent-minded condition but rather a state that one might describe as "innocent," in which one's actions leave no trace behind. There is a Zen saying, "Active all day, he does nothing."

• *Independent, like a thousand-fathom cliff.* This refers to the unshakably independent condition of the Zen mind.

• *Seppō, Chōkei, Gensha, Ummon.* Seppō first appears in Case 13 of *Mumonkan*, Chōkei in Case 8 of *Hekiganroku*, Ummon in Case 15 of *Mumonkan*, and Gensha in Case 41 of *Mumonkan*. Chōkei, Ummon, and Gensha were all disciples of Seppō.

• *A turtle-nosed snake.* This is an age-old, bent-headed, venomous serpent. All the Buddhas, patriarchs, and Zen masters were once swallowed by this snake. They came out enlightened and themselves became venomous serpents. The allegory of the snake may seem strange at first, but it is common in Zen literature. It means that you must once undergo the Great Death.

• *There is obviously one man who has lost his life.* Chōkei is saying, "It must be particularly mentioned that there is a man here who has experienced the Great Death." He is speaking of himself. He wants to respond to his teacher's instruction.

• *As for me, I am different.* Zen masters always wished to be original in their actions.

• *What use is there in making use of the South Mountain?* Zen is everywhere. It is pointless to try to localize it. (Remember Gensha once said, "Bodhidharma did not come from the West, the Second Patriarch did not go to India.") Gensha meant, "If I were Chōkei, I would have said, 'What use is there in making use of the South Mountain?' " The South Mountain was a hill located to the south of Seppō's temple.

• *Ummon threw his staff down . . . and made a gesture as if he were afraid of it.* Ummon threw himself into the staff and, becoming the serpent, sprang into Seppō's presence. His gesture as if he were afraid is another matter. When you are the serpent itself, you are the serpent itself; when observing the serpent, you are observing the serpent.

• *Chōkei and Gensha made nothing of it.* This is a poetic figure of speech. In fact, they performed very well. Chōkei, Gensha, and Ummon were all veteran snake-charmers. But their abilities, and the parts they played, were different. Setchō appreciated Ummon's action most of all.

• *How many truly lost their lives?* Setchō is asking the reader, "Did you truly lose your life?"

• *Ummon knew how to beat the bushes.* He was a master hand, and well versed in this sort of exercise.

• *The snake—its nature so—was nowhere to be found.* It is the nature of the snake not to be seen by those who try to grasp it by conceptual understanding.

• *Now it is hidden on this peak of Nyūhō.* The snake is here now, on this peak of Nyūhō (another name for Mount Setchō).

• *If you want to see it, look at it directly.* Anyone who has the eye to see it intuitively should come and see it directly.

• *Look out beneath your feet!* This is a popular Zen saying. It is often shouted by a master to his students and means "Watch your step." The serpent is under your feet; keep your footing.

Case 23 Hofuku Points to Myōhōchō

ENGO'S INTRODUCTION Jade is tested by fire, gold by a stone, a sword by a hair, water by a staff. In Zen training the degree of one's attainment and one's progress is known by one's words and phrases, one's attitude and actions, one's coming and going, one's asking and responding. Tell me, how will it be done? See the following.

MAIN SUBJECT When Hofuku and Chōkei went out for a walk, Hofuku, pointing with his finger, said, "This is Myōhōchō" [*myō*, marvelous; *hō*, peak; *chō*, top]. Chōkei said, "What you say is well said, but alas!" [Setchō puts in his comment, saying, "Today, walking with this man, what is he plotting?" But again he says, "I don't say we do not find such men as this once in a hundred or a thousand years, but they are rare."] A monk related this to Kyōsei, who said, "But for Chōkei's remark, the field would have been littered with skulls."

SETCHŌ'S VERSE

This is Myōhōchō! Now weeds grow rampant.
You see it clearly, but to whom could you impart it?
If you, O Chōkei, didn't discriminate,
Many would never know, and their skulls would litter the field.

NOTES   *Hofuku, Chōkei, Kyōsei.* Hofuku (d. 928) also appears in Cases 8, 76, 91, and 95; Chōkei (854–932) in Cases 8, 22, 74, 76, 93, and 95; and Kyōsei (868–937) in Cases 16 and 46. They were all disciples of Seppō. Chōkei was the eldest, Hofuku the youngest—perhaps twenty or a little older at the time of this story.

• *A sword [is tested] by a hair.* To test the sharpness of a sword, one blew a hair against the blade to see if it would be cut. Such a sharp sword was called *suimōken* (*sui*, blow; *mō*, hair; *ken*, sword). This image appears again in Case 100.

• *Water [is tested] by a staff.* The depth of water is ascertained by a staff.

• *Coming and going.* One's daily life.

• *Hofuku, pointing with his finger, said, "This is Myōhōchō."* Myōhōchō is a mythological sacred mountain, mentioned in the *Avatamsaka Sutras*, which symbolizes ultimate reality. In these sutras it is related that an earnest seeker after truth named Zenzai, following Manjusri's instructions, ascended this mountain to see and study with a certain famous *bhikkhu*, or monk, named Tokuun. He searched for seven days and failed to find Tokuun, who was well known never to descend the mountain. But Tokuun met Zenzai on another peak. What does this mean? The peak of Myōhōchō represents absolute samadhi, in which no nen-thought stirs and there is neither seeing nor hearing. When coming from absolute samadhi into positive samadhi, one can for the first time truly meet others. The seven days during which Zenzai searched for Tokuun denote the seven senses of consciousness: seeing, hearing, feeling, tasting, smelling, knowing, and reflecting. When these are all transcended, absolute samadhi appears. When one returns to these seven senses, one's positive samadhi appears, which constitutes another peak.

In one's experience of realization, one finds Myōhōchō everywhere. One finds the Buddha-land even in a blade of grass. Hofuku must recently have had such an experience and have been full of exaltation. It was a great thing, and therefore Setchō says, "I don't say we do not find men such as this once in a hundred or a thousand years, but they are rare."

• *What you say is well said, but alas!* What you say is true, but alas! Your condition is still far from true maturity.

• *Today.* Today is all in all. Today is the present. Apart from this present time, there is no existence. Therefore you must fill it up all the more. But how is one to fill it up? By indulgence in momentary pleasures, as so many think? Definitely not.

• *This man.* "This man" is a term indicating a man of maturity. Here it alludes to Chōkei.

• *What is he plotting?* Setchō is criticizing Hofuku. This is an important point in this case, and one to which Setchō draws special attention. Hofuku may simply have been eager to express himself. But he should have outgrown this exaltation of his if he wanted to achieve maturity. He still had to eradicate the traces of his achievement by undertaking the so-called cultivation of Holy Buddhahood after enlightenment.

It might be suggested that Hofuku was perhaps testing his elder, Chōkei, and a Zen story may indeed admit of a number of interpretations. However, if this was the case his attempt was rebutted by Chōkei's words.

• *But for Chōkei's remark, the field would have been littered with skulls.* If people think Hofuku's words perfect and remain at that level of understanding, they will be led astray. They will become dead people, their skulls littering the ground as on an old battlefield.

• *This is Myōhōchō! Now weeds grow rampant.* It is true, as Hofuku says, that here is Myōhōchō. But the peak is now overgrown and spoiled by rampant weeds because of Hofuku's words.

• *You see it clearly, but to whom could you impart it?* Myōhōchō can be attained only by one's own efforts. It cannot be given to one by others. It cannot be taught or even talked about.

Case 24 Ryūtetsuma the Old Female Buffalo

ENGO'S INTRODUCTION Standing on the highest mountaintop, no devil or heretic can approach him. Descending to the farthest depths of the sea, he is not to be seen even by the Buddha's eyes. Even if your eye is like a shooting star and your spirit like lightning, you are still like the turtle, which cannot avoid dragging its tail. At such a juncture, what do you do? See the following.

MAIN SUBJECT Ryūtetsuma came to Isan. Isan said, "Old Female Buffalo, so you have come!" Tetsuma said, "Tomorrow there is a great festival at Taisan. Will you be going?" Isan lay down and stretched himself out. Tetsuma went away.

SETCHŌ'S VERSE
Riding an iron horse, the general entered the double-walled fortress;
The imperial proclamation: the six kingdoms are at peace.
Still gripping the golden whip, he urges the returning troops;
In the quiet depths of the night, no one goes with him through the king's streets.

NOTES *Standing on the highest mountaintop, no devil or heretic can approach him.* When an enlightened one is in positive samadhi, he truly experiences the state described as "silver mountains and iron cliffs." No devil or heretic can approach him. Positive samadhi is the exercise of pure cognition in ordinary active life.
• *Descending to the farthest depths of the sea, he is not to be seen even by the*

Buddha's eyes. In absolute samadhi, which develops in the most profound depths of his meditation, he goes deep down to the bottom of the fathomless sea; even the Buddha's eye cannot peep into his samadhi.

• *Even if your eye is like a shooting star and your spirit like lightning, you are still like the turtle, which cannot avoid dragging its tail.* These lines are concerned with the student's condition. Even if your understanding is as quick as a shooting star and your actions are like lightning, it will take many more years of training before you can totally eradicate the traces of your realization, attachment, and pride. You are like the turtle, who is clever enough to erase her footprints with the movements of her tail in order to conceal the whereabouts of the eggs she has laid in the sand, but still cannot help leaving the traces of the movements of her tail, which allow the eggs to be discovered.

• *Ryūtetsuma* had Ryū as her family name, Tetsuma as a nickname (*tetsu*, iron; *ma*, mill) referring to her tendency to crush her opponents in Dharma battle into pieces or grind them into powder. She is mentioned in Case 17, where Shiko took the initiative and hit her. Now she has appeared before Isan. What will his response be?

• *Isan*, who appeared in Case 4, was the student of Hyakujō. Case 40 of *Mumonkan* describes how Hyakujō recognized his worth. Once Isan said, "After a hundred years, I shall be born in a farmhouse in the village as a buffalo, with the words 'Isan-sō Reiyū' (*sō*, monk; Reiyū, Isan's personal name) marked on its side. At that time, what will you call it: Monk Isan or a buffalo?" Isan's ideal, as well as the Bodhisattva Kannon's, was embodied in the saying, "He goes among the different creatures to save them."

• *Ryūtetsuma came to Isan.* She may have come just to have a chat with Isan, but in the old days they were always ready for Dharma battle. Ryūtetsuma, especially, was a bomb that might explode at any time.

• *Old Female Buffalo.* Isan called himself a buffalo, and now he calls Ryūtetsuma a female buffalo. This was an intimate greeting with a touch of humor.

• *Tomorrow there is a great festival at Taisan.* Taisan was a sacred mountain dedicated to Manjusri. Many learned and virtuous priests lived there, and there were many Buddhist temples, making it a place of Buddhist pilgrimage. It is located in Shansi Province in North China, while Mount Isan is situated in Hunan Province. They are hundreds of miles apart, and the journey could not be made in a few days, let alone one day.

But Engo puts in his comment here: "If you beat the drum in China, they dance to the sound in Korea." And Gensha said, "Bodhidharma did not come from the West, the Second Patriarch did not go to India."

• *Will you be going?* The question is quite unreasonable. In Zen we often meet with paradoxical and unreasonable questions.

• *Isan lay down and stretched himself out.* Peace reigns over Isan's land.

• *Tetsuma went away.* She found it was impossible to start a disturbance in Isan's territory.

• *Riding an iron horse, the general entered the double-walled fortress.* Ryūtetsuma (the general) was fully prepared for Dharma battle (riding an iron horse) and came to Isan's fortress.

• *The imperial proclamation: the six kingdoms are at peace.* In Chinese history there was an age of civil wars, called the Warring States period (480–221 B.C.), when China was divided into six kingdoms which fought against each other. They were eventually amalgamated in the empire of Ch'in (221–207). Ryūtetsuma met with Isan's peaceful greeting, "Old Female Buffalo, so you have come!" There was no chance for her to take advantage of Isan and open an attack. The six kingdoms may also be interpreted as referring to the activities of consciousness: seeing, hearing, feeling, tasting, smelling, and knowing.

• *Still gripping the golden whip, he urges the returning troops.* Tetsuma asked, "Will you be going?" The festival was an informal, light-hearted entertainment. But Isan was not to be found there. He lay down, sprawled out. There was nothing for Tetsuma to do but go away.

• *In the quiet depths of the night, no one goes with him through the king's streets.* All was quiet and peaceful. There was no holy one in the emerald palace (see Case 18). Isan left no trace of his tail.

Case 25   The Master of Rengehō's Staff

ENGO'S INTRODUCTION   If the action of one's ki is not independent of one's degree of enlightenment, one falls into a sea of poison. If one's words do not astonish the crowd, one slips into the conventional. If you can distinguish black from white in the moment of a spark's being struck and can tell life from death in the instant of a flash of lightning, then you will be able to command all quarters and stand firm like a thousand-fathom cliff. Who could ever be so? See the following.

MAIN SUBJECT   The master of Rengehō cottage held out his staff and said to his disciples, "When, in olden times, a man reached the state of enlightenment, why did he not remain there?" No one could answer, and he replied for them, "Because it is of no use in the course of life." And again he asked, "After all, what will you do with it?" And once again he said in their stead,

> "Taking no notice of others,
> Throwing his staff over his shoulder,
> He goes straight ahead and journeys
> Deep into the recesses of the hundred thousand mountains."

SETCHŌ'S VERSE
> His eyes filled with sand, his ears with clay,
> Even among the thousand mountains he does not remain.
> Falling blossoms, flowing streams: he leaves no trace.
> Open your eyes wide, and you'll wonder where he's gone.

NOTES   *The master of Rengehō.* Little is known of him except that in Dharma lineage he was Ummon's grandson and was called by the name Shō. Rengehō (*ren*, lotus; *ge*, flower; *hō*, peak) is said to have been located at Taisan, in Shansi Province, where he built his cottage. He did not become the master of a fine large temple, but he had some disciples, as is shown by the present case.

• *Ki.* Direct, free-flowing activity of the Zen mind is called Zen-ki, or simply ki. I said in the notes to Case 3 that "in mental activity . . . a certain strain or tension arises before an action is performed. This mental strain is called ki." But putting it simply, it is the action of the first nen (see the notes to Case 6).

• *Degree of enlightenment.* The original text simply says "rank"; this means one's level or degree of enlightenment. In one's Zen training certain grades of achievement naturally appear: a beginner's understanding, deeper experience, kenshō (realization), and the cultivation of Holy Buddhahood. But if you are fascinated by the experience of kenshō and, thinking it ultimate, settle down there, self-satisfaction will set in and you will inevitably find yourself "fallen into a sea of poison." The eradication of the slightest trace of enlightenment is of the utmost importance. It is this that constitutes the main theme of the present case.

• *If one's words do not astonish the crowd.* Zen-ki is demonstrated in word and action. It is expected to be always fresh and original, springing from one's own individuality. If not, it will not astonish other people. We might compare this with the originality displayed by creative thinkers, such as Galileo, Descartes, and Freud.

• *You will be able to command all quarters.* Zen-ki works like a sharp sword and immediately cuts away all complications. The literal translation of the original text here is "cut down ten directions."

• *Stand firm like a thousand-fathom cliff.* This denotes the unshakable, deep-rooted condition of the Zen mind.

• *The master of Rengehō cottage held out his staff.* Zen mind is symbolized by the staff, with which the master demonstrates Zen spirit.

• *When, in olden times, a man reached the state of enlightenment, why did he not remain there?* A truly enlightened man never stays in the same place. He always pushes on, leaving behind no trace of his footprints. Remaining in the same old condition inevitably leads to retrogression and deterioration.

• *It is of no use in the course of life.* Even if you become experienced in entering absolute samadhi, when you come out into the world of the activity of consciousness you will find yourself helpless unless you have attained positive samadhi, which is the condition in which the cultivation of Holy Buddhahood is carried on. Zen has two aspects: one is the world of pure wisdom, represented by Manjusri; the other is the world of action, represented by Samantabhadra and Avalokitesvara (Kannon). This explains why Manjusri and Samantabhadra are always represented standing one on each side of Shakyamuni Buddha. To put it another way, when you attain enlightenment, you must come out into the world of ordinary activity and life and help others. In fact, you must do this not only for the sake of others but for your own benefit as well. Man is made, on the one hand, to live by himself, for himself, and in himself; and on the other, to live with other people and work for them. To work for others is really to work for yourself, because it develops the fullness of your mind. Without this fullness, or richness, of mind you find yourself helpless in the actual world of the activity of consciousness. This is the point the master of Rengehō is stressing when he says, "It is of no use in the course of life." True enlightenment must include both the experience of realization and the free and unobstructed activity of mind in daily life.

Clara Barton, who was the founder of the American Red Cross, was a vigorous woman who by nature belonged to Samantabhadra's world of action. When eleven years old she voluntarily took charge of her ailing cousin, vowing to herself that she would not leave the sickroom until her cousin recovered. She said to herself, "While he is sick in bed, I shall never be happy." And she carried out her vow to the end. When fifteen, she was already a teacher of little children and behaved like a mature woman, sacrificing youthful pleasures. In the Civil War, on her own initiative, she acted as a nurse, taking up the work spontaneously before anyone else had thought of performing such a task. She could not help launching into the job at the sight of the wretched condition of the wounded soldiers. With her, working for others was an indispensable condition of her happiness. In conspicuous contrast to Clara Barton, some people think only of themselves. They are acutely sensitive to their own troubles and generally self-centered. They complain of their miserable condition and the wretchedness of life. They think of escaping from the society they find themselves in, from their homes, from their spouses, and eventually from themselves. Often they are driven into mental disturbances. Character is to some extent inborn. But it can be reformed by Zen training.

You must not stop at the top of the hundred-foot pole but must proceed on further from it. How is one to do this? You have to come down and mingle with people and help them. But how is one to come down? Let go your hands that are clutching the pole (the ego) and step forward into space (emptiness). In the physical world this would mean certain death. It does in the mental world, too. But this death of the self-centered ego is absolutely necessary. When you kill your petty ego, you will find a more developed one in its place. The ego has more than nine lives.

• *Taking no notice of others.* Paying no attention to the whisperings of delusive thought, either of his own mind or of other people, he advances eagerly and single-mindedly.

• *Throwing his staff over his shoulder.* This symbolizes his free, unconstrained condition.

• *He goes straight ahead and journeys | Deep into the recesses of the hundred thousand mountains.* This does not mean he escapes from the world but rather that in the most vigorous activity of consciousness he is quite innocent and displays no trace of egocentric thinking. In his daily life his ego is empty.

• *His eyes filled with sand, his ears with clay.* Literally this means that he does not see because his eyes are filled with sand, and he does not hear because his ears are filled with clay. The true meaning is that he sees but leaves no trace of the seeing, and hears but leaves no trace of the hearing.

• *Even among the thousand mountains he does not remain.* He remains nowhere.

• *You'll wonder where he's gone.* You cannot find him because he leaves no trace.

Case 26   Hyakujō Sits on the Great Sublime Peak

MAIN SUBJECT   A monk asked Hyakujō, "What is the most wonderful thing?" Jō said, "I sit alone on this Great Sublime Peak." The monk made a bow. Jō struck him.

SETCHŌ'S VERSE
Across the patriarch's field went galloping
The heavenly horse, Baso's successor,
Different, however, in way of teaching,
In holding fast and letting go.

His actions were quick as lightning,
Always fitting.
The monk came to tweak the tiger's whiskers,
But his efforts made him a laughingstock.

NOTES   *Hyakujō* first appears in *Mumonkan*, Case 2.

• *What is the most wonderful thing?* Monks often invented quite unexpected questions to take the master by surprise and received marvelous answers.

• *I sit alone on this Great Sublime Peak.* The original text says *dokuza dai yūhō* (*doku*, alone; *za*, sit; *dai*, great; *yū*, sublime; *hō*, peak): I sit alone on the Great Sublime Peak. There was in fact a rocky peak one hundred fathoms high on Mount Hyakujō (the name itself means one hundred fathoms: *hyaku*, one hundred; *jō*, fathom). This peak was called the Great Sublime Peak. Now, this Great Sublime Peak was Hyakujō himself. But Hyakujō was not bragging. He was simply the Great Sublime Peak, which is Myōhōchō (Case 23), the ultimate truth of the universe.

• *The monk made a bow.* The monk made a gesture of astonishment at the appearance before him of so wonderful a thing as the Great Sublime Peak. He made his bows with an exaggerated degree of ceremony. Of course, he was expressing his admiration of Hyakujō and his answer. At the same time, there was an element of bantering in his action. This was a normal part of a Dharma battle.

• *Jō struck him.* This was a Dharma battle, and the blow was the finishing touch.

• *Across the patriarch's field went galloping / The heavenly horse, Baso's successor.* The patriarch's field is the realm of Zen. A fine horse, capable of a thousand miles a day, often appears in Chinese literature. Here the horse means Hyakujō, Baso's successor. Both these masters cut conspicuous figures in the realm of Zen, like fine horses galloping freely across a field. The comparison is especially apt in Baso's case, as his name contains the ideograph for horse (*ba*, horse; *so*, patriarch).

• *Different, however, in way of teaching, / In holding fast and letting go.* Every Zen master has his own individual method of teaching. This comment is not necessarily limited to Baso and Hyakujō. "Holding fast" and "letting go" are explained in the notes to Case 4.

• *His actions were quick as lightning.* Hyakujō had the quickness of speech and action characteristic of a great master.

• *Always fitting.* A Zen teacher sometimes adapts himself to the level of his disciples, while at other times he is unyielding and unaccommodating. That is to say, he sometimes lets go, sometimes holds fast, always doing what is best suited to the situation. He changes from one approach to the other intuitively and rapidly. Hyakujō's answer in the present case was well suited to the questioner.

• *The monk came to tweak the tiger's whiskers, | But his efforts made him a laughingstock.* The monk came intending to test Hyakujō and, if possible, to take him by surprise. But it was like pulling a tiger's whiskers, and the upshot was to make him a laughingstock among Zen people. But the laughter is kindly and appreciative.

Case 27 Ummon's "Golden Breeze"

ENGO'S INTRODUCTION One question, and he answers ten; one corner, and the other three are made clear. Seeing the hare, he lets go the hawk; using the wind, he makes fire. Now, not sparing the eyebrows may be put aside for a while—how about your entering the tiger's cave? See the following.

MAIN SUBJECT A monk asked Ummon, "What will it be when trees wither and leaves fall?" Ummon said, "You embody the golden breeze."

SETCHŌ'S VERSE
Significant the question,
Pregnant the answer, too!

The three phrases are satisfied,
The arrow penetrates the universe.

The wind blows across the plain,
Soft rain clouds the sky.

Don't you see the master of Shōrin Temple,
Not yet returning, wall-gazing,
Meditating quietly now on Yūji Peak?

NOTES *One question, and he answers ten.* If a student asks about one thing, the master's answer will make him understand ten.

• *One corner, and the other three are made clear.* See the notes to Case 1.

• *Seeing the hare, he lets go the hawk; using the wind, he makes fire.* This refers to the teacher's ability to adapt himself to any situation. He trims his sail according to the wind.

• *Now, not sparing the eyebrows may be put aside for a while—how about your entering the tiger's cave?* As we have already learned in Case 8, there is a popular Zen saying that talking too much makes one's eyebrows fall off. (However, the teacher does not spare his eyebrows.) But it is also said, "Unless you enter the tiger's cave, you cannot get the cub." Zen training is like entering the tiger's cave. This is so not only with the student but also with the teacher, who often enters the tiger's cave for the sake of his students.

• *What will it be when trees wither and leaves fall?* You encounter such a scene when you walk through the park and, greatly impressed, think you have already understood this question. But as you advance in Zen training, you will come to realize that there are many levels of understanding such a question. In truth, it is not a matter of understanding but of experiencing, and the experience is deepened according to how far your training has advanced.

• *You embody the golden breeze.* The golden breeze is the autumnal breeze. When you embody it you know the meaning of "trees wither and leaves fall." This saying of Ummon's may sound commonplace, but to one who has an intuitive understanding of it, it is ever fresh and original. This embodying of the golden breeze constitutes the principal theme of Setchō's verse.

• *Significant the question, | Pregnant the answer, too!* Answering ten questions when asked one, letting go the hawk when he sees the hare, he does not spare his eyebrows but goes into the tiger's cave. What is the tiger's cave?

• *The three phrases are satisfied.* Ummon's three phrases are (1) heaven and earth meeting squarely (question and answer fit intimately), (2) following the coming and going of the waves (the teacher adapts himself to the condition of the student), and (3) cutting off the stream of thought (all complications are cut off once and for all). These constitute the essential features of the teacher's method. "Satisfied" means that

Ummon's answer fulfills the requirements embodied in his three phrases.

• *The arrow penetrates the universe.* The arrow is Ummon's answer, which goes directly to the heart of the matter. Ummon is ushering the questioner into the tiger's cave.

• *The wind blows across the plain.* Simply listen to the sound of the wind. Simply watch the misty rain. Place yourself in those scenes in your positive samadhi.

• *The master of Shōrin Temple.* Bodhidharma, after meeting Emperor Wu (see Case 1), retired to Shōrin Temple and there sat for nine years in silent meditation.

• *Not yet returning.* When Bodhidharma died, he was buried on Yūji Peak. He did not return to India. However, a legend relates that an official who was sent to India saw, on his way, Bodhidharma traveling alone, carrying one of his sandals in his hand.

• *Wall-gazing.* Bodhidharma sat in meditation facing the sheer wall of the cliff that rose in front of his hermitage. It is from this that the term "wall-gazing" derives.

• *Meditating quietly now on Yūji Peak.* Setchō is seeing in his mind's eye Bodhidharma quietly sitting in meditation on Yūji Peak. In his verse to Case 47, Setchō says, "Lo! Since last night he has been here facing Nyūhō!" Nyūhō is another name for Mount Setchō.

Case 28 What the Holy Ones Have Not Preached

MAIN SUBJECT Nansen came to see Hyakujō Nehan Oshō. Jō said, "Is there any Dharma that the holy ones have not preached to the people?" Nansen said, "There is." Jō said, "What is the Dharma that has not been preached to the people?" Nansen said, "It is not mind, it is not Buddha, it is not things." Jō said, "You have preached." Nansen said, "I am like this. How about you?" Jō said, "I am not a man of great wisdom. How can I tell if there is preaching or no preaching?" Nansen said, "I don't follow you." Jō said, "I have talked quite enough for you."

SETCHŌ'S VERSE

Patriarchs and Buddhas have not preached,
Yet monks run after preachers.

Clear mirror on the stand, sharply imaging.
Looking southward, see the Great Bear.

The shaft hangs down. Where do you find it?
Saving your nostrils, you have lost your mouth.

NOTES   *Nansen came to see Hyakujō Nehan Oshō.* Hyakujō Nehan Oshō, Hyakujō Ekai (the great Hyakujō), and Nansen were all disciples of Baso. Hyakujō Nehan succeeded Hyakujō Ekai as master of Hyakujō Mountain. Nehan is his surname; Oshō is a term of respect applied to a priest.

• *Is there any Dharma that the holy ones have not preached to the people?* "Dharma" here means truth, law, or teaching. This case is also found in *Mumonkan* (Case 27). When the Buddha was dying he said, "In forty-nine years I have preached not a word." Ōbaku said to his monks, "Do you know that in all the land of T'ang there is no Zen teacher?" (Case 11). There is a saying that Zen truth cannot and should not be preached. One must learn Zen for oneself and master it by oneself. But if this is so, why do so many people go on talking about Zen? This is an old question, and the answer is obvious. In the most fundamental sense, from the viewpoint of the first principle of Zen, talking about Zen *is* nonsense. But to initiate the novice, it is absolutely necessary to talk about it. We have already encountered this problem in Case 13. In the present case Nehan Oshō was talking in terms of the first principle. How could Nansen answer him?

• *Nansen said, "There is."* This is a Dharma battle, in which both participants are attempting to bring out what it is impossible to bring out. Both Nansen and Nehan knew from the outset that they were tackling an impossible problem. Nevertheless, the Dharma that has not been preached by anyone must exist. What is it? The question must be asked.

• *It is not mind, it is not Buddha, it is not things.* This saying derives from some words of Baso, who once said, "This very mind is the Buddha" (*Mumonkan*, Case 30). On another occasion he said, "No mind, no Buddha." Then a monk asked him, "What do you say when a man comes who has finished these two?" Baso said, "I would say to him, 'No things.'" "How about when a man comes who has finished all these?" "I would make him understand the Great Way." (See *Mumonkan*, Case 33.)

• *You have preached.* Your words are not a direct expression of Zen truth—that is, they do not spring from the first principle—but belong to a secondary level: you are talking *about* Zen, in other words, preaching.

• *I am like this. How about you?* When you speak from the first principle, you speak from the first principle. It does not matter whether the listener sees this or interprets your words as belonging to a secondary level. Nansen, therefore, could say nonchalantly, "I am like this." Then he assumed the offensive and said, "How about you?"

• *I am not a man of great wisdom. How can I tell if there is preaching or no preaching?* This was the answer of a man of maturity.

• *I don't follow you.* Nansen (748–834) was one of the greatest Zen masters. (See *Mumonkan*, Cases 14, 19, 27, and 34; and *Hekiganroku*, Cases 31, 40, 63, 64, and 69.) But at the time of the present case he was perhaps still rather young and inclined to be aggressive. Possibly he wanted to make the Dharma battle an animated one. If his first answer had been different, the whole conversation might have taken another course. Tōzan Ryōkai, the founder of the Sōtō sect, once said on a similar occasion, "Take my head and carry it away with you, if you want." And on another occasion, "Coming to this point, my heart is breaking." Nehan's words were "I am not a man of great wisdom." Another teacher said, "Good morning." They were quiet and showed maturity. But variety is also important, and Nansen's youthful bravery is greatly to be admired. A Dharma battle is not something to be won or lost but a matter of finding a way to express the inexpressible.

• *Patriarchs and Buddhas have not preached.* As usual, Setchō summarizes the essence of the case in his first line.

• *Clear mirror on the stand, sharply imaging.* You have in yourself a mirror which reflects objects clearly. Why don't you look into your own mind? But how is this to be done?

• *Looking southward, see the Great Bear.* You have to overturn the delusive way of looking at things. If I say, "Look southward and get a true view of the Plow," it may sound nonsensical. But sometime you have to change your whole way of looking at things.

• *The shaft hangs down.* The shaft of the Plow is reaching into this room of yours. It flowers as the chair, the table, the tablecloth, and everything else. It is said, "Preaching, preaching, all creatures are preaching!" Why don't you hear them and achieve genuine cognition of them?

• *Saving your nostrils, you have lost your mouth.* Preserving your reasoning, conceptual understanding of things, you have lost your intuitive cognition of them.

Case 29   Daizui's "It Will Be Gone with the Other"

ENGO'S INTRODUCTION   Fish swimming, the water is disturbed; a bird flying, a feather falls. Host and guest are clearly distinguished; black and white are sharply divided. It is like a clear mirror on the stand and a bright jewel in the hand. When a man of Han appears, he is reflected; if a man of Ho comes, he is mirrored. Sound is manifest, color is apparent. How will it be like that? See the following.

MAIN SUBJECT   A monk asked Daizui, "When the kalpa fire flares up and the great cosmos is destroyed, I wonder, will 'it' perish, or will it not perish?" Zui said, "It will perish." The monk said, "Then will it be gone with the other?" Zui said, "It will be gone with the other."

SETCHŌ'S VERSE
  Blocked by the double barrier,
  The monk asked from the heart of the kalpa fire.
  Wonderful the words, "It will be gone with the other."
  Thousands of miles he wandered in vain, seeking a master.

NOTES   *Daizui* (878–963) was a disciple of Taian, who was in turn a disciple of Hyakujō Ekai. When young, Daizui studied with Tōzan, Isan, and others. After attaining enlightenment he retired to Mount Daizui in Szechwan Province and for over ten years did not descend the mountain. He lived in a hollow in the trunk of a large tree. Later, monks came to study with him.

• *Fish swimming, the water is disturbed.* As the swimming fish can be detected by the disturbance of the water, so the teacher can gauge the condition of the student by his attitude.

• *A bird flying, a feather falls.* A flying bird leaves no trace in the air, but a falling feather betrays its passage.

• *Host and guest are clearly distinguished.* In a Dharma meeting, host is host, guest is guest; they are clearly distinguished from each other. In the tea ceremony, too, the host gives hospitality to the guest and the guest receives it.

• *Black and white are sharply divided.* In an interview with the teacher, good and bad in the student are immediately separated by the teacher.

• *It is like a clear mirror on the stand.* This clause corresponds to the next sentence: "When a man of Han appears, he is reflected; if a man of Ho comes, he is mirrored."

• *A bright jewel in the hand.* This phrase corresponds to "Sound is manifest, color is apparent." Jade is judged by its sound and color.

• *How will it be like that?* The following story will tell you the secret.

• *The kalpa fire.* A kalpa is the period of time between the creation and re-creation of a universe. It is divided into four periods: formation, existence, destruction, and annihilation (void). The kalpa fire is the conflagration that destroys the universe.

• *"It."* The ultimate thing. In a narrow sense this means our being. More generally, it means the being or existence of the universe, or absolute reality.

• *Will "it" perish, or will it not perish?* The monk was greatly concerned about the immortality of his soul, or self. He was hoping that Daizui would say that it would not perish, and set his mind at rest. This anxiety is not, of course, restricted to the monk but must be the greatest problem for everyone.

• *It will perish.* This is an example of Ummon's "cutting off the stream of thought" (see the notes to Case 27).

• *Then will it be gone with the other?* "The other" means the great cosmos. The monk was dismayed by Daizui's answer. But like a drowning man clutching at a straw, he repeated his question in another form.

• *It will be gone with the other.* This was the finishing blow.

• *Blocked by the double barrier.* To say that it will perish is all right; to say it will not perish is all right. If you are blocked, this will constitute the double barrier. What really exists is this present moment. Moment after moment, the four phases of the kalpa are repeated.

• *The monk asked from the heart of the kalpa fire.* He cried for help from the heart of the flames.

• *Wonderful the words, "It will be gone with the other."* These words of Daizui's are much admired. What a penetrating statement!

• *Thousands of miles he wandered in vain, seeking a master.* The monk did not understand Daizui and was greatly discouraged. He traveled all the way to visit another famous Zen teacher, Tōsu, who lived at Anking in Anhwei Province, which is located along the lower Yangtze River, while Mount Daizui is situated on the upper reaches of the river. Tōsu, having heard the monk's story, offered incense toward distant Mount Daizui, paid profound homage to Daizui, and said, "Another holy one has appeared in Szechwan. Daizui is a great master. Go back to him quickly, confess your error, and follow him." The monk returned to Daizui, only to find that he had already died. He journeyed back to Tōsu but found that he too had died.

This story is almost certainly not wholly true. Tōsu died long before Daizui. But the important point about the story is that it urges you to be diligent and alert, and to take care not to miss what may be your sole opportunity.

Case 30   Jōshū's "A Big Radish"

MAIN SUBJECT   A monk asked Jōshū, "I have heard that you closely followed Nansen. Is that true?" Jōshū said, "Chinshū produces a big radish."

SETCHŌ'S VERSE
Chinshū produces a big radish;
Monks have taken it as their model.
They know only how it was and would be.
How can they truly realize
The swan is white, the crow black?
Plunderer! Plunderer!
The monk had his nostrils threaded through.

NOTES *I have heard that you closely followed Nansen. Is that true?* Nansen settled on Mount Nansen as a Zen master in 795, when Jōshū was seventeen years old. At that age Jōshū had his first experience of kenshō. Jōshū followed Nansen until Nansen's death in 834. Perhaps he observed three years' mourning for Nansen according to the Chinese custom of the time, and then in his sixtieth year set out on a journey, visiting Zen teachers in various places. At eighty he settled down in the town of Jōshū as a Zen master and lived there until his death at the age of one hundred nineteen. That Jōshū had finished his Zen training under Nansen and succeeded him was well known among Zen students of those days. But this monk asked, "Is that true?" This was a Dharma battle. He was asking not about historical fact but what Jōshū had got from Nansen—in other words, what Jōshū had attained. This was an unpleasant question. The monk had come to Jōshū with an ax to grind. A clumsy answer might well have led to some kind of trouble. Engo puts in his comment here, saying, "A thrust."

• *Chinshū produces a big radish.* Chinshū was a district near the town of Jōshū famous for producing fine big radishes. What did Jōshū mean by his answer? Had he been an Englishman, he might have said, "England has produced Shakespeare"; if an American, "America has produced Lincoln." In plain words, Jōshū was saying, "Like father, like son." But he gave the monk nothing to take advantage of.

• *Chinshū produces a big radish [Setchō's verse].* Engo's comment here is "It supports the heavens and sustains the earth." Jōshū's radish seems to be that big and strong.

• *Monks have taken it as their model.* Monks have followed the pattern of Jōshū's example in their answers.

• *They know only how it was and would be.* They have kept in mind only the old example and presumed that it would be all right in the future, too.

• *How can they truly realize?* They do not realize that their answers must be truly their own.

• *The swan is white, the crow black.* Children truly cognize the whiteness of the swan swimming on the blue waters of the lake, or the bee flying through the clear morning air. Theirs is the intuitive, direct cognition of the object, while most adults look at things only through the medium of their conceptual understanding. If we genuinely recognize the whiteness of the swan and the blackness of the crow, our study of Zen is fairly under way.

• *Plunderer!* Jōshū was a plunderer.

• *The monk had his nostrils threaded through.* As a man threads the rope of a halter through the nostrils of a bull and is able to control it, so Jōshū took the nose of the monk and handled him skillfully. The image of threading the nostrils is often used in this way in Zen literature.

Case 31   Mayoku Comes to Shōkei

ENGO'S INTRODUCTION   With subconscious stirring, images appear; with awareness, ice forms. Even if there is no stirring and no awareness, you have not yet escaped from the confinement of the fox's hole. If you truly penetrate in your practice and become master of it, you will experience not a trace of obstruction. You will be like a dragon supported by deep waters, like a tiger that commands its mountain retreat. Then, if you let go, even tiles and pebbles become illuminating; if you hold fast, even pure gold loses its luster. And the koans of the old masters will become tedious. Tell me, what am I talking about? See the following.

MAIN SUBJECT   Mayoku came to Shōkei carrying his bell staff with him, walked around Shōkei's seat three times, shook his staff, ringing the bells, stuck it in the ground, and stood up straight. Kei said, "Good." [Setchō says, "A mistake."] Mayoku then came to Nansen, walked around Nansen's seat, shook his staff, ringing the bells, stuck it in the ground, and stood up straight. Nansen said, "Wrong." [Setchō says, "A mistake."] Mayoku said, "Shōkei said, 'Good'; why do you say, 'Wrong'?" Nansen said, "Shōkei is 'good,' but you are wrong. You are blown about by the wind. That will lead to destruction."

SETCHŌ'S VERSE
This mistake, that mistake,
Never take them away!
In the four seas, the waves subside;
A hundred rivers flow quietly to the sea.

The twelve bells of the staff tinkled up high;
Empty and silent is the road to the gate.
No, not empty and silent;
The enlightened man must take medicine
For the illness of "having no illness."

NOTES   *Mayoku, Shōkei, Nansen.* They were all disciples of Baso. Nansen (748–834) was the eldest; Shōkei (755–815) was a little younger. Mayoku's dates are uncertain, but he is believed to have been the youngest.

• *With subconscious stirring, images appear.* If, in your meditation, the slightest nen-action occurs, various images appear in your mind. The ancient Buddhists had no term equivalent to the modern "subconscious," but they were aware of such an activity of the mind. The literal translation of the original text would be "If stirring, images appear," that is, "If the mind stirs subconsciously, images appear."

• *With awareness, ice forms.* When, in your meditation, you become aware of a nen-action within you, your mind stiffens. The inner conflict brings about a sort of frozen blockage, and it is to this that the phrase "ice forms" refers.

• *Even if there is no stirring and no awareness.* No stirring, no awareness, indicates a blurred condition of mind that is close to sleep. It implies the loss of your jishu-zammai, or self-mastery.

• *You have not yet escaped from the confinement of the fox's hole.* Zazen can be a sham, a matter of superficial pretense. This is called "fox's Zen." One is lying content, so to speak, in a fox's den, and is reluctant to leave it. It can sometimes be very difficult to persuade a person in this condition to emerge from it.

• *If you truly penetrate your practice and become master of it.* If you become truly experienced in the practice of genuine samadhi.

• *You will experience not a trace of obstruction.* In your ordinary daily life there will be no hindrance to the free activity of your mind.

• *Like a dragon supported by deep waters, like a tiger that commands its mountain retreat.* See the notes to Case 8.

• *If you let go.* See the notes to Case 4. When you work at some constructive activity, even tiles and pebbles come alive.

• *If you hold fast.* See the notes to Case 4. When you enter the "sweeping away" phase of Zen activity, there is no place even for the Buddha.

• *The koans of the old masters will become tedious.* Compared to your own quick, keen Zen activity, the words and actions of the old Zen masters will seem sluggish.

• *What am I talking about?* Whose story will it be? The following provides a good example.

• *Mayoku came to Shōkei carrying his bell staff with him.* As we have noted, Mayoku was probably much younger than Shōkei, and this incident seems to have occurred soon after Mayoku had his first experience of kenshō, which makes one feel exalted. One feels like a dragon ascending to heaven. Tokusan, in Case 4, provides another example of this. Mayoku, full of self-confidence, came to Shōkei to demonstrate his attainment. He adopted a proud attitude quite naturally, as is seen in what follows.

• *Walked around Shōkei's seat . . . and stood up straight.* The customary salutation was to walk three times around the host's seat, stand in front of him, then retire to a corner to await his direction. But Mayoku, a tiger on its mountain, haughtily stuck his staff in the ground and stood up straight before Shōkei, awaiting his word.

• *Kei said, "Good."* Shōkei knew all about this. Everyone is the same when he has his first experience of kenshō. So "Good" issued forth from his mouth. Shōkei was letting go.

• *Setchō says, "A mistake."* Mayoku was right, and at the same time wrong. He had still to go much further. But Zen is not a matter of designating things "good" or "bad." However, Shōkei for the moment committed that fault for Mayoku's sake.

- *Mayoku then came to Nansen.* He was puffed up with success.
- *Nansen said, "Wrong."* This was a decisive blow, unexpected by Mayoku. Nansen was holding fast.
- *Setchō says, "A mistake."* This is negation of negation. Neither holding fast nor letting go can avoid being one-sided. Everything has its advantages and disadvantages.
- *Mayoku said, "Shōkei said, 'Good'; why do you say, 'Wrong'?"* Of what use is it to be now glad, now cast down, at others' words?
- *Nansen said, "Shōkei is 'good,' but you are wrong. You are blown about by the wind. That will lead to destruction."* Shōkei said, "Good," but your useless demonstration is wrong. You are like dust before the wind. Nansen was sweeping everything away. As the Zen saying goes, "When you kill, kill exhaustively."
- *This mistake, that mistake, / Never take them away!* Mayoku, Shōkei, and Nansen were all right, and at the same time they were mistaken. Setchō is saying, never forget this "mistake."
- *In the four seas, the waves subside; / A hundred rivers flow quietly to the sea.* If you can really master this mistake, you will attain a peaceful condition of mind.
- *The twelve bells of the staff tinkled up high.* The staff has twelve bells at the top. They are said to symbolize the gate to enlightenment and also the twelve stages of causation, which are ignorance, action, consciousness, form, sense, touch, pleasure, love, attachment, existence, life, and death.
- *Empty and silent is the road to the gate.* The road to the gate of enlightenment is empty and silent. This symbolizes the emptiness and silence of absolute samadhi. However, that is only one side of Zen.
- *No, not empty and silent.* The positive side of Zen, the world of vigorous activity, is equally important.
- *The enlightened man must take medicine / For the illness of "having no illness."* The cure of the malady of "having no illness" is the central theme of the present case. It is often supposed that when you achieve enlightenment there is no further illness of mind. However, in Zen the belief that one is free from illness is itself held to be an illness. The cure is cultivation of Holy Buddhahood after enlightenment.

Case 32   Jō Jōza Stands Still

ENGO'S INTRODUCTION   Once the delusive way of thinking is cut off, a thousand eyes are suddenly opened. One word blocking the stream of thought, and all nen-actions are controlled. Is there anyone who would undergo the experience of dying the same death and living the same life as the Buddha? Truth is manifest everywhere. If you do not see it, here is an ancient example. See the following.

MAIN SUBJECT   Jō Jōza asked Rinzai, "What is the essence of Buddhism?" Rinzai, getting up from his seat, seized him, slapped him, and pushed him away. Jō Jōza stood still. A monk standing by said, "Jō Jōza, why don't you bow?" When Jō Jōza bowed, he suddenly became enlightened.

SETCHŌ'S VERSE
    Inheriting the spirit of Dansai,
    How could he be gentle and quiet?
    Not difficult for Kyorei
    To lift his hands and split Mount Kasan,
    Letting the Yellow River through.

NOTES   *Jō Jōza.* Jō was his personal name; Jōza (*jō*, upper; *za*, seat) was a term of respect applied to a senior monk. The dates of his birth and death are not recorded. According to the few anecdotes related of him he was a strong and somewhat violent man but also a man of great determination, willing to go through every hardship for the sake of Zen.
• *Once the delusive way of thinking is cut off, a thousand eyes are suddenly opened.* A Zen master's words and actions, and his way of dealing with his disciples, can cut through all the complications and entanglements under which his students groan. And then their eyes are suddenly opened.
• *One word blocking the stream of thought, and all nen-actions are controlled.* A single word from a Zen master may be sufficient to change the direc-

tion of the listener's thinking, and all the delusive activity of consciousness is uprooted.

• *Is there anyone who would undergo the experience of dying the same death and living the same life as the Buddha?* In studying Zen one goes through life and death with one's teacher, and the teacher does the same with his disciples. Such extravagant actions as striking, pushing, knocking down, and pinching are part of the mental grappling that goes on in a Dharma battle (though generally, because the student is so much weaker than the master, such exchanges are one-sided).

• *Truth is manifest everywhere.* Truth is there for you to see, in front of your nose. You can be aware of it, however, only if you can exercise genuine cognition. Usually the delusive activity of consciousness masks and distorts your cognition.

• *What is the essence of Buddhism?* Every time this question is raised it seems fresh and new. That is why it is so often asked, and why there are so many answers to it.

• *Rinzai, getting up from his seat, seized him, slapped him, and pushed him away.* This can happen only when a close relationship exists between teacher and disciple. Although the disciple is not aware of his own condition, the teacher perceives it as clearly as if he were looking at an aerial photograph and could point out on it the precise mountain that the student is struggling up. He can do this because he has himself been through that experience.

• *Jō Jōza stood still.* His condition at this moment is aptly described by the Zen saying, "The bottom of his pail had fallen out." Imagine you were carrying water in a pail and its bottom suddenly fell out. This is a subtle moment. If chance favors you, openness and emptiness will suddenly appear within you. That is to say, if the state of your mind happens to chime with the situation, all the complications that beset you will suddenly be gone, and you will truly understand the emptiness of which you have heard so much but hitherto could not grasp.

• *A monk standing by said, "Jō Jōza, why don't you bow?"* A chance event or remark, such as that unwittingly provided by the monk in this episode, may count for much in the kenshō experience, just as it does when one has a sudden idea while trying to solve an intellectual problem.

• *When Jō Jōza bowed, he suddenly became enlightened.* Kenshō means seeing into one's own true nature. When this occurs, there is first an intuitive looking into the object (the action of the first nen), and then comes reflection on it by the second and third nen, as we have discussed elsewhere (see the notes to Case 6 and *Zen Training*, chapter 10). The moment Jō Jōza became aware of the necessity of bowing, he was reminded of himself, and this reflection upon himself brought about his kenshō experience. To put it another way: the first nen's intuitive action of looking into the object is an action of pure ego. Reflecting upon this pure ego is seeing into one's own true nature, and the kenshō experience is brought about. However, we are every moment reflecting upon ourselves (and thus are conscious of ourselves), but the kenshō experience does not normally occur. Why is this?

The reason is that the third nen, which carries out the reflecting, integrating, and synthesizing operations of the mind, and has come to assume the position of representing man's self-consciousness itself, is permeated through and through with a utilitarian way of thinking. Our consciousness, in its ordinary daily life, is wholly occupied by thoughts of what is beneficial, helpful, and useful to us or what is harmful. Consciousness typically operates in an individualistic, egocentric fashion. This necessarily causes our cognition of the world to be distorted. We call this state of affairs the deluded, habitual way of consciousness. It is this which blocks the intuitive, pure cognition of the first nen.

For example, although life and death is the rule of the universe, we hate death and cling to life. However, in a moment of emergency, such as that experienced by Jō Jōza in the present case, the deluded way of thinking may drop away and the pure cognition of the first nen be set free. In that moment the third nen itself is also purified from its delusive way of thinking. Thus, kenshō is not only the recognition of the intuitive action of the first nen (pure ego) but also the recognition of the purified condition of the third nen (this is also pure ego). All three nen-actions, in fact, have now regained the activity of pure ego, which we call original nature. Kenshō is ultimately the recognition of one's own pure ego.

Why is it said that "self-nature is not nature"? Each nen-action occurs momentarily. In other words, it operates in this present moment; the next moment there is another present and another nen-thought. Pure ego is also momentary. Each moment there is pure ego, but the next moment it is replaced by another ego. Everything is changing, and the continuous stream of changes flows on perpetually. Hence, ego is no ego, and self-nature, no nature.

• *Inheriting the spirit of Dansai, | How could he be gentle and quiet?*

Dansai (*dan*, cutting; *sai*, complications) was a surname of Ōbaku, given him by Emperor Taichū (Sensō). Ōbaku, who was Rinzai's teacher, appears in Case 11 and also in Case 2 of *Mumonkan*. There is a well-known story that Ōbaku once struck Sensō, who was at that time still a prince (see the notes to Case 11). He struck Rinzai, too, causing him to become enlightened. The name Dansai implies cutting powerfully and decisively through all the knotty complications that beset the student. Rinzai inherited Ōbaku's spirit and was also direct, quick, and sometimes rough in his handling of his disciples.

• *Not difficult for Kyorei* . . . Kyorei was a deity endowed with great strength. According to legend, he cleaved Mount Kasan with his hands and let the Yellow River flow through. In like manner Rinzai, with his slapping, cut through the complications that beset Jō Jōza and exposed his original nature.

Case 33   Chinsō Shōsho
Comes to Visit Shifuku

ENGO'S INTRODUCTION   He does not distinguish east from west, nor north from south. From morning to evening, from evening to morning, so he remains. Can he be called asleep? Sometimes his eyes are like shooting stars. Can we call him wide awake? Sometimes he points to the south, calling it the north. Tell me, is he mindful or mindless; is he a man of enlightenment or a mediocrity? If you thoroughly understand this topic and know the secret of it, you will realize how the ancient masters went this way and that. Tell me, what season of life is this? See the following.

MAIN SUBJECT   Chinsō came to see Shifuku. Shifuku drew a circle in the air. Chinsō said, "I have no object in coming here. Why do you bother to draw a circle?" Shifuku closed the door of his room. [Setchō says, "Chinsō has only one eye."]

SETCHŌ'S VERSE
Perfect the circle, pure the sound,
Bright and abundant the encircling jade,
Loaded on horses and mules,

Loaded on board the iron boats,
Given to those who know
The peace and freedom of land and sea.

He put down the tackle to fish the turtle.
Setchō comments here:
"Monks throughout the world can't jump out of it."

NOTES *Chinsō Shōsho* was a layman. Chin was his family name, Sō his personal name. Shōsho was the title of a government official corresponding to a minister or deputy minister. He studied Zen with Bokushū, who appears in Case 10. Chinsō had a subtle understanding of the Zen spirit and tested monks who came to see him. None could cope with him. One day Ummon came. Chinsō said to him, "I shall not ask you about the teaching in the sutras, but I ask you, why do you journey to visit Zen masters?" "How many monks have you asked this question?" said Ummon. "I am asking you just now." Ummon said, "Put aside these things for the moment. What is the Buddha's teaching?" "One is at a loss for words to expound it; one's mind is blocked when one tries to think about it." (This was a popular saying, expressing the subtlety of the Buddha's teaching.) Ummon said, "Being at a loss for words comes from using words; being blocked comes from delusive thinking. Tell me, what is the Buddha's teaching?" Chinsō could not answer.

After further exchanges, Ummon said, "Shōsho, don't flatter yourself. Zen masters cast off all worldly things and all learning, give ten or twenty years of undivided attention to this matter, and still find themselves helpless. How could you easily solve it?" Chinsō bowed and said, "It was a mistake on my part." (Why did he not say, in first answering Ummon, "Many in the world are starving. How much I want to save them"?)

• *Shifuku* must have been an outstanding Zen master, but little is known of him except that he was, in Dharma lineage, the grandson of Kyōzan, who, in collaboration with Isan, founded the Igyō school. This school was famous for using objects and gestures in its teaching, especially the circle. Kyōzan once pushed forward a cushion in answer to the question, "What is Buddha?" but more often he used the circle. Shifuku seems often to have used the same technique, as related in the present case.

• *He does not distinguish east from west, nor north from south.* This is a figure of speech. He behaves like a child and does not display his shrewdness and sagacity. Sometimes he seems to be nodding, and to be failing to distinguish right from wrong, advantage from disadvantage.

• *Sometimes his eyes are like shooting stars.* However, occasionally a brilliant observation issues from his lips, like a ray of sunshine piercing dark clouds.

• *Sometimes he points to the south, calling it the north.* In the introduction to Case 25, Engo says, "If one's words do not astonish the crowd, one slips into the conventional."

• *Chinsō came to see Shifuku. Shifuku drew a circle in the air.* The opponents in Dharma battle are like two tennis players. The server starts from a position of advantage, but he must be a skillful player if he is to take advantage of it. The receiver is in a difficult position, but if he is a good player he can quickly change his defensive position to an attacking one. Shifuku instantly took the offensive (as did Ummon in the episode related above) and drew a circle in the air. Chinsō has the choice of letting himself be encircled by it voluntarily (not involuntarily) or of trying to leap out of it (if he has the ability).

• *Chinsō said, "I have no object in coming here. Why do you bother to draw a circle?"* To be purposeful is much admired in the world at large, as are being useful, meaningful, profitable, and so on. But in its pursuit of the useful and profitable, consciousness has fallen into its delusive way of thinking. Chinsō says he has come without any object. Here Engo puts in his comment: "A sleepyhead." In a way, Chinsō's answer was splendid. He did not want to be enclosed within Shifuku's circle. But if you truly and naively appreciate the truth of the universe that is symbolized by the circle, there is no way of leaping out of it. Everything has its advantages and disadvantages. Chinsō refused and was rebuffed by Shifuku.

• *Shifuku closed the door of his room.* This was Shifuku's response. Chinsō came to a standstill, unable either to advance or to retreat.

• *Setchō says, "Chinsō has only one eye."* If Chinsō had had another eye with which to see the other side of the matter, he would have avoided this dead end. In such an emergency, what should he have done? Engo's comment here is "Why did you not give a fine greeting that would have left Shifuku no way out?" But how?

• *Perfect the circle, pure the sound, | Bright and abundant the encircling jade.* The circle of jade is perfect in shape, sound, color, and luster.

• *Loaded on horses and mules, | Loaded on board the iron boats.* It is everywhere on land and sea.

• *Given to those who know | The peace and freedom of land and sea.* Those who enjoy the circle must be those who are free from all cares and enjoy the peace of the mountains and sea.

• *He put down the tackle to fish the turtle.* The turtle is a mysterious, legendary creature popular in Zen literature. Sometimes it is blind, sometimes lame. Sometimes it carries three mountains on its back. Here it represents something big. A Zen master always wants to land something big like the turtle.

• *Monks throughout the world can't jump out of it.* There is one way to leap out of it. That is to be in it. He does not distinguish east from west, and sometimes points to the south, calling it the north. What season of life is this?

Case 34   Kyōzan's "You Have Not Visited Rozan"

MAIN SUBJECT   Kyōzan asked a monk, "Where are you from?" "Mount Rozan," answered the monk. "Have you ever visited Gorōhō Peak?" asked Kyōzan. "No, not yet," said the monk. Kyōzan said, "You have not visited Rozan."

Later, Ummon said, "This talk of Kyōzan's was falling into the weeds, all out of kindness."

SETCHŌ'S VERSE
Falling or not falling, who can tell?
White clouds piling up,

Bright sun shining down,
Faultless the left, mature the right.

Don't you know Kanzan?
He went very fast;
Ten years not returning,
He forgot the way he had come.

NOTES *Kyōzan* (814–90) first studied Zen with Tangen (see Case 18). After Tangen's death he studied with Isan, under whom he attained his greatness. He and Isan jointly established the Igyō school.

• *Where are you from?* This question was commonly asked by a master of a monk when the latter first came to him. The monk's answer generally revealed his condition.

• *Mount Rozan.* Rozan was a mountain four thousand feet high, famous both as a seat of Buddhist learning, having a great many temples, and for its beautiful scenery. It was regarded as a sort of earthly paradise. Many fine poems have been written about this mountain. To say "from Rozan" suggested an association with something spiritual and refined.

• *Have you ever visited Gorōhō Peak?* Gorōhō consisted of five peaks shaped like old men greeting each other, and was the most famous part of Mount Rozan. Kyōzan's question was aimed at discovering if the monk had attained a true, subtle insight into Zen.

• *No, not yet.* If this answer had come from a monk with a background of diligent training and study in Zen, it would have indicated that he was not an easy fellow to deal with. But in the present case there was nothing to suggest that the monk had such experience.

• *You have not visited Rozan.* With these words Kyōzan dealt the monk a decisive blow. A more severe master, such as Tokusan or Rinzai, would have used his stick on the monk. However, a gentle word can sometimes be more telling in its effect than a blow.

• *This talk of Kyōzan's was falling into the weeds, all out of kindness.* "Falling into the weeds" means disgracing oneself for the sake of one's disciples by talking too much. It is a hackneyed saying that the truth of Zen cannot and should not be talked about. But what cannot be talked about must be talked about if students are ever to progress. However, it must always be remembered that the truth must be reached by each student through his own immediate experience, not through others' words, hence Ummon's comment.

• *Falling or not falling, who can tell?* All words, all actions, are Zen. The Buddha said, when he was dying, that he had not preached a word in the forty-nine years of his Buddha life. Yet he had preached hundreds of thousands of words. It is said, "All creatures deliver sermons."

• *White clouds piling up,* | *Bright sun shining down.* At one level this is a description of the spectacular scenery of Rozan: peak upon peak crowned with white clouds, the trees, rocks, and streams, and the tiled roofs of the temples shining in the bright sunlight. At the same time, ti is a symbolic description of Kyōzan's condition.

• *Faultless the left, mature the right.* Left and right are both the Pure Land. That is the condition of mind of Kyōzan, Ummon, and so on, as well as the appearance of Rozan.

• *Kanzan* was a legendary figure. The priest of Kokusei Temple on Mount Rozan once found on the mountain a strange fellow clad in beggar's rags. It was difficult to make out whether he was an old man or a child. The priest, Bukan, took him back to his temple and kept him as a servant, calling him Jittoku (*jitsu* [*jit-*], pick up; *toku*, a find). Jittoku had a friend who was a sort of counterpart to him. He often came to visit Jittoku at the temple, where he might be given leftovers to eat. This person was Kanzan. They were a shabby, dirty pair, half madmen, half hermits, talking and laughing loudly and reciting poems. One day they disappeared before the eyes of the monks and were never seen again. People searched for them and came upon a cave where Kanzan had lived. Poems were written all over the walls of the cave. According to legend, the poems were copied down, and we have today a collection called *Kanzan's Poems*, which contains about four hundred masterpieces.

• *He went very fast.* Stories are told of *sennin* (*sen*, wizardlike hermit; *nin*, human being) who went over mountains and dales so fast that no ordinary climber could follow them, and were soon lost to sight.

• *Ten years not returning,* | *He forgot the way he had come.* These lines are a quotation from *Kanzan's Poems*. The poem runs:

> This is my resting place,
> Kanzan knows the best retreats;
> The breeze blows through the pines,
> Sounding better the nearer it is.

Under a tree I'm reading
Lao-tzu, quietly perusing.
Ten years not returning,
I forgot the way I had come.

This is the condition of a mature Zen master. He has gone into the world of unworldliness and forgotten the way back to the world of worldliness. Setchō is singing in praise of Kyōzan.

Case 35 Manjusri's "Threes and Threes"

ENGO'S INTRODUCTION In distinguishing dragon from snake, jewel from stone, black from white, irresolute from decisive, if one does not have the clear eye of the mind and the amulet under the arm, one invites instant failure. Just at this moment, if one's vision and hearing are clear, and color and sound are truly cognized, tell me, is he black or white, crooked or straight? The subtle difference—how could you discern it?

MAIN SUBJECT Manjusri asked Muchaku, "Where have you recently come from?" Muchaku said, "From the south." "How is Southern Buddhism faring?" asked Manjusri. "The monks of the latter days of the Law observe the Buddha's precepts a little," Muchaku answered. "Are there many or few?" "Here about three hundred, there around five hundred."

Then Muchaku asked Manjusri, "How does Buddhism fare in your part of the world?" Manjusri said, "The worldly and the holy are living together; dragons and snakes are mingled." "Are there many or few?" "The former threes and threes, the latter threes and threes."

SETCHŌ'S VERSE
The thousand hills, peak upon peak, deep blue;
Who can converse with Manjusri?

How I laugh at "many or few"!
How I admire
"The former threes and threes,
The latter threes and threes"!

NOTES *Muchaku* (821–900) had the personal name Bunki. Muchaku (*mu*, no; *chaku*, attachment) was an honorific name given him in his later years by the emperor. As a youth Muchaku traveled all over the country visiting Zen teachers, and the story of the present case seems to have been an incident occurring during this journey. He studied under Kyōzan and eventually succeeded him.

It is related that Muchaku made a pilgrimage to Mount Godai, a holy mountain long dedicated to Manjusri. It was evening when he arrived, and he found a temple at the foot of the mountain and stayed there overnight. The master priest of the temple met him and the conversation related in the present case took place.

The next morning, when Muchaku was leaving, he was accompanied to the gate of the temple by a boy who had been deputed by the master priest to see Muchaku off. Muchaku asked the boy who the master was and what was the name of the temple. The boy, without saying anything, pointed to the mountain. Muchaku looked up and saw the mountain above him, colored a beautiful deep blue. When he looked back he found that the temple, the boy, and everything had disappeared. In their place he saw a lonely valley. Muchaku realized that the master priest had been Manjusri himself, who had appeared for the sake of his devotee.

• *In distinguishing dragon from snake.* In distinguishing a promising, dragonlike monk from a commonplace one.

• *Irresolute from decisive.* "Irresolute" denotes a monk who lacks force and determination; "decisive," a determined, earnest one.

• *The clear eye of the mind.* A literal translation is "the eye on top of the head." The god Daijizai-ten (*dai*, great; *jizai*, free, unrestricted; *ten*, heaven), or Mahesvara (Siva), has three eyes: two ordinary ones and a third placed lengthwise in the middle of the forehead, which represents the clear eye of the mind. "The clear eye" here denotes the penetrating insight of a Zen master.

• *The amulet under the arm.* The amulet is a talisman believed to confer upon the man who carries it under his arm the mystical power to do whatever he wants. The amulet here symbolizes the Zen master's remarkable abilities in dealing with his disciples, in deciding matters of daily routine, in doing calligraphy, painting, garden design, and so on.

• *Manjusri asked Muchaku.* In Zen literature Manjusri is often portrayed approaching his eager devotee in the guise of a human being. As the host of the phantasmal temple he talked kindly to the visitor, Muchaku.

• *From the south.* Speaking from the viewpoint of absolute samadhi, there are no north and south, no east and west. From this point of view, Muchaku's answer can be faulted. However, from the viewpoint of positive samadhi, there are north and south, there are mountains and rivers, and so on. If he has the strength and ability to do it, his saying "From the south" cannot be faulted. The present case is a fiction invented by someone, perhaps Muchaku himself, to help clarify the subtle problem of the absolute and relative (or positive) aspects of the mind.

• *How is Southern Buddhism faring?* Southern Zen is so called because it flourished mainly in the south of China, centered in the districts around the Yangtze River. It attached importance to practice and the attainment of sudden enlightenment. Its traditions went back to the Sixth Patriarch, Sōkei (Enō). Northern Zen thrived chiefly in North China and emphasized theoretical learning and the gradual attainment of realization. The geographical separation of these schools was not absolute: some great masters of Southern Zen were to be found in northern China.

• *The monks of the latter days of the Law observe the Buddha's precepts a little.* The five hundred years after the death of Shakyamuni Buddha are called "the age of the genuine Law," in which the true Law, or Dharma, was observed. The next thousand years are called "the age of the pseudo-genuine Law," and the following ten thousand years are "the latter days of the Law."

• *Are there many or few?* From the absolute point of view there is no question of many or few, coming or going, being born and dying, and so on. To be asked this question was a disgrace for Muchaku. If he had the power, he should have covered Manjusri's mouth. But at the same time, from the viewpoint of positive samadhi, what is wrong with talking of many and few?

• *Here about three hundred, there around five hundred.* Muchaku answered in terms of the situation as it really was. Perhaps he gave these answers without having a clear idea of their meaning. Afterward, he (or some other author) achieved a clear idea and developed this story.

• *Then Muchaku asked Manjusri.* Now Muchaku, living up to his fame, took the offensive.

• *In your part of the world.* In a narrow sense this means on Mount Godai; more widely, it means in North China. It can also be taken as referring to Manjusri's condition.

• *The worldly and the holy are living together; dragons and snakes are mingled.* This describes the real state of the world, not only at present but in the past and in the future. Dragons fulfill their lives as dragons and snakes their lives as snakes, and the worldly and holy do the same.

• *Are there many or few?* Muchaku perhaps simply repeated Manjusri's question without understanding its true significance.

• *The former threes and threes, the latter threes and threes.* This answer of Manjusri's is very much admired, especially the words "threes and threes." It answers the question in terms of numbers but without specifying a particular number. Imagine those people passing in endless succession, in twos and threes, through eons of time.

• *The thousand hills, peak upon peak, deep blue.* With his first line Setchō gives the essence of the case. Recite it in language samadhi and you will see floating before your eyes the image of Manjusri himself, who is, in truth, the best part of yourself. Setchō has described this scene in his verse to Case 20:

> Beautiful, the evening clouds,
> Endless, the distant hills, blue upon blue, peak upon peak!

• *Who can converse with Manjusri?* Whoever has the power to do so can do it.

• *How I laugh at "many or few"!* Setchō laughs at the idea of asking the number.

• *The former threes and threes, | The latter threes and threes.* This is the real condition of things in the world.

Case 36   Chōsha Went for a Walk

MAIN SUBJECT   One day Chōsha went for a walk. When he returned to the gate, the head monk said, "Oshō, where have you been strolling?" Chōsha said, "I have come from walking in the hills." The head monk said, "Where have you been?" Chōsha said, "First I went following the fragrant grasses, and now I have returned in pursuit of the falling blossoms." The head monk said, "You are full of the spring." Chōsha said, "Better than the autumn dews falling on the lotus leaves." [Setchō says, "Thank you for your answer."]

SETCHŌ'S VERSE
   The world without a speck of dust!
   What man's eyes are not opened?
   First following the fragrant grasses,
   Returning in pursuit of falling blossoms,
   The slender stork perched in the wintry tree,
   A crazy monkey shrieking on the age-old heights.
   Chōsha's eternal meaning—ah!

NOTES   *Chōsha* was a disciple of Nansen and a contemporary of Tokusan, Rinzai, and Isan. One of his poems ("You, who sit on the top of a hundred-foot pole") forms part of Case 46 of *Mumonkan*, and another ("Clinging to the deluded way of consciousness") is quoted by Mumon as his verse to Case 12.
   One evening Chōsha was enjoying the moonlight with Kyōzan, who said, "Everyone has 'this one thing' but does not know how to use it." ("This one thing" is a widely used Zen term meaning Buddha Nature.) Chōsha said, "Perhaps I should employ you and use it." Kyōzan said, "Try it." Instantly, Chōsha trampled on Kyōzan. Kyōzan said, "Uncle, you are like a fierce tiger!" (Chōsha was Kyōzan's "uncle" in terms of Dharma lineage; see the genealogical table at the back of the book.)
   Case 23 ("This is Myōhōchō") is a parallel case to this incident, though Chōsha was more direct in his answer than Chōkei. Chōsha was a man of a poetic nature, though the incident related above (to which he owes his

name, meaning "fierce tiger") shows that he was capable of vigorous action. Kyōzan, who later became a great master, was still young at the time he met with Chōsha's rough treatment.

• *One day Chōsha went for a walk.* Engo puts in comments here: "Today, all today" and "He has fallen head over heels in the grass." "Today, all today" means not yesterday, not tomorrow, but all today—only the present. "Falling in the grass" means that he has walked wholeheartedly in the grass. This is positive samadhi.

• *The head monk said, "Oshō, where have you been strolling?"* Engo's comment is "You must examine this old master." This is a Dharma battle.

• *I have come from walking in the hills.* Engo's comment is "You should not fall in the grass." With Chōsha, falling in the grass is itself ascending Myōhōchō (Case 23), while an ordinary person will tumble down helplessly.

• *Where have you been?* Engo's comments are "A thrust" and "If he has anywhere to go, he has fallen in the grass." Purposelessness is admired in Zen, in contrast to the usual attitude of the world. Here purposeless means innocent, that is, free from any plotting activity of the mind.

• *First I went following the fragrant grasses, and now I have returned in pursuit of the falling blossoms.* Chōsha followed the grasses like a child chasing after a butterfly. "Pursuit" may seem to imply a purpose, but Chōsha's action was childlike, untainted by the calculated activity of an ordinary adult's utilitarian mode of consciousness.

• *You are full of the spring.* You are a little too much possessed by the buoyant mood of spring, a little too merry, aren't you?

• *Better than the autumn dews falling on the lotus leaves.* The dews and frosts of autumn and the winter snows represent absolute samadhi; the spring grasses and flowers represent positive samadhi. The former is the foundation of Zen and must come first in zazen practice, but positive samadhi is samadhi in actual life and is much more highly valued. Hakuin Zenji says, "Samadhi in actual life is a hundred thousand times better than samadhi in quietude."

• *Setchō says, "Thank you for your answer."* The head monk's reaction to Chōsha's words is not recorded, so Setchō puts in these words for him. Setchō wants to make sure that you value Chōsha's words correctly.

• *The world without a speck of dust!* Chōsha's world is pure, like a clear blue sky. Engo's comment is "Who is it that has thrown open the door and stands towering above the eaves?" He is a giant.

• *What man's eyes are not opened?* Who is unable to open his eyes when confronted with the pure land of Chōsha?

• *First following the fragrant grasses.* Ten years not returning . . .

• *Returning in pursuit of falling blossoms.* . . . I forgot the way I had come. (See Case 34.)

• *The slender stork perched in the wintry tree.* Spring represents the positive side of Zen; the absolute side is symbolized by lonely, wintry scenes.

• *A crazy monkey shrieking on the age-old heights.* Trackless mountains and the bleak plateau. Positive samadhi always implies absolute samadhi as its background, and Setchō did not neglect to allude to this. The fragrant grasses and falling blossoms of spring correspond to positive samadhi, while a slender stork perching in a wintry tree and a monkey shrieking on the mountain heights signify winter, which represents absolute samadhi. Readers familiar with Chinese poetry would associate the slender stork with an old man of noble character who has undergone all the hardships of life, and the monkey's shrieks in the desolate mountains with a lonely traveler's deep, speechless feeling. These two images are now poetically connected by Setchō with the severe side of absolute samadhi.

• *Chōsha's eternal meaning—ah!* Full of admiration, which he can no more withhold than a monkey can avoid shrieking, Setchō is speechless and can only say, "Ah!"

Case 37   Banzan's "Three Worlds, No Dharma"

ENGO'S INTRODUCTION   The spirit which moves like lightning you fail to follow. When the bolt descends from the blue, you have no time to cover your ears. The scarlet banner flutters over the master's head; the two-edged sword is being brandished behind the student's neck. Unless your eyes are sharp and your hands move quickly, how can you cope with the situation? One will lower his head and ponder, following the delusive ways of thought. Don't you know that countless skulls are haunted by ghosts? I want to ask you, without falling into the delusive way of thinking and without halting irresolutely, how can you respond to the teacher's words? See the following.

MAIN SUBJECT   Banzan said to his disciples, "In the three worlds, there is no Dharma. Where could you find the mind?"

SETCHŌ'S VERSE
Three worlds, no Dharma,
Where could you find the mind?
White clouds crown the heavens,
The streams draw music from the harp—
Tunes and harmonies which none can understand.
The night's rain has brought the autumn waters deep.

NOTES   *Banzan* (720–814) was a disciple of Baso. Once, when he was young, Banzan went to a butcher's shop to buy some meat and said, "Give me some good meat." The butcher said, "It is all good meat." At these words Banzan had a certain experience, and he commenced the study of Buddhism. The main subject of the present case comes from some words of his to his disciples: "You have to look into it for yourselves. No one can do it for you. In the three worlds, there is no Dharma. Where could you find the mind? The four elements are originally empty. Where does the Buddha abide? The Plow does not move and it says nothing, yet it reveals itself immediately. And there is nothing else."

• *The spirit which moves like lightning you fail to follow.* A Zen master's spirit operates like lightning, and you find it hard to follow him.

• *When the bolt descends from the blue, you have no time to cover your ears.* Here is an example. A monk once handed a kettle to his teacher with the spout turned toward the teacher. Instantly there came a loud scolding, like a thunderbolt. He had no time to cover his ears. But the monk says that he has never again disregarded the teacher's precepts.

• *The scarlet banner flutters over the master's head; the two-edged sword is being brandished behind the student's neck.* The scarlet banner, denoting victory, is always above the master's head. The disciple's defeat comes abruptly, as if a sword were suddenly thrust at his neck.

• *Unless your eyes are sharp and your hands move quickly.* Such terms as "eyes" and "hands" are often used in Zen literature to express spiritual and mental actions. Engo means, "If your spirit is not quick and your mind does not work freely."

• *One will lower his head and ponder, following the delusive ways of thought.* When a student who has no confidence in himself is examined by his teacher, he lowers his head and stops to think, trying to solve the problem by conceptual thinking.

• *Countless skulls are haunted by ghosts.* This is a figurative description of the condition of a student who is beset by doubts and fears.

• *How can you respond to the teacher's words?* Banzan's words in the present case will come like a bolt from the blue to the ears of an ordinary student. He may be astonished and discouraged. But unless one's words astonish the crowd, one will fall into the conventional.

• *In the three worlds, there is no Dharma.* The three worlds are (1) the realm of desire, (2) the realm of form, and (3) the realm of no-form. Together, these embrace the whole universe, spiritual and physical. To say that there is no Dharma means that there is no universe. But this means that there is no universe such as we conceive of by the operation of our ordinary thought processes.

• *Where could you find the mind?* The idea of the Dharma, or the mind, is a concept produced by thought. It is quite a different thing from our real, immediate experience. When Banzan says there is no Dharma, no mind, he is refusing to equate the idea with the direct experience. The *Diamond Sutra* says, "The world is not the world, and it is called the world." The mind is not the mind, and it is called the mind. How can you recognize the mind, then? No, there is no mind. There is only a certain internal pressure, a nen-thought, which momentarily appears and then disappears. Banzan transcends all conceptual treatment of the problem. The question can be solved only by returning to the intuitive grasp of the present.

• *White clouds crown the heavens, / The streams draw music from the harp.* Heaven and earth play together to produce harmonious music.

• *Tunes and harmonies which none can understand.* But there are few who can appreciate this.

• *The night's rain has brought the autumn waters deep.* The night's rain, the autumn waters, their depths—recite this line in language samadhi. You will discover an exquisite poetic demonstration of Banzan's "no Dharma, no mind." It is very difficult to give a plausible explanation of Banzan's words in philosophical terms. It is not so difficult to grasp his meaning, however, if you attain the state of absolute samadhi, because in that condition there are no space, no time, and no causation, which is another version of "no Dharma, no mind." Conceptual and philosophical thinking is, of course, necessary to the human mind, but such thinking must follow experience and explain it, not the reverse.

Case 38   Fuketsu and the Dharma Seal of the Patriarch

ENGO'S INTRODUCTION   When one adopts the gradual method, though it is not normal, one can nevertheless be on the right road, and in the busiest marketplace one will be able to enjoy unhindered movement. When one adopts the sudden method, one leaves behind no trace, and even the thousand Buddhas cannot spy one out. Now, how about when one uses neither the gradual nor the sudden method? A word is sufficient to the wise, as a flick of the whip is to a fine horse. Taking such a course, who can be the master? See the following.

MAIN SUBJECT   Fuketsu took the high seat in the government office of Eishū and said, "The Dharma Seal of the patriarch is like the iron ox's spirit. If the seal is removed, the impression is left; if it is not removed, the impression does not appear. If you want neither of them, tell me, should you or should you not press the seal down?"

Then a senior monk, Rohi, came forward and said, "I have the iron ox's spirit. I ask you not to press down the seal." Fuketsu said, "For a long time now I have been used to fishing the whale in the great oceans, and I feel rather annoyed at finding a little frog tumbling about in the muddy water." Rohi stopped to think. Fuketsu gave a shout and said,

"Why don't you go on with what you were saying?" Rohi faltered. Fuketsu made as if to strike him with his hossu and said, "Do you remember the topic? Try to recite it." Rohi tried to open his mouth. Fuketsu struck with his hossu once more.

The governor said, "The Buddha's law and the king's law are just the same." Fuketsu said, "Why do you say that?" The governor said, "When punishment is called for, it should not be neglected. Otherwise one invites trouble." Fuketsu descended from the seat.

SETCHŌ'S VERSE
Holding Rohi to let him ride the iron ox,
He used the armor of Rinzai's three mysteries.
The stream that ran to greet the lord's palace—
With one shout he made it flow backward.

NOTES   *Fuketsu* (896–973) was, in Dharma relation, Rinzai's great-grandson. The governor of Eishū was a follower of Fuketsu and often asked him to lecture. Fuketsu also appears in Case 61 and *Mumonkan*, Case 24.

• *Gradual method.* Satori (realization) generally comes suddenly because it is normally a matter of intuitive cognition. However, a more gradual attainment of realization is also possible. It may happen that a man has a good conceptual understanding of Zen and a long experience of samadhi but has not undergone the experience of realization. He is in a delicate condition. Sometimes his attainment is superior to that of a man who has had an insecurely based kenshō. The important point lies in the experience of samadhi. If you have attained an advanced state of samadhi, you have already achieved that much realization of Zen. However, you lack confidence in yourself because you have not had the sudden experience. A competent teacher can detect your condition but will wait until the great time comes, when everything bursts into glorious bloom. Some modern people, particularly those with a highly developed intellectual way of thinking, find that the sudden experience eludes them. The intuitive activity of their mind has retrogressed too far. But such people sometimes achieve a good understanding of Zen. In short, the gradual method is a way of reaching realization by the progressive development of one's samadhi and of one's conceptual understanding of it.

• *In the busiest marketplace one will be able to enjoy unhindered movement.* In busy daily life he enjoys the free activity of his mind.

• *When one adopts the sudden method, one leaves behind no trace.* To leave behind no trace whatever is the real condition of genuine enlightenment. But generally speaking, and to our shame, we leave behind all too many traces in our daily life (see Case 6).

• *How about when one uses neither the gradual nor the sudden method?* If you can go about the world leaving no trace of your activity, it is all right whether you use either the gradual or the sudden method, or neither.

• *A word is sufficient to the wise.* His world is as free of tracks as outer space. The slightest sign is enough for him to direct his course anywhere.

• *Took the high seat.* A Zen teacher delivered his lecture or sermon from an elevated platform in front of an image of the Buddha. This denoted that he took the place of the Buddha. The students stood in rows and listened to him.

• *The Dharma Seal of the patriarch.* The patriarch is Bodhidharma. The Dharma Seal is the mind of the Buddha.

• *The iron ox.* In legendary times Emperor Yu built a gigantic embankment along the Yellow River to prevent it from flooding. In memory of the work he constructed a huge iron statue of an ox, with its head in Honan Province, on the south bank of the river, and its tail in Hopei Province, on the north. It was intended as a guardian deity to prevent the flooding from which the people had suffered so many disasters. Fuketsu uses this image to represent unsurpassed strength and firmness.

• *If the seal is removed, the impression is left; if it is not removed, the impression does not appear.* The two alternatives can be compared to subjectivity and objectivity. The former is action itself, which is not reflected upon. This corresponds to the impression not appearing. Objectivity is action which is reflected upon, corresponding to the appearance of an impression. Alternatively, we might compare them to holding fast and letting go: the former is an exacting, annihilating action, which leaves no trace; the latter is open and constructive, and there an impression appears.

• *If you want neither of them.* In other words, if you want to transcend both subjectivity and objectivity, both holding fast and letting go. This may sound like asking the impossible, but at the moment of kenshō you find that the impossible is happening. Kenshō is a subjective action, but at the same moment one recognizes (objectively) that one is attaining one's own true self.

• *Should you or should you not press the seal down?* This is the challenge in the Dharma battle.

• *I have the iron ox's spirit. I ask you not to press down the seal.* I have already realized the Dharma Seal within me. I am not going to ask you for it.

• *I feel rather annoyed at finding a little frog tumbling about in the muddy water.* A teacher sometimes immediately rejects the student's answer to see if his attainment is genuine.

• *Why don't you go on with what you were saying?* Rohi had not come up to Fuketsu's expectation, hence this urging on.

• *Fuketsu made as if to strike him with his hossu.* For "hossu," see the notes to *Mumonkan*, Case 30. Fuketsu was showing his disapproval.

• *Do you remember the topic?* The topic was "the iron ox's spirit." For Rohi to have to be reminded of it was a disgrace, and his confusion was extreme.

• *Rohi tried to open his mouth.* Even if he could say anything, it was too late.

• *When punishment is called for, it should not be neglected.* When you kill, kill exhaustively.

• *Rinzai's three mysteries.* Rinzai once said, "Each statement must have three mysteries." The three mysteries can be interpreted in several ways, which we need not enter into here. We may take them as representing Rinzai's keen spiritual discernment and actions.

• *The stream that ran to greet the lord's palace.* A river ran through the town of Eishū.

• *With one shout he made it flow backward.* So powerful was Fuketsu's way of teaching that it completely reversed the direction of Rohi's mind.

Case 39   Ummon's "Kayakuran"

ENGO'S INTRODUCTION   When one is enlightened and enjoys perfect freedom of mind in ordinary life, one is like a tiger that commands its mountain retreat. If one is not enlightened and drifts about in the affairs of the world, one is like a monkey in a cage. If you want to know Buddha Nature, you must pay attention to time and causation. If you aspire to the condition of pure gold that has been refined a hundred times over, you must be shaped in the teacher's forge. I want to ask you this: How would you identify the one who has mastered the Way of the absolute?

MAIN SUBJECT   A monk asked Ummon, "What is the pure body of the Buddha?" Ummon said, "Kayakuran" [the fence around a flower garden]. The monk said, "How about if I understand it like that?" Ummon said, "The golden-haired lion."

SETCHŌ'S VERSE
   Don't mistake "Kayakuran."
   The mark is on the balance, not the tray;
   Saying "like that" betrays ignorance;
   Master hand, beware the golden lion.

NOTES   *Like a monkey in a cage.* True freedom is the mind's freedom. And the mind's freedom is freedom from one's own mind. The freedom that people ordinarily talk about—social, political, or economic freedom, for example—relates merely to external matters and is of a limited kind. Freedom from one's own mind has nothing to do with external circumstances.
   • *If you want to know Buddha Nature, you must pay attention to time and causation.* If you want to attain enlightenment, you must respect causation and spend time in training yourself in zazen.
   • *The one who has mastered the Way of the absolute.* This phrase means a teacher like Ummon, who knows and understands every condition the disciple goes through in his training.
   • *The pure body of the Buddha.* This is the Dharmakaya, which can be identified with the Great Perfect Mirror Wisdom.
   • *Kayakuran.* Like Tōzan's "Masagin" (*Mumonkan*, Case 18) or Ummon's "Kanshiketsu" (*Mumonkan*, Case 21), "Kayakuran" (*ka*, flower;

yaku, medicine; *ran*, fence) cannot be understood conceptually. You must just recite it. At first it will be meaningless, just a strange word. But recite it with deep attention in your language samadhi. The recitation will bring out whatever you have within yourself. If you have anything profound, that much profundity will appear. If there are no depths, you cannot get beyond that shallowness. Ummon's words often disturb us, but at the same time, they are attractive.

• *How about if I understand it like that?* The monk's question is open to two interpretations. One is that he was ignorant and simply wanted to be told what to believe. The other is that he was experienced and had an advanced understanding of Zen but feigned ignorance. His question, meaning "How about if I take it literally as the fence around a flower garden?" was intended to provoke Ummon to further speech, which might throw light on his meaning. In dealing with a Zen koan we are less interested in historical truth than in finding varieties of possible meanings.

• *The golden-haired lion.* This was a common phrase used to indicate one's approval. But Ummon's approval was subtle. He was giving it on condition that the monk had truly understood "like that." Ummon meant that the fence around a flower garden and the pure body of the Buddha, or Dharmakaya, are just the same, and that he would give his approval if the monk truly understood this.

• *Don't mistake "Kayakuran."* Then, how is one to take it? That is the point.

• *The mark is on the balance, not the tray.* The measuring mark is engraved on the balance, not on the tray or some other part of the scales. Ummon's true meaning is not to be found in the literal meaning of his words. You must read between the lines.

• *Saying "like that" betrays ignorance.* For "betrays ignorance" the original text has *tai-mu-tan* (*tai*, very; *mu*, not; *tan*, direct). This means that he was ignorant. But this ignorance, as we have noted, may have been either real or feigned.

• *Master hand, beware the golden lion.* If you are a master hand, you will understand the true meaning of "The golden-haired lion."

Case 40　Nansen's "This Flower"

ENGO'S INTRODUCTION　When the action of the mind is stopped and swept away, the iron tree will bloom. Can you demonstrate it? Even a crafty fellow will come a cropper here. Even if he excels in every way, he will have his nostrils pierced. Where are the complications? See the following.

MAIN SUBJECT　Riku Taifu, while talking with Nansen, said, "Jō Hosshi said, 'Heaven and earth and I are of the same root. All things and I are of one substance.' Isn't that absolutely fantastic?" Nansen pointed to a flower in the garden, called Taifu to him, and said, "People of these days see this flower as though they were in a dream."

SETCHŌ'S VERSE
Hearing, seeing, touching, and knowing are not one and one;
Mountains and rivers should not be viewed in the mirror.
The frosty sky, the setting moon—at midnight;
With whom will the serene waters of the lake reflect the shadows
　in the cold?

NOTES　*When the action of the mind is stopped and swept away, the iron tree will bloom.* In absolute samadhi the activity of your consciousness is stopped and the source of your thoughts is swept away. And when the activity of your consciousness resumes, it is just like an iron tree coming out in full bloom. You enjoy a beautiful world of pure cognition. Even a single blade of grass becomes illuminating and wonderful.
• *Can you demonstrate it?* Engo is urging his disciples on.
• *Even a crafty fellow will come a cropper here.* One may act as if one understands, but the man whose understanding is purely conceptual and not based on repeated personal experience will someday be caught out.
• *Even if he excels in every way, he will have his nostrils pierced.* He may act like a triton among the minnows, but when he meets an able master he will have a ring put through his nose and be led along like a cow.

• *Nansen.* See Case 28.

• *Riku Taifu* (764–834) was a high government official. He studied Zen with Nansen and attained an advanced understanding.

• *Jō Hosshi* (382–414) was one of the four distinguished disciples of Kumarajiva, who went from India to China in 401, translated many Buddhist scriptures, and generally had great influence on the development of Chinese Buddhism. Jō collaborated with his teacher and was also a great Buddhist scholar in his own right. Hosshi (*ho*, Dharma; *shi*, teacher) is a title of honor for a priest. Jō is said to have met an untimely death by execution when, for religious reasons, he refused to obey an order of the ruler of the state.

• *Heaven and earth and I are of the same root. All things and I are of one substance.* Riku quoted Jō Hosshi to demonstrate his understanding. But understanding can be of various kinds: direct, indirect, conceptual, shallow, profound, and so forth. What was the nature of Riku's understanding?

• *Isn't that absolutely fantastic?* In the original text the word we have translated as "fantastic" is *kikai* (*ki*, strange; *kai*, weird). It has the implication of absurd extravagance. Riku had achieved an advanced understanding of Zen, and in using the word "kikai" he meant to say that Jō Hosshi's proposition was so true that it sounded absurd to ordinary ears. He demonstrated thereby that his understanding went beyond the ordinary conception of such matters. But the question whether Riku's understanding came from pure cognition or from intellectual learning still remained.

• *Nansen pointed to a flower in the garden.* When "a flower" was mentioned in China, without further specification, it meant a flower of the tree peony. In pointing to the flower, Nansen was saying, "See this flower! The Tathagata sees Buddha Nature with his naked eyes. Can you see Buddha Nature in this flower?" Seeing Buddha Nature is exercising pure cognition. But how is one to perform that kind of cognition? It is really a simple matter of looking in positive samadhi. Look at a rose in the garden, and watch it—watch and watch. Or better, if that does not lead to positive samadhi, simply go out into the garden one fine sunny afternoon, lie down on your back on the grass, and watch the floating clouds. Forget all your busy daily affairs and simply watch the white clouds. Watch and watch and watch. Suddenly you will find your condition of mind is quite different from your ordinary one. The clouds and the sky have become totally absorbing. Only a few writers have ever described this sort of experience. There is an example in *Anna Karenina*, where Tolstoy describes Levin looking at a fleecy, mother-of-pearl cloud vanishing in the morning sky and having a certain mental experience as a result.

It is not too difficult to get into positive samadhi by these sorts of methods, but to be able to practice it in the routine of ordinary life is most difficult. However, if you once become mature in this practice you will find that you have only to look at the tiniest flower or a pebble by the roadside and you will be able to get into the spirit of the flower or the pebble. When you do this you are really looking into your own spirit. It is a matter of intuitive, direct cognition. Nansen wanted Riku's cognition to be of that kind, but Riku was not capable of it. He saw only a peony in the ordinary way and nothing more. His understanding of the flower was a conceptual matter. It was this that led to Nansen's next words.

• *People of these days see this flower as though they were in a dream.* Nansen's meaning is that for people now, including Riku, cognition is done vacantly, as if they were in a dream. Perhaps it is true that the activity of consciousness is something like dreaming, but Nansen dreamed a dream of pure cognition, while Riku dreamed a conceptual one. The difference is great.

• *Setchō's Verse.* This is a eulogy of pure cognition, of seeing Buddha Nature.

• *Hearing, seeing, touching, and knowing.* Hearing, seeing, and touching represent the sensations, mediated by the intuitive action of the first nen. Knowing is the reflecting, integrating action of the third nen, which results in recognized cognition.

• *Not one and one.* This is a commonly used phrase to denote that two things are not separate and distinct from each other. Thus, sensation and cognition are not strangers to each other, and further, since sensation gives us direct knowledge of external objects, nor are cognition and the cognized object. What Setchō is saying directly contradicts the view of the idealists, who have been unable to establish a connection between subjective cognition and external objects. In fact, these two have been closely interrelated from the earliest times in evolution, when cognition began to occur. Setchō knew this not as a result of theorizing but from his experience of samadhi.

• *Mountains and rivers should not be viewed in the mirror.* Mountains and rivers represent the external world. The mirror corresponds to your subjectivity. The idealist philosopher supposes our subjectivity to be totally isolated from the external world, and thus that mountains and rivers are nothing but the projection of the subjective action of one's mind—the creation of the mirror. However, the truth is the exact opposite. Pure cognition is achieved by the unification of the subjective action and the external world.

• *The frosty sky, the setting moon—at midnight.* The serenity and sublimity of this image are intended to convey the profound beauty of the meeting of object and sensation in pure cognition.

• *With whom will the serene waters of the lake reflect the shadows . . . ?* The serene waters of the lake represent your purified, cognizing mind. "Reflect" means, in fact, not reflecting but performing pure cognition. "Shadows" are external objects. "With whom" implies that no one else can peep into your cognition.

• *Cold.* This is intended to convey the serene, untroubled state of the mind when it performs pure cognition. In profound silence, at midnight, the serene waters of the lake reflect (cognize) the frosty sky, the setting moon, mountains, rivers, trees, and grass. The cognition is done solemnly and exclusively between you and the objects. Cognition is accomplished in two stages: pure cognition and the recognition of pure cognition. The moment your hand touches the cup on the table there is only the touch. Hand and object interact, and at that moment pure cognition is performed. The next moment you recognize that you felt the touch, the pure cognition is recognized by the reflecting action of consciousness, and recognized cognition is completed. Then there arise subjectivity and objectivity, and you say there is a cup on the table. I have discussed these topics in greater detail in *Zen Training*.

Case 41   Jōshū and the Great Death

ENGO'S INTRODUCTION   When right and wrong are intermingled, even the holy ones cannot distinguish between them. When positive and negative are interwoven, even the Buddha fails to discern one from the other. The most distinguished man of transcendent experience cannot avoid showing his ability as a great master. He walks the ridge of an iceberg, he treads the edge of a sword. He is like the *kirin*'s horn, like the lotus flower in the fire. Meeting a man of transcendent experience, he identifies with him as his equal. Who is he? See the following.

MAIN SUBJECT Jōshū asked Tōsu, "What if a man of the Great Death comes back to life again?" Tōsu said, "You should not go by night; wait for the light of day and come."

SETCHŌ'S VERSE
Open-eyed, he was all the more as if dead;
What use to test the master with something taboo?
Even the Buddha said he had not reached there;
Who knows when to throw ashes in another's eyes?

NOTES *Jōshū, Tōsu.* Tōsu was born in 819 and died when he was ninety-five years old. He appears again in Cases 79, 80, and 91. Jōshū was almost forty years older than Tōsu. Their meeting, described in the present case, took place in the course of the journey which Jōshū undertook after the death of his master, Nansen (see the notes to Case 30).
• *Right and wrong are intermingled.* The present case is a good example of right and wrong intermingled.
• *Even the holy ones cannot distinguish between them.* Engo exaggerates in order to set the heroes of the case in relief.
• *Positive and negative are interwoven.* In Zen practice, positive and negative may be so interwoven that distinguishing between them is almost impossible.
• *The most distinguished man of transcendent experience cannot avoid showing his ability as a great master.* This alludes to Jōshū and Tōsu.
• *He walks the ridge of an iceberg, he treads the edge of a sword.* His maturity and experience enable him, like a skillful circus performer, to tread with his bare feet on the edge of the death-dealing blade, to walk on the life-giving sword.

- *He is like the kirin's horn.* The kirin is a legendary creature famous for being difficult to capture. Its horn is as rare as the unicorn's.
- *The lotus flower in the fire.* Imagine the lotus flower, which does not shrivel and fade in the fire but radiates a brilliant light like flashing jewels blazing in the heart of the flames.
- *Meeting a man of transcendent experience, he identifies with him as his equal.* One devil knows another. Jōshū and Tōsu were well able to recognize each other's abilities.
- *Who is he?* He must be a great master, such as Jōshū or Tōsu.
- *What if a man of the Great Death comes back to life again?* The Great Death is the condition that appears in absolute samadhi, in which the activity of consciousness is stopped and the state called "body and mind fallen off" is reached. In other words, the delusive thinking of ordinary consciousness is cut off and your mind is purified. When you then come back once more to the ordinary activity of consciousness, you will find that it has undergone a great change. It is released from its spell, and suddenly you come to realize your true nature. That is called realization. This experience is wonderful because the old self-centered world, with which you have so long been familiar and to which you could not help clinging, has dropped away, and a new world of unity and equality has taken its place. This, in brief, is what happens when a man of the Great Death comes back to life again.

However, you should not think that Zen training stops here. On the contrary, this is the starting point of real Zen practice. The cultivation of Holy Buddhahood after realization is awaiting you. It is a process of ripening, of becoming mature. Unless you do this, everything remains green and unsatisfactory. First you must cast off what is called *hōshū* (*hō*, Dharma; *shū*, attachment), the attachment to your own realization. When you stick to anything, it will blind you. You must forsake what you attain as it is attained, and try to reach a wider world—wider and wider, until it is as boundless as outer space. Then you will understand what so-called emptiness is. When you look back from this emptiness to the realization for which you struggled so hard, you will see that even the realization was a burden of bygone days. You must, in other words, be emancipated from your own satori (realization). When this has happened, it is childishly simple to talk about such a topic as the Great Death and coming back to life again. Jōshū knew all this perfectly well, as he was a mature Zen master. But he had a reason for asking about it.

• *You should not go by night; wait for the light of day and come.* Tōsu was saying, "A thief goes by night; you must not go stealing about like a thief. Come to me when you have attained the light of the mind."

• *Open-eyed, he was all the more as if dead.* Jōshū knew everything, which made him all the more like one who had undergone the Great Death. He behaved like an ignorant man and asked this question.

• *What use to test the master with something taboo?* In the original text the word translated here as "taboo" is *yakuki* (*yaku,* medicine; *ki,* evasion: a kind of food to be avoided when one is taking medicine or is on a special diet). Setchō means that Jōshū tried Tōsu with something that should have been avoided. But his question elicited a fine answer: "You should not go by night; wait for the light of day and come."

• *Even the Buddha said he had not reached there.* Setchō's intention is not to assert that the Buddha did not reach there but rather to emphasize the extreme difficulty and importance of doing so. It is a matter of the greatest difficulty to become a man of the Great Death in ordinary life.

• *Who knows when to throw ashes in another's eyes?* Zen masters sometimes talk affirmatively, sometimes negatively. They enter into subtle problems where right and wrong are intermingled, positive and negative interwoven. Now students must be exhorted to undergo the Great Death, now they must be urged to undertake the cultivation of Holy Buddhahood. First one must be praised, then the other. The masters' words are like ashes thrown into someone's eyes to make a true blind man of him. Setchō means that Jōshū and Tōsu were great Zen masters who knew how and when to throw ashes into their disciples' eyes. This idea of throwing ashes into other people's eyes may sound strange. But think of the examples of Copernicus, who made the earth go around the sun; of Darwin, who diminished man to being the descendant of an ape; of Einstein, who distorted space. Did not they, in a sense, throw ashes into people's eyes, blinding them and astounding them?

Case 42 Hō Koji's "Beautiful Snowflakes"

ENGO'S INTRODUCTION He talks independently, acts independently; and he trudges through the mire for the sake of others. He talks with others, acts with others; and he stands alone, like silver mountains and iron cliffs. If you doubt and hesitate, you will be a ghost haunting a skull. If you stop to think, you will fall into hell. Don't you see the bright sun shining in the sky and feel the cool breeze blowing across the face of the earth? Was any of the great ones of ancient times like this? See the following.

MAIN SUBJECT Hō Koji was leaving Yakusan. Yakusan let ten *zenkaku* [Zen students] escort him to the temple gate to bid him farewell. Koji pointed to the falling snowflakes and said, "Beautiful snow-flskes, one by one; but they fall nowhere else." Then one of the zenkaku, named Zen Zenkaku, said, "Then where do they fall?" Koji gave him a slap. Zen said, "Koji! You shouldn't be so abrupt." Koji said, "If you are like that and call yourself a zenkaku, Emma will never let you go." Zen said, "What about yourself?" Koji gave him another slap and said, "You look, but you are like a blind man; you speak, but you are like a deaf-mute." [Setchō adds his comment: "Why didn't you hit him with a snowball in place of your first question?"]

SETCHŌ'S VERSE
Hit him with a snowball, hit him with a ball!
Even the best will fail to reply.
Neither heaven nor earth knows what to do;
Eyes and ears are blocked with snow.
Transcendent serenity and purity!
Even the blue-eyed old monk can't explain.

NOTES *Hō Koji* (Hō was his family name, Koji a title of respect for a lay student of Zen) studied first with Sekitō and then with Baso, whom he succeeded. When he first met Sekitō, he asked, "Who is he that is independent of all things?" Before he had finished asking this, Sekitō covered Koji's mouth with his hand. At this Koji underwent an experience and expressed himself in the following verse:

> Daily, nothing particular,
> Only nodding to myself,
> Nothing to choose, nothing to discard.
>
> No coming, no going,
> No person in purple,
> Blue mountains without a speck of dust.
>
> I exercise occult and subtle power,
> Carrying water, shouldering firewood.

When he came to Baso he again said, "Who is he that is independent of all things?" Baso said, "When you have drunk all the water in the Yangtze River, I will tell you." At this, Koji underwent his great experience and composed another verse:

> The ten directions converging,
> Each learning to do nothing,
> This is the hall of Buddha's training;
> Mind's empty, all's finished.

• *He talks independently, acts independently; and he trudges through the mire for the sake of others.* Sometimes a Zen master talks and acts independently, but he is nonetheless giving everything he has, sparing no effort and going through everything for the sake of his students.

• *He talks with others, acts with others; and he stands alone, like silver mountains and iron cliffs.* A Zen master will at times talk and act amiably with others, but at the same time he is totally independent.

• *You will be a ghost haunting a skull.* If the student is irresolute he will become a wandering ghost, ever returning to the old skull.

• *If you stop to think, you will fall into hell.* When your teacher asks you a question that you cannot answer, you lower your head and try to think. That is falling into hell. The Zen student has to go through hell many times; then he will one day be free of it. That is Zen training.

• *Yakusan let ten zenkaku escort him.* Yakusan (751–834) succeeded Sekitō and was himself an outstanding Zen master. He appears also in Case 81. One day, when he was still studying with Sekitō, he was sitting in meditation, and Sekitō asked him, "What are you doing there?"

"I am doing nothing at all," answered Yakusan. "Then you are sitting idle." "If sitting is idle, then I am idly sitting." "You say you are doing nothing. What is it you are not doing?" Yakusan answered, "Even thousands of old Buddhas do not know." Sekitō expressed his approval of Yakusan in a verse:

> Living long together, and not knowing his name;
> Naturally you have worked along with him.
> But even the ancient Buddhas did not know;
> How can an ordinary soul know him?

Hō Koji stayed with Yakusan for seventeen years, although he was not a monk, and now he was leaving. Yakusan thought highly of him and let ten Zen students escort him to the gate.

· *Beautiful snowflakes, one by one; but they fall nowhere else.* Heaven and earth became one.

· *Then where do they fall?* Zen Zenkaku's question was asked from the viewpoint of an ordinary man.

· *Koji gave him a slap.* He meant, "Don't you understand my meaning?"

· *You shouldn't be so abrupt.* Again, this is what an ordinary man might say.

· *If you are like that and call yourself a zenkaku, Emma will never let you go.* If, not understanding the first thing about Zen, you still call yourself a zenkaku, Emma (Yama, the king of hell) will not let you go when you are in hell.

· *What about yourself?* What do you say, then? All through this exchange, Zen Zenkaku could not escape from a defensive position.

· *Koji gave him another slap.* This was a preliminary to the words that followed.

· *You look, but you are like a blind man; you speak, but you are like a deaf-mute.* Hō Koji was scolding Zen Zenkaku for his spiritual blindness and deafness but at the same time was answering Zen Zenkaku's question. Engo says, "He talks independently, acts independently; and he trudges through the mire for the sake of others." When you act in pure subjectivity, you are like a blind man when you look and like a deaf-mute when you speak, because you are then your looking itself and your speech itself. That is what Sekitō says in his verse, "Living long together, and not knowing his name."

• *Why didn't you hit him with a snowball . . . ?* Hitting with a snow-ball makes the whole universe as pure and clean as snow, bringing about oneness of heaven and earth. But this does not mean that Hō Koji should have been spattered with snow.

• *Hit him with a snowball, hit him with a ball!* All through this verse, Setchō sings in praise of his "Hit him with a snowball."

• *Even the best will fail to reply.* A Zen master as able as Hō Koji would have had no response to being hit with a snowball—except to laugh—because it would have been the actualization of what he meant.

• *Neither heaven nor earth knows what to do.* At this point, all things throughout heaven and earth are dumbfounded.

• *Eyes and ears are blocked with snow. | Transcendent serenity and purity!* Eyes and ears are blinded and blocked when confronted by the purity and serenity of the whole universe.

• *Even the blue-eyed old monk can't explain.* Even Bodhidharma (who is said to have been blue-eyed), not to mention all the Buddhas, cannot tell the secret.

Case 43   Tōzan's "No Cold or Heat"

ENGO'S INTRODUCTION   The words which command the universe are obeyed throughout the ages. The spirit able to quell the tiger amazes even thousands of the holy ones. His words are matchless, his spirit prevails everywhere. If you want to go through with your advanced training, you must enter the great master's forge. Tell me, who could ever show such spirit? See the following.

MAIN SUBJECT   A monk said to Tōzan, "Cold and heat descend upon us. How can we avoid them?" Tōzan said, "Why don't you go where there is no cold or heat?" The monk said, "Where is the place where there is no cold or heat?" Tōzan said, "When cold, let it be so cold that it kills you; when hot, let it be so hot that it kills you."

Setchō's Verse
A helping hand, but still a thousand-fathom cliff;
Shō and *Hen*: no arbitrary distinction here.
The ancient emerald palace shines in the bright moonlight.
Clever Kanro climbs the steps—and finds it empty.

Notes *Tōzan*. This is not Tōzan Shusho, who appeared in Case 12, but Tōzan Ryōkai (807–69), who was one of the most distinguished Zen masters and the founder of the Sōtō Sect. Tōzan visited several masters. When he was with Nansen, one of Baso's disciples, Nansen observed the anniversary of Baso's death and said to the assembly, "Will Baso come back to us?" Tōzan said, "If there is company fit for him, he will." Nansen appreciated this answer.

When Tōzan was studying with Isan, he asked Isan about Chū Kokushi's "Sermons by insentient creatures." Isan said, "Sermons by insentient creatures are given here for us, too, but few can hear them." Tōzan said, "I am not yet certain about them. Would you please teach me?" Isan said nothing, but raised his hossu straight up. Tōzan said, "I do not understand. Would you explain it to me?" Isan said, "I would never tell you about this with the mouth given to me by my parents." This was his way of teaching.

He suggested that Tōzan visit Ungan (whom Tōzan later succeeded). Coming to Ungan, Tōzan asked, "Who can hear the sermons of insentient creatures?" "Insentient creatures can hear them," answered Ungan. "Why can I not hear them?" Ungan raised his hossu straight up and said, "Do you hear?" "No, I don't." Ungan said, "Don't you know the sutra says, 'Birds and trees, all meditate on the Buddha and Dharma'?" At this, Tōzan suddenly became enlightened. He wrote the following verse:

Wonderful! How wonderful!
Sermons by insentient creatures;
You fail if you listen with your ears;
Listening with your eyes, you hear them.

Tōzan continued practicing zazen carefully, with close attention. This close attention characterized his Zen and his school, and made him a great master. He was ever watchful, and one day, while he was wading a stream, he saw his shadow cast on the water and experienced his great enlightenment. His verse on that occasion was:

> Long seeking it through others,
> I was far from reaching it.
> Now I go by myself;
> I meet it everywhere.
> It is just I myself,
> And I am not itself.
> Understanding this way,
> I can be as I am.

• *The words which command the universe are obeyed throughout the ages.* Such powerful words as those of Tōzan in the present case come to be the unquestioned authority for all the ages to come.

• *The spirit able to quell the tiger.* The spirit so full of strength that it can overcome the tiger among men astonishes even the holy ones (Buddhas).

• *The great master's forge.* As iron is shaped in the forge, so monks are molded by their teacher's instruction. This metaphor is common in Zen literature.

• *Cold and heat descend upon us.* Death and disease stare us in the face. How can we hope to escape from them?

• *Why don't you go where there is no cold or heat?* Where is the place that is without cold or heat? We all madly, pointlessly seek it, to no avail.

• *When cold, let it be so cold that it kills you.* Freedom of mind comes when we free ourselves of what was burdening our minds. If you bravely face even the most appalling prospect with all your strength and resolution, that is positive samadhi, and what had frightened you will become enjoyable.

• *A helping hand, but still a thousand-fathom cliff.* In saying, "Go where there is no cold or heat," Tōzan was lending his pupil a hand to pull him up into a safe place. But for the monk it was still like being faced with a thousand-fathom cliff.

• *Shō and Hen: no arbitrary distinction here.* This is a reference to Tōzan's five ranks, which are a philosophical treatment of the relation between the real (Shō) and the apparent (Hen). I have discussed the five ranks at some length elsewhere (see *Zen Training*, chapter 17, and the notes to Case 61 and to *Mumonkan*, Case 13). In fact, Tōzan's words,

"When cold, let it be so cold that it kills you," resolve the question very simply and directly, and render it unnecessary to enter into a complicated philosophical discussion. And when you understand this, you will find, as Setchō says, that Shō and Hen are not a matter of mere philosophizing.

• *The ancient emerald palace shines in the bright moonlight.* The ancient emerald palace is the place where there is no cold or heat. It represents the realm of samadhi. In samadhi, your subjectivity and objectivity are unified. In other words, when it is cold, you do not evade it but become one with it. When it is hot, you immerse yourself in the heat and become one with it. In samadhi you are doing this all the time. Now the emerald palace appears before you, lit by the bright moon.

• *Clever Kanro climbs the steps—and finds it empty.* A legend tells of a clever, fast-running dog, Kanro, that chased a hare. Both ran so fast that eventually they fell dead of exhaustion. The monk who asked the question in the present case is being compared to Kanro. He pursued the problem of life and death, entered the emerald palace, and found it empty. But what is empty?

Case 44   Kasan's "Beating the Drum"

MAIN SUBJECT   Kasan said, "Learning by study is called 'hearing'; learning no more is called 'nearness'; transcending these two is 'true passing.' " A monk asked, "What is 'true passing'?" Kasan said, "Beating the drum." The monk asked again, "What is the true teaching of the Buddha?" Kasan said, "Beating the drum." The monk asked once more, "I would not ask you about 'This very mind is the Buddha,' but what is 'No mind, no Buddha'?" Kasan said, "Beating the drum." The monk still continued to ask: "When an enlightened one comes, how do you treat him?" Kasan said, "Beating the drum."

SETCHŌ'S VERSE
Dragging a stone, carrying earth,
Use the spiritual power of a thousand-ton bow.

Zōkotsu Rōshi rolled out three wooden balls;
How could they surpass Kasan's "Beating the drum"?
I will tell you, what is sweet is sweet,
What is bitter, bitter.

NOTES   *Kasan* (891–960) entered Seppō's monastery when he was seven years old. Seppō was then seventy-six. At the age of twenty, after Seppō's death, Kasan went to Kyūho, whom he eventually succeeded. Kyūho himself succeeded Sekisō and is famous for an episode in which his pressing Sekisō's head monk for an answer ended in the latter's death. This happened as follows. When Sekisō died, everyone except Kyūho expected that the head monk would succeed him. Kyūho said, "Our late teacher said, 'You should be completely finished up, emptied away; one nen, one eon; you should be like cold ashes and the dead tree, like the incense burner on the deserted shrine, like the frozen lake, like a piece of glazed silk.' Tell me, what does this mean?" The head monk said, "It means the realm of one color" (that is, great enlightenment). Kyūho said, "You do not understand our teacher's meaning." The head monk ordered someone to fetch a packet of incense and said, "If I cannot pass away while this incense is burning, your words will be proved true." He threw the incense into the burner. A cloud of white smoke rose, and while it still hung in the air, the monk passed away, sitting up straight. Kyūho, stroking the dead monk's back, said, "You could pass away sitting up straight, but you could never dream of our late teacher's meaning."

• *Learning by study is called "hearing."* Even after experiencing enlightenment, you are still learning, that is, "hearing."

• *Learning no more.* Logically, the state of learning no more can be imagined, but who can really say that he has reached a condition where there is nothing more to learn?

• *True passing.* This is attainment to Buddhahood. Everyone is endowed with Buddha Nature. But its fulfillment is a matter of unceasing practice.

• *Beating the drum.* The original text says *getaku* (*ge*, understand; *ta*, beat; *ku*, drum). When you are beating a drum in positive samadhi, you are truly beating the drum: you are exercising Buddha Nature, and that is not too difficult to do. The difficulty lies in keeping it up moment after moment through life. That condition of mind is called *shōnen sōzoku* (*shō*, genuine; *nen*, nen-thought; *sō*, in succession; *zoku*, continue: maintaining genuine nen-thoughts in continuous succession).

• *This very mind is the Buddha . . . No mind, no Buddha.* Both mean one and the same thing, provided you are directly working in it and not understanding it conceptually. "I allow the barbarian's realization, but I do not allow his understanding" (*Mumonkan*, Case 9).

• *Dragging a stone, carrying earth.* This is an allusion to certain Zen stories. It is enough for us to imagine that we are dragging a stone with ropes and carrying earth in straw baskets over our shoulders.

• *Use the spiritual power of a thousand-ton bow.* When working, work in positive samadhi. Its spiritual power is immense.

• *Zōkotsu Rōshi rolled out three wooden balls.* Zōkotsu Rōshi is a surname of Seppō, Zōkotsu being the name of a peak on Mount Seppō. One day, Seppō rolled out three wooden balls before his students. What was the meaning of this? Movement! Dragging a stone, carrying earth, and Kasan's beating the drum are all movements. Setchō presents these examples of Zen movement (positive samadhi) to bring out Kasan's meaning.

• *How could they surpass Kasan's "Beating the drum"?* Kasan, Seppō, and others are all excellent. None surpasses the others. Setchō exaggerates to draw attention to the "Beating the drum" of the present case.

• *What is sweet is sweet, / What is bitter, bitter.* Positive samadhi is that intuitive state of activity in which we simply call what is sweet, sweet, and what is bitter, bitter. If one can existentially realize one's movements, one will be able to understand Kasan's "Beating the drum." What does "existentially" mean? Simply that one does not lose one's sense, the intuitive action of the first nen. In other words, one is not spoiled by conceptual thinking. Beating a drum or striking a match and lighting a candle: if it is done in true positive samadhi, in that moment one is demonstrating one's existence.

Case 45   Jōshū's Seven-Pound Hempen Shirt

ENGO'S INTRODUCTION   If he wants to speak, he speaks, and none can rival him throughout the whole universe. When he wants to act, he acts, and his activity is peerless. The one is like shooting stars and flashing lightning, the other like crackling flames and flashing blades. When he sets up his forge to discipline his disciples, they lay down their arms and lose their tongues. I will give an example. See the following.

MAIN SUBJECT   A monk asked Jōshū, "All the Dharmas are reduced to oneness, but what is oneness reduced to?" Jōshū said, "When I was in Seishū I made a hempen shirt. It weighed seven pounds."

SETCHŌ'S VERSE
> You brought a piece of logic
> To trap the old gimlet,
> But do you know the meaning
> Of the seven-pound hempen shirt?
>
> Now I have thrown it away
> Into Lake Seiko
> And sail before the wind.
> Who will share the coolness with me?

NOTES   *If he wants to speak, he speaks, and none can rival him.* A master like Jōshū speaks with total freedom. His words are so superbly original that all are amazed.

• *Like shooting stars and flashing lightning.* His words are dazzling and illuminate things like a flash of lightning in the dark night.

• *Like crackling flames and flashing blades.* His actions are quick, full of energy, and unceasing.

• *They lay down their arms and lose their tongues.* His disciples pay their respects to him and follow his teaching obediently.

• *All the Dharmas are reduced to oneness.* The Dharmas include all the sentient and insentient beings of the universe. This saying is a reference to a passage in the *Gandavyuha Sutra* which says, "All things of the three realms are reduced to one mind."

• *What is oneness reduced to?* The *Gandavyuha Sutra* stops at one mind, but this monk wanted to go further and tried to get Jōshū to answer his impossible question. There is, of course, no possible philosophical answer to the question, and the monk knew this quite well. He was hoping to trap Jōshū into saying something like "emptiness" or "nothingness." Jōshū, however, could not be caught out in this way.

• *When I was in Seishū I made a hempen shirt. It weighed seven pounds.* This resembles another of Jōshū's answers, "Chinshū produces a big radish" (Case 30), and also Tōzan's "Masagin" (*Mumonkan*, Case 18). Seishū seems to have been famous for fine hemp. Jōshū's words remind us of the keen sensibilities of people who lived in the days when things were made by hand. They enjoyed a close, fond relationship to the materials of their clothes and the processes by which they were made. The seven pounds of hemp had first to be prepared, and in the course of its being gathered, washed, and spun, it was constantly being touched, felt, and handled. Then it was woven into cloth and cut and sewn into a shirt, all by the exercise of skillful craftsmanship. And at the end, when Jōshū put on his hempen shirt, he experienced a keen sensation, which was a direct recognition of the shirt for what it was. With Jōshū, touching and feeling were pure cognition of the object.

Philosophically speaking, reality, oneness, being, existence, and so on constitute the most difficult problems, but when one recognizes one's own sensations (the action of the first nen), matters become very simple, because sensation gives one pure cognition of the object: there reality is. It is not that the Dharmas are reduced to oneness but that the Dharmas are oneness and are this seven pounds of hemp. There is no coming and going, no need to ask questions like "What is oneness reduced to?"

• *You brought a piece of logic.* For "a piece of logic" the original text says *henpeki-mon* (*hen*, braiding; *peki*, pressing or approaching; *mon*, question), hence, "a question approaching step by step." This is one of the eighteen kinds of questions of the Zen mondō, or dialogue.

• *To trap the old gimlet.* "Old gimlet" is a Zen term that means a mature, preeminent master. The idea comes from the saying, "A nail in a bag cannot help sticking out."

• *Do you know the meaning / Of the seven-pound hempen shirt?* Can you truly cognize the shirt, as Jōshū can?

• *Now I have thrown it away.* Setchō says that though it is to be greatly valued, he has no need now of such a thing as Jōshū's hempen shirt, so he has thrown it away. In Zen practice everything must be cast away, even enlightenment.

• *Into Lake Seiko.* Lake Seiko was famous for its fine scenery. Setchō's temple was situated nearby.

• *And sail before the wind. | Who will share the coolness with me?* The unloaded boat sails along the lake before the wind. Buddhism, oneness, Zen, realization, Nirvana, emptiness—all have been thrown away. With whom shall I share this peaceful coolness of my mind?

Case 46 Kyōsei's "Voice of the Raindrops"

ENGO'S INTRODUCTION   In a single action he transcends both the ordinary and the holy. With a single word he cuts away all complications and encumbrances. He walks the ridge of an iceberg, he treads the edge of a sword. Seated amid the totality of form and sound, he rises above them. Leaving aside the freedom of such subtle activity, tell me, what about finishing it in a moment? See the following.

MAIN SUBJECT   Kyōsei asked a monk, "What is the noise outside?" The monk said, "That is the voice of the raindrops." Kyōsei said, "Men's thinking is topsy-turvy. Deluded by their own selves, they pursue things." The monk asked, "What about yourself?" Kyōsei said, "I was near it but am not deluded." The monk asked, "What do you mean by 'near it but not deluded'?" Kyōsei said, "To say it in the sphere of realization may be easy, but to say it in the sphere of transcendence is difficult."

SETCHŌ'S VERSE
  The empty hall resounds with the voice of the raindrops.
  Even a master fails to answer.

If you say you have turned the current,
You have no true understanding.
Understanding? No understanding?
Misty with rain, the northern and southern mountains.

NOTES Kyōsei (868–937) also appears in Cases 16 and 23. The following examples illustrate his way of teaching. A monk asked Kyōsei, "Why don't you do something to make me enlightened quickly?" Kyōsei said, "If I did that I should deprive you of your own property." Another monk asked Kyōsei, "What is the meaning of the saying, 'Man, being innocent, accords with the Way'?" Kyōsei said, "Why don't you ask me about 'The Way, being innocent, accords with man'?" The monk did as he was told. Kyōsei said, "Although the white clouds reach the green peak, the bright moon does not leave the blue sky."

• In a single action he transcends both the ordinary and the holy. This means the same as "When he wants to act, he acts, and his activity is peerless"(Case 45).

• With a single word he cuts away all complications and encumbrances. Again, this resembles "If he wants to speak, he speaks, and none can rival him" (Case 45).

• He walks the ridge of an iceberg, he treads the edge of a sword. The same sentence occurs in the introduction to Case 41.

• Seated amid the totality of form and sound, he rises above them. Form and sound represent the objective world; the subjective counterparts are the activities of hearing, seeing, touching, tasting, smelling, and thinking. This sentence means that in the busiest circumstances, he keeps himself above them and does not lose his shōnen sōzoku (see the notes to Case 44).

• Leaving aside the freedom of such subtle activity. Putting to one side such subtle activities as those just mentioned.

• What about finishing it in a moment? We live moment by moment. In other words, we live in this present moment. As a matter of fact, we think of the future and remember the past, but the thinking and the remembering are this moment's thinking and remembering. The words of the original text are setsuna ben kyo ji ikan (setsuna, a moment; ben, immediately; kyo, leave; ji, when; ikan, what about: hence, what about when one immediately leaves in a moment?). The strict meaning might be taken as "What about when one abandons the delusive way of thought and achieves enlightenment?" However, Engo is here referring to a more advanced condition than merely experiencing realization.

• *What is the noise outside?* This is the teacher's leading question. It is the mother hen tapping at the eggshell (Case 16).

• *That is the voice of the raindrops.* The chick is pecking from inside. Zen has two aspects, the absolute and the positive. The absolute side is that of absolute samadhi, where there are no objects—no mountain, no river, no man, no woman, no plant, no animal, no rain, no raindrops. The positive side is that of positive samadhi, where all these things exist. Whatever answer you may make is all right if you truly realize it. Shuzan Oshō once held up a shippei (a bamboo baton) before his disciples and said, "If you call it a shippei, you oppose its reality. If you do not call it a shippei, you ignore the fact. Tell me, you monks, what will you call it?" (*Mumonkan*, Case 43).

• *Men's thinking is topsy-turvy.* People in general are led astray by their egocentric thinking.

• *Deluded by their own selves, they pursue things.* Our ordinary consciousness has acquired an egocentric way of thinking. It is always looking for what is most profitable for "me." The result is a distorted view of life and the world, which has led to endless disasters: deceiving, fighting, killing, wars, and so on. But still men go on pursuing the nonexistent profit, with calamitous results. You may ask what relation the raindrops have to man's appalling condition. The answer is that they have a close relationship, because this case is dealing with the fundamental question of cognition, and hence with the essential nature of our underlying mental attitude.

• *What about yourself?* The monk's question was inevitable, and Kyōsei had intended to elicit it.

• *I was near it but am not deluded.* Kyōsei had first asked, "What is the noise outside?" He asked as any ordinary person might have done. The difference is this. A baby may be unaware of danger even if it crawls near the edge of a cliff. Kyōsei was as close to danger as anyone else when he asked the question, but he did it with full knowledge. He was not deluded.

• *To say it in the sphere of realization may be easy, but to say it in the sphere* of transcendence is difficult. To say it in the dimension of absolute samadhi is rather easy, but to say it in positive samadhi—that is, having transcended the busiest activity of consciousness in ordinary life—is difficult. Kyōsei is stressing the importance of transcending actual daily life while being busily engrossed in it. This is what Engo means by his sentence, "Seated amid the totality of form and sound, he rises above them."

• The empty hall resounds with the voice of the raindrops. Keeping these explanations in mind, recite this line in your language samadhi. At first you may get nothing out of it, but if you do it persistently you will someday come across the true meaning.

• Even a master fails to answer. At first sight Kyōsei seems to have failed to answer, but in fact he answered splendidly, as we explained above. It is you who failed to catch the true meaning of Kyōsei's answer.

• If you say you have turned the current. "Turn the current" comes from a passage in the Surangama Sutra: "The Buddha instructed me to enter samadhi starting from hearing. . . . First in hearing I turned the current [the flow of consciousness] until I forgot the object, and then, both the current and the object being silent, both subjectivity and objectivity dropped away."

The word which, in accordance with usual practice, we have translated as "turn" is, in the original, nyū, which means "enter." The reason "enter" can be translated as "turn" in this passage is as follows. Ordinarily, when you hear something, your reflecting action of consciousness accompanies your hearing and makes you aware of it. However, in samadhi you become the hearing itself. No reflecting action of consciousness occurs to make you aware of your hearing, and neither your subjectivity nor your objectivity is noticed. In other words, you have redirected, or "turned," the stream of your mental activity. Another way to put this is to say that you have "entered" the stream of the first nen and become the first nen's hearing alone.

In brief, the line means: If you have entered absolute samadhi and forgotten all about subjectivity and objectivity.

• You have no true understanding. Unless you can emerge from absolute samadhi and return to positive samadhi, in which your subjectivity and objectivity are recognized and you enjoy freedom of mind in ordinary life, your understanding of Zen is imperfect.

• Understanding? No understanding? | Misty with rain, the northern and *southern mountains.* Whether one fully understands it or not is a very subtle (misty) matter. You should first shut out the sound of the raindrops in absolute samadhi, and then, returning to positive samadhi, enjoy the sound of them as it is. Reality is things as they are.

Case 47 Ummon's "Beyond the Six"

ENGO'S INTRODUCTION Heaven never speaks, yet the four seasons follow their courses. Earth does not talk, but all things prosper. Where the four seasons follow their courses, you can see the substance. Where all things prosper, you can find the use. Now tell me, where do you see the monk? Stop your speech, your actions, your daily routine, and, closing your throat and lips, say it.

MAIN SUBJECT A monk asked Ummon, "What is the Dharmakaya?" Ummon said, "Beyond the six."

SETCHŌ'S VERSE
One, two, three, four, five, six . . .
Even the blue-eyed Indian monk cannot count it.

Rashly they say Shōrin passed it on to Shinkō,
Or he, clad in the robe, journeyed back to India.

India is vast and far; he is not to be found.
Lo! Since last night he has been here facing Nyūhō!

NOTES *You can see the substance . . . you can find the use.* The substance and the use represent the two sides of reality, the absolute and the relative (or positive).

• *Where do you see the monk?* This monk represents Ummon or a similar great master.

• *Stop your speech, your actions, your daily routine, and, closing your throat and lips, say it.* If you want to see the Dharmakaya, the pure body of the Buddha, you must first get into absolute samadhi.

• *Ummon said, "Beyond the six."* The literal translation of "beyond the six" would be "six not-containable." Six, seven, or a hundred—any number will do. And within or beyond, containable or not containable, makes little difference.

A superficial explanation of Ummon's statement would be that the Dharmakaya is so great that the six elements (earth, water, fire, wind, space, and consciousness) cannot contain it. But we want to contain the Dharmakaya within ourselves, so the six must be the six senses (seeing, hearing, tasting, smelling, touching, and consciousness). However, all such explanations miss the point.

Ummon's "Beyond the six," like his "Kayakuran" (Case 39) and "Kanshiketsu" (*Mumonkan*, Case 21), and like Tōzan's "Masagin" (Case 12; *Mumonkan*, Case 18), seems highly obscure. But this obscurity arises because we are in the habit of working with sharply defined concepts arrived at by the operation of our intellect. If only we return to direct intuitive understanding, such seeming obscurity, along with all pointless elaborations, will vanish like mist.

• *One, two, three, four, five, six . . . / Even the blue-eyed Indian monk cannot count it.* One, two, three, and countless things are all expressing the Buddha's true body. (All sentient creatures and insentient objects deliver their sermons.) And even Bodhidharma, "the blue-eyed Indian monk," cannot count them.

• *Rashly they say Shōrin passed it on to Shinkō.* Shōrin was the name of the temple where Bodhidharma lived, and it became his surname. Shinkō was another name of Eka, the Second Patriarch (see Case 96). People say that Bodhidharma handed the Dharma Seal on to Shinkō. But the Dharmakaya, which the Dharma Seal represents, can be attained only in one's own realization.

• *Or he, clad in the robe, journeyed back to India.* There is a legend that after Bodhidharma died and had been buried on Yūji Mountain, he came to life again and returned to India. An official on his way back from India, where he had been sent on business, met Bodhidharma in the mountains, returning to India carrying a single sandal in his hand. Following the official's report, the authorities opened Bodhidharma's tomb and found he was gone, leaving one sandal behind. Here Bodhidharma is to be taken as representing the Dharmakaya.

• *India is vast and far; he is not to be found.* There is no need to search for him far and wide; he is very close at hand.

• *Lo! Since last night he has been here facing Nyūhō!* Since last night he has been sitting in meditation, facing the mountain. Setchō's temple was on Mount Nyūhō (another name for Mount Setchō).

Case 48 Ō Taifu and the Tea Ceremony

MAIN SUBJECT Ō Taifu went to Shōkei Temple for the tea ceremony. Rō Jōza, lifting the kettle to bring it to Myōshō, happened to overturn it. Ō Taifu said, "What is under the kettle?" Rō said, "The god of the hearth." Taifu said, "If it is the god of the hearth, why has it upset the kettle?" Rō said, "A thousand days of government service, and one accident!" Taifu swung his sleeves and left the room. Myōshō said, "Rō Jōza, you have long had food from Shōkei Temple, and still you wander about the countryside, working with a stump." Rō said, "What about you?" Myō said, "That is where the devil gets the better of you." [Setchō says, "Why didn't you, at that moment, trample on the hearth?"]

SETCHŌ'S VERSE
  Cleaving the air, the question came;
  The answer missed the point.
  Alas! The one-eyed dragon monk
  Did not show his fangs and claws.

  Now fangs and claws are unsheathed,
  Lightning flashes, stormy clouds!
  Surging billows rage around,
  Falling back against the tide.

NOTES *Ō Taifu, Rō Jōza, Myōshō.* Ō Taifu was governor of the district of Senshū. He installed Chōkei as abbot of Shōkei Temple, and patronized him and the temple. Myōshō was vice-abbot of the temple, and Rō Jōza was a senior monk. All the personages in this case were descended in Dharma lineage from Tokusan. The episode related took place in the temple, perhaps at a time when Chōkei was absent.

• *Ō Taifu went to Shōkei Temple for the tea ceremony.* Myōshō held the tea ceremony in honor of Ō Taifu. Acting as host, he told Rō Jōza to fetch the teakettle. As was the Chinese custom, they would have been sitting on chairs or stools, and perhaps the kettle had to be fetched from the hearth in the corner of the room and placed on the table.

• *Rō Jōza, lifting the kettle to bring it to Myōshō, happened to overturn it.* In the Japanese tea ceremony, which is that best known in the West, the host's first consideration is the comfort of the guest. The guest, in turn, is supposed to attend closely to his host, so that together they produce a harmonious atmosphere. Their concentration is such that even the slightest mishap is rare. If, by any chance, a minor accident happens, it is dealt with quietly and may even enhance the composed spirit in which the ceremony is conducted. Everything is done with seeming nonchalance, but in reality with collected serenity. The Chinese tea ceremony was performed in the same spirit, though with many differences in detail. In this context, Rō Jōza upset the kettle.

• *What is under the kettle?* According to ancient folklore, there were gods or spirits in many parts of the house—in the kitchen, the hearth, the fireplace, the bathroom, the lavatory, the central pillar of the house, the well, and even the corners of the garden. These gods, especially those concerned with the more important domestic affairs, were greatly revered, and the housewife presented offerings to them. There was wisdom in these ancient beliefs, for they led to things being done carefully in the household. In Ō Taifu's question, "under" has special significance. "Watch out under your feet" is a Zen saying reminding one to maintain a firm footing of mind and body lest one be led into error. Ō Taifu's question meant "Is your footing secure?" It made a good opening to a Zen mondō, which Setchō appreciates ("Cleaving the air, the question came").

• *The god of the hearth.* This was a natural but ordinary response to Ō Taifu's question. In Zen terms it was a poor answer because it simply followed the lead already given.

• *If it is the god of the hearth, why has it upset the kettle?* This is empty theorizing. The mondō started brightly enough, but the ending is dull.

• *A thousand days of government service, and one accident!* Rō Jōza is excusing himself by saying, "Even Homer nods." However, this is far removed from the proper spirit of a Zen mondō.

• *Taifu swung his sleeves and left the room.* This gesture expressed displeasure.

• *You have long had food from Shōkei Temple.* You have lived in Shōkei Temple for a long time and studied under an outstanding master, Chō-kei.

• *Still you wander about the countryside, working with a stump.* This is a common phrase used to condemn a person who wanders about dabbling in worthless affairs.

• *What about you?* What is the use of asking someone else's opinion? Why don't you make your own original answer?

• *That is where the devil gets the better of you.* Your lack of originality and your insecure footing have given the devil a chance to take advantage of you and cause you to blunder.

• *Why didn't you, at that moment, trample on the hearth?* Setchō is saying, "If I were you, I would have trampled on the hearth." But that does not mean scattering ashes all over the room. When Emperor Shukusō asked Chū Kokushi, "What is the ten-bodied herdsman?" Chū Kokushi said, "Go trampling on Vairocana's head" (Case 99). One may sit quietly performing the tea ceremony while one's mind goes trampling on the head of the Buddha.

• *Alas! The one-eyed dragon monk.* "One-eyed dragon" is a standard phrase applied to a one-eyed person, the word "dragon" sometimes implying possession of heroic qualities. Myōshō was one-eyed, and a sort of dragon among the monks.

• *Did not show his fangs and claws.* Fangs and claws symbolize a dragon's power to evoke a storm, accompanied by thunder and lightning, in which he ascends to the heavens. But alas, Setchō says, Myōshō failed to display his dragonlike qualities. However, Myōshō's "That is where the devil gets the better of you" is admirable.

• *Now fangs and claws are unsheathed . . .* The last four lines of Setchō's verse are in praise of his own words, "trample on the hearth."

Case 49 Sanshō's "The Golden Carp out of the Net"

ENGO'S INTRODUCTION Seven piercing and eight breaking through, seizing the drums and capturing the banners, a hundred barriers and a thousand checkpoints, watching the front and guarding the rear, holding the tiger's head and securing its tail—even all these are not comparable to the veteran master's ability. The ox-head disappearing, the horse-head appears—that also is not a great wonder. Tell me, what do you do when a man of transcendent experience comes? See the following.

MAIN SUBJECT Sanshō said to Seppō, "The golden carp is out of the net! Tell me, what will it feed on?" Seppō said, "When you have got out of the net, I will tell you." Sanshō said, "The renowned teacher of fifteen hundred monks cannot find even one word to say about this topic." Seppō said, "I am the chief abbot and have much to attend to."

SETCHŌ'S VERSE
The golden carp comes out of the net!
Don't say it remains in the water still.
It shakes the heavens and moves the earth,
Swinging its fins, lashing its tail.
It blows like a whale, raising great waves;
Then the thunder sounds, and a cool breeze comes;
A cool breeze—yes! a cool breeze comes.
Who in the whole universe knows this?

NOTES Sanshō was so called after the name of his temple. The dates of his birth and death are not known. He succeeded Rinzai and was the compiler of Rinzairoku. He was an outstanding Zen master. After finishing his studies under Rinzai he traveled to various places visiting Zen masters and trained himself assiduously in the cultivation of Holy Buddhahood after realization. We have another story of him in Case 68. It is recorded that when he visited Kyōgen (see *Mumonkan*, Case 5), Kyōgen asked him, "Where are you from?" Sanshō said, "From Rinzai." "Have you brought Rinzai's sword with you?" Before Kyōgen had finished speaking, Sanshō dashed forward, picked up a cushion, and struck Kyōgen with it. Kyōgen said nothing but only smiled.

• *Seven piercing and eight breaking through.* In a Dharma battle the protagonists try to pierce and break through each other's defenses. In an interview with a teacher the disciple's weak points, as well as those he prides himself upon as his strong ones, are picked on and relentlessly criticized.

• *Seizing the drums and capturing the banners.* The teacher deprives his disciples of their views and understanding.

• *A hundred barriers and a thousand checkpoints.* The teacher examines his students from every aspect.

• *Holding the tiger's head and securing its tail.* Even a tiger among the monks is seized by its head and brought under control.

• *Even all these are not comparable to the veteran master's ability.* Even though possessing the wonderful abilities mentioned, one still cannot be called a man of transcendent experience, such as appears in the present case.

• *The ox-head disappearing, the horse-head appears.* As we have already explained in the notes to Case 5, the appearance and disappearance of the ox-head and the horse-head represent the momentary comings and goings of nen-thoughts. In the present context they denote the quick mental activity of a mature Zen master.

• *A man of transcendent experience.* This refers to the masters who appear in the present case, Sanshō and Seppō.

• *The golden carp is out of the net!* We have already met, in Setchō's verse to Case 7, the saying, "Ascending the falls, the carp became a dragon." The net is not a fisherman's net but the mental restrictions that bind the mind of man. A monk who has broken free from these and achieved a great enlightenment is the golden carp that has ascended the falls and become a dragon. Sanshō is declaring himself to be such a person.

• *What will it feed on?* Sanshō is saying that he is satiated with enlightenment, samadhi, and everything else. What treatment is Seppō going to give him now?

• *When you have got out of the net, I will tell you.* Although you claim to have got out of the net, I find you to be still in it. Come back to me after you have got free from being "satiated." Bashō Oshō once said, "If you have a staff, I will give you a staff. If you have no staff, I will take it from you" (*Mumonkan*, Case 44).

• *The renowned teacher of fifteen hundred monks cannot find even one word to say about this topic.* Sanshō was not saying this recklessly. He was sure of his footing and could withstand Seppō's rebuff. He took the offensive.

• *I am the chief abbot and have much to attend to.* I am too busy to pay attention to your false accusation.

• *The golden carp comes out of the net!* As usual, Setchō puts the important point in the first line of his verse.

• *Don't say it remains in the water still.* This refers to Seppō's words, "When you have got out of the net, I will tell you."

• *It shakes the heavens and moves the earth.* Now it causes a storm, filling the stage of heaven and earth.

• *Swinging its fins, lashing its tail.* A tremendous operation!

• *It blows like a whale, raising great waves.* This refers to Sanshō's cry, "The renowned teacher of fifteen hundred monks cannot find even one word to say about this topic."

• *Then the thunder sounds.* This refers to Seppō's "I am the chief abbot and have much to attend to." His words were quiet but came like a thunderclap.

• *A cool breeze comes.* A clap of thunder, and the storm is gone. See the breeze stirring the leaves of the trees.

• *Who in the whole universe knows this?* Enjoy this cool breeze to your heart's content.

Case 50   Ummon's "Particle After Particle's Samadhi"

ENGO'S INTRODUCTION Transcending all ranks, rising above all expedients; spirit corresponding to spirit, words answering words— unless he has undergone the great emancipation and attained the great use of it, how could he rank with the Buddhas and be a faultless exponent of the teachings? Now, tell me, who can be so direct and adaptable to all occasions, and have the free command of transcendent words? See the following.

MAIN SUBJECT   A monk asked Ummon, "What is particle after particle's samadhi?" Ummon said, "Rice in the bowl, water in the pail."

SETCHŌ'S VERSE
Rice in the bowl, water in the pail!
Even the most talkative can add nothing.

The North and the South stars do not change places,
Heaven-touching waves arise on land.

If you doubt, if you hesitate,
Though heir to millions—trouserless!

NOTES   *Transcending all ranks.* Buddhist theory recognizes fifty-two ranks through which one is supposed to pass, one by one, before reaching the rank of Buddha. But Zen enjoins sudden enlightenment, which brings one with a single bound to the rank of Buddha. The ranks are transcended.
• *Rising above all expedients.* Men find it very difficult to attain to Buddhahood, so various expedients have been invented to give them temporary footholds. But zazen passes beyond these expedients by leading to the attainment of sudden enlightenment.
• *Spirit corresponding to spirit, words answering words.* The direct communication of truth from mind to mind is the principle of Zen practice.
• *The great emancipation.* The man who is emancipated from his own passions and desires attains command of his own mind. Hakuin Zenji says, "Young men, if you do not want to die, die now; if you die once, you will never die again." In other words, if you want to live, die now and you will live forever. And you will enjoy true freedom of mind. That is the great emancipation.
• *Attained the great use of it.* If you once attain true emancipation, you

achieve the free command of your mind, and you can go out into the world and act like a Buddha.

• *Transcendent words.* Ummon's words in the present case.

• *Particle after particle's samadhi.* This means the samadhi of each and every entity. When an ox-head appears, it is the ox-head's samadhi; when a horse-head appears, it is the horse-head's samadhi; when Tom, Tom's; when Susan, Susan's; a dog, a dog's; a rose, a rose's; a stone, a stone's. In short, all sentient and insentient beings deliver their sermons. The phrase also means moment after moment's samadhi, that is, the samadhi of the ever renewed present. Just look at the watch on the table. Stare at it with all the power of your breathless concentration, and you will experience the samadhi of present moment after present moment.

• *Rice in the bowl, water in the pail.* Look at the rice in your bowl, gaze at the water in the pail. If you do this in samadhi, you will find that the rice becomes illuminating and the water starts breathing. Just now, look at the table in front of you: watch it, gaze at it. This is not self-hypnosis but the exercise of positive samadhi. Presently you will enter into unity with the table. Likewise, how easy it is to enter into unity with the rice in the bowl!

• *The North and the South stars do not change places.* Both the North Star and the South Star are fixed and immobile. It is just the same with your samadhi, in which you lord it over the universe, just as the North Star exercises its silent command over the night sky.

• *Heaven-touching waves arise on land.* In your positive samadhi the sublime serenity of mind reigns everywhere, while your consciousness may be working violently, like angry waves. It is said, "The white clouds do not move; the green mountains are ever shifting." Ummon's words are as powerful as the heaven-touching waves, the more so in that they arise on land.

• *If you doubt, if you hesitate.* You are Buddha from the beginning, but unless you once attain to realization you will have no confidence in yourself.

• *Though heir to millions—trouserless!* This refers to a parable in the *Saddharma Pundarika Sutra,* or *Lotus Sutra,* that tells of a millionaire's son who ran away from home. He was reduced to such poverty that he had no trousers. By the time he was found by his father and taken home, he had lost his memory. His father tried every means to restore his memory and eventually succeeded in getting the son to recognize himself as the heir to a millionaire. The meaning of this parable is, of course, that we have Buddha Nature from the outset, but because of our deluded thinking we have lost sight of it. The Buddha's teaching restores to man's mind its own true nature.

Case 51 Seppō's "What Is This?"

ENGO'S INTRODUCTION If you have the slightest choice of right and wrong, you will fall into confusion of mind. If you are not caught up in the ranks, there will be no groping in the dark. Tell me, which is advisable, letting go or holding fast? At this point, if you deal in terms of concepts and remain attached to sophisticated thinking, you are a ghost clinging to weeds and bushes. Even if you become innocent of such vulgarity, you are still thousands of miles from your homeland. Do you understand? If not, just study the present koan. See the following.

MAIN SUBJECT When Seppō was living in his hermitage, two monks came to pay their respects. As Seppō saw them coming he pushed open the gate and, presenting himself before them, said, "What is this?" The monks also said, "What is this?" Seppō lowered his head and returned to his cottage.

Later the monks came to Gantō, who said, "Where are you from?" The monks answered, "We have come from south of the Nanrei Mountains." Gantō said, "Have you ever been to see Seppō?" The monks said, "Yes, we have been to him." Gantō said, "What did he say to you?" The monks related the whole story. Gantō said, "Alas! I regret that I did not tell him the last word when I was with him. If I had done so, no one in the whole world could have pretended to outdo him."

At the end of the summer session the monks repeated the story and asked Gantō for his instruction. Gantō said, "Why didn't you ask earlier?" The monks said, "We have had a hard time struggling with this topic." Gantō said, "Seppō came to life in the same way that I did, but he does not die in the same way that I do. If you want to know the last word, I'll tell you, simply—This! This!"

SETCHŌ'S VERSE
The last word, let me tell you—
Light and darkness intermingled,
Living in the same way, you all know;
Dying in different ways—beyond telling!
Absolutely beyond telling!
Buddha and Dharma only nod to themselves.
East, west, north, and south—homeward let us go,
Late at night, seeing the snow on the thousand peaks.

NOTES   *Seppō, Gantō.* See *Mumonkan,* Case 13.
• *If you have the slightest choice of right and wrong.* Paradoxically, with true freedom of mind one has no choice. The mind that is free is decided from the beginning. Imagine you are an official and are offered a bribe. If your mind is made up from the beginning, there is no possibility of doing anything but refuse, and you enjoy freedom of mind. Political freedom is restricted by laws and regulations, social freedom by social organization, and in these contexts there are necessarily choice and decision. Freedom of mind is different. If you feel a possibility of choosing, your mind is divided and disturbed, and that is not freedom.
• *You will fall into confusion of mind.* Confusion arises in your own mind, not externally. Everything depends on whether you are free from delusive thoughts.
• *If you are not caught up in the ranks.* The ranks are discussed in the notes to Case 50.
• *There will be no groping in the dark.* In Zen practice everything becomes clear, and there is no need to try to approach realization by intellectual means.
• *Which is advisable, letting go or holding fast?* For "letting go" and "holding fast" see the notes to Case 4. This sentence refers to Seppō's behavior in the present case. Was he letting go or holding fast when he lowered his head and returned to his cottage?
• *A ghost clinging to weeds and bushes.* One who has not attained enlightenment.
• *Your homeland.* This land is the land of the mind.
• *When Seppō was living in his hermitage.* There were several great persecutions of Buddhism in China, the severest of which was in 845,

when over a quarter of a million monks were forced to leave their temples and return to secular life. However, at that time Seppō was twenty-four years old and Gantō only eighteen. The incident related in the present case must have occurred at the time of another persecution when they were mature masters and had been obliged to retire temporarily to their hermitages.

• *Two monks came to pay their respects.* To judge by their actions and the way Seppō received them, these monks could not have been entirely immature. Probably they had studied under Seppō earlier and achieved some degree of attainment.

• *He pushed open the gate and, presenting himself before them.* Such an action is part of a teacher's individual method, and such methods vary in a thousand ways. Therefore Gantō said, "He does not die in the same way that I do."

• *What is this?* In the notes to Case 17 we related the story of Ummon, who called every day to his attendant, Kyōrin. When the latter answered, "Yes, sir," Ummon said, "What is this?" He continued this for eighteen long years. One day Kyōrin exclaimed, "Oh, I understand." Ummon said, "Why don't you say it in a transcending way?" And Kyōrin spent another three years studying with Ummon to become fully mature. Zen teachers do not impart knowledge to their disciples prematurely. They wait patiently. Seppō was delighted to see the well-known faces of the two monks coming to see him. He expected good news from them, judging by their vigorous, self-confident attitude. So he cheerfully came out to the garden gate to meet them, pushed it open, and presenting himself suddenly before them, said, "What is this?" His expectations were high, but he was disappointed.

• *The monks also said, "What is this?"* Their answer was not so bad. Had they not been trained in Zen mondō they could not have made such a quick reply. But that was a different thing from their showing true realization. If their experience had been genuine, whatever they may have said and however they may have acted, their words and actions would have been full of power. But their words were only conventional, and Seppō was not satisfied.

• *Seppō lowered his head and returned to his cottage.* After years of Zen practice, some clever monks develop a crafty technique of meeting the master's questions. Seppō saw through them. Hence this lowering of his head, which he did with a certain intention in mind. But the monks did not understand Seppō. They may at first have been rather pleased at what they supposed to be the success of their answer, but they were in fact repeating the very same error that Seppō himself had once fallen into when he was studying with Tokusan. That story is related in Case 13 of *Mumonkan*, and it is there that Gantō uses the phrase "the last word."

• *Later the monks came to Gantō.* After staying for a certain period with Seppō the monks went, at his suggestion, to see Gantō. "The last word" cannot be taught, and one should not attempt to do so. But Seppō expected something from Gantō, whose phrase this was.

• *Alas! I regret that I did not tell him the last word when I was with him.* In saying this, Gantō does not really mean that Seppō does not understand the last word; he is drawing the monks' attention to the last word. This also applies to his next sentence.

• *Seppō came to life in the same way that I did.* The way to enlightenment is the same for everybody.

• *He does not die in the same way that I do.* After attaining enlightenment, various ways of conducting oneself are open. Who could have predicted Seppō's pushing open the gate and presenting himself suddenly before the monks? Why did Gantō use the peculiar word "die"? Does he mean egoless activity? Study it for yourself. That is the best way to study Zen.

• *If you want to know the last word.* This was being like a talkative old woman, which is deplored in Zen. But a true Zen master knows when to be talkative and when not.

• *I'll tell you, simply—This! This!* Gantō's tongue will fall to the ground! Nevertheless, his words may provide a first foothold for the student who wants to climb the cliff.

• *Light and darkness intermingled.* Letting go and holding fast, living and dying, the first and the last, and so forth, intermingled. (Was Seppō's lowering his head letting go or holding fast?)

• *Living in the same way, you all know.* Who knows?

• *Dying in different ways—beyond telling.* Living relates to absolute samadhi and dying to positive samadhi, not the reverse. In absolute samadhi you first experience the Great Death, then you come back to life again. In positive samadhi your consciousness is in vigorous activity, but you attach to nothing. In other words, you are dying moment by moment, and this transcends everything.

• *Absolutely beyond telling!* Dying is fathomless. It is absolutely individual and transcends description.

• *Buddha and Dharma only nod to themselves.* Coming to this point even Shakyamuni and Bodhidharma can only nod to themselves.

• *East, west, north, and south—homeward let us go.* Each person has his own way to go.

> Oh, this town gate!
> People coming and going,
> Strangers and friends,
> Meeting and parting,
> All going their separate ways . . .

• *Late at night, seeing the snow on the thousand peaks.*

> . . . But each and every one sees the snow
> On the distant mountain peaks!

Case 52 Jōshū's Stone Bridge

MAIN SUBJECT A monk said to Jōshū, "The stone bridge of Jōshū is widely renowned, but coming here I find only a set of steppingstones." Jōshū said, "You see only the steppingstones and do not see the stone bridge." The monk said, "What is the stone bridge?" Jōshū said, "It lets donkeys cross over and horses cross over."

SETCHŌ'S VERSE
> No show of transcendence,
> But his path was high.
> If you've entered the great sea of Zen,
> You should catch a giant turtle.
> I can't help laughing at old Kankei,
> His contemporary, who said,

"It is as quick as an arrow"—
A mere waste of labor.

NOTES   *The stone bridge of Jōshū is widely renowned.* The so-called three famous stone bridges of China at that time were the stone bridge of Tendai, the stone bridge of Nangaku, and the stone bridge of Jōshū. They were not bridges of the kind we are familiar with but a series of rocks placed across a river as steppingstones. The monk was asking not about the bridge but about Jōshū himself. His real meaning was "Jōshū is renowned throughout the whole country, but coming here to see him I find only an insignificant-looking monk."

• *You see only the steppingstones and do not see the stone bridge.* You see only Jōshū's external appearance; you do not see the real Jōshū.

• *It lets donkeys cross over and horses cross over.* To cross over is to cross from one side of a river to the other. The river is the river of samsara (the realm of existence, of birth and death). Donkeys and horses represent all living creatures. Jōshū is saying that anyone who comes to him will be led to cross the river of birth and death.

• *No show of transcendence.* Jōshū used plain language and acted like an ordinary man. There was nothing transcendent about his behavior.

• *But his path was high.* He was a great master who followed a high and noble path.

• *If you've entered the great sea of Zen, / You should catch a giant turtle.* If you are a Zen master you should get good students of Zen. But how are they to be acquired? With good words and actions, like Jōshū's in the present case. Various overtones can attach to the word "turtle" in Zen literature. In the present case it simply represents an outstanding student. There is an allusion here to an old Chinese legend, which tells that in a land called Lung-po, ninety thousand miles north of the Kun-lun Mountains, there lived a giant five hundred feet tall. He took three or four strides, which carried him into China, and there, with one scoop, fished six giant turtles out of the water. He returned to his country carrying them on his shoulder.

• *I can't help laughing at old Kankei.* Kankei (d. 895) was a disciple of Rinzai and a contemporary of Jōshū, who died in 897 (though since Jōshū was one hundred nineteen years old when he died, he was probably a good deal older than Kankei). His name came from the place where his temple was situated (*kan*, pouring; *kei*, ravine).

• *It is as quick as an arrow.* A monk came to visit Kankei and said, "Kankei is widely renowned, but coming here I find only a hemp-bleaching pond." Kankei said, "You see only a hemp-bleaching pond and do not see Kankei." The monk said, "What is Kankei?" Kankei said, "It is as quick as an arrow."

• *A mere waste of labor.* Kankei's answer shows him straining to achieve a show of power. Jōshū's answer is quiet; he does not strain himself, but his answer is far more profound.

Case 53 Hyakujō and a Wild Duck

ENGO'S INTRODUCTION   The universe is not veiled; all its activities lie open. Whichever way he may go, he meets no obstruction. At all times he behaves independently. His every word is devoid of egocentricity, yet still has the power to kill others. Tell me, where did the ancient worthy come to rest? See the following.

MAIN SUBJECT   When Ba Daishi [Baso] was out walking with Hyakujō, he saw a wild duck fly past. Daishi said, "What is it?" Hyakujō said, "It is a wild duck." Daishi said, "Where is it?" Hyakujō said, "It has flown away." Daishi at last gave Hyakujō's nose a sharp pinch. Hyakujō cried out with pain. Daishi said, "There, how can it fly away?"

SETCHŌ'S VERSE
   The wild duck! What, how, and where?
   Baso has seen, talked, taught, and exhausted
   The meaning of mountain clouds and moonlit seas.
   But Jō doesn't understand—"has flown away."

Flown away? No, he is brought back!
Say! Say!

NOTES   *The universe is not veiled; all its activities lie open.* It is not the case that reality is hidden and only the apparent lies open. The apparent is itself reality. You should see the real in the apparent.

• *Whichever way he may go, he meets no obstruction.* In active life, in all circumstances, he enjoys freedom of mind.

• *At all times he behaves independently.* He never loses presence of mind.

• *His every word is devoid of egocentricity, yet still has the power to kill others.* His words are without bias, yet devastating in effect. Engo has in mind Baso's demanding questions.

• *Where did the ancient worthy come to rest?* How did he come to be emancipated? The question refers to Hyakujō, but it is a matter for everyone.

• *When Ba Daishi was out walking with Hyakujō.* Waking or sleeping, they never forgot Zen.

• *What is it?* Beware! Danger is at hand!

• *It is a wild duck.* This would have been a good answer if Hyakujō had offered it with proper understanding of the "it." But he did not.

• *Where is it?* Hyakujō had failed with the first question. Now the same question was asked again in different words.

• *It has flown away.* Has it? What is it, after all? Baso is asking not about the duck but about Hyakujō's "it." If "it" has flown away, this is a serious matter indeed.

• *Daishi at last gave Hyakujō's nose a sharp pinch.* A direct physical action of this kind is not recorded of any master prior to Baso. Quite possibly he was the initiator of a new sort of Zen spirit, which used beating, pushing, shouting, and other violent measures. A Zen teacher expects you to understand before a word has been uttered. Hyakujō had already failed twice.

• *Hyakujō cried out with pain.* Pain has often been accompanied by realization. Gensha stumbled over a stone and stubbed his toes. Pain pervaded his body, and when he came to himself he found he was enlightened. Bokushū pushed Ummon out of his room and slammed the door so quickly, and with such force, that Ummon's leg was caught in it and broken. He cried out with pain and at that moment had a great experience. It is not, of course, pain alone that accompanies realization. The activity of any of the senses may be involved. This is because sensation is the intuitive action of the first nen, which performs direct cognition of external objects. Why, then, is it that though everyone uses his five senses every day, he does not become enlightened? This question is answered throughout this book.

• *There, how can it fly away?* The universe is not veiled; all its activities lie open. There is no going and no coming. When Gensha bruised his toes and became enlightened he said, "Bodhidharma did not come to China, and the Second Patriarch did not go to India." This saying is much appreciated.

• *What, how, and where?* The universe is not veiled; all its activities lie open.

• *Baso has seen, talked, taught.* Baso knew Hyakujō's condition perfectly well. It was as if he were looking at an aerial photograph and could point out on it the exact position that the climber had reached in his ascent of the mountain. He saw through Hyakujō, talked to him and taught him, and used every means to lead him on.

• *Exhausted | The meaning of mountain clouds and moonlit seas.* This is a popular phrase. When one has traveled widely, one will have many cherished recollections of mountains and seas—fine days and stormy ones, moonlit nights and peaceful evenings. The path of life, and Zen activities, too, leave us with many memories and stories. All such recollections and thoughts are represented by this phrase. Setchō is saying that Baso has related all those stories and used every possible measure to teach Hyakujō and lead him to realization.

• *Flown away? No, he is brought back!* Pinching Hyakujō's nose was the last resort to bring him back to life.

• *Say! Say! What do you say?* It is too clear. The universe is open; everything is exposed.

Case 54   Ummon Stretches Out His Hands

ENGO's INTRODUCTION   Transcending life and death, actualizing Zen spirit, he casually cuts through iron and nails, lightly moves heaven and earth. Tell me, whose doing can that be? See the following.

MAIN SUBJECT   Ummon asked a monk, "Where have you recently come from?" The monk said, "From Saizen." Ummon said, "What words has Saizen offered lately?" The monk stretched out his hands. Ummon struck him. The monk said, "I had something to tell you." Ummon now stretched out his own hands. The monk was silent. Ummon struck him.

SETCHŌ's VERSE
> Controlling the head and tail of the tiger,
> Exerting invincible influence
> Over the four hundred provinces,
> How precipitous he is!
> The master says,
> "One further word, I leave it open."

NOTES   *Transcending life and death.* This is realized in absolute samadhi.
• *Actualizing Zen spirit.* This is done in positive samadhi.
• *He casually cuts through iron and nails.* Iron and nails represent the complications of life. He cuts through them, hard though they are, in an almost indifferent, casual way.
• *Tell me, whose doing can that be?* This refers to Ummon's actions in the present case.
• *Where have you recently come from?* One question, one answer, and everything is quite obvious.
• *From Saizen.* Saizen is said to have been a disciple of Nansen, but little is known about him. The monk answered Ummon's question with a simple statement of fact, apparently without any attempt at guile, though such an answer often proved to be a trick.

• *What words has Saizen offered lately?* Ummon was asking how the monk had understood Saizen.

• *The monk stretched out his hands.* Now the trick has appeared. Perhaps the monk spread out his arms and hands, showing his palms.

• *Ummon struck him.* Ummon is holding fast.

• *I had something to tell you.* The attempt at vindication is already an acknowledgment of defeat.

• *Ummon now stretched out his own hands.* Ummon is now letting go. He adopted a defensive position from choice: "Come, attack me how you will, if you can." But with a good player the defensive can quickly become the offensive.

• *The monk was silent.* The monk was dumbfounded by Ummon's unexpected move. Engo puts in a comment here: "Ummon watches the front and guards the rear, but the monk watches only the front."

• *Ummon struck him.* This was a punishing blow. Up to this moment Ummon had been going along with the monk's maneuvers—in his own phrase, "following the waves," like a mother with a baby that she follows as it totters away. You may say that this whole episode is a mere game. That is true, but it is a serious game, called Dharma battle, which can be played only by masters who are well versed in Zen. The monk knew something of Zen, but when he came to measure himself against Ummon the difference in capacity was only too obvious.

• *Controlling the head and tail of the tiger.* He watches the front and guards the rear.

• *Exerting invincible influence | Over the four hundred provinces.* Ummon's influence spread over the whole of China.

• *How precipitous he is!* He is a difficult rock face to tackle.

• *The master says, | "One further word, I leave it open."* Try to write the last line. If you are successful, you will rival not only Setchō but Ummon as well.

Case 55 Dōgo's "I Would Not Tell You"

ENGO'S INTRODUCTION Absolute truth—direct enlightenment; positive activity—immediate understanding. Quick as sparks and lightning, he cuts through the complications. Sitting on the tiger's head and grasping its tail, he is still like a thousand-foot cliff. Be that as it may, is there any case for giving a clue for others' sake? See the following.

MAIN SUBJECT One day Dōgo, accompanied by his disciple Zengen, went to visit a family in which a funeral was to take place, in order to express sympathy. Zengen touched the coffin and said, "Tell me, please, is this life or is this death?" Dōgo said, "I would not tell you whether it is life or it is death." Zengen said, "Why don't you tell me?" Dōgo said, "No, I would not tell you." On their way home, Zengen said, "Oshō, please be kind enough to tell me. If not, I will hit you." Dōgo said, "Strike me if you like, but I would not tell you." Zengen struck Dōgo.

Later Dōgo passed away. Zengen came to Sekisō and told him the whole story. Sekisō said, "I would not tell you whether it is life or it is death." Zengen said, "Why don't you tell me?" Sekisō said, "No, I would not tell you." Upon these words, Zengen attained sudden realization.

One day Zengen, carrying a hoe, went up and down the lecture hall as if he were searching for something. Sekisō said, "What are you doing?" Zengen said, "I am searching for the spiritual remains of our dead teacher." Sekisō said, "Limitless expanse of mighty roaring waves; foaming waves wash the sky. What relic of the deceased teacher do you seek?" [Setchō says, "Alas! Alas!"] Zengen said, "It is a way of acquiring strength." Taigen Fu said, "The deceased teacher's spiritual remains still exist."

SETCHŌ'S VERSE
Hares and horses have horns,
Cows and goats have none.
It is quite infinitesimal,

It piles up mountain-high.
The golden relic exists,
It still exists now.
Foaming waves wash the sky.
Where can you put it?—No, nowhere!
The single sandal returned to India
And is lost forever.

NOTES   *Dōgo, Zengen, Sekisō, Taigen Fu.* Dōgo (769–835) was a disciple of Yakusan and the teacher of Zengen and Sekisō. He appears again in Case 89. Zengen's dates are not recorded. Sekisō is Sekisō Keisho (807–88), who became an outstanding Zen master. He was famous for disciplining his students strictly. His monks sat like tree stumps and were called "the stock monks of Sekisō." A monk once said to him, "I am very close to you, separated only by the window; why is it that I do not see your face?" Sekisō said, "The universe is never veiled." Tōzan once said to his monks, "After the summer session you disperse, some going east, some west; but you should go through the thousands of miles of country where there is not a blade of grass." On this Sekisō said, "When I go out the gate, there I find grass." (The Sekisō who appears in Case 46 of *Mumonkan* is a different Zen master, Sekisō Soen.) Taigen Fu was a disciple of Seppō and well versed in Zen, though he does not seem to have become master of any monastery.

• *Absolute truth—direct enlightenment.* If you are familiar with genuine absolute samadhi, enlightenment will unfailingly come to you.

• *Positive activity—immediate understanding.* Then in active life you achieve true understanding.

• *Quick as sparks and lightning, he cuts through the complications.* His words cut through the student's difficulties like a razor through paper. Zengen came to understand Dōgo's words only many years after they were spoken. But when he understood them, they cut him to the quick, and it was as if the episode had happened yesterday.

• *Sitting on the tiger's head and grasping its tail.* He watches the front and guards the rear.

• *Like a thousand-foot cliff.* While Zengen did not understand, Dōgo seemed as unapproachable as a thousand-foot cliff face. When he understood, the cliff was himself.

• *Is there any case for giving a clue for others' sake?* This is a reference to Dōgo's "I would not tell you," which told so much.

• *Dōgo . . . went to visit a family in which a funeral was to take place.* In those days it was not the custom for Buddhist monks to conduct funerals. Dōgo and Zengen went purely to express their sympathy.

• *Tell me, please, is this life or is this death?* Zengen was deeply troubled about the problem of death. From death there is no escape. It is the extinction of one's self. When one becomes truly aware of this, one can find no place to take refuge. Zengen was crying inwardly. He had seen death with his own eyes. He was hanging on Dōgo, asking for help, like a frightened child clinging to its mother.

• *I would not tell you whether it is life or it is death.* Dōgo's answer was cruel because he understood the matter too well. He knew Zengen's heart-rending misery. He gave a direct answer. This problem of death cannot be solved by discussion, that is, by conceptual manipulation. Although it appears cruel, Zengen must be left to solve this problem for himself, with his own mind and body. In the end, you have to solve it for yourself through your own zazen practice.

Truth is cruel. Man has to pay for it with his own blood. Today, after World War II, in which thousands shed their blood, we have perhaps learned something. How foolish it is, but how inevitable. This inevitable foolishness has been repeated over and over again since man first appeared on earth. It is not obvious whether man's present condition is to be regarded as representing progress or retrogression. But one thing is clear: in the course of long ages man's elaborate mental activity has come into being, and this is now equipped with an eye to see into itself. Being was blind, but now being can see itself and realize itself. If there is any object in the universe, it must be the development of this ability of being to see itself. In order to reach this condition, innumerable sacrifices have been made. Life and death repeat endlessly. Living and dying, man creates the stream of being. Can it be called life or can it be called death? But this sort of discussion will not help you to meet the problem of death.

• *Why don't you tell me?* Zengen was anxiously questioning. Though an individual may be only the tiniest component in the stream of being, one's individuality constitutes a whole world for oneself. It needs to solve this question as a matter of desperate importance.

• *No, I would not tell you.* Life is cruel. Nature is cruel. The cliff is cruel. This cruelty itself constitutes a topic for study. It is said that in your study of Zen you must treat your teacher like an enemy.

• *Please be kind enough to tell me.* Zengen was thinking of only one thing. He did not understand Dōgo and was upset with him for not telling the secret.

• *If not, I will hit you.* The urgency of the question for Zengen drove him to this extremity. At such a crisis one feels like using any means to force the other to answer.

• *Strike me if you like, but I would not tell you.* This cruel persistence! Will it not end as a "case for giving a clue for others' sake"?

• *Zengen struck Dōgo.* Striking one's teacher was regarded as a great transgression. Dōgo told Zengen to leave the temple for a while lest harm befall him, for if the other monks discovered what had happened they would take some action against Zengen. While Zengen was on his travels he came to a little temple and there heard a monk reciting the *Avalokitesvara Sutra.* When the monk came to the passage that runs, "To him who is to be enlightened as a monk, he [the Bodhisattva Avalokitesvara] manifests himself as a monk and gives his teaching," Zengen suddenly achieved an insight and said to himself, "I was mistaken in doubting my teacher. Now I know it is not a matter to be understood through words."

• *Later Dōgo passed away. Zengen came to Sekisō.* Dōgo had already died by the time Zengen attained realization, so he came to Sekisō, who had succeeded Dōgo, to express his views.

• *Sekisō said, "I would not tell you."* Sekisō knew his teacher's method and repeated his words. But it was not imitation. Engo comments here, "Very fresh."

• *Sekisō said, "No, I would not tell you."* Engo says, "If the teaching descended from the Sixth Patriarch harps on the same string, many a man will be drowned on land." (See the notes to Case 20.) The teaching must be fresh every time.

• *Upon these words, Zengen attained sudden realization.* One experience of realization may be enough, but an ordinary person usually has to go through realization after realization before genuine enlightenment is established.

• *Zengen, carrying a hoe, went up and down the lecture hall.* His action was intended to express his understanding.

• *I am searching for the spiritual remains of our dead teacher.* Zengen was still green.

• *Limitless expanse of mighty roaring waves; foaming waves wash the sky.* This is a popular saying among monks. In this case it means that the dead teacher's spiritual remains pervade the entire universe.

• *What relic of the deceased teacher do you seek?* You are face to face with it. What need is there to seek after it?

• *Setchō says, "Alas! Alas!"* It is regrettable that you do not understand it.

• *It is a way of acquiring strength.* This is an idiomatic phrase meaning "Thank you for your teaching."

• *Taigen Fu said, "The deceased teacher's spiritual remains still exist."* This is bringing the story to its ultimate conclusion.

• *Hares and horses have horns, / Cows and goats have none.* Life is not life, death is not death. Therefore hares and horses have horns, cows and goats have none.

• *The single sandal returned to India.* Legend says that after his death Bodhidharma returned to India carrying a single sandal (see Case 47).

• *And is lost forever.* Don't be worried about it, because it is lost forever. In *Rinzairoku* it is related that when Rinzai was about to die, he said, "After I have passed away, do not let my True Dharma Eye be extinguished." Sanshō said, "How could I let your True Dharma Eye be extinguished!" Rinzai said, "Later on, when somebody asks you about it, what will you say to him?" Sanshō gave a shout. Rinzai said, "Who would have thought that my True Dharma Eye would be extinguished on reaching this blind ass!"

Case 56   Kinzan and One Arrow Piercing the Three Barriers

ENGO'S INTRODUCTION   No Buddha has ever come into the world; no Law has ever been handed down. Bodhidharma did not come to China; no transmission from mind to mind took place. People of today do not understand the truth but seek after it out in the external world. They do not know that even the thousand holy ones cannot discover the great cause that lies at each person's feet. Now, at this moment, how does it happen that while seeing, you do not see; hearing, you do not hear; speaking, you do not speak; and knowing, you do not know? If you have not yet understood this, study it in an old koan. See the following.

MAIN SUBJECT   Ryō Zenkaku asked Kinzan, "What about when one arrow pierces the three barriers?" Kinzan said, "Bring out the master of the barriers and let me see him." Ryō said, "If that is the case, recognizing my fault, I will withdraw." Kinzan said, "How long will you keep me waiting?" Ryō said, "A good arrow! But it has achieved nothing." And he was about to leave. Kinzan said, "Wait a bit. Just come here." Ryō turned his head. Kinzan took hold of him and said, "Leaving aside for a moment the arrow that breaks through the three barriers—just shoot an arrow at me!" Ryō hesitated. Kinzan gave him seven blows and said, "I should let you go on puzzling over this for thirty years."

SETCHŌ'S VERSE
I'd take out the master of the barriers for you!
Be mindful, you who loose the arrow.

If you stick to the eyes, the ears are deafened;
If you discard the ears, the eyes are blinded.

How I like the arrow piercing the barriers;
The arrow's path is clearly seen!

Don't you recall, Gensha once said,
The man of might is master of the mind, prior to heaven.

NOTES   *Kinzan* was a disciple of Tōzan, the founder of the Sōtō sect, and became the master of Kinzan Mountain when only twenty-seven years old. His dates of birth and death are not known. His actions and teachings display some debatable features, perhaps because he left his teacher too early.

• *Ryō Zenkaku.* Little is known about him except his appearance in the present case. The term *zenkaku* (*zen*, Zen; *kaku*, guest or visitor) occurs twice in *Hekiganroku* (the other instance is in Case 42). It probably meant a senior Zen student, either a monk or a layman who was staying at the temple.

• *No Buddha has ever come into the world.* You must find your own Buddha within yourself. If, instead, you seek Buddha in the external world, you will miss it forever.

• *No Law has ever been handed down.* No Law (truth of the universe) has ever been discovered except by you yourself.

• *Bodhidharma did not come to China.* The true Bodhidharma is present within you from the beginning.

• *No transmission from mind to mind took place.* Here "mind" is Zen mind, which cannot be given to or by others.

• *The great cause that lies at each person's feet.* The ultimate, vital thing, which demands one's immediate attention.

• *Seeing, you do not see; hearing, you do not hear; speaking, you do not speak; and knowing, you do not know.* In samadhi you do not see or hear anything, and while speaking you do not speak. Knowing, you do not engage in conceptual knowing but have direct, intuitive cognition.

• *An old koan.* The original text here has "complications." This word is frequently used to mean koan, and I have translated it that way here.

• *What about when one arrow pierces the three barriers?* What about when one gets sudden and direct enlightenment, as if one arrow were to pierce the three barriers which are supposed to check the Zen student's gaining enlightenment?

• *Bring out the master of the barriers.* Bring out the Buddha who is to be found in yourself. But how do you bring him out?

• *If that is the case, recognizing my fault, I will withdraw.* I have already presented him to you. But I will withdraw if you tell me to.

• *How long will you keep me waiting?* What use is there in your dilly-dallying?

• *A good arrow! But it has achieved nothing.* I started a good mondō, but it was not properly carried on.

• *He was about to leave.* If he had actually left, it would have obviated the complications which ensued.

• *Wait a bit. Just come here.* Kinzan is using a teacher's old trick.

• *Ryō turned his head.* This action is rejected as being irresolute. So it is. Yet if he was really enlightened, what fault was there in his looking back?

• *Just shoot an arrow at me!* Kinzan was ushering the burglar in. This is a teacher's hazardous gambit for the sake of his student. If Ryō had been powerful enough, Kinzan would have paid dearly for it.

• *Ryō hesitated.* This hesitation is rejected.

• *I should let you go on puzzling over this for thirty years.* It seems that Kinzan was wholly victorious. But is that really so? I am sick of declaring who is the winner. But I want to ask why it was that they could not cut the knot once and for all with one stroke. A great Zen master, such as Baso or Jōshū, would have done something different. Baso once said, "Sun-faced Buddha, Moon-faced Buddha" (Case 3), and everyone was dumbfounded with admiration.

• *I'd take out the master of the barriers for you!* In treating this case, Setchō is interested only in this master of the barriers and characteristically states his view in the first line of his verse.

• *If you stick to the eyes, the ears are deafened.* The state of mushin (*mu*, no; *shin*, mind: no-mind, that is, innocence) is much advocated. See the following line of the verse.

• *If you discard the ears, the eyes are blinded.* Don't be too discriminating in your choice. The real Way is not difficult. It only abhors choice and attachment. (See Case 2.)

• *How I like the arrow piercing the barriers.* Setchō speaks of the delight of enlightenment.

• *The arrow's path is clearly seen!* If you once have the great experience, you may thereafter close your eyes and see the route you took, like the wake of a ship drawn across the waters.

• *Gensha.* See Cases 22 and 88, and *Mumonkan*, Case 41.

• *The man of might is master of the mind, prior to heaven.* The man of might, that is, the man of great strength, is the master of the mind before heaven manifests itself, that is, before the creation of all beings.

Case 57　Jōshū's "I Alone Am Holy Throughout Heaven and Earth"

ENGO'S INTRODUCTION　When you have not yet penetrated it, it is like silver mountains and iron cliffs. When you have penetrated it, you find you yourself are the silver mountains and iron cliffs. If you ask how to do it, I would say that if you attain realization in the exercise of ki, you will occupy the pinnacle of attainment and will allow not even the holy ones to spy on you. If you cannot do this, see and study the ancient's doings as follows.

MAIN SUBJECT　A monk said to Jōshū, "It is said, 'The real Way is not difficult. It only abhors choice and attachment.' Now, what are non-choice and non-attachment?" Jōshū said, "I alone am holy throughout heaven and earth." The monk said, "It is still choice and attachment." Jōshū said, "You country bumpkin! Where are choice and attachment?" The monk was speechless.

SETCHŌ'S VERSE
　Deep as the sea, high as the mountains!
　The fly's attempt to face the gale!
　The ant trying to attack the pillar!
　Choice and attachment! Non-choice and non-attachment!
　A cloth-covered drum that reaches the eaves!

NOTES　*When you have not yet penetrated it, it is like silver mountains and iron cliffs.* When you have not yet realized Buddha Nature, it blocks you like the silver, snow-clad Himalayas and their cliffs.
　• *When you have penetrated it, you find you yourself are the silver mountains and iron cliffs.* When you have realized Buddha Nature, you find that you have been Buddha from the beginning.
　• *In the exercise of ki.* Ki is Zen-ki, that is, the intense, momentary

concentration of mind and body (see Case 3). It appears, for instance, at the moment of making the starting dash in a hundred-meter sprint or when making a thrust in fencing. It is refined in Zen practice, and even in your ordinary quiet moments it fills your body and mind. It appears then even in the casual movement of your hand, in lifting your foot or moving your eyebrows. You look at the rice in the bowl or glance at the water in the pail, and you see there Buddha Nature. One who can do this is the master of the barriers who appeared in the previous case.

• *You will occupy the pinnacle of attainment.* You are the master everywhere.

• *Will allow not even the holy ones to spy on you.* The holy ones are the Buddhas and patriarchs. Even these cannot see into your realization.

• *The real Way is not difficult. It only abhors choice and attachment.* The sun shines brightly, the moon shines serenely. They give impartially. When clouds come, it is cloudy. When it rains, it is rainy. Every day is a good day. However, man introduces discrimination and differentiation, calling things good or bad. All evils stem from this practice, that is, from choice and attachment. (See Case 2.)

• *What are non-choice and non-attachment?* Man has consciousness, which is equipped with the eye to see itself. Being has succeeded in seeing (realizing) itself. That is enlightenment. Enlightenment is empty. It is non-preference, non-attachment.

• *I alone am holy throughout heaven and earth.* Enlightenment represents being itself. When you attain enlightenment, you realize you are being itself, and this exclamation, "I alone am holy," emerges naturally.

• *It is still choice and attachment.* Jōshū spoke from the point of view of transcendence. But this monk was still seeing things from the relative point of view, and to him Jōshū's words sounded discriminating. In fact, the monk had thought up his question with the intention of shutting up Jōshū, whatever answer he might make.

• *You country bumpkin!* Jōshū usually spoke calmly but to the point. However, he did not hesitate to utter a forthright condemnation when it was called for.

• *The monk was speechless.* The monk's attack was repulsed because of the inescapable difference in ability between him and Jōshū.

• *Deep as the sea, high as the mountains!* Jōshū was as deep as the sea and as steep and high as the mountains.

• *The fly's attempt to face the gale!* The monk's attempt to rival Jōshū.

• *The ant trying to attack the pillar!* Jōshū was as solid and immovable as the central pillar of a house.

• *Choice and attachment! Non-choice and non-attachment!* With the truly mature Zen master, preference (choice and attachment) is all right, and so is non-preference, because his words and actions issue from emptiness.

• *A cloth-covered drum that reaches the eaves!* This is an idiomatic expression denoting something that drives people to their wits' end. A cloth-covered drum is useless, and to make matters worse, it is gigantic, reaching the eaves of the house and blocking the door. Setchō identifies this bizarre object with Jōshū. He is saying that however people approach Jōshū, tapping him and sounding him in every possible way in an attempt to get a normal response, they always get some quite unexpected repercussion that bowls them over. This drum (Jōshū) is a monster—spirits shriek and gods groan (see Case 59, Setchō's verse).

Case 58   Jōshū's "No Justification"

MAIN SUBJECT   A monk said to Jōshū, "You so often quote the words, 'The real Way is not difficult. It only abhors choice and attachment.' Isn't that your point of attachment?" Jōshū said, "A man asked me the same question once before, and five years later I have still found no justification for it."

SETCHŌ'S VERSE
  King Elephant's yawn!
  King Lion's roar!
  Plain words
  Stop men's mouths.
  North, south, east, and west,
  The crow swoops, the hare bounds.

NOTES *Isn't that your point of attachment?* A monk asked Jōshū whether, in so often quoting the Third Patriarch's words, "The real Way is not difficult. It only abhors choice and attachment" (these are Jōshū's words in Case 2), he was not himself showing attachment to those words. The monk had no doubt racked his brains and hit on this idea, and was confident that he could trap Jōshū.

• *A man asked me the same question once before.* Jōshū, fully aware of the monk's intention, quietly said that the question came as no surprise to him. This was the first step in frustrating the monk.

• *Five years later.* Your question has been around for five years—the second step in deflating the monk.

• *I have still found no justification for it.* Jōshū calmly stated the fact as it was, thus showing that he was not in any dilemma. He was not operating in the realm of old-fashioned logic. In Zen a sort of intuitive logic develops, which works with something of the immediacy of a computer. Jōshū's answer stemmed from such an intuitive understanding.

• *King Elephant's yawn! | King Lion's roar!* King Elephant and King Lion denote Jōshū himself. The elephant symbolizes the Buddha's actions; the lion, the Buddha's wisdom. The yawn means casual speech. Even Jōshū's seemingly casual words expound the truth with the force of a lion.

• *North, south, east, and west, | The crow swoops, the hare bounds.* The crow and hare occur in Setchō's verse to Case 12, and the symbolism is explained in the notes to that case. These lines are intended to convey Jōshū's total freedom of action.

Case 59   Jōshū's "Why Not Quote to the End?"

ENGO'S INTRODUCTION   Controlling the heavens, commanding the earth, transcending the holy, rising above the mundane, he shows us even in the myriad weeds the Wonderful Mind of Nirvana, and in the midst of Dharma battle holds the lifeline of the monk. Tell me, by what blessing can he be like that? See the following.

MAIN SUBJECT A monk said to Jōshū, " 'The real Way is not difficult. It only abhors choice and attachment. If you say a word, there arise choice and attachment.' How, then, can you go about helping someone?" Jōshū said, "Why don't you quote it to the end?" The monk said, "I have only this much in mind." Jōshū said, "You know, the real Way is not difficult. It only abhors choice and attachment."

SETCHŌ'S VERSE
Spit in his face—he is not sullied;
Call him names—it doesn't touch him.
He walks like a tiger, moves like a dragon.
Spirits shriek, gods groan and weep.
His head is three feet long. Who is he?
Facing you, he stands silent, on a single leg.

NOTES *Controlling the heavens, commanding the earth, transcending the holy, rising above the mundane.* Such is the ordinary daily activity of the Zen master.

• *He shows us even in the myriad weeds the Wonderful Mind of Nirvana.* Not only weeds but flowers, trees, mountains, animals, and so on manifest the Wonderful Mind of Nirvana. Only man does not realize it. It is said in the Bodhisattva's Vow, "Then on each moment's flash of thought, there will grow a lotus flower, and on each lotus flower will be revealed a Buddha. These Buddhas will glorify Sukhavati, the Pure Land, every moment and everywhere."

• *By what blessing can he be like that?* By going through and through the practice of samadhi, he becomes mature in such activity.

• *If you say a word, there arise choice and attachment.* He says as much as he likes, and there is no choice and attachment.

• *How, then, can you go about helping someone?* If you cannot use words, how can you help others in their training? The monk or monks in this and the two preceding cases are trying every means to checkmate Jōshū.

• *Why don't you quote it to the end?* The whole quotation (Case 2) is: "The Real Way is not difficult. It only abhors choice and attachment. With but a single word there may arise choice and attachment, or there may arise clarity. This old monk does not have that clarity. Do you appreciate the meaning of this or not?" As explained in the notes to Case 2, this is Jōshū's modification of a passage from the writings of the Third Patriarch.

• *I have only this much in mind.* The monk is saying that he is concerned with just this point and has therefore recited only this much. It seems at first like a clever evasion of Jōshū's criticism, but in fact the monk shows that he has himself exercised a choice, hence Jōshū's next words.

• *Spit in his face . . .* The first two lines of Setchō's verse refer to Jōshū's famous words, "If you want to spit on me, do it as if you were pouring water; if you want to abuse me, do it with your mouth touching me."

• *He walks like a tiger, moves like a dragon.* This is a poetic description of Jōshū's behavior.

• *Spirits shriek, gods groan and weep.* They shriek and weep to express their demonic excitement. Jōshū's heaven-born words were enough to make even spirits and gods cry out, shout, and weep.

• *His head is three feet long. Who is he?* This must be some kind of monster.

• *Facing you, he stands silent, on a single leg.* This is a quotation from Tōzan. The monster stands silently facing you, and look! it stands on a single leg. I don't know where he is from or what manner of fearful being he is! Who is he?

Case 60   Ummon's Staff Becoming a Dragon

ENGO'S INTRODUCTION   Buddhas and sentient beings are not, by nature, different. Mountains, rivers, and your own self are all just the same. Why should they be separate and constitute two worlds? Even if you are well versed in Zen koans and know how to deal with them, if you stop there everything is spoiled. If you do not stop, the whole world will be dissolved, with not a particle of it left behind. Now tell me, what does it mean to be well versed in Zen koans? See the following.

MAIN SUBJECT Ummon held out his staff and said to the assembled monks, "The staff has transformed itself into a dragon and swallowed up the universe! Where are the mountains, the rivers, and the great world?"

SETCHŌ'S VERSE
The staff has swallowed up the universe.
Don't say peach blossoms float on the waters.
The fish that gets its tail singed
May fail to grasp the mist and clouds.
The ones that lie with gills exposed
Need not lose heart.
My verse is done.
But do you really hear me?
Only be carefree! Stand unwavering!
Why so bewildered?
Seventy-two blows are not enough,
I want to give you a hundred and fifty.

[Setchō descended from the rostrum waving his staff. The whole crowd ran away.]

NOTES *Buddhas and sentient beings are not, by nature, different.* When Shakyamuni, sitting under the Bodhi tree and catching sight of the morning star, suddenly came to his Great Awakening, he exclaimed, "How wonderful! Every sentient being is endowed with the innate wisdom and virtue of the Tathagata." When one is enlightened, he is Buddha; there is no difference between the Buddha and sentient beings.

• *Mountains, rivers, and your own self are all just the same.* Mountains and rivers represent the external world; your own self represents inner experience. Together, these two—objective and subjective, matter and mind—constitute one world. They are not distinct from each other.

• *If you stop there everything is spoiled.* However proficient the student may be in handling koans, he has still to undertake the cultivation of Holy Buddhahood.

• *The whole world will be dissolved, with not a particle of it left behind.* The condition of absolute samadhi (in which mountains, rivers, men, women, animals, and everything are gone) will prevail even in his active life. In the middle of the busiest activity of consciousness, he will enjoy calmness of mind, as if he were deep in the mountains, far from the sight and sound of human beings.

• *The staff has transformed itself into a dragon and swallowed up the universe.* The staff represents Zen mind; a dragon signifies an enlightened man. To speak more plainly, you have swallowed up the universe; you have realized that mountains, rivers, and your own self are just the same thing.

• *Where are the mountains, the rivers, and the great world?* You and they are unified.

• *The staff has swallowed up the universe.* The essence of the case is expressed in this line. Setchō wants to go over Ummon's head: "Instead of saying, 'The staff has transformed itself into a dragon,' and so on, I want to say directly that the staff has swallowed up the universe."

• *Don't say peach blossoms float on the waters.* The allusion is to the Dragon Gate falls on the Yellow River, which we encountered in Case 7. Every spring, when the crimson petals of the peach blossoms flutter down onto the waters, hundreds of fish congregate below the falls. The energetic ones leap the falls to reach the waters above. Their tails are scorched by lightning, and they are transformed into dragons. Seizing clouds and mist, they ascend to heaven. Those who fail to make the leap fall back on the rocks below and die, their gills exposed to the sun. But Setchō is saying in his first two lines that there is really no need to talk in this roundabout way: the staff (you yourself) has swallowed up the universe.

• *The fish that gets its tail singed.* The fish that has leaped the falls, hence, the enlightened man.

• *May fail to grasp the mist and clouds.* This alludes to those who talk so much of their experience of kenshō. It is not necessarily they who eventually attain the deepest understanding of Zen. If they stop there, everything will be spoiled.

• *The ones that lie with gills exposed | Need not lose heart.* Some Zen students spend many years in zazen training and find it hard to attain kenshō. They need not be discouraged. Many of them have already come to understand something of Zen. Even if they have not, they are Buddha from the beginning. Someday they will come across the genuine experience if they only keep up their practice diligently.

• *My verse is done.* Setchō says, "I have said all I want to say about this case." But he notices a certain agitation among his monks.

- *But do you really hear me?* Have you really understood me?
- *Only be carefree! Stand unwavering!* Maintain the ordinary mind, that is, the truly innocent condition of mind.
- *Seventy-two blows are not enough, | I want to give you a hundred and fifty.* Since you are still wondering about it, I must resort to my final measure. I will not spare you a hundred and fifty blows.

Case 6 1 Fuketsu's "One Particle of Dust"

ENGO'S INTRODUCTION   Setting up the Dharma banner and establishing the Dharma teaching—such is the task of the teacher of profound attainment. Distinguishing a dragon from a snake, black from white— that is what the mature master must do. Now let us put aside for a moment how to wield the life-giving sword and the death-dealing blade, and how to administer blows with the stick: tell me, what does the one who lords it over the universe say? See the following.

MAIN SUBJECT   Fuketsu said to the assembled monks, "If one particle of dust is raised, the state will come into being; if no particle of dust is raised, the state will perish."

Setchō [at a later time], holding up his staff, said to his disciples, "Is there anyone among you who will live with him and die with him?"

SETCHŌ'S VERSE
Let the elders knit their brows as they will;
For the moment, let the state be established.
Where are the wise statesmen, the veteran generals?
The cool breeze blows; I nod to myself.

NOTES   Fuketsu. See Case 38 and *Mumonkan*, Case 24.
- *Setting up the Dharma banner and establishing the Dharma teaching.*

Organizing a monastery (setting up the Dharma banner) and teaching disciples (establishing the Dharma teaching).

• *Distinguishing a dragon from a snake, black from white.* This is a repetition of the above in more concrete form. The teacher must distinguish between a dragonlike monk and a snakelike one and decide whether a student is on a wrong path (black) or a right one (white).

• *How to wield the life-giving sword and the death-dealing blade, and how to administer blows with the stick.* This is a still more concrete description of the teacher's technique. The life-giving sword and the death-dealing blade denote the two tactics of letting go and holding fast (see the notes to Case 4).

• *What does the one who lords it over the universe say?* Before interpreting these words, let us go briefly through Tōzan's five ranks, which we encountered in Case 43 and *Mumonkan*, Case 13, and which I have discussed in detail in chapter 17 of *Zen Training*. The five ranks are (1) the apparent within the real (Hen in Shō), (2) the real within the apparent (Shō in Hen), (3) coming from within the real (coming from Shō), (4) arrival at mutual integration (integration in Hen), and (5) unity attained (perfection in integration).*

The first two ranks correspond to absolute samadhi and positive samadhi, respectively. One may interchange between these two ranks, but in the first, emphasis is placed on the real, and in the second, on the apparent. "Coming from within the real" (the third rank) is the condition in which the interchange of real and apparent has been successfully achieved. Such a condition manifests itself in a fully mature Zen master. In the busiest activity of consciousness he enjoys the same quietness of mind as if he were in absolute samadhi. We are supposed to remain in this condition in our daily life.

Then what is the meaning of the remaining two ranks? "Arrival at mutual integration" is the situation in which the teacher is engaged in setting up the Dharma banner, establishing the Dharma teaching, distinguishing a dragon from a snake and black from white, wielding the life-giving sword and the death-dealing blade, administering blows with the stick, and so on. His activity of consciousness is polished like a precious stone. In this condition, human existence itself becomes a work of art. In aesthetic perception, in insight into human nature, in understand-

---

*This translation of the ranks is from Miura and Sasaki, *Zen Dust*.

ing and teaching Zen, the master in this condition attains a state of perfection. The fifth rank, "unity attained," is that to which Engo refers when he says the master "lords it over the universe." In this rank, the master becomes forgetful even of Zen itself.

• *If one particle of dust is raised, the state will come into being.* If the slightest activity of consciousness occurs, the whole universe appears. In saying this, Fuketsu refers to the condition represented by the second rank, that is, positive samadhi.

• *If no particle of dust is raised, the state will perish.* Here Fuketsu means the condition of absolute samadhi (the first rank). His words may be paraphrased as follows: If a particle of dust is raised, the state will come into being and the elders of the village will frown. If no particle of dust is raised, the state will perish and the elders of the village will be pleased. The elders are dreaming of remote times, when there were no troublesome laws and regulations, and no heavy taxes. The prevailing philosophy was that of Lao-tzu, who said, "He who loves the people will practice non-action when ruling the country."

• *Setchō [at a later time], holding up his staff, said to his disciples.* Setchō conveyed his meaning by holding up his staff.

• *Is there anyone among you who will live with him and die with him?* Living and dying, coming into being and perishing, are the two wheels of the Zen cart.

• *For the moment, let the state be established.* The teacher is supposed to operate in the state corresponding to the fourth rank, in which he sets up the Dharma banner, establishes the Dharma teaching, and so on.

• *Where are the wise statesmen, the veteran generals?* In order that the state (that is, Zen) may flourish, competent men are required to run it. Setchō looks for such men among his disciples.

• *The cool breeze blows; I nod to myself.* The cool breeze symbolizes an independent and easy mind. What does Setchō nod to himself about? One must go through the five ranks over and over again, returning repeatedly to the first after reaching the last. Then every rank is enriched.

Case 62 Ummon's "One Treasure"

ENGO'S INTRODUCTION With untaught wisdom he engages in the subtle action of inaction. With unsolicited compassion, he becomes your true friend. With a single word, he kills you and saves you. In one move he lets you go and holds you fast. Tell me, who is it that comes in that way? See the following.

MAIN SUBJECT Ummon said to the assembled monks, "Between heaven and earth, within the universe, there is one treasure. It is hidden in the mountain form. You take the lantern, entering the Buddha hall, and take the temple gate, placing it above the lantern!"

SETCHŌ'S VERSE
Look!
On the ancient bank,
Who is that
Holding the fishing rod?

Quietly moving clouds,
Boundless waters,
The bright moon, the white flowers of the reeds,
You see by yourself!

NOTES *With untaught wisdom he engages in the subtle action of inaction.* True wisdom is attained without the aid of a teacher, especially Zen wisdom, which can be learned only by yourself. Ōbaku said, "I do not say that there is no Zen, but that there is no Zen teacher" (Case 11). With your ordinary mind you carry out the subtle act of inaction. In getting up in the morning, putting on your clothes, washing your face, going and coming, walking downstairs, you are performing the act of inaction without knowing it. The least stirring of egocentric thought, and you depart from your ordinary mind and become stiff and unnatural. The first nen, if not interfered with by the deluded third nen, acts intuitively.

That is untaught wisdom. You have been endowed with this from the beginning. Even the third nen, when freed from its delusive mode of action, comes to cooperate with the first nen and exercises intuitive pure reason. To recover this untaught wisdom it is essential to undertake Zen training, in which the third nen is purified.

• *With unsolicited compassion, he becomes your true friend.* The Bodhisattva Avalokitesvara (Kannon) invariably feels and displays compassion toward all suffering beings even if they are hostile toward him. This is unsolicited compassion.

• *Tell me, who is it that comes in that way?* This alludes to Ummon, the hero of the present case.

• *Between heaven and earth, within the universe, there is one treasure. It is hidden in the mountain form.* The treasure fills the whole universe. At the same time, it is hidden in your own body (the mountain form).

• *You take the lantern, entering the Buddha hall, and take the temple gate, placing it above the lantern!* Your ordinary mind is the lantern, and with that lantern you enter the Buddha hall. Going out or coming in, with the lantern, through the temple gate (the Buddha's Way), you go innocently.

• *Look! | On the ancient bank, | Who is that | Holding the fishing rod?* The ancient bank is the bank along the stream of the Buddha's teaching. Who can it be, casting his line to fish the monks, but Ummon himself?

• *Quietly moving clouds, | Boundless waters.* Clouds move innocently and waters stretch boundlessly, quite free of any selfish motive. This is the quiet scene which we see from the bank. At the same time, these lines symbolize the activity of ordinary mind.

• *The bright moon, the white flowers of the reeds.* This is a further description of the scene viewed from the bank. When the bright moon sheds its light upon the clumps of flowering reeds, the scene is mantled in a frosty whiteness. Then it will be difficult to distinguish the feathery flowering heads of the reeds from one another. Nevertheless, each one is still there, separate and independent.

• *You see by yourself!* You must come to see by yourself the one treasure, which is hidden in the mountain form, and which is equally manifest in the bright moonlight and the flowering reeds. And again, you must find within yourself the untaught wisdom to carry out the subtle action of inaction.

Case 63 Nansen Cuts the Cat in Two

ENGO'S INTRODUCTION   What is beyond thinking must be the topic for serious discourse. What transcends words should be the subject of earnest investigation. When lightning flashes and shooting stars fall, you should display the power to drain the deepest lakes and overturn mountains. Has any of you acquired such ability? See the following.

MAIN SUBJECT   Nansen one day saw the monks of the Eastern and Western halls quarreling over a cat. He held up the cat and said, "If you can give an answer, I will not kill it." No one could answer. Nansen cut the cat in two.

SETCHŌ'S VERSE
Thoughtless the monks of both halls;
Raising dust and smoke,
Out of control.
Fortunately, Nansen was there;
His deeds squared with his words.
He cut the cat in two
Regardless of who was right,
Who wrong.

NOTES   *What is beyond thinking must be the topic for serious discourse.* What is beyond thinking is the topic the teacher must take up for his discourse.
• *What transcends words should be the subject of earnest investigation.* Zen students frequently come to a point which cannot be described in words. That is the point which they should earnestly investigate.
• *When lightning flashes and shooting stars fall.* In a Zen mondō (Dharma battle) a situation often flares up which is like a thousand flashes of lightning and a hundred shooting stars all at once.
• *You should display the power to drain the deepest lakes and overturn moun-*

tains. These are superhuman feats, but this is what is expected of you in actual life, in Dharma battle, and throughout your Zen training.

• *Main Subject*. This and Case 64 appear as Case 14 in *Mumonkan*. See the notes to that case.

• *Thoughtless the monks of both halls*. But they believed themselves to be very much the reverse.

• *Raising dust and smoke*. "Dust and smoke" means the tumult of war.

• *Out of control*. Men are foolish beings, unable to control themselves. How are we to escape from this karmic curse?

• *Fortunately, Nansen was there*. Fortunately, man has a monitor in his own mind.

• *His deeds squared with his words*. Do yours?

• *He cut the cat in two*. What is the cat? It is your own ego. If you get rid of your ego's demands, there is no dread, no anger, no fear of death. "Cut the cat in two" implies a decisive, determined action. The original text runs *ittō ryō dan* (*ittō*, one knife; *ryō*, two; *dan*, cutting: hence, one act of cutting, and cutting it all).

• *Regardless of who was right, / Who wrong*. The words of the original text are *nin henpa* (*nin*, indifferent; *henpa*, one-sidedness: hence, indifferent to one-sided treatment). Nansen was indifferent to who was right, who wrong, and indifferent to all possible criticism. His attitude was wholly decisive.

Case 64   Jōshū Puts His Sandals on His Head

MAIN SUBJECT   Nansen told the previous story [Case 63] to Jōshū and asked his opinion. Jōshū then took off his sandals and, putting them on his head, went away. Nansen said, "If you had been there, the cat would have been saved."

SETCHŌ'S VERSE
He asked Jōshū to complete the koan.
It was their leisure time in Ch'ang-an.

The sandals on the head—who has guessed?
Returning home, they were at rest.

NOTES *Main Subject.* See the notes to *Mumonkan*, Case 14.
• *He asked Jōshū to complete the koan.* Cutting the cat in two did not complete the koan; Jōshū's action supplied the finishing touch.
• *It was their leisure time in Ch'ang-an.* Ch'ang-an was the ancient capital.
• *The sandals on the head—who has guessed?* Zen students have long found it difficult to make an adequate guess about this point.
• *Returning home, they were at rest.* This is an established phrase to describe the condition of a mature Zen master who has long finished attaining enlightenment and is now relaxed and at ease at home.

Case 65 A Non-Buddhist Philosopher Questions the Buddha

ENGO'S INTRODUCTION It has no form and yet appears. It extends in every direction and is boundless. It responds spontaneously and works in emptiness. Even though you may be clever enough to deduce three from one instance, and to detect the slightest deviation at a glance, and though you may be so powerful that the blows fall from your stick like raindrops and your shouts sound like thunderclaps, you are not yet to be compared with the man of advanced enlightenment. What is the condition of such a man? See the following.

MAIN SUBJECT A non-Buddhist philosopher said to the Buddha, "I do not ask for words; I do not ask for non-words." The World-honored One remained silent for a while. The philosopher said admiringly, "The World-honored One, in his great mercy, has blown away the clouds of my illusion and enabled me to enter the Way."

After the philosopher had gone, Ananda asked the Buddha, "What did he realize, to say he had entered the Way?" The World-honored One replied, "A fine horse runs even at the shadow of the whip."

SETCHŌ'S VERSE

The spiritual wheel does not turn;
When it turns, it goes two ways.
The brilliant mirror on its stand
Divides beauty from ugliness,
Lifts the clouds of doubt and illusion.
No dust is found in the gate of mercy.
A fine horse watches for the shadow of the whip;
He goes a thousand miles a day.
Once the Buddha made his mind turn back.
Should the horse come back when I beckon,
I'll snap my fingers thrice at him.

NOTES *It has no form and yet appears.* Being has in itself no definite form, but it manifests itself in the form of men, women, plants, animals, mountains, and rivers.

• *It extends in every direction and is boundless.* Being is everywhere and has no limits.

• *It responds spontaneously and works in emptiness.* Spontaneity arises naturally from within; actions flow freely and naturally.

• *The blows fall from your stick like raindrops and your shouts sound like thunderclaps.* The Zen teacher uses every means to instruct his students. He does not spare the rod.

• *Not yet to be compared with the man of advanced enlightenment.* The man of advanced enlightenment is the Buddha, or a completely mature master, who embodies in himself the quality of being formless and yet appearing, of extending in all directions and spontaneously responding with absolute freedom.

• *What is the condition of such a man?* The following story gives a good example.

• *Main Subject.* This case also occurs in *Mumonkan* as Case 32. See the notes to that case.

- *The World-honored One remained silent for a while.* "World-honored One" was one of the ten honorary titles given to the Buddha. The Buddha remained silent for a while at the philosopher's question. This silence was the embodiment of Engo's words, "It has no form and yet appears. It extends in every direction and is boundless. It responds spontaneously and works in emptiness." In *Mumonkan*, Case 32, the text is slightly different, reading, "The Buddha just sat there," instead of "The World-honored One remained silent for a while." But these two sentences are saying the same thing, namely, that the Buddha demonstrated a working samadhi, which combined both absolute and positive samadhi. Samadhi is the ever renewed continuation of the present, which is the very nature of being. Being is formless (absolute) but appears every moment (positive). Being extends in every direction and is immortal. Being is in perpetual motion. All things flow. You live in samadhi, you die in samadhi. This is the Middle Way of Buddhism.
- *Ananda.* See *Mumonkan*, Case 22.
- *The spiritual wheel does not turn.* In absolute samadhi, nothing moves. In positive samadhi, everything moves.
- *When it turns, it goes two ways.* When it moves, it goes either in the way of words or in the way of non-words.
- *The brilliant mirror on its stand.* The Buddha's remaining silent for a while is symbolized by the exquisite appearance of the brilliant mirror on its stand.
- *Divides beauty from ugliness.* This sings the praises of the mirror.
- *Lifts the clouds of doubt and illusion.* This refers to the philosopher's realization.
- *No dust is found in the gate of mercy.* "Gate" represents the whole structure of Buddhism, and "gate of mercy" symbolizes the Buddha's compassionate mind. The first six lines of Setchō's verse are in praise of the Buddha. The remainder is devoted to the philosopher's achievement.
- *A fine horse watches for the shadow of the whip.* The philosopher is likened to Emperor Shiko's famous horse, said to be able to go a thousand miles a day. This line describes the manner of the philosopher's asking and understanding the Buddha.
- *Should the horse come back when I beckon, / I'll snap my fingers thrice at him.* There is a Zen saying, "Even if you strike him, he does not look back." This describes the attitude of a truly independent man. If the horse comes at my beckoning, he is not worthy to be called truly independent.

Case 66 Gantō Laughed Loudly

ENGO'S INTRODUCTION Adapting himself adroitly to circumstances, displaying the spirit to capture a tiger; attacking now from the front, now in the flank, planning to seize the rebel; combining light and dark, holding fast and letting go; dealing with deadly serpents—this is the master's task.

MAIN SUBJECT Gantō asked a monk, "Where are you from?" The monk said, "From the western capital." Gantō said, "After the rebellion of Kōsō had been suppressed, did you get the sword?" The monk said, "Yes, I have got it." Gantō stretched out his neck before the monk and let forth a great yell. The monk said, "Your head has fallen." Gantō laughed loudly.

Later, the monk visited Seppō, who asked, "Where are you from?" The monk said, "From Gantō." Seppō said, "What did he say to you?" The monk recounted the story. Seppō gave him thirty blows and drove him out.

SETCHŌ'S VERSE
Since the rebel was suppressed,
The sacred sword has been restored;
Why the laughter, the master knows.
Too small a reward, the thirty blows;
One gains, one loses.

NOTES *Gantō, Seppō.* See *Mumonkan,* Case 13.
• *Adapting himself adroitly to circumstances, displaying the spirit to capture a tiger.* The Zen master, in his interviews with his students, always displays a decisive, forceful spirit. But he adapts himself to the condition of his students.
• *Attacking now from the front, now in the flank, planning to seize the rebel.* These are the teacher's tactics. The disciple often tries to surprise him. He is a rebel.

• *Combining light and dark.* Dark represents the condition of absolute samadhi, light that of positive samadhi. You must combine them both in yourself.

• *Serpents.* Students.

• *The western capital.* Lo-yang was called the eastern capital, Ch'ang-an the western. At the time of the incident in the present case, Ch'ang-an was the capital.

• *After the rebellion of Kōsō had been suppressed, did you get the sword?* At the time of the decline and fall of the T'ang dynasty the central government, in an attempt to tide over a financial crisis, tried to levy unjustly heavy taxes. Riots broke out. Kōsō was the leader of a rebellious faction. It is recorded in a chronicle that "an object fell from heaven. It was found to be a sword, which bore the inscription, 'Heaven gives this to Kōsō.' " From then on, Kōsō's group developed into a powerful force. In 880 Kōsō seized Ch'ang-an. Emperor Kisō fled from the imperial palace, and his relatives who failed to escape were massacred. Kōsō was killed four years later, and his followers were subjugated. But other riots followed throughout the country. Towns and villages were plundered, and the unrest accelerated the fall of the T'ang dynasty. Gantō's temple was located at Wuchang in the province of Hupei, far from Ch'ang-an, but it was nonetheless raided by rioters. Finding nothing worth stealing, they stabbed Gantō with a dagger. As he died, he gave a great shout, which is famous as "Gantō's shout." This took place in April 887, when Gantō was fifty-nine. The story of the present case must have occurred between Kōsō's execution in 884 and Gantō's death three years later.

Gantō asked the monk, "Did you get the sword?" This sword is something which everyone has innately. But unless he is enlightened, he is unaware of it. Gantō was asking the monk whether he had become aware of the sword.

• *Yes, I have got it.* This was a poor answer.

• *Gantō stretched out his neck before the monk and let forth a great yell.* Gantō's gesture meant, "If you have got the sword, try it on my head." It was a demonstration of Engo's "displaying the spirit to capture a tiger," and it was also a combination of a frontal and a flank attack, of holding fast and letting go.

• *The monk said, "Your head has fallen."* Invited to say this, he said it. There is no originality whatever. But the monk seems to have mistaken it for a success and, puffed up with it, went to Seppō.

• *Gantō laughed loudly.* The laughter was a demonstration of holding fast and letting go. But the monk did not understand.

• *Seppō gave him thirty blows and drove him out.* The monk deserved to be kicked out.

• *Since the rebel was suppressed, | The sacred sword has been restored.* Since your rebellious ego was toppled, you have realized your own nature.

• *Why the laughter, the master knows.* Only the mature master understands Gantō's laughter.

• *Too small a reward, the thirty blows.* The punishment was too light.

• *One gains, one loses.* The monk derived a false profit. Gantō had all his trouble for nothing, and with Seppō it was so much labor lost. But this is the inescapable lot of the teacher. His work is beyond price.

Case 67 Fu Daishi Concludes His Lecture on the Sutra

MAIN SUBJECT Emperor Wu of Liang asked Fu Daishi to give a lecture on the *Diamond Sutra.* Fu Daishi mounted the platform, struck the reading desk with his baton, and descended from the platform. The emperor was dumbfounded. Shikō said to him, "Your Majesty, have you understood?" The emperor said, "No, I do not understand." Shikō said, "Daishi has concluded his lecture."

SETCHŌ'S VERSE
    Instead of staying in his hut,
    He gathered dust in Liang.
    Had Shikō not lent a hand,
    He would have had to leave the country,
    As Bodhidharma did, by night.

NOTES *Fu Daishi* (497–569) had the family name Fu and the personal name Kyū. *Daishi* (*dai*, great; *shi*, virtuous gentleman) was the Chinese translation of "Bodhisattva." There is another *daishi* with a different second ideograph (*dai*, great; *shi*, teacher) that means a great teacher of Buddhism.

• *Emperor Wu of Liang* appears in Case 1. See the notes to that case.

• *Shikō* (d. 514) also appears in Case 1, to which the present case bears a close resemblance. Some Zen stories are fictitious, and this one probably is, as there is difficulty in reconciling the dates of Shikō and Fu.

• *Fu Daishi mounted the platform, struck the reading desk with his baton, and descended from the platform.* Here Engo puts in a comment: "Shooting star." The scene was the magnificent imperial lecture hall. A great array of dignitaries was no doubt present. Fu Daishi, in positive samadhi, ascended the platform and sat down. There was a hushed silence. Then he took up his baton, struck the lectern, and quietly descended from the platform. The audience, which had been holding its breath in anticipation, was astounded. But this was a genuine demonstration of the *Diamond Sutra*, in which we find such expressions as "There is no Dharma to be preached, and that is called Dharma preaching"; "The past mind is not attainable, the present mind is not attainable, the future mind is not attainable"; and "Abiding nowhere, let the mind work." Another sutra says, "You preached nothing, I heard nothing. No preaching and no hearing: that is true *prajna* [wisdom]."

• *The emperor was dumbfounded.* He was a devout Buddhist, but his interest lay chiefly in studying the Buddhist scriptures. He had no true understanding of Zen.

• *Shikō said to him, "Your Majesty, have you understood?"* Someone had to ask this. Shikō was a well-known priest in whom the emperor had great confidence.

• *The emperor said, "No, I do not understand."* The mature Zen master also says he does not understand Zen. There are many kinds of not-understanding Zen. Nowadays, there are many who do understand Zen.

• *Daishi has concluded his lecture.* It was an admirable conclusion.

• *Instead of staying in his hut, / He gathered dust in Liang.* There are two kinds of Zen students. One lives a life of retirement and seclusion. The other goes out into the world (in the Zen phrase, he goes into the marketplace) and, not bothering to shake the dust of the world from his feet, works for others. The latter is much appreciated in Zen.

• *He would have had to leave the country, / As Bodhidharma did, by night.*

In Case 1, Bodhidharma failed to meet with Emperor Wu's approval and left the land of Liang to go to Lo-yang.

Case 68   Kyōzan Asks Sanshō's Name

ENGO'S INTRODUCTION   Commanding the center of the heavens, overturning the axis of the earth; capturing the tiger, distinguishing the dragon from the snake: displaying such abilities, one can for the first time be called active and enlightened. And then words can meet words, spirit meet spirit. Tell me, who has ever been like that? See the following.

MAIN SUBJECT   Kyōzan asked Sanshō, "What is your name?" Sanshō said, "Ejaku!" Kyōzan said, "Ejaku is my name!" Sanshō said, "My name is Enen!" Kyōzan laughed heartily.

SETCHŌ'S VERSE
  Both grasping, both releasing—what fellows!
  Riding the tiger—marvelous skill!
  The laughter ends, traceless they go.
  Infinite pathos, to think of them!

NOTES   *Commanding the center of the heavens, overturning the axis of the earth.* Engo writes in an extravagant style appropriate to the massive Dharma battle between these two great Zen masters. They make a toy of heaven and earth, and lead Buddhas by the nose. In truth, it is no exaggeration to say that the activity of consciousness alone can change the course of existence. Every day and every moment of one's life must be a desperate struggle, a struggle which can be engaged in only once. The stream of consciousness never repeats itself; the path of life can never be retraced. Every moment's thought creates our karma.

• *Capturing the tiger, distinguishing the dragon from the snake.* See the notes to Case 35. Genuine existence is moment by moment's fighting and creation.

• *Words can meet words, spirit meet spirit.* This often occurs in the true Dharma battle. The present case is a typical example.

• *Kyōzan asked Sanshō, "What is your name?"* Kyōzan appears in Case 34, Sanshō in Case 49. Both were great masters. Kyōzan was the elder, being, in Dharma relation, a grandson of Hyakujō, while Sanshō was Hyakujō's great-grandson. The exchange recorded in the present case seems to have taken place when Sanshō first visited Kyōzan. The latter must long have been familiar with Sanshō's name, but he pretended not to know it. Was he really asking Sanshō's name or inquiring about Sanshō himself? Engo comments here, "He ignored both the name and the reality." Kyōzan ignored Sanshō's name, that is, he deprived Sanshō of his name and reality. What answer should Sanshō give?

• *Sanshō said, "Ejaku!"* This was Kyōzan's personal name. In other words, if you deprive me of my name, I shall deprive you of yours.

• *Kyōzan said, "Ejaku is my name!"* In holding fast, or grasping (see Case 4), the whole universe vanishes. In letting go, or releasing, the individual world appears, in which everyone asserts his existence. When he asked his first question, Kyōzan was standing in the absolute world, where others are ignored. But now he has come out into the world where everyone has his name, and he has himself confirmed his own name.

• *Sanshō said, "My name is Enen."* All right, if you come out into the world and confirm yourself, I shall do the same. Of course, the two masters' actions were not the outcome of this sort of intellectual reasoning but flowed from an intuitive understanding.

• *Kyōzan laughed heartily.* Kyōzan found that his words were met by Sanshō's, and so was his spirit. And quite naturally, he laughed delightedly.

• *Both grasping, both releasing—what fellows!* When holding fast, they both held fast; when letting go, they both let go.

• *Riding the tiger—marvelous skill!* The opponents in the great Dharma battle come out in splendid armor, riding their tigers.

• *The laughter ends, traceless they go.* One cannot help yearning after them.

• *Infinite pathos, to think of them!* In the sublime culmination of love, one wants above all to become one with the other person, but one knows the impossibility of such union—hence the pathos, which is infinite and eternal. We feel this same pathos when faced with beautiful scenery, with solemn mountains, rivers, the boundless oceans, the endless expanse of great plains; and we feel it too, and no less, when confronted with an exalted human spirit.

Case 69   Nansen Draws a Circle

ENGO'S INTRODUCTION   Where entry is barred, the Dharma Seal is like the iron ox's spirit. The monk who has passed through the thorny entanglements is like a snowflake on a red-hot hearth. Putting aside for a moment the "seven piercing and eight breaking through," what about acting independently of words and logic? See the following.

MAIN SUBJECT   Nansen, Kisu, and Mayoku were on their way together to pay their respects to Chū Kokushi. When they were halfway there, Nansen drew a circle on the ground and said, "If you can say a word, I will go on with you." Kisu sat down in the middle of the circle. Mayoku, seeing this, made a bow just as a woman does. Nansen said, "Then I will not go." Kisu said, "What an attitude of mind!"

SETCHŌ'S VERSE
  Yūki's arrow shot the monkey;
  How straight it flew,
  Circling the tree.

  Out of thousands, even tens of thousands,
  How many have hit the mark?
  Come, let us go home together.

  No need to pay respects to Sōkei!
  But again—why not?
  Isn't it a smooth road to Sōkei?

NOTES   *The Dharma Seal is like the iron ox's spirit.* See Case 38.

• *The thorny entanglements.* See Case 16. In brief, "thorny entanglements" means deluded thoughts.

• *A snowflake on a red-hot hearth.* It melts immediately and evaporates, leaving no trace behind. A monk who has passed through the thorny entanglements is like that. He is the embodiment of emptiness.

• *Seven piercing and eight breaking through.* See Case 49.

• *Acting independently of words and logic.* Acting with perfect freedom in all ways.

• *Nansen, Kisu, Mayoku, Chū Kokushi.* For Nansen see *Mumonkan,* Case 14. Mayoku appears in Case 31. For Chū Kokushi see *Mumonkan,* Case 17. Nansen, Kisu, and Mayoku were all students of Baso.

• *Nansen drew a circle on the ground.* The use of the circle as a Zen symbol is said to have originated with Chū Kokushi. The circle represents the universe, ultimate truth, Buddhism, and so on. Everybody is encircled in it; no one can get out of it. But in Zen you are supposed to embody it in yourself.

• *If you can say a word, I will go on with you.* A Zen story is not something old and remote; it refers to yourself. Now, how are you going to answer Nansen's question? It is no use imitating Kisu.

• *Kisu sat down in the middle of the circle.* Kisu's action must have seemed very fresh and original when he produced it.

• *Mayoku, seeing this, made a bow.* Nansen produced Chū Kokushi's circle, Kisu demonstrated his mastery of the circle, and Mayoku paid his respects to the master.

• *Just as a woman does.* When a monk bows, he falls on his knees. A woman does not kneel but only bows from the waist.

• *Nansen said, "Then I will not go."* Homage has already been paid to Chū Kokushi. There is no need to go to see him.

• *What an attitude of mind!* You rascal!

• *Yūki's arrow.* In remote times, a king named Sō went hunting. He saw a white monkey and ordered his attendants to shoot it. But the monkey seized the arrows as they were shot and played with them mockingly. No one could shoot it. At length, Yūki, a master archer, was called for and told to shoot the monkey. When Yūki drew his bow the monkey clutched the tree, screaming with fear. When the arrow was loosed the monkey leaped around the tree to dodge it. The arrow, too, went around the tree in circles and shot the monkey.

• *How straight it flew*. Nansen, Kisu, and Mayoku, too, went directly to Chū Kokushi.

• *Out of thousands, even tens of thousands, | How many have hit the mark?* Of countless Zen students, how many have truly attained enlightenment?

• *Come, let us go home together*. We have it from the beginning. Stop searching after it. Return home, and be at ease.

• *No need to pay respects to Sōkei!* There is no longer any need to go to Sōkei, where Chū Kokushi lived. The Sixth Patriarch also lived at Sōkei initially, and Sōkei generally refers to the Sixth Patriarch. In the present case, however, it means Chū Kokushi.

• *But again—why not?* Zen practice must be done. It must be carried through.

• *Isn't it a smooth road to Sōkei?* It is a level road to Sōkei. Go on and reach your destination, and be at home.

Case 70   Isan's "I Would Ask You to Say It"

ENGO'S INTRODUCTION   A word is sufficient to the wise, as a flick of the whip is to a fine horse. One eon, one nen. One nen, one eon. What is immediacy? It is prior to words. Tell me, how do you attain to it? See the following.

MAIN SUBJECT   Isan, Gohō, and Ungan were standing together in attendance on Hyakujō. Hyakujō said to Isan, "With your mouth and lips closed, how would you say it?" Isan said, "I would ask you to say it." Hyakujō said, "I could say it. But if I did so, I fear I should have no successors."

SETCHŌ'S VERSE
    "I would ask you to say it."
    The tiger has got a crest
    And sprung from the jungle!

In the ten lands, spring is over.
Eternal under the golden sun
The fields of coral lie.

NOTES   *A word is sufficient to the wise.* See Case 38.
• *One eon, one nen. One nen, one eon.* A nen is the smallest fraction of thought. Hence, this moment is endless time; endless time is this moment.
• *What is immediacy?* Immediacy is direct pure cognition.
• *Isan, Gohō, Ungan, Hyakujō.* Isan appears in Cases 4 and 24 and in *Mumonkan*, Case 40. For Hyakujō, see Case 53 and *Mumonkan*, Case 2. Not much is known of Gohō, and his dates are not recorded. Ungan (782–841) entered Hyakujō's temple in 794, when he was twelve years old. He studied under Hyakujō for twenty years and, at Hyakujō's death in 814, went to Yakusan (see Case 42), under whom he attained enlightenment. He appears again in Cases 72 and 89.
• *With your mouth and lips closed, how would you say it?* How do you demonstrate the immediate truth? If you really become the immediate truth itself, it will be easy for you to do so quite freely in ordinary daily life. Saying "Good morning" or sitting down will demonstrate it. Whether you open your mouth or not makes little difference. This and the following two cases present three answers to Hyakujō's question.
• *I would ask you to say it.* Isan is turning the tables on his teacher.
• *I could say it. But if I did so, I fear I should have no successors.* The answer lies in the question. The question tells us that the immediate truth is beyond words. Hyakujō says that if he were to talk too much about this it would spoil his students.
• *"I would ask you to say it."* Setchō reproduces Isan's words to emphasize that this is the essence of the case.
• *The tiger has got a crest | And sprung from the jungle!* The tiger has no crest. But the one to which Isan is compared is helmeted for battle, a fierce and powerful creature. The first three lines of the verse are in praise of Isan.
• *In the ten lands, spring is over.* The ten lands are legendary islands where spring lasts a hundred years and in which all the objects of worldly desire are produced: the elixir of eternal life, incense which summons up the ghosts of the dead, delicious wine, precious jewels, auspicious ani-

mals, birds, flowers, and so on. However, when spring is over, all the flowers and treasures decay. In other words, all the objects of worldly desire will eventually crumble to dust. In this line, however, Setchō is also alluding to such sayings as Ummon's "[When trees wither and leaves fall,] you embody the golden breeze" (Case 27).

• *Eternal under the golden sun | The fields of coral lie.* This is an image of everlasting beauty, symbolizing the condition of Isan and Hyakujō and to be set against the evanescent spring of the ten lands.

Case 71 Gohō's "Shut Up"

MAIN SUBJECT Hyakujō said to Gohō, "With your mouth and lips closed, how would you say it?" Gohō said, "Oshō! You should shut up!" Hyakujō said, "In the distant land where no one stirs, I shall shade my eyes with my hand and watch for you."

SETCHŌ'S VERSE
"Oshō! You should shut up!"
Upon the dragon's line
He plans his counterattack.

Let's think of General Li,
Who shot the eagle
In the distant sky.

NOTES *Oshō! You should shut up!* This case follows from the previous one. There Isan was letting go; now Gohō is holding fast.

• *In the distant land where no one stirs, I shall shade my eyes with my hand and watch for you.* Gohō's answer was full of vigor, and that is much to be admired. He was holding fast, and that, too, is good in itself. But by doing this he excluded others and isolated himself. This is what Hyakujō refers to in his words, "In the distant land where no one stirs." In absolute samadhi, you are in total seclusion and purify yourself. This is called "planning profit for yourself." Then you are expected to come out into the busy world in positive samadhi and work for others. That is called "planning profit for others." When mature, one is supposed to be able to do both. Though Gohō's answer was to be admired, he was not equal in maturity to Isan.

• *"Oshō! You should shut up!"* Setchō begins his verse with the essence of the case.

• *Upon the dragon's line | He plans his counterattack.* The dragon's line is the battle line constructed by Hyakujō. If you hit the head, the tail will descend upon you in a counterattack. If you hit the tail, the head will descend on you. If you hit the body, both head and tail will counterattack. Strictly speaking, both Gohō and Hyakujō have constructed their lines and taken up their positions confronting each other.

• *Let's think of General Li, | Who shot the eagle | In the distant sky.* General Li was a good archer, and Gohō is compared to him. Gohō's arrow shot the eagle that Hyakujō loosed.

Case 72 Ungan's "Do You Have Them or Not?"

MAIN SUBJECT   Hyakujō asked Ungan, "With your mouth and lips closed, how would you say it?" Ungan said, "Oshō, do you have them or not?" Hyakujō said, "My successors will be missing."

SETCHŌ'S VERSE
"Oshō! Do you have them or not?"
The golden-haired lion
Does not crouch.

In twos and threes, they go the old way;
The master of Mount Taiyu
Snaps his fingers in vain.

NOTES *Ungan was slow in maturing.* When this question was asked him he was still immature. Later he became a great Zen master. This case follows from the previous two.

• *Oshō, do you have them or not?* This counter-question of Ungan's can be paraphrased in two ways: (1) Have you (representing Buddha Nature) any mouth or lips? or (2) Have you, on your part, asked your question with your mouth and lips closed? Had Ungan said this with good understanding, it would have produced an excellent effect. But Ungan was still groping blindly in the dark, and his attitude was irresolute and dull. He was not keen-edged, as were Isan and Gohō in the two previous cases, and his answer was rejected by Hyakujō.

• *My successors will be missing.* If you are still in such an irresolute condition, I shall have no successors.

• *The golden-haired lion / Does not crouch.* In China, a crouching lion meant a lion crouched to spring upon its prey. Ungan, who is compared to the golden-haired lion, showed no sign of being ready to spring upon his oppponent.

• *In twos and threes, they go the old way.* Monks, in groups of two and three, idle away their time irresolutely, as some of them have always done.

• *The master of Mount Taiyu.* Hyakujō.

• *Snaps his fingers in vain.* One may snap one's fingers to arouse others or to indicate one's rejection of them. Hyakujō tried to arouse Ungan, but in vain.

Case 73 Baso and the Hundred Negations

ENGO'S INTRODUCTION Preaching is non-preaching and non-teaching. Hearing is non-hearing and non-attaining. If preaching is non-preaching and non-teaching, what use is there in preaching? If hearing is non-hearing and non-attaining, what use is there in hearing? But this non-preaching and non-hearing are worth something. You are listening to me now, preaching here. How can we escape that criticism? Those who have eyes, see the following.

MAIN SUBJECT   A monk said to Ba Taishi, "Independent of the four propositions and transcending the hundred negations, tell me plainly the meaning of Bodhidharma's coming from the West." Bashi said, "Today I am tired and cannot tell you. Ask Chizō about it." The monk asked Chizō, who said, "Why don't you ask the master?" The monk said, "He told me to ask you." Chizō said, "Today I have a headache and cannot tell you about it. Ask Brother Kai." The monk asked Brother Kai, who said, "Coming to this point, I do not understand." The monk told this to Ba Taishi, who said, "Zō's head is white, Kai's head is black."

SETCHŌ'S VERSE
"Zō's head is white, Kai's head is black!"
It defies understanding.

Ba's horses trampled over the world;
Rinzai wasn't such a daylight robber.

Putting aside the four propositions, the hundred negations,
You can only nod to yourself.

NOTES   *Preaching is non-preaching and non-teaching. Hearing is non-hearing and non-attaining.* When you really understand the truth of Zen, you realize that you have attained nothing particularly profound but just a very simple and commonplace understanding. To come to that simple understanding, however, you had to listen intently to a great deal of instruction. When you started Zen practice, you expected to attain to some profound, mysterious truth. And certainly in absolute samadhi, where the activity of consciousness is stopped, you shook off the old world, and in kenshō (realization) you found yourself in quite a different world from the ordinary one (though that different world is none other than the ordinary world where you have always lived). When you return to the ordinary activity of consciousness, you find yourself again in the old common-sense world, only now you have established positive samadhi and your nen-actions are purified. What is positive samadhi? In brief, it is the acknowledgment of the present world as it is. Dōgen Zenji said, "I have returned from my study in China realizing that my eyes lie horizontally and my nose is vertical."

• *What use is there in preaching? . . . What use is there in hearing?* Now that pure cognition is restored to you, you can calmly recognize the objects of the external world. In achieving liberation from your own ego, you become free of all delusive thoughts and sufferings.

• *This non-preaching and non-hearing are worth something.* The sun shines silently. Mountains, rivers, plants, and animals all deliver their silent sermons. Heaven and earth go quietly around, and the universe continues on its course.

• *Independent of the four propositions and transcending the hundred negations.* The four propositions are existing, non-existing, both existing and non-existing, and neither existing nor non-existing. The hundred negations are arrived at by multiplying the four propositions in the characteristic fashion of Indian philosophy. In short, they represent all the varieties of philosophical thinking. Disregarding all such philosophizing, what is the true nature of Buddhism?

• *The meaning of Bodhidharma's coming from the West.* No-meaning is the meaning of Bodhidharma's coming from India, and at the same time the meaning of Buddhism. This no-meaning is the true meaning of the universe, which continues blindly on its course.

• *Bashi.* Ba Taishi (*tai*, great; *shi*, teacher), Bashi, and Baso all denote the same person, Baso. (See *Mumonkan*, Case 30.)

• *Today I am tired and cannot tell you.* "Tired" and "cannot" are a splendid exemplification of the direct preaching of non-preaching.

• *Ask Chizō.* Chizō was one of Baso's outstanding pupils. How he would deal with this topic was the point of interest.

• *Why don't you ask the master?* Every sentence is an expression of non-preaching.

• *He told me to ask you.* Although himself exercising non-hearing, the monk is not aware of it.

• *Today I have a headache and cannot tell you about it.* He tells so much.

• *Brother Kai.* "Brother" here means "elder." Kai is the shortened, familiar name of Hyakujō Ekai, who was fifteen years older than Chizō.

• *Coming to this point, I do not understand.* This was most direct.

• *Zō's head is white, Kai's head is black.* The rose is red, the peony scarlet. The northern mountain is high, the southern hill low.

• *"Zō's head is white, Kai's head is black!"* This is the same as saying, "My eyes lie horizontally and my nose is vertical."

• *It defies understanding.* There is no difficulty in understanding it.

• *Ba's horses trampled over the world.* Baso's name inevitably brings to mind the image of a horse (*ba*, horse; *so*, patriarch). Ba's horses are Baso's disciples, who were all distinguished Zen students. They rose above the heads of ordinary people.

• *Rinzai wasn't such a daylight robber.* A great Zen master can be called a daylight robber because he deprives his students of their most treasured achievements. Rinzai was called a daylight robber, but he is not to be compared with Baso. This is, of course, intended simply as a way of emphasizing Baso's greatness.

• *Putting aside the four propositions, the hundred negations, / You can only nod to yourself.* Preaching is non-preaching, hearing is non-hearing. You can only nod your head to yourself.

Case 74 Kingyū Oshō and the Rice Pail

ENGO'S INTRODUCTION The Bakuya sword in hand, he cuts through all complications. The clear mirror hung high, he himself utters the words of Vairocana. In self-mastery he quietly puts on his clothes and takes his meal. In occult and playful samadhi, what will he do? See the following.

MAIN SUBJECT At every midday mealtime, Kingyū Oshō would himself bring the pail of boiled rice and, in front of the refectory, dance and laugh loudly, saying, "Dear Bodhisattvas, come and take your meal." [Setchō says, "Although Kingyū did this, he was not simple-minded."]

A monk said to Chōkei, "The ancient worthy said, 'Dear Bodhisattvas, come and take your meal.' What does it mean?" Chōkei said, "He seems to observe reflection and thanksgiving before the midday meal."

SETCHŌ'S VERSE
From among the white clouds, laughter rings out;
He brings the rice himself to give to the monks.

If golden-haired, they will follow him,
Even thousands of miles away.

NOTES *Kingyū* was one of the eighty-four outstanding disciples of
Baso. When Rinzai, after attaining enlightenment, was traveling about
visiting Zen masters in various places, he came one day to Kingyū's
temple. Kingyū, seeing Rinzai coming, sat in his room holding his stick
crosswise. Rinzai struck the stick three times with his hand, then entered
the monks' hall and sat down in the first seat. Kingyū came in, saw Rinzai, and said, "In an encounter between host and guest, each should observe the customary formalities. Where are you from? And why are you
so rude?" "What are you talking about, old oshō?" answered Rinzai.
As Kingyū was about to open his mouth to reply, Rinzai struck him.
Kingyū pretended to fall down. Rinzai hit him again. Kingyū said, "Today things were not to my advantage."

At a later time, Isan asked Kyōzan, "In the case of these two venerable
ones, was either the winner or loser?" Kyōzan said, "When one wins,
one wins unconditionally; when one loses, one loses unconditionally."

• *The Bakuya sword in hand, he cuts through all complications.* The Bakuya
sword was famous in an early warring period of Chinese history. Here
Engo uses it to symbolize the sword of wisdom, which Manjusri holds.

• *The clear mirror hung high, he himself utters the words of Vairocana.* The
clear mirror is the Great Perfect Mirror Wisdom, which represents
the Dharmakaya, or Vairocana. The Zen master, uttering Vairocana's
words, himself takes the place of the Buddha.

• *In self-mastery he quietly puts on his clothes and takes his meal.* Self-
mastery appears in absolute samadhi. The phrase in the original text
which we have translated as "self-mastery" is *onmitsu denji* (*on*, subtle;
mitsu, mysterious; *denji*, field). If you progress to maturity in your cultivation of Holy Buddhahood after realization, self-mastery appears in
ordinary life and presides over your mind. We generally pay little attention to such ordinary actions as putting on our clothes or eating a
meal. But from the Zen point of view such actions are of great importance. They are expressions of ordinary mind. True peace of mind is
demonstrated there.

• *In occult and playful samadhi, what will he do?* Playful samadhi is the
joyful demonstration of positive samadhi, in which the person com-

munes freely with others. The behavior of Kingyū Oshō in the present case is a good example of this. What is occult samadhi? There is nothing mysterious in this from the Zen point of view. The only mystery is that of one's own being. Hō Koji (see Case 42) says,

> "I exercise occult and subtle power,
> Carrying water, shouldering firewood."

• *At every midday mealtime.* Every day Kingyū Oshō would bring the rice pail and would dance and laugh loudly, saying, "Dear Bodhisattvas, come and take your meal." He did not miss even one day. It was wonderful. What was in his mind? Sometimes the Zen teacher has these peculiar ways, which he sticks to. Ummon used to ask Kyōrin every day, "What is this?"

• *Setchō says, "Although Kingyū did this, he was not simple-minded."* Setchō is reminding you that Kingyū had a definite intention in behaving as he did, although he was as innocent as a baby.

• *He seems to observe reflection and thanksgiving before the midday meal.* At every mealtime the monks recite certain prescribed sutras, some reflective, some giving thanks.

• *From among the white clouds, laughter rings out.* Dense clouds of steam rise from the hot boiled rice, like white clouds moving across the sky. The old oshō's bizarre face appears among the clouds, and a great peal of laughter issues from his mouth.

• *He brings the rice himself.* In occult and playful samadhi he brings the meal.

• *To give to the monks.* He is giving something to others every moment. But what is the "it" that he gives?

• *If golden-haired, they will follow him.* If they are golden-haired lions they will understand Kingyū's present.

• *Even thousands of miles away.* You can understand even if you are separated by thousands of miles and hundreds of years.

Case 75   Ukyū's Unfair Blows

ENGO'S INTRODUCTION   The sacred sword is ever in hand: it is death-dealing and life-giving. It is there, it is here, simultaneously giving and taking. If you want to hold fast, you are free to hold fast. If you want to let go, you are free to let go. Tell me how it will be when one makes no distinction between host and guest, and is indifferent to which role one takes up. See the following.

MAIN SUBJECT   A monk came from Jōshū Oshō's assembly to Ukyū, who said to him, "What do you find in Jōshū's teaching? Is there anything different from what you find here?" The monk said, "Nothing different." Ukyū said, "If there is nothing different, why don't you go back there?" and he hit him with his stick. The monk said, "If your stick had eyes to see, you would not strike me like that." Ukyū said, "Today I have come across a monk," and he gave him three more blows. The monk went out. Ukyū called after him and said, "One may receive unfair blows." The monk turned back and said, "To my regret, the stick is in your hand." Ukyū said, "If you need it, I will let you have it." The monk went up to Ukyū, seized his stick, and gave him three blows with it. Ukyū said, "Unfair blows! Unfair blows!" The monk said, "One may receive them." Ukyū said, "I hit this one too casually." The monk made bows. Ukyū said, "Oshō! Is that how you take leave?" The monk laughed aloud and went out. Ukyū said, "That's it! That's it!"

SETCHŌ'S VERSE
    Easy to call the snakes, hard to scatter them.
    How splendidly they crossed swords!
    Although the sea is deep, it can be drained;
    The kalpa stone is hard, but wears away.
    Old Ukyū! Old Ukyū!
    Who is there like you?
    To give the stick to another—
    That was truly thoughtless!

NOTES *Ukyū.* Like Kingyū in Case 74, Ukyū was one of Baso's outstanding disciples. Apart from the story of the present case, another is recorded of him. After he had left Baso and was living in his own temple, two monks, Gen and Shō, came from Baso's monastery to have an interview with him. Ukyū asked Gen, "Where are you from?" "From Kozei," replied Gen. (Kozei was the location of Baso's temple.) Before Gen had finished these words, Ukyū gave him a blow with his stick. Gen said, "I have heard that you treat visitors like this." "You do not understand me," said Ukyū, and turning to Shō, he said, "Come before me." When Shō came forward, he was hit before he had said anything. Ukyū was one of the first Zen masters to use the stick in his teaching. The idea of being struck is repugnant to most modern people, but in the early days of Zen in China it was an accepted element in Zen training. Some blows expressed approval, others disapproval.

• *The sacred sword is ever in hand.* "The sacred sword" means spiritual power. It is called by many other names: the diamond treasure sword, the sword of prajna, the Bakuya sword (Cases 9 and 74), and so on. Everyone has this spiritual sword, but unless it is sharpened it remains dull and useless.

• *When one makes no distinction between host and guest.* The episode related in the present case is a fine example of this.

• *Jōshū Oshō.* This is not the famous Jōshū Jūnen, who appears in many cases in *Mumonkan* and *Hekiganroku*, but Jōshū Sekizō, who was related in Dharma lineage to Shinshū, the founder of the Northern Zen school. Ukyū belonged to the Southern Zen school, as did Setchō. Both Ukyū, in his treatment of the monk, and Setchō, in selecting this story, showed no discrimination between the Northern and Southern schools.

• *I have come across a monk.* Here "a monk" means one who is worthy of that name.

• *If you need it, I will let you have it.* This is what Engo refers to when he says, "One makes no distinction between host and guest, and is indifferent to which role one takes up."

• *The monk made bows.* This marks a return to the normal relationship between host and guest.

• *Oshō! Is that how you take leave?* For Ukyū to say "Oshō" is to talk to the monk on equal terms. "Is that how you take leave?" marks the renewal of the dialogue.

• *The monk laughed aloud and went out.* From the beginning in a Dharma battle, there is no ego at work. Surging waves may arise in the encounter, but they pass away like clouds moving across the bright face of the autumn moon. Nothing is left behind.

• *That's it! That's it!* The original text says *sho toku inmo, sho toku inmo* (*sho*, do; *toku*, could; *inmo*, like this). These are Ukyū's words of acknowledgment.

• *Easy to call the snakes, hard to scatter them.* The snake-catcher plays on a leaf flute and the snakes, attracted by the sound, gather around him. He catches those that he wants. It is rather easy up to this point. But it is said that after that he finds it hard to make the rest of the snakes scatter. To start a Dharma battle is easy, but to bring it to a successful conclusion, as Ukyū and the monk did, is difficult.

• *How splendidly they crossed swords!* Spiritual swords were crossed by host and guest, each alternately taking the other's role.

• *Although the sea is deep, it can be drained.* Though even the deep sea can be drained, Ukyū's and the monk's performance will last forever.

• *The kalpa stone is hard, but wears away.* The kalpa stone is forty miles square. Every hundred years a nymph comes and passes the sleeve of her silken robe lightly over it. When the stone has wholly worn away, one kalpa, or eon, has passed. The kalpa stone will eventually cease to exist, but the achievement of Ukyū and the monk will last forever.

• *Old Ukyū! Old Ukyū!* This affectionate calling of Ukyū's name implies Setchō's unreserved admiration for him.

• *That was truly thoughtless!* Ukyū's action stems from his pure cognition, which is totally free of any element of calculation. Such cognition is here characterized as "thoughtless" in the literal sense of the word. The line gains its effect from the fact that in its usual sense "thoughtless" means careless or not paying proper attention.

Case 76 Tanka's "Have You Had Your Dinner?"

ENGO'S INTRODUCTION   It is as small as a particle of flour, as cold as ice and frost. It fills the universe, transcends light and darkness. Its depths cannot be fathomed, its summit is beyond reach. Holding fast and letting go are all contained within it. Where is your absolute freedom, transcending all restrictions? See the following.

MAIN SUBJECT   Tanka asked a monk, "Where are you from?" The monk replied, "From the foot of the mountain." Tanka said, "Have you had your dinner?" The monk said, "I have had it." Tanka said, "Is he open-eyed who brings food to a fellow like you and lets you eat it?" The monk could make no reply.

Later Chōkei asked Hofuku, " To give food to others is surely worthy. How could he fail to be open-eyed?" Hofuku said, "Both giver and receiver are blind." Chōkei said, "Are you still blind, even though you exhaust every means?" Hofuku said, "How can you call me blind?"

SETCHŌ'S VERSE
Exhaust every means, and you will not be blind;
You hold the cow's head to let it graze.
The four sevens, the two threes, the following band
Have handed down the Dharma treasure,
Raising dust and trouble to make men drown on land.

NOTES   *Tanka* (739–824) was a contemporary of Nansen, Isan, Ryūtan, Hō Koji, and Yakusan. He first studied Zen with Baso and then, at Baso's suggestion, went to Sekitō. Three years later he returned to Baso's temple and, before paying his respects to Baso, went into the monks' hall and climbed up onto the shoulders of a statue of Manjusri. The monks were astonished and went to tell Baso, who came down to the hall. He saw Tanka and said, "My son Tennen" [son of nature]. Tanka climbed down from Manjusri's shoulders and made bows to Baso, saying, "Thank you, master, for giving me my Dharma name." And thereafter he was called Tennen.

After Baso's death Tanka went on a journey visiting Zen masters, and one winter's day he stayed at a certain temple. It was very cold that night. Tanka took down an image of Buddha from the platform, put it in the hearth to burn, and warmed himself at the fire. The priest of the temple reproached him for his audacity. Tanka said, "I am going to take out the Buddha's bones." "How can you get the Buddha's bones from the wood?" the priest asked. Tanka said, "Then I am not to blame for burning the wood."

When he was eighty-one years old he retired to his temple at Mount Tanka in Hunan Province. One day, four years later, he said to his disciples, "I am starting on my journey." He equipped himself with hat, leggings, socks, and staff, and put on a shoe. Before his foot touched the ground he had died.

• *Where are you from?* This is a hackneyed question, but from the way the visitor answers it the master can get a general idea of his condition.

• *From the foot of the mountain.* In point of fact, he could hardly have dropped from the sky. This answer is too obvious. Is he pretending ignorance?

• *Have you had your dinner?* The question has a double meaning. It refers to both the monk's material food and his spiritual food, that is, his realization.

• *I have had it.* This reply revealed the monk's immaturity.

• *Is he open-eyed who brings food to a fellow like you and lets you eat it?* "Open-eyed" means having a good understanding of Zen. Tanka is saying that he who gives food to a foolish one like you cannot have an eye to discern a genuine student of Zen.

• *Later Chōkei asked Hofuku.* Chōkei (854–932) appears in seven cases in *Hekiganroku*. He was born thirty years after Tanka died, so this conversation took place long after the episode related in the first part of the case. Hofuku appears also in Cases 8, 23, 91, and 95. His dates are not recorded, but he seems to have been younger than Chōkei. In asking his question Chōkei perhaps was examining Hofuku's level of attainment.

• *To give food to others is surely worthy. How could he fail to be open-eyed?* Setchō took a special interest in this question, regarding it as the most important part of the case. As part of their routine activities, Zen monks go begging. This is called *takuhatsu* (*taku*, holding up; *hatsu*, bowl). It is not begging in the ordinary sense. They receive food and other things with an "empty mind," which means that there is no sort of personal discrimination about the giver and the receiver or about the things given. The giver, too, is supposed to be empty-minded in giving things. There is no thought of charity or almsgiving: he simply gives. Emptiness also pertains to the things given: they are not evaluated. A penny and a thousand dollars are regarded as equal. This attitude of mind is called "triple emptiness."

Takuhatsu is carried out with the utmost gravity and makes the people concerned solemn-minded. If you once participate in a takuhatsu trip, you will inevitably feel its solemnity. The thanksgiving for donations is purely thanksgiving. Chōkei's meaning is that a man who gives with an empty mind must have a genuine understanding of Zen and be demonstrating the spirit of Zen. How can he be said not to be open-eyed?

• *Hofuku said, "Both giver and receiver are blind."* As explained in the notes to Case 10, there are five kinds of spiritual blindness from the Zen point of view. The blindness referred to in Hofuku's answer is that of the last category and also of the third.

• *Are you still blind, even though you exhaust every means?* Chōkei is cross-examining Hofuku. Chōkei is asking whether, if you do everything you can for the benefit of others, you are still blind. He means here common blindness. Chōkei is saying that the man who works for others must be enlightened, though Tanka seemingly says the contrary.

• *How can you call me blind?* Hofuku's answer is that you cannot call such a person blind. There is a confusion here simply because "blindness" is being used in different senses. Why is this? The Zen masters of old did not bother to define their terms precisely, as Western philosophers do. They often used a word quite loosely, giving it various shades of meaning. This gave rise to a great deal of confusion and often made it difficult for students to understand the meaning of certain ambiguous and even illogical expressions. Students therefore had first to arrive at a true understanding of Zen for themselves, from their own practice, and then to work out the meaning of the paradoxical statements and equivocal terms. Zen is not intrinsically illogical or paradoxical, as a casual acquaintance with it might suggest. It can be explained perfectly logically. But Zen masters refused to do this, and they indulged in paradoxes particularly in order to forestall attempts at conceptual understanding. You must attain to the truth yourself, on the basis of your own hard practice, and not attempt to reach it indirectly through the medium of other people's explanations.

• *Exhaust every means, and you will not be blind.* Setchō emphasizes this. His verse concentrates on Chōkei's question. Tanka and the questioning monk are ignored in his verse. Why? Because to do everything you can for others is the soul of Buddhism.

• *You hold the cow's head to let it graze.* The Bodhisattva's Vow is to act as a friend to his fellow creatures even though uninvited, and to help others if nevenot asked. He exhausts every possible means to save others. The cow may not want to eat, but he uses every means to feed it. The following lines are a paraphrase of the Bodhisattva's Vow.

• *The four sevens, the two threes, the following· band.* The twenty-eight Indian patriarchs, the six Chinese patriarchs, and the patriarchs and teachers who followed them.

• *Have handed down the Dharma treasure, / Raising dust and trouble.* The patriarchs and other teachers handed down the Dharma Seal, offering it to people as if they were holding a cow's head to let it graze. They caused much trouble because, as a result of their teaching, many people have been led to practice zazen and torment themselves with hard training. In Case 41 of *Mumonkan*, Mumon's verse says:

> You entrusted the Dharma, and trouble arose;
> The clamor of the monasteries
> Is all because of you.

And in Case 17 his verse reads:

> He carried an iron yoke with no hole
> And left a curse to trouble his descendants.
> If you want to hold up the gate and the doors,
> You must climb a mountain of swords with bare feet.

• *To make men drown on land.* Zazen practice and getting into absolute samadhi, where one suffers the Great Death, are like drowning on land. The Buddha and the patriarchs and teachers who followed him all drowned on land. With infinite compassion and kindness they have guided others along the same path. They cannot help doing this. The traditional interpretation of Setchō's lines is that the Buddha and the patriarchs handed down the Dharma treasure and that the people who received it were thrown into an irrational, unreasonable state. This appears different from my interpretation, but if you understand it thoroughly you will find that the difference is superficial. In Case 93 Setchō's verse includes the line, "Many would drown on land," which there has a slightly different meaning.

Case 77   Ummon's "A Sesame Bun"

ENGO'S INTRODUCTION   If you work in the upward, transcendent way, you lead others by the nose; you are like a hawk taking a dove. If you work in the downward way, you place yourself at others' disposal, like a tortoise in its shell. If any of you come forward and say: There is originally no upward and downward; what use is it to talk in that way? I will say to them: I know you are living among dead spirits. Now, tell me, how do you distinguish black from white? [Here Engo pauses a while, then goes on to say:] If there is a rule, follow it; if not, follow a precedent. See the following.

MAIN SUBJECT   A monk asked Ummon, "What is the teaching that transcends the Buddha and patriarchs?" Ummon said, "A sesame bun."

SETCHŌ'S VERSE
　Talking about transcendence,
　Men come up with countless puzzles.
　Just look! All patched up,
　Full of holes.
　Ummon stopped the gaps
　With his sesame bun.
　But problems still remain
　To torture you.

NOTES   *If you work in the upward, transcendent way, you lead others by the nose.* Holding fast, or grasping, you control others, as Baso did by pinching Hyakujō's nose (Case 53).
• *If you work in the downward way, you place yourself at others' disposal.* Letting go, or releasing, you behave as Ukyū did, letting his opponent use his stick (Case 75).
• *There is originally no upward and downward.* In the realm of the absolute there is neither upward nor downward movement, no right and wrong, no loss and gain, and so on.

• *How do you distinguish black from white?* In daily life there appear good and evil, equality and difference, the koan and the studying of the koan, holding fast and letting go, and so on.

• *Follow a precedent.* A koan constitutes a precedent.

• *What is the teaching that transcends the Buddha and patriarchs?* The monk is saying, I have already transcended the Buddha and patriarchs; now I want to discuss with you the transcendent teachings.

• *A sesame bun.* This is a Chinese bun with sesame seeds sprinkled on top. It is a very ordinary, common sort of bun. Jōshū once said, "Have a cup of tea."

• *Talking about transcendence,* / *Men come up with countless puzzles.* Like the philosophers, who have written so many difficult passages about transcendence, Buddhist monks often brought up knotty problems.

• *Just look! All patched up,* / *Full of holes.* Zen practice aims at directly mastering truth by intuitive experience. Those who discuss truth in conceptual terms show that they have not mastered it directly. Their understanding is a makeshift thing, full of holes.

• *Ummon stopped the gaps* / *With his sesame bun.* Ummon abruptly put an end to conceptual discussion.

• *But problems still remain* / *To torture you.* There is no end to the people who talk about transcendence, right up to the present time, and there is no end to the conceptual tangles they create.

It is not wrong to say that reason is the master of the mind. Reason brings together and synthesizes various nen-actions, and may develop a system of thinking. Reason works with ideas and concepts. Conceptual thinking can result in apparent clarity and accuracy, from which one derives a sense of security. Conceptual thinking, it is true, may repeat error after error. This is shown by the way in which long-held popular beliefs are constantly being shown to be erroneous and are discarded. But man's thinking becomes deeper as it continues, even though it may contain errors. Nowadays we have at our disposal a great deal of very sophisticated intellectual equipment. We have reached a stage at which even Zen can be conceptually explained. In writing about Zen in these comments and elsewhere, my aim is to recapture in conceptual terms what has once been intuitively experienced. I do not at all condemn conceptual thinking, but the immediate, intuitive experience must come first.

Case 78   Bodhisattvas in the Bath

MAIN SUBJECT   In ancient times, there were sixteen Bodhisattvas. At the monks' bathtime, following the rule, they had baths. They suddenly experienced realization through the touch of the water. You reverend Zen students, do you understand their words? "We experienced the subtle and clear touch, have attained Buddhahood, and still retain it." You will be able to attain this condition after seven times piercing and eight times breaking through.

SETCHŌ'S VERSE
The enlightened man is master of one single thing,
Stretches at ease on his bed.
If, in a dream, the ancients said they were enlightened,
Let them emerge from the scented water, and I would spit at them!

NOTES   Sixteen Bodhisattvas. In the Surangama Sutra there is an episode in which twenty-five Bodhisattvas relate their experiences of attaining realization. First, Kyōchinnyo and four others (the first five disciples of the Buddha) stand up and describe their paths to realization. Kyōchinnyo says, "As for my realization, seeing a sight was the primary cause of it." Second, Kyōgon Dōji (kyō, smell; gon, solemn; dōji, student of Zen) says, "Smelling a scent was the cause of my realization." Third, Yakuō and Yakujō (yaku, medicine; ō, king; jō, superb) cite tasting as the cause of their realization. Fourth, Baddabara and the fifteen other Bodhisattvas of the present case rise and make obeisance to the Buddha, and Baddabara says, "We formerly heard the preaching of Ion-ō [the first Buddha] and became monks. At the monks' bathtime, following the rule, we entered the bathroom. We suddenly experienced realization through the touch of the water. We did not wash off dirt, did not wash the body. We achieved peace of mind and obtained the state of no-possession. The aforementioned Buddha named me Baddabara, saying, 'You have experienced subtle and clear touching, and attained Buddhahood, and retain it.' The answer to your question, therefore, is that touching was the primary cause of our realization." Other Bodhisattvas in turn tell of their experiences, and finally the Bodhisattva Kannon (Avalokitesvara) cites the importance, in his case, of "listening to sound."

It will be seen that the primary causes of realization named here are all sensations: seeing, smelling, tasting, touching, and hearing. Sensing is the action of the first nen, which performs pure cognition. In fact, other Bodhisattvas cite examples of thinking—thinking of the emptiness of the ego, of the body, of mental processes, and so on—as the cause of their realization. Some of their examples sound like conceptual manipulation. I admit that even conceptual manipulation may lead to pure cognition. But sensation always takes the lead.

Why did they not wash off dirt and clean the body? What is no-possession? These points will be explained in the notes on subsequent cases.

• *Seven times piercing and eight times breaking through.* See the notes to Case 49.

• *Stretches at ease on his bed.* This is a figure of speech. It does not mean that the enlightened man idles away his time but that he is quite at ease and enjoys peace of mind.

• *If, in a dream, the ancients said they were enlightened, | Let them emerge from the scented water, and I would spit at them!* Setchō is saying that while you are claiming merit because of your realization, it is not genuine. Such a realization must be thrown away. "In a dream" implies that they were not properly awakened. "The ancients" means the sixteen Bodhisattvas. But in fact Setchō is not belittling them. He acknowledges that theirs was genuine enlightenment. His intention is to remind monks in general of the importance of going on to a higher level of enlightenment.

Case 79 Tōsu and "Every Voice Is the Buddha's Voice"

ENGO'S INTRODUCTION The Great Way manifests itself naturally; it is bound by no fixed rules. The teacher does not have to exert himself to bring his students under control. Tell me, who has ever given such an example? See the following.

MAIN SUBJECT   A monk said to Tōsu, "It is said, 'Every voice is the Buddha's voice.' Is that true?" Tōsu said, "Yes, it is true." The monk said, "Master, don't let me hear you breaking wind." Tōsu gave him a blow with his stick.

The monk asked again, "The sutra says, 'Rough words and soft words, both lead to the first principle.' Is that true?" Tōsu said, "Yes, it is true." The monk said, "Master, may I call you a donkey?" Tōsu gave him a blow with his stick.

SETCHŌ'S VERSE
Tōsu! Tōsu! The wheel turns unchecked.
One shot, two victories! That blow, this blow!
Pity him who mocks the tide:
He will fall in it and die!
If he suddenly comes alive—
A hundred surging, roaring rivers!

NOTES   *Tōsu* appears also in Cases 41, 80, and 91. He succeeded Suibi (Case 20), who succeeded Tanka (Case 76). He was a contemporary of Isan, Kyōzan, and Seppō.
• *The Great Way manifests itself naturally.* The Great Way is the activity of being. The phrase in the original text is *tai yū* (*tai*, great; *yū,* use).
• *It is bound by no fixed rules.* Being is its own ruler.
• *The teacher does not have to exert himself to bring his students under control.* The mature Zen master embodies the Great Way in himself and need make no special exertion to deal with his disciples.
• *Every voice is the Buddha's voice.* This is a popular Buddhist saying, which appears in various sutras.

> Streams and birds,
> Trees and woods,
> All recite
> The name of the Buddha,
> The honor of the Dharma,
> The peace of the Sangha.

• *Don't let me hear you breaking wind.* When you are by yourself you may break wind and it is as if you were humming to yourself. You do not even laugh, much less scold yourself.

• *Tōsu gave him a blow with his stick.* This rascal!

• *Rough words and soft words, both lead to the first principle.* The *Parinirvana Sutra* says:

> Buddhas use soft words;
> For the ignorant they speak roughly.
> Rough words and soft words, both lead to
> The first principle.

"Use soft words" here means to give a comprehensive, detailed explanation of the truth; "speak roughly" means to give a rough outline of the truth, suitable for a beginner. This monk, however, understood soft words to mean polite, courteous ones and rough words to mean harsh, rude ones.

• *Tōsu! Tōsu!* Tōsu was so brilliant that Setchō could not help crying out his name twice.

• *The wheel turns unchecked.* The spiritual wheel of Tōsu turns splendidly.

• *One shot, two victories! That blow, this blow!* With one "Yes" he achieved two victories.

• *Pity him who mocks the tide.* The beach of Chechiang was famous for its splendid surf, especially in summer and autumn. Many visitors came to sport in it, and quite often reckless people lost their lives in the incoming tide.

• *If he suddenly comes alive— / A hundred surging, roaring rivers!* The questioning monk may have been something of a daredevil, but he must also have been an earnest student. If he suddenly achieves realization he will be as mighty as a hundred surging rivers.

Case 80   Jōshū's "A Newborn Baby"

MAIN SUBJECT   A monk asked Jōshū, "Does a newborn baby possess the six senses or not?" Jōshū said, "It is like throwing a ball into the rapids." The monk later asked Tōsu, "What is the meaning of 'throwing a ball into the rapids'?" Tōsu said, "Nen after nen, without ceasing."

SETCHŌ'S VERSE
   The question: the six senses. Purposeless.
   Well acquainted with it, the masters.
   A ball is thrown into the rapids;
   Do you know where it is carried?

NOTES *Jōshū, Tōsu.* Tōsu was forty-one years younger than Jōshū. He settled down in his temple when he was sixty-one years old. The incident related in the present case must have taken place when both he and Jōshū were quite old.

• *Does a newborn baby possess the six senses or not?* In Buddhist psychology the six senses are seeing, hearing, touching, smelling, and tasting, together with the activity of consciousness. The Buddhist psychologist also conceives of seventh and eighth senses. These relate to deeper levels or activities of consciousness. The seventh bears a certain relationship to the modern psychologist's subconscious. The eighth is thought of as having no particular activity of its own but as constituting the foundation of all other conscious activities. We experience it at the deepest level of absolute samadhi. The experience of it gives the Zen student the firm conviction of returning to his original nature. This enables him to imagine that the mental life of a newborn baby must be largely at the level of this eighth sense, its senses and consciousness being not yet fully developed. The monk in this case had come to see this from his own experience but was still not certain of it, and hence asked Jōshū this question.

• *It is like throwing a ball into the rapids.* Moment after moment, the ball floats on with the stream. It has no time to stop and reflect upon itself. It corresponds to the action of the first nen. A newborn baby's senses may not yet be fully developed, but such as they are, they are pure, not yet overlaid by the delusive activity of consciousness as in an adult. The baby is capable of pure cognition, though that cognition is not fully developed. Full-fledged pure cognition is achieved by the practice of zazen, in which the delusive action of the third nen is cast off.

• *Nen after nen, without ceasing.* Nen follows nen, each passing away moment by moment. In ancient times, before scientific research had begun, this knowledge could be attained only through Zen practice, in which the different sorts of nen-actions are clearly perceived. Zen students attained through their practice a wonderful insight into the nature of consciousness, and this insight gave them a deep understanding of human nature.

• *The six senses. Purposeless.* The sun shines silently, without purpose, without motive, without seeking profit or trying to earn merit. In this sense, Bodhidharma's coming to China was purposeless and meaningless. A mirror's reflecting is purposeless, meaningless, and empty. A Zen master's activities are also purposeless. Of course they are purposeful, too, but from the viewpoint of the self-centered, deluded activity of consciousness, they are purposeless. Pure cognition through the medium of the six senses is also done purposelessly.

• *Well acquainted with it, the masters.* These two great masters, Jōshū and Tōsu, were fully acquainted with the pure cognition of the newborn baby and also with that achieved by purified nen-action in the adult's positive samadhi.

• *A ball is thrown into the rapids; | Do you know where it is carried?* Over a thousand years ago, Zen students were familiar with the subtle activities of consciousness through experiencing various phases of samadhi.

Case 81 Yakusan's King of the King Deer

ENGO'S INTRODUCTION When he seizes the opponent's banners and captures the enemy's drums, even the thousand holy ones cannot hold him. When he cuts through the complications, even a battle-hardened veteran cannot touch him. This is not due to his using occult powers, nor to his returning to the absolute itself. Tell me, how can he attain such wonderful ability?

MAIN SUBJECT A monk said to Yakusan, "On the grassy plain there is a herd of deer, with the king deer among them. How could one shoot the great king of the king deer?" Yakusan said, "Watch the arrow!"

The monk threw himself on the floor. Yakusan called his attendant and said, "Boy! Take this dead fellow away!" The monk ran away. Yakusan said, "There is no end to these people who play with mud pies." [Setchō says in a comment here, "For three steps he might be alive, but he would not survive five."]

SETCHŌ'S VERSE

The king of the king deer: watch him!
One arrow, and he ran three steps;
Five steps, and he might drive a tiger.
The hunter had a true eye, you know.
Now Setchō cries, "Watch the arrow!"

NOTES   *Yakusan.* See Case 42.

• *When he seizes the opponent's banners and captures the enemy's drums.* In the Dharma battle the master seizes the student's flying banners and captures his drums.

• *When he cuts through the complications, even a battle-hardened veteran cannot touch him.* "Complications" are koans and other knotty problems which the student finds it hard to solve. But the master easily cuts through everything of this kind.

• *This is not due to his using occult powers.* It is because of his long and hard training, which has often caused him pain and often delight.

• *On the grassy plain there is a herd of deer, with the king deer among them.* This incident occurred when Yakusan was living in his monastery at Heiden (*hei*, level; *den*, field: *heiden* denotes a grassy plain). The monk is using the image of a herd of deer on a grassy plain to represent the monks of the monastery.

• *How could one shoot the great king of the king deer?* Among the deer there are some, the king deer, that protect and take care of the herd. The great king is the king of the herd. We are dealing in metaphors, as is often the case in Dharma battles. The great king represents a great enlightened one, and the monk fancies himself to be such a person. He is saying, "I am king of the king deer. How will you deal with me?"

• *Watch the arrow!* Yakusan took the pose of drawing a bow and said, "Watch the arrow!"

• *Take this dead fellow away.* When the master kills, he kills exhaustively.

• *The monk ran away.* Don't worry, I can still walk.

• *There is no end to these people who play with mud pies.* Yakusan's final words are highly effective. Without them the present case would have come to a lame conclusion.

• *For three steps he might be alive, but he would not survive five.* People start Zen practice with great determination and an earnest desire to master it. Their determination may be maintained for some time, and they may reap certain rewards. Unfortunately, however, many of them drop away, by and by.

• *Five steps, and he might drive a tiger.* If he were to continue Zen training to the end, he would become so strong he could drive even a tiger.

• *The hunter had a true eye.* Yakusan had a keen eye and was not beguiled by the monk.

• *Setchō cries, "Watch the arrow!"* Be on the watch to the last, and you will suddenly find the wide world open before you.

Case 82   Tairyū's "Indestructible Dharma Body"

ENGO'S INTRODUCTION   The fishing line at the end of the rod—the one with eyes will know. The spiritual activity which transcends the ordinary—the enlightened one will discern. What, then, is the fishing line at the end of the rod, and the spiritual activity which transcends the ordinary? See the following.

MAIN SUBJECT   A monk said to Tairyū, "Man's body will ultimately decompose; what is the indestructible Dharma body?" Tairyū said,

> "Flowers cover the hillside like brocade,
> The vale lies deep in shade."

SETCHŌ'S VERSE

The question came from ignorance;
The answer was not understood.
The moon is clear, the wind is cool,
The wintry pine stands on the peak.

I laugh heartily to hear the saying,
"When you encounter a man of the Way,
Meet him with neither words nor non-words."

He held the crystal whip and smashed the jewels;
Otherwise, faults develop.
For there are laws in the land,
With three thousand regulations.

NOTES   *Tairyū* was descended in Dharma lineage from Tokusan, but not much is known of him. Once a monk asked him, "What is the Buddha?" Tairyū said, "That is you." Another asked, "What is subtlety?" Tairyū said,

"The wind brings the murmuring of the stream to my pillow;
The moon casts the shadow of the hill at my bedside."

He seems to have been a man of poetic inclination.
• *The fishing line at the end of the rod—the one with eyes will know.* The teacher is always casting a line. The student with eyes will understand the teacher's intention, and sometimes he will knowingly take the bait. The inexperienced fellow will be caught. The clever one sometimes will have a narrow escape, carrying away the bait.
• *The spiritual activity which transcends the ordinary—the enlightened one will discern.* The spiritual activity of the teacher transcends that of the ordinary man. The student who is enlightened will discern both the subtle merits and the tiny defects that the teacher intentionally displays.
• *Man's body will ultimately decompose; what is the indestructible Dharma body?* Many people begin their practice of Zen in order to escape the fear of death. They are terrified at the thought that their egos will eventually perish. They ask whether there is any sort of eternal soul, whether there is anything to hold onto. What is the indestructible Dharma body? The monk's question in the present case was prompted by such fears.

• *Flowers cover the hillside like brocade, | The vale lies deep in shade.* It will probably not be difficult for you to arrive at a conceptual understanding of Tairyū's meaning in these words: that the phenomenal is the real. The blooming flowers, the dark valley are themselves the indestructible Dharma body. But such understanding will not give you true peace of mind. That can be attained only through your practice of zazen. In samadhi you will one day find that you are freed from your nervous turmoil, and that is all. If you then look at the flowers on the hillside, you will find that they are so close to you that they sink into your eyes and penetrate your body; but at the same time, they are there on the hillside. This is what we call pure cognition. The pure, intuitive activity of your first nen has been unified with the object. You will realize that you are cognizing the Dharma body in the flowers. This kind of realization is quite different from conceptual understanding, and it brings true peace of mind.

To the monk in the present case, who had not yet attained genuine samadhi, Tairyū's answer must have seemed remote and irrelevant. However, the teacher must sometimes be cruel. Tairyū had no qualms about depriving the monk of his treasured belief in the indestructibility of the Dharma body, for that belief was based on nothing more than a conceptual understanding.

• *The moon is clear, the wind is cool, | The wintry pine stands on the peak.* Tairyū's words are springlike, and represent positive samadhi. Setchō supplies the complementary autumnal and wintry quietude of absolute samadhi.

• *I laugh heartily to hear the saying . . .* Setchō's laughter expresses his appreciation of Goso's saying (*Mumonkan*, Case 36), "When you meet a man of the Way on the path, do not meet him with words or with silence." It is also appreciative of Tairyū's words in the present case. Did Tairyū meet the monk's question with words or non-words?

• *He held the crystal whip and smashed the jewels.* The jewels are the Dharma body. Tairyū smashed the Dharma body which the monk had erroneously conceived and was treasuring in his mind.

• *Otherwise, faults develop.* The Dharma body, as understood by the monk, must be smashed, or it will lead to error.

• *For there are laws in the land.* Just as there are laws in the country, so, in Zen, there is an unshakable discipline which cannot be ignored.

Case 83　Ummon's "The Old Buddha Communes with the Pillar"

MAIN SUBJECT　Ummon spoke to his disciples and said, "The old Buddha communes with the pillar. What level of spiritual activity would that be?" And he himself gave the answer for them, saying, "Clouds gather over the southern hill, rain falls on the northern mountain."

SETCHŌ'S VERSE
Rain on the northern mountain, clouds over the southern hill;
Four sevens and two threes, I see them face to face!
In Korea they assemble in the lecture hall,
In China they have not beaten the drum or rung the bell.
Joy in the midst of pain, pain in the midst of joy;
Who dares to say, "Gold is the same as soil"?

NOTES　*The old Buddha communes with the pillar.* In pure cognition you commune with the object. Your nen-action is the old Buddha, and the pillar is the object. The intuitive action of the first nen holds intercourse with the object. This comes first, and then come the successive actions of the second and third nen. To put it in other terms, the image of the Buddha on the platform looks at the pillar all day and all night, and never complains of being tired. In the same way, if you look at the pillar in front of you in positive samadhi, you will never find yourself tiring of it.

• *What level of spiritual activity would that be?* As has already been explained (Case 6), the only direct communication is between the object and the first nen. The third nen carries through and presides over a more remote, integrated final cognition. It should be emphasized that the first, second, and third nen-actions are not sharply distinct but simply represent different phases of the activity of the mind, which acts now as a receiver of impressions, now as a reflecting inspector of those impressions, now as the integrator of all its actions. The third nen is the master of the mind because it knows everything that is occurring in the mind.

• *Rain on the northern mountain, clouds over the southern hill.* Now, in positive samadhi, look at the clouds and the southern hill. What a marvelous world you find before you! Nature's living work of art, which has never been painted so splendidly, even by the greatest artist! Now turn your face toward the northern mountain, on which the rain is falling. Here again you find the greatest work of art. It closes in upon you. It penetrates you through and through. You are unified with the object. Such is the first nen's direct communication with the external object. There is no time and no space. Time and space are products of the synthesizing activity of the third nen, which has retired into the background for the time being. As with a newborn baby, the first nen is occupying the stage of consciousness.

• *Four sevens and two threes, I see them face to face!* The twenty-eight Indian patriarchs and the six Chinese patriarchs. Setchō sees them face to face because the mountains and hills, the clouds and rain, have the character of the Buddha.

• *In Korea they assemble in the lecture hall, / In China they have not beaten the drum or rung the bell.* There is no time and no space in your samadhi, only a succession of present moments; and events occur in succession in these present moments, just as in a battle or an emergency you have no experience of time but are aware only of present moment after present moment. "They have not beaten the drum" is just the same as "they have beaten the drum."

• *Joy in the midst of pain, pain in the midst of joy.* Gensha once stumbled over a stone and bruised his toes. The pain penetrated his whole body, and he suddenly became enlightened. When pain fills your whole existence, the pain is pain no more, but your existence itself. It is the same in the case of joy. Then pain and joy are one and the same thing. At the same time, it must be remembered that pain is pain and joy is joy: they are different things.

• *Who dares to say, "Gold is the same as soil"?* The allusion is to a story of two politicians, Chōji and Chinyo, who were at first sworn friends. They declared that, compared with the depth and purity of their friendship, gold was no better than night soil. But later they quarreled because of a clash of personal interests and became estranged, eventually coming to harbor implacable hostility toward each other. Setchō's intention is first to say that the communion of the Buddha with the pillar is not this sort of relationship but a matter of pure cognition; and second to say that in reality, gold is gold and soil is soil: they should not be falsely equated, as Chōji and Chinyo did. There is a Zen saying that equality without differentiation is bad equality; differentiation without equality is bad differentiation.

Case 84 Yuima's "The Gate to the One and Only"

ENGO'S INTRODUCTION There is nothing right that can truly be called right. There is no wrong that can truly be called wrong. With right and wrong eliminated, gains and losses are forgotten. It is all naked and exposed. Now I want to ask you, what is in front of me and what is behind me? Some monk may come forward and say that in front there are the Buddha hall and the temple gate, and behind, the bedroom and the sitting room. Tell me, is that man open-eyed? If you can see through him, I will acknowledge that you have seen the ancient worthy.

MAIN SUBJECT Yuima asked Manjusri, "What is the Bodhisattva's Gate to the One and Only?" Manjusri answered, "To my mind, in all Dharmas, there are no words, no preaching, no talking, no activity of consciousness. It is beyond all questions and answers. That is entering the Gate to the One and Only." Then Manjusri said to Yuima, "Each of us has had his say. Now I ask you, what is the Bodhisattva's Gate to the One and Only?" [Setchō says, "What did Yuima say?" And again he says, "I have seen through him."]

SETCHŌ'S VERSE
   You foolish old Yuimakitsu,
   Sorrowful for sentient beings,

You lie sick in Biyali,
Your body all withered up.

The teacher of the Seven Buddhas comes,
The room is cleared of everything,
You ask for the Gate to the One and Only;
Are you repulsed by Manju's words?

No, not repulsed; the golden-haired lion
Can find you nowhere.

NOTES   *Yuima.* The main subject of the present case is based on the *Vimalakirti-nirdesa Sutra* (*Vimalakirti*, Yuimakitsu, Yuima; *nirdesa*, preached). Vimalakirti, or Yuima, was a semilegendary person, a lay disciple of the Buddha, who was living in Biyali, where the Buddha was preaching. One day he failed to appear at the Buddha's gathering, and word was sent that he was sick. He was sick because "sentient beings are sick." The Buddha sent Manjusri to inquire after him. Manjusri was followed by thirty-one Bodhisattvas and thirty-two thousand Arhats (see the notes to Case 95) and others, all of whom could fit into Yuima's room, which was ten feet square. Yuima asked the Bodhisattvas, "What is the Bodhisattva's Gate to the One and Only [absolute oneness]?" Each of them gave his answer. Some said: The Dharma is unborn, therefore it cannot perish; this is the Gate to the One and Only. Some said: There is no ego, therefore there is no external world; this is the Gate to Non-relativity. Many other sayings followed, such as: Sin and blessing are all empty and not different; Samsara and Nirvana are the same; There are no gains and no losses. When all thirtyone had finished, Yuima put the same question to Manjusri, who answered as in the present case.

• *There is nothing right that can truly be called right.* In the original text the word which we have translated as "right" is *ze*, which has many meanings: affirmative, good, right, and so forth. Affirmation and negation are relative ideas. Absolute truth transcends relativity. What is absolute truth? It can be experienced only in absolute samadhi, where there are no words and no conceptual understanding.

• *There is no wrong that can truly be called wrong.* The word in the original text which we have translated as "wrong" is *hi*, which also has the meanings of negation, not good, not right, and so on.

• *With right and wrong eliminated, gains and losses are forgotten.* In absolute samadhi you transcend right and wrong, gains and losses.

• *It is all naked and exposed.* It is not veiled to the eye that can see it.

• *In front there are the Buddha hall and the temple gate, and behind, the bedroom and the sitting room.* Absolute truth is not a remote thing but is manifested in actual life.

• *Is that man open-eyed?* If he says what he says with true understanding, he is.

• *The ancient worthy.* Yuima.

• *What is the Bodhisattva's Gate to the One and Only?* How do you enter the gate?

• *To my mind, in all Dharmas, there are no words, no preaching, no talking, no activity of consciousness. It is beyond all questions and answers.* Absolute truth is to be found in absolute samadhi. If you try to find it in the external Dharmas—in philosophy, in science, and so on—you will never be successful. "Dharma" has two meanings: first, law, truth, religion, the doctrine and teachings of the Buddha, and Buddhism; and secondly, the elements of existence, things, phenomena.

• *Then Manjusri said to Yuima, "Each of us has had his say. Now I ask you, what is the Bodhisattva's Gate to the One and Only?"* How can one answer this, when, in the absolute truth of nonrelativity, there is no word, no talking, and no activity of consciousness?

• *Setchō says, "What did Yuima say?"* The *Vimalakirti-nirdesa Sutra* says, "At this point, Yuima remained silent, and had no words." Manjusri had expressed himself in words. It was not bad, because he spoke independently of words and non-words. But Yuima was more direct; he remained silent. Setchō does not simply say that Yuima was silent, because he was not merely silent. His silence, properly understood, was a thunderous roar.

• *I have seen through him.* Like knows like.

• *You foolish old Yuimakitsu.* Yuimakitsu is Yuima's full name. Because of the sickness of sentient beings, he also suffers from sickness. A foolish thing, isn't it? This is Setchō's usual paradoxical mode of expression.

• *Your body all withered up.* The word which we have translated as "withered up," *koko*, is often also used to mean "elegantly slender." Setchō here implies that all worldly things have been cast off.

• *The teacher of the Seven Buddhas comes.* This refers to Manjusri. The

Seven Buddhas are the most ancient Buddhas, including Shakyamuni Buddha as the last one. They represent all Buddhas. Manjusri is officially regarded as a Bodhisattva second to the Buddha in rank, but he is especially appreciated because of his Zen wisdom.

• *The room is cleared of everything.* Yuima's tiny room was cleared so as to be spacious enough to accommodate the thirty-two Bodhisattvas and the thirty-two thousand Arhats.

• *No, not repulsed.* Yuima's silence was powerful enough to repel Manjusri's counterattack.

• *The golden-haired lion | Can find you nowhere.* "Golden-haired lion" is an epithet of Manjusri. He can find Yuima nowhere because of Yuima's silence.

Case 85   The Master of Tōhō Hermitage Roars Like a Tiger

ENGO'S INTRODUCTION   Controlling the world, he allows not the least speck of dust to escape; and all men on earth give up their weapons and still their tongues. This is the enforcement of the monk's ordinance. The beams from his forehead pierce the four directions. This is the activity of the monk's diamond eye. He turns iron into gold and gold into iron, and both holds fast and lets go. This is the action of the monk's staff. He stops the mouths of all people under the sun, making them silent and as if driven three thousand miles away. This is the force of the monk's spirit. But what would you say when one falls short of these abilities? See the following.

MAIN SUBJECT   A monk came to visit the master of Tōhō hermitage and said to him, "If, on this mountain, you were suddenly to meet a tiger, what would you do?" The master roared like a tiger. The monk pretended to be frightened. The master roared with laughter. The monk said, "You old robber!" The master said, "Try as you may, you cannot do anything to me." The monk stopped short. [Setchō says, "They were both veteran robbers, but they stopped their ears and tried to steal the bell."]

SETCHŌ'S VERSE
    A chance, and if you fail to seize it,
    You miss by a thousand miles.
    The tiger had fine stripes
    But no fangs and claws.
    Remember the battle on Mount Taiyu:
    Their words and actions shook the earth.
    If you have eyes to see, you see
    They caught both head and tail of it.

NOTES   *The master of Tōhō hermitage.* His name is not recorded. He was a disciple of Rinzai and lived in a hermitage on Mount Tōhō. This case gives an example of how even veterans may fail in Dharma battle.
• *The monk's ordinance . . . the monk's diamond eye . . . the monk's staff . . . the monk's spirit.* The monk's ordinance is the teacher's method of teaching. The monk's diamond eye is the teacher's keen observing eye. The monk's staff is the teacher's activity. The monk's spirit is Zen mind.
• *If, on this mountain, you were suddenly to meet a tiger, what would you do?* This monk is presenting himself as if he were a tiger. He is saying, "I have the strength of a tiger. I will devour you if you don't take care!"
• *The master roared like a tiger.* The master himself adopted the role of the tiger.
• *The monk pretended to be frightened.* The monk was letting go. Why did he not strike the tiger dead?
• *You old robber!* The answer is a little too easy.
• *Try as you may, you cannot do anything to me.* This is dull.
• *The monk stopped short.* A poor ending! There was no keen cut and thrust in their dialogue.
• *They were both veteran robbers.* They knew how to carry on a Dharma battle, but in this case they ended in failure.
• *They stopped their ears and tried to steal the bell.* This is like saying that

the cat shuts its eyes while stealing cream. A Dharma battle is something that demands the keenest attention.

• *You miss by a thousand miles.* This is an allusion to the popular belief that a tiger goes a thousand miles a day. Seize the tiger while it is within your reach.

• *Remember the battle on Mount Taiyu.* Setchō refers to a story of Ōbaku and Hyakujō. Once Ōbaku came back from working outside, and Hyakujō asked what he had been doing. Ōbaku said he had been gathering mushrooms. Hyakujō, starting a Dharma battle, asked whether Ōbaku had seen a tiger. Ōbaku, knowing what Hyakujō was about, gave a tiger's roar. Hyakujō brandished an ax to cut the tiger down, but Ōbaku ducked under it and, catching hold of Hyakujō, gave him a blow. That evening, Hyakujō spoke to his assembly and said, "There is a tiger on Mount Taiyu [the mountain where Hyakujō lived]. Beware of him. Today he gave me a bite."

• *Their words and actions shook the earth.* Ōbaku and Hyakujō carried through a fine Dharma battle.

• *They caught both head and tail of it.* At a later date Isan asked his disciple Kyōzan his opinion of the story of Ōbaku and Hyakujō. Kyōzan said, "They knew how to catch hold of both the head and the tail of it." Isan said, "Ejaku [Kyōzan's personal name] uses strong words."

Case 86   Ummon's "Everybody Has His Own Light"

ENGO'S INTRODUCTION   Controlling the world, he allows not the least speck of dust to escape. He cuts off the deluded stream of thought, leaving not a drop behind. If you open your mouth, you are mistaken. If you doubt for a moment, you have missed the way. Tell me, what is the eye that has pierced the barriers? See the following.

MAIN SUBJECT   Ummon spoke to his assembly and said, "Everybody has his own light. If he tries to see it, everything is darkness. What is everybody's light?" Later, in place of the disciples, he said, "The halls and the gate." And again he said, "Blessing things cannot be better than nothing."

SETCHŌ'S VERSE
   It illuminates itself,
   Absolutely bright.
   He gives a clue to the secret.
   Flowers have fallen, trees give no shade;
   Who does not see, if he looks?
   Seeing is non-seeing, non-seeing is seeing.
   Facing backward on the ox,
   He rides into the Buddha hall.

NOTES *Controlling the world, he allows not the least speck of dust to escape.* This is holding fast.
   • *If you open your mouth, you are mistaken.* The truth is there before you speak.
   • *If he tries to see it, everything is darkness.* You are the light itself. If you try to reflect upon yourself, your subjectivity is turned into objectivity. In samadhi alone can you catch hold of your own subjectivity.
   • *The halls and the gate.* Ummon asked, "What is everybody's light?" but no one could reply, so he gave the answer himself. In saying, "The halls and the gate," he means that truth is not remote but is under your nose. "See the halls and the gate. You find it there, don't you?"
   • *Blessing things cannot be better than nothing.* Anything cannot surpass nothing.
   • *It illuminates itself.* It does not borrow its light from others.
   • *Flowers have fallen, trees give no shade.* Such a condition is found in your absolute samadhi.
   • *Who does not see, if he looks?* If you have the eye, you can see it.
   • *Seeing is non-seeing, non-seeing is seeing.* This is found to be true in your samadhi.
   • *Facing backward on the ox.* The ox represents one's true nature. Now he rides the ox facing backward. He is wholly free to go facing any way —backward or forward, right or left, up or down.
   • *He rides into the Buddha hall.* He is the Buddha himself.

Case 87 Ummon's "Medicine and Sickness Cure Each Other"

ENGO'S INTRODUCTION The clear-eyed man knows no restriction. At one time he stands on the top of the mountain, with the weeds thick around him. At another time he is in the bustle of the marketplace, enjoying perfect ease of mind. When he displays the wrath of Nada, he is three-faced and six-armed. When he shows the mercy of the Sun-faced and Moon-faced, he gives forth the all-embracing light of blessing. In every particle, he reveals all the bodies of the Buddha; mixing with people, he trudges through the mire. When he performs a transcendent action, even Buddhas cannot follow him, and they are driven back thousands of miles. Is there anyone among you who can go with him and act with him? See the following.

MAIN SUBJECT Ummon said to his disciples, "Medicine and sickness cure each other. All the earth is medicine. Where do you find yourself?"

SETCHŌ'S VERSE
All the earth is medicine;
Ancient and modern, men make a great mistake.
Shut the gate, but do not build the cart;
The universe is the highway, vast and wide.
Mistaken, all is mistaken.
Though their noses are stuck up to heaven,
They will still be pierced for a rope.

NOTES *He stands on the top of the mountain, with the weeds thick around him.* To stand on the top of the mountain corresponds to absolute samadhi, that is, to holding fast. "The weeds thick around him" refers to letting go. This state, then, is one in which holding fast is manifest while letting go. In Tōzan's five ranks (see Cases 43 and 61) it corresponds to "arrival at mutual integration (integration in Hen)."

• *He is in the bustle of the marketplace, enjoying perfect ease of mind.* This corresponds to Tōzan's "unity attained (perfection in integration)."

• *The wrath of Nada.* Nada is a kind of deva, or devil, but here refers to the Buddha.

• *He is three-faced and six-armed.* He performs the great deeds of the three-faced, six-armed Buddha.

• *The Sun-faced and Moon-faced.* See Case 3.

• *In every particle.* The Bodhisattva's Vow says, "Then on each moment's flash of thought, there will grow a lotus flower, and on each lotus flower will be revealed a Buddha. These Buddhas will glorify Sukhavati, the Pure Land, every moment and everywhere."

• *He reveals all the bodies of the Buddha.* The Bodhisattva Kannon (Avalokitesvara) has thirty-three bodies. When a lord comes, he meets him in the body of a lord; when a child, in the body of a child; and so on.

• *He trudges through the mire.* He does not mind going through mud and dirt for the sake of his fellow creatures.

• *When he performs a transcendent action.* For instance, when silent, as was Yuima (Case 84).

• *Medicine and sickness cure each other.* Buddhism is necessary, like medicine, because man is sick. When the sickness is cured, Buddhism can be discarded. Medicine is a kind of poison; it acts as medicine only to a sick person. When the sickness is gone, the medicine must go, too. If not, it turns into a poison. There really is a so-called sickness of Buddhism (see Cases 31 and 98), which Zen masters are vigilant in eradicating.

• *All the earth is medicine.* Manjusri once asked Zenzai, an earnest Zen student, to bring him something that was not a medicine. Zenzai could find nothing that could not work as a medicine. Manjusri then asked him to bring something that was definitely a medicine. Zenzai handed Manjusri a blade of grass. Manjusri held it up and said to his assembly, "This single blade of grass can give life to a man and can also bring death to him." Used as medicine, everything is medicine; used as poison, everything is poison.

• *Where do you find yourself?* Medicine and your delusive ego cure each other. Both are neutralized and reduced to nothing. There is no ego. Where do you find your own self? At the same time, all the earth is medicine, and all the universe is yourself, because they cure each other and become unified.

• *All the earth is medicine [Setchō's Verse].* When sickness comes, let it; when the remedy comes, let it. And all the earth is you yourself.

• *Ancient and modern, men make a great mistake.* They do not know the true meaning of Ummon's words.

• *Shut the gate, but do not build the cart.* The ancient Chinese philosopher Chuang-tzu says that even if one shuts the gate and builds the cart within, it still fits the road. But here Setchō says: Don't build the cart; that is, don't set up Buddhism and all that sort of thing. There is no need to be in such a bustle. The universe is vast and wide, and you can go anywhere, as you like.

• *Mistaken, all is mistaken.* Six hundred monks under the Fifth Patriarch all understood Buddhism. Only Enō did not understand Buddhism, and he became the Sixth Patriarch. (See *Mumonkan*, Case 23.)

• *Though their noses are stuck up to heaven.* Though they may be successful in studying and understanding Buddhism, that remains in the realm of merit. You must transcend merit and become meritless.

• *They will still be pierced for a rope.* Like an ox, their nostrils will be pierced and they will be led by a rope.

Case 88 Gensha's Man of Three Disabilities

ENGO'S INTRODUCTION In his teaching, the master often turns two into three. Talking of the profound, he goes through and through it, seven times piercing and eight times breaking through. He adapts himself to all circumstances, penetrates the most mysterious secrets. Acting on the principles of the Buddha, he leaves no trace of his actions. Where do the complicated koans come from? If you have an eye to see, see the following.

MAIN SUBJECT Gensha said to the assembly, "Every teacher in the land talks of saving things and delivering mankind. When a man of three disabilities comes to you, how do you deal with him? A blind man does not see you holding up the hossu, a deaf person does not hear your words, a dumb person will not talk even if you want him to. How do you approach him? If you cannot, Buddhism can bestow no benefit."

A monk asked Ummon about this topic. Ummon said, "Make your bows." The monk did so. Ummon made as if to push the monk with his staff. The monk retreated, and Ummon said, "You are not blind." He then said, "Come close to me." The monk approached Ummon, who said, "You are not deaf." Ummon asked the monk, "Do you understand?" The monk replied, "No, I do not understand." Ummon said, "You are not dumb." The monk attained an insight.

SETCHŌ'S VERSE

Blind, deaf, and dumb: none can come near;
Throughout the country, none could understand.
Rirō did not discern the true color,
Nor Shikō the subtle sound.
Let us sit quietly by the window
And enjoy the falling leaves, the spring flowers.
I say, "Do you understand?
It is a holeless iron hammer."

NOTES *Gensha.* See Cases 22 and 56, and *Mumonkan*, Case 41.
• *In his teaching, the master often turns two into three.* In the Christian Trinity, we develop three from one. Buddhism also speaks of one Buddha and three bodies: the Dharmakaya, Sambhogakaya, and Nirmanakaya. As thesis and antithesis come to synthesis, so you can cancel good and evil and arrive at emptiness. There is a Zen question, "Before your father and mother were born, what is your true self?"
• *Talking of the profound, he goes through and through it, seven times piercing and eight times breaking through.* See Case 49.
• *He leaves no trace of his actions.* Leaving no trace behind is a principle of Buddhism.
• *When a man of three disabilities comes to you, how do you deal with him?* There is a Zen saying that the question contains the answer. When Gensha asked this question, he was at the same time answering it. The

man of three disabilities is a man in samadhi, in which he sees nothing, hears nothing, and says nothing. This is literally true in absolute samadhi. In positive samadhi he sees but is not affected by it; he hears but is as if deaf; he speaks, but it is said, "He speaks all day long but says nothing." Gensha asked his question only in order to introduce his man of three disabilities to you.

• *A blind man does not see you holding up the hossu.* A hossu is a baton with a tuft of horsehair at one end. Manipulating it beautifully, the master uses it to express Zen spirit. This manipulation is a method of teaching, referred to in Engo's introduction. But the man of three disabilities cares nothing for this. He enters directly into the profound.

• *A deaf person does not hear your words.* This person has already gone through and through absolute samadhi (the profound). He is in no need of your words.

• *A dumb person will not talk even if you want him to.* This person has finished everything he has to say.

• *How do you approach him?* If you understand his condition, you will know how to do so.

• *If you cannot, Buddhism can bestow no benefit.* To bestow no benefit is most effective in Buddhism.

• *A monk asked Ummon about this topic.* The monk's actions—making bows, retreating, approaching, listening, and speaking—were all activities in samadhi, whether he was aware of it or not. But he could attain his insight only when he understood this.

• *Blind, deaf, and dumb: none can come near.* When you are in profound samadhi, no one can approach you.

• *Rirō did not discern the true color, / Nor Shikō the subtle sound.* Rirō was famous for his eagle eye, Shikō for his good ear, but from the Zen point of view the one could not truly discern colors and the other was not a good listener.

• *Let us sit quietly by the window.* This refers to one's samadhi, in which one enjoys quiet reading, meditation, or looking at nature.

• *I say, "Do you understand?"* Have you understood the true meaning of Gensha and Ummon?

• *It is a holeless iron hammer.* How do you fix a handle to a hammer without a hole? This is a popular Zen saying, meaning how do you solve a puzzling problem? When you achieve realization, you can fix a handle onto this hammer.

Case 89 Ungan's "The Whole Body Is Hand and Eye"

ENGO'S INTRODUCTION When the entire body is the eye, while seeing you do not see; when the entire body is the ear, while hearing you do not hear; when the entire body is the mouth, while speaking you do not speak; when the entire body is the mind, while thinking you do not think. Putting aside the entire body, if there are no eyes, how do you see? If there are no ears, how do you hear? If there is no mouth, how do you speak? If there is no mind, how do you think? If you are familiar with this point, you are in the company of the ancient Buddhas. However, putting aside being in the company of the Buddhas, with whom should you study Zen?

MAIN SUBJECT Ungan asked Dōgo, "What use does the great Bodhisattva of Mercy make of all those hands and eyes?" Dōgo said, "It is like a man straightening his pillow with his outstretched hand in the middle of the night." Ungan said, "I have understood." Dōgo said, "How do you understand?" Ungan said, "The whole body is hand and eye." Dōgo said, "You have had your say, but you have given only eight-tenths of the truth." Ungan said, "How would you put it?" Dōgo said, "The entire body is hand and eye."

SETCHŌ'S VERSE
To say "the whole" is all right;
"The entire" is also well said.
If you take it conceptually,
You are a million miles away.

When the giant roc spreads its wings,
The clouds of six directions vanish.
Its wingbeats lash the seas
Of the four realms.

This is raising a speck of dust:
Much bleating but little wool!

Don't you see!
The net of jewels reflect each other!
Where does the eye of the staff come from?
I cry, "Tut! Tut!"

NOTES   *Ungan.* See Cases 70 and 72.
- *Dōgo.* See Case 55.
- *When the entire body is the eye, while seeing you do not see* . . . Subjectivity is unaware of its own seeing, hearing, speaking, and thinking.
- *If there are no eyes, how do you see?* . . . In absolute samadhi you have no eyes, ears, mouth, or mind.
- *With whom should you study Zen?* Jōshū said, "If an eight-year-old child is superior to me in understanding, I will learn from him."
- *The great Bodhisattva of Mercy.* This is Kannon (Avalokitesvara), who has a thousand hands and eyes. He has empathy with all sentient creatures, looking into them individually and using a thousand different methods to save them.
- *It is like a man straightening his pillow* . . . He has no thought but to arrange the pillow. He acts with his entire body and soul.
- *The whole body* . . . *The entire body* . . . There can be no difference between these. But there can be a great difference in your degree of attainment and understanding.
- *To say "the whole" is all right;* / *"The entire" is also well said.* Words and conceptions only point the way. To understand, you must experience for yourself.
- *When the giant roc spreads its wings,* / *The clouds of six directions vanish.* The word *taihō* means a giant bird (*tai*, great; *hō*, phoenix or roc). With one flap of its wings it is said to fly ninety thousand miles, and the clouds of six directions are dispersed. This line refers to Ungan's action.
- *Its wingbeats lash the seas* / *Of the four realms.* Its wingbeats cause the seas to part, exposing the dragon that lurks in the depths and that the bird catches and eats. Setchō compares this to Dōgo's action.
- *This is raising a speck of dust:* / *Much bleating but little wool!* In the previous lines Setchō praised Ungan and Dōgo, but now he belittles

them, saying that their actions are as nothing compared with those of the Bodhisattva Kannon.

• *The net of jewels reflect each other!* In the deity Indra's net of jewels, each jewel reflects not only the others but the reflection of each of the others, and the reflection of the reflections, ad infinitum. This metaphor comes from the *Avatamsaka Sutras.* The Kegon doctrine based upon these sutras is said to represent the highest development of Buddhist philosophy in China. Of the four Dharmadhatu which this doctrine sets up (see the notes to *Mumonkan*, Case 16), the image of the net of jewels represents the last, the unhindered mutual interpenetration of phenomena.

• *Where does the eye of the staff come from?* From your own attainment, not from others' words or demonstrations.

• *I cry, "Tut! Tut!"* Setchō decries all conceptual understanding.

Case 90   Chimon and the Essence of Prajna

ENGO'S INTRODUCTION   As to what stands prior to the Word, not one phrase has been handed down, even by the thousand holy ones. One thread maintains its continuity before your eyes through countless eons. It is all pure and naked, with hair erect and ears pricked up. Tell me, what is this about? See the following.

MAIN SUBJECT   A monk asked Chimon, "What is the essence of prajna?" Chimon said, "The oyster swallows the full moon." The monk said, "What is the action of prajna?" Chimon said, "The hare conceives by the full moon."

SETCHŌ'S VERSE
    A piece of emptiness transcends description;
    This has made heaven and earth remember Sunyata.
    The oyster conceives by the moon—amazing!
    Monks ever since have done Dharma battle on it.

NOTES   *Chimon.* See Case 21.

• *As to what stands prior to the Word.* See Case 7. This denotes the absolute. In terms of Tōzan's five ranks (see Cases 43 and 61) it is Shō (the real), the condition that manifests itself in absolute samadhi.

• *Not one phrase has been handed down, even by the thousand holy ones.* The thousand holy ones are the successive Buddhas and patriarchs. They find it hard even to talk about the absolute; they cannot hand it down to others. Each person must arrive at it by his own efforts.

• *One thread maintains its continuity before your eyes.* This refers to the phenomenal world; in terms of Tōzan's five ranks it is Hen (the apparent). This is the condition of positive samadhi in conscious activity.

• *Through countless eons.* This moment's nen-thought corresponds to eons of time. Conversely, eons are contained in this moment's nen-thought. In short, eternity is just this moment. In samadhi you realize for yourself the truth of this proposition.

• *It is all pure and naked.* When you have achieved this realization, you find truth exposed in all its purity and nakedness.

• *With hair erect and ears pricked up.* This seems bizarre, but such realization or understanding led painters and poets of successive generations to depict Kanzan and Jittoku (see Case 34) with hair disheveled, mouths gaping, and ears pricked up.

• *What is the essence of prajna?* "Essence" means substance or nature. "Action" (in the monk's subsequent question) means activity. "Prajna" is Zen wisdom. Essence and action correspond to absolute and positive samadhi, respectively.

• *The oyster swallows the full moon.* This alludes to a folk tale according to which the oyster rises to the surface of the sea at the time of the full moon, swallows the moonlight, and conceives a pearl.

• *What is the action of prajna?* The monk thought there was a difference between the essence and the action of prajna.

• *The hare conceives by the full moon.* In another folk tale the hare is said to conceive its young after swallowing the light of the full moon. Chimon's answers to the two questions are expressed in different ways but have essentially the same meaning. He implies that there are both similarity and difference between essence and action.

• *A piece of emptiness transcends description.* Emptiness, found in absolute samadhi, transcends explanation. You must experience it yourself.

• *This has made heaven and earth remember Sunyata.* Sunyata was famous for his meditation on emptiness (see Case 6).

• *The oyster conceives by the moon—amazing!* The oyster swallows the moonlight and produces a pearl. The hare conceives its young by the full moon. These are mysterious happenings. But the same thing happens in absolute samadhi, in which the pearl of the mind is produced before one is aware of it, and also in positive samadhi, in which one's consciousness is brilliantly illuminated as if by bright moonlight.

• *Monks ever since have done Dharma battle on it.* Ever since Chimon said this, Zen masters and students have been discussing it—the writer of these notes being no exception.

Case 91   Enkan and the Rhinoceros Fan

ENGO'S INTRODUCTION   Transcend delusive attachments, deceptive ideas, and all kinds of entanglements. Proclaim the marvelous teachings and uphold the precious treasury of the true Dharma. Secure the free command of the ten directions and the perfect serenity of the eight dimensions. Let the land of peace be realized. Now, tell me, is there anyone who will go hand in hand with the Buddha, testifying to the same realization, living the same life and dying the same death? See the following example.

MAIN SUBJECT   Enkan one day called to his attendant and said, "Bring me the rhinoceros fan." The attendant said, "The fan has been broken." Enkan said, "If the fan is broken, bring the rhinoceros to me." The attendant made no reply.

Tōsu [at a later time, speaking in place of the attendant] said, "I would not refuse to bring it out, but I fear the head and horns would not be perfect." [Setchō says, "I want that imperfect one."]

Sekisō said, "If I return it to you, there will be no more of it." [Setchō says, "There is still the rhinoceros."]

Shifuku drew a circle and wrote the character for "ox" in it. [Setchō says, "Why didn't you bring it out earlier?"]

Hofuku said, "My master, you have grown old; employ someone else to attend you." [Setchō says, "Long labor lost."]

SETCHŌ'S VERSE

You have long used the rhinoceros fan.
If asked, however, you know nothing of it.
Infinite, the cool breeze, and the head and horns.
Like clouds and rain which have passed, it cannot be captured.

[Setchō again said, "If you want the cool breeze to return and the head and horns to be regained, each of you say a turning word." And he said, "If the fan is broken, bring the rhinoceros to me." Then a monk came forward and said, "You monks, go back to the meditation hall." Setchō said, "I wanted to catch a giant whale, but only a toad came up." And he descended from the rostrum.]

NOTES   *Enkan, Tōsu, Sekisō, Shifuku, Hofuku.* Enkan succeeded Baso. The exact date of his birth is not known, but he is said to have been ninety-two years old when he died in 842. He was invited to go to Japan but, because of his age, sent his disciple Gikū in his place. This was the first introduction of Southern Zen into Japan. Gikū led Empress Sachiko to enlightenment. Her poem on that occasion runs:

> The clouds which arise
> Above the hills of T'ang
> Are the smoke of the fire
> We kindle in this land.

Tōsu also appears in Cases 41, 79, and 80, Sekisō in Case 55, and Shifuku in Case 33. For Hofuku, see Case 8.

• *The precious treasury of the true Dharma.* The phrase in the original text is *shōbō genzō* (*shō*, genuine; *bō*, Dharma; *gen*, eyes, and thus, as precious as eyes; *zō*, treasury).

• *The ten directions . . . the eight dimensions.* This means all regions, both material and mental.

• *Living the same life and dying the same death.* In other words, sharing the same realization as the Buddha.

• *Bring me the rhinoceros fan.* This fan was one on which a picture of a rhinoceros viewing the moon was painted. In Zen literature the ox is used to symbolize the Zen mind, and the rhinoceros is looked upon as a kind of ox. The original text says *sai-gyū-ji* (*sai*, rhinoceros; *gyū*, ox; *ji*, an affectionate suffix). The rhinoceros here represents the enlightened mind. Enkan is asking his attendant to present such a mind to him.

• *The fan has been broken.* When one attains realization, one is supposed to transcend it. If one sticks to it and stays there, the so-called Dharma malady will start to develop. Being attached to anything, even Buddhahood, is looked upon with great aversion. The attendant knew this well, and when he said, "The fan has been broken," he was saying that before he experienced realization he had yearned for it greatly, but once he attained it he found it as useless as a broken fan and threw it away. Up to this point he was doing well, but Enkan had another, more difficult question.

• *If the fan is broken, bring the rhinoceros to me.* When you have cast away your mean ego, another ego will stand in the place of the one cast out. There is never complete absence of ego. However, repeated elimination will ultimately lead to an egoless ego. Enkan was asking his attendant to display such an ultimate condition.

• *The attendant made no reply.* He was driven into a corner and could not answer.

• *I would not refuse to bring it out, but I fear the head and horns would not be perfect.* Before I attained to Buddhahood I painted a splendid picture of it in imagination, but now I have reached it I find it as worthless as a dog's droppings. If you need such a shabby thing, I would not refuse to give it back to you.

• *Setchō says, "I want that imperfect one."* That shabby one is what I require of you (meaning, of course, you yourself).

• *If I return it to you, there will be no more of it.* If I try to hand it over to you, it will be all gone. Bodhidharma said to the Second Patriarch (Eka), "Bring your mind here, and I will pacify it for you." Eka said, "I have searched for my mind, and I cannot take hold of it." Bodhidharma said, "Now your mind is pacified" (*Mumonkan*, Case 41).

• *There is still the rhinoceros.* You say it is no more, but I find the rhinoceros still there.

• *Shifuku drew a circle and wrote the character for "ox" in it.* Drawing a circle with an ox in it was a favorite teaching method of certain Zen masters, especially those of the Igyō (Isan and Kyōzan) school. Shifuku was a grandson of Kyōzan in Dharma lineage. But a drawn ox is worthless.

• *Why didn't you bring it out earlier?* If you have prepared such a fine dinner, why don't you bring it to me?

• *My master, you have grown old; employ someone else to attend you.* You are in your dotage and talk nonsense. I want none of your grumbling. This was another answer to Enkan's questioning.

• *Long labor lost.* This is work that came to nothing in spite of good intentions. The work of Zen masters is almost always done by stealth. Their labor goes unnoticed and unappreciated. Zen transcends right and wrong, good and evil, sage and fool, successful and unsuccessful. Setchō simply says, "Long labor lost." All the teachers who appear in this case— Enkan, Tōsu, Sekisō, Shifuku, and Hofuku—are employed in thankless labor, being compelled by the desire to lead others to enlightenment. Such thankless labor is of the greatest value. This is Setchō's conclusion.

• *You have long used the rhinoceros fan; / If asked, however, you know nothing of it.* Everybody is using the rhinoceros fan (Buddha Nature) without knowing it, because subjectivity does not reflect upon itself, just as the eyes do not see themselves. But the Zen masters know they are using it.

• *Infinite, the cool breeze, and the head and horns.* When enlightened, you enjoy anything and everything. The cool breeze represents the serene, peaceful condition of the mind, like a moonlit night.

• *Like clouds and rain which have passed, it cannot be captured.* You can enjoy it in your samadhi, but you cannot catch hold of it.

• *Setchō again said.* Every time it is brought out it is still fresh.

• *If you want the cool breeze to return and the head and horns to be regained.* That is, to construct the Buddha's image, or Buddhahood.

• *If the fan is broken, bring the rhinoceros to me.* Why this persistent questioning, this returning again and again to the same topic? Because it is a most important part of Zen practice and it forms the core of this case. But how are you to answer it? The case gives us a number of answers from former great teachers. But you must not simply accept their words. You must bring out your own answer from the bottom of your mind.

• *A monk came forward and said, "You monks, go back to the meditation hall."* These were the words said by the teacher when his lecture was finished. But here the monk took the initiative. If you are sufficiently accomplished, you may say what you like. If you are doing something beyond your powers, however, it becomes merely a show of bravado.

• *Only a toad came up.* Setchō seems not to be satisfied with the monk's words. In the exchanges of Zen mondō, one is required to polish one's expression. This monk's answer is less subtle, less refined than those of the great masters, such as Ummon and Jōshū, whose seemingly nonchalant utterances admit of no criticism. Hence Setchō's criticism.

Case 92   The World-honored One Takes His Seat

ENGO'S INTRODUCTION   One string is plucked, and he discerns the whole tune. Such insight is hardly to be met with even in a thousand years. Like a hawk pursuing the hare, he at once demonstrates his superiority. He embodies all the teachings in one phrase, encompasses the thousand great worlds in a single grain of dust. Can any of you go with him, living the same life and dying the same death? Can you testify to the truth by going through and through it yourself? See the following example.

MAIN SUBJECT   The World-honored One one day took his seat on the platform. Manjusri struck the table with the gavel and said, "Clearly understand the Lord of Dharma's Law, the Lord of Dharma's Law is like this." The World-honored One descended from his seat.

SETCHŌ'S VERSE
  The brilliant ones among the constellation
  Know the Lord of Dharma's Law is not like this.

Had Saindhava been there,
Manjusri need not have struck with the gavel.

NOTES *One string is plucked, and he discerns the whole tune.* This is a reference to an old story which tells of a skilled musician, Hakuga, and his close friend Shōshiki, who liked to listen to Hakuga playing the harp. When thoughts of the high mountains ran in Hakuga's mind while he was playing, Shōshiki said, "Oh! It is as rugged as the great mountain." When Hakuga had in mind a stream, Shōshiki said, "Now it flows like the great river." When Shōshiki died, Hakuga broke his harp, saying, "Not in a thousand years will there be another Shōshiki to understand my playing as he did."

• *He embodies all the teachings in one phrase.* When he was dying, the Buddha said, "In my forty-nine years of teaching I did not preach even one word." This saying embodies all the teachings of his lifetime. Bodhidharma said, "Emptiness, no holiness," in reply to Emperor Wu's query, "What is the first principle of the holy teachings?" (See Case 1.)

• *The thousand great worlds.* A thousand small worlds make up one medium world, and a thousand medium worlds make up one great world. The worlds are thus as numerous as the sands of the Ganges—in other words, innumerable. This ancient cosmology agrees with the findings of modern astronomy.

• *Clearly understand the Lord of Dharma's Law, the Lord of Dharma's Law is like this.* This was the formula pronounced at the end of the Buddha's preaching. At the beginning of the preaching the phrase used was "Illustrious disciples assembled here, listen to the first principle of the Dharma." But in this case, Manjusri said the closing words when the Buddha had just ascended the platform and the audience was attentively waiting to hear him speak. By this strange action Manjusri demonstrated that "before a word is spoken, the sermon is already delivered." The Buddha agreed with Manjusri and descended from his seat.

• *The brilliant ones among the constellation | Know the Lord of Dharma's Law is not like this.* "The constellation" is the splendid array of disciples that surrounded the Buddha, including the patriarchs and teachers of successive generations. Among them there were, of course, many brilliant ones who understood all this before Manjusri struck with the gavel.

• *Had Saindhava been there.* Saindhava was a clever retainer who always knew what his master needed and had it ready before he was asked for it.

• *Manjusri need not have struck with the gavel.* Setchō is saying that if there had been a clever disciple who knew what was in the Buddha's mind before he opened his mouth, there would have been no need for Manjusri to strike with the gavel and say, "The Lord of Dharma's Law is like this."

Case 93 Taikō's "You Fox-Devil"

MAIN SUBJECT A monk asked Taikō, "What is the meaning of Chōkei's words, 'He seems to observe reflection and thanksgiving before the midday meal'?" Taikō performed a dance. The monk made bows. Taikō said, "What makes you make the bows?" The monk performed a dance. Taikō said, "You fox-devil!"

SETCHŌ'S VERSE
  One arrow glanced off, the second struck deep;
  Don't tell me yellow leaves are gold.
  If the waves of Sōkei were all the same,
  Many would drown on land.

NOTES *Taikō* (837–903) succeeded Sekisō, who appears in Cases 55 and 91. He was a contemporary of Gensha, Seppō, and Gantō.

• *Chōkei* also appears in Cases 8, 22, 23, 74, 76, and 95. The monk's question is a reference to Case 74.

• *Taikō performed a dance.* This was not an imitation of Kingyū's dance (see Case 74) but Taikō's own dance, performed in his samadhi.

• *The monk made bows.* This is the customary way of expressing one's gratitude when one has understood one's teacher's words or instruction.

• *What makes you make the bows?* The teacher is shaking his disciple to make sure of his degree of understanding. If he has reached a true understanding, it will be only the more firmly rooted by the shaking. If not, his deficiences—of which he may have been unaware—will be exposed.

· *The monk performed a dance.* This may be accepted as evidence of true understanding or not, according to the student's degree of attainment, which will now be clearly apparent to the teacher. Either way, the teacher does not easily give his approval. "Whip the horse even when it runs" is the teacher's watchword.

· *You fox-devil!* Setchō liked this saying of Taikō's and so included the story in his collection of a hundred cases.

· *One arrow glanced off, the second struck deep.* Taikō's words, "You fox-devil!" made a deep impression.

· *Don't tell me yellow leaves are gold.* "Yellow leaves" comes from a passage in the *Parinirvana Sutra*: "It is like parents soothing their crying child by giving him some yellow leaves from a willow tree and saying, 'Don't cry, here is some gold for you.' " Yellow leaves are false, while gold is genuine. Setchō is saying that you must discern clearly whether or not the monk was a fraud.

· *If the waves of Sōkei were all the same.* Sōkei was the name of the place where the Sixth Patriarch, Enō, lived, and became his surname. If his descendants acted merely as he did, without originality, they would inevitably lead students astray, and Zen would only decline.

· *Many would drown on land.* Such an absurdity as drowning on land will occur if deceptive imitations are allowed to pass without censure. In Case 76 we suggested a somewhat different meaning for the phrase "drown on land." However, you must penetrate to the true, inward meaning of such phrases and not try to understand them through their exact wording. Consistency of expression is sometimes ignored in Zen literature.

Case 94   The Surangama
Sutra and "Unseeing"

ENGO'S INTRODUCTION   As to what stands prior to the Word, not one phrase has been handed down, even by the thousand holy ones. One thread maintains its continuity before your eyes through countless eons. Entirely pure, entirely naked is the white ox under the blue sky. The golden-haired lion stands with eyes upturned, ears erect. Put the lion aside for a while and tell me, what is the white ox under the blue sky?

MAIN SUBJECT In the *Surangama Sutra* the Buddha says, "When unseeing, why do you not see the unseeing? If you see the unseeing, it is no longer unseeing. If you do not see the unseeing, it is not an object. Why isn't it yourself?"

SETCHŌ'S VERSE
  Entire the figure of an elephant,
  Complete the image of an ox;
  To have seen is a defect of the eyes.
  The wisest have groped in the dark.
  Do you want to see the golden-headed Buddha?
  Through countless eons, none is more than halfway there.

NOTES *As to what stands prior to the Word.* See the notes to Case 7.
• *The thousand holy ones.* Even Buddhas could not talk about the essence of Buddha Nature.
• *One thread maintains its continuity before your eyes through countless eons.* See the notes to Case 90.
• *Entirely pure, entirely naked is the white ox under the blue sky.* The white ox stands for Buddha Nature. Buddha Nature is pure and is revealed in all its nakedness. "Under the blue sky" refers to its openness. But the unenlightened person is not aware of it.
• *The golden-haired lion stands with eyes upturned, ears erect.* The golden-haired lion refers to Manjusri, who represents the four wisdoms (Great Perfect Mirror Wisdom, Universal Nature Wisdom, Marvelous Observing Wisdom, and Perfecting of Action Wisdom). The first two of these represent the essence of Buddha Nature, the latter two its manifestation in activity. The upturned eyes and erect ears symbolize the quick insight of Manjusri's wisdom. In the present case the golden-haired lion is taken as representing Buddha Nature in activity. In Zen literature gen-

erally, both the white ox and the golden-haired lion are used to stand sometimes for the essence of Buddha Nature, sometimes for its manifestation in action. As we saw in Case 90, essence and activity are one and the same thing, being separated only in conceptual thinking.

• *What is the white ox under the blue sky?* What is the essence of Buddha Nature?

• *When unseeing . . .* "Unseeing" is pure subjectivity. It appears in absolute samadhi. It is what Engo refers to in his phrase "what stands prior to the Word." Pure subjectivity is not aware of itself, just as the eye does not see itself. If it is seen—and it can be seen when it has turned into a direct past—it is no longer pure subjectivity but is an object, which is being viewed by another subject. Thus, "If you see the unseeing, it is no longer unseeing." If you do not see the unseeing, it is not an object and hence is pure subjectivity. Why isn't it yourself?

• *Entire the figure of an elephant.* This image is from a parable told by the Buddha. A blind man who touched the trunk of an elephant said an elephant was like a pipe, one who touched a leg said an elephant was like a pillar, and so on. Each perceived only a small part of the whole.

• *Complete the image of an ox.* This comes from an ancient story in which an expert butcher says that although he sees nothing of the ox, his knife works efficiently and the cutting up is carried out precisely.

• *To have seen is a defect of the eyes.* To say that one has seen the elephant or has not seen the ox is equally mistaken.

• *Through countless eons, none is more than halfway there.* One's study of Zen must continue endlessly. Everyone is still on the way. It is the pursuit of a whole lifetime. Engo says, "Even the old master Shakya does not know. How can I demonstrate it?"

Case 95 Chōkei and Hofuku Discuss the Buddha's Words

ENGO'S INTRODUCTION Do not remain where Buddha is; if you do, horns will grow on your head. Run quickly past the place where there is no Buddha; if not, weeds will grow like a jungle. Even if you are entirely naked and absolutely bare, and the unhindered interpenetration of mind and circumstances is attained, you still cannot avoid resembling the fool who watched the tree stump to catch a hare. Now tell me, what are you to do in order to be free from these faults? See the following.

MAIN SUBJECT   Chōkei one day said, "Even if you say that the Arhats still have three poisons, you should not say that the Tathagata has two languages. I do not say that the Tathagata has no language but that he does not have two languages." Hofuku said, "What is the Tathagata's language?" Chōkei said, "How can a deaf person hear it?" Hofuku said, "I know you are speaking from a secondary principle." Chōkei said, "What is the Tathagata's language?" Hofuku said, "Have a cup of tea."

SETCHŌ'S VERSE
Who speaks from the first, who from the second principle?
Dragons do not lie in puddles;
Where dragons lurk,
Waves arise when no wind blows.
Oh! You Ryō Zen monk,
You've bruised your head on the Dragon Gate.

NOTES   *Chōkei, Hofuku.* See Case 8.
• *Do not remain where Buddha is.* If you stick to anything, even the Buddha and enlightenment, you will deviate from your ordinary mind and will become the demon of attachment.
• *Run quickly past the place where there is no Buddha.* In the previous sentence, Buddha was denied. Here, no Buddha is also denied.
• *Even if you are entirely naked and absolutely bare.* The original text says *jō ra-ra, shaku sha-sha* (*jō*, pure; *ra-ra*, naked-naked; *shaku*, bare; *sha-sha*, free and easy). You are supposed to be stark naked, just as you came from the hands of nature. That is, you carry nothing with you and have nothing to lose.
• *The unhindered interpenetration of mind and circumstances.* The literal

translation of the original is: "There is no spiritual activity beyond object, and no object beyond spiritual activity." In the Kegon doctrine, the four categories are (1) the realm of the absolute, (2) the realm of the relative, phenomenal world, (3) the realm of the unhindered interpenetration of these two, and (4) the realm of the unhindered interpenetration of phenomena. It is the last category which is supposed to represent the most advanced condition of Zen practice. Engo is urging us to go beyond the third category to reach this state.

• *You still cannot avoid resembling the fool who watched the tree stump to catch a hare.* See Case 8.

• *Even if you say that the Arhats still have three poisons, you should not say that the Tathagata has two languages.* It is said that there are fifty-two holy grades. The highest is the Buddha, the second is the Bodhisattva, the third is the Pratyeka Buddha, and the Arhat comes fourth. The Arhats are thought to be free of the three poisons: covetousness, anger, and folly. Chōkei says that the Arhats are, of course, free of these, but even if you suppose they are not, you should not say that the Tathagata (the Buddha) has two languages. The Buddha is often said to have adapted himself to the condition of his hearers and to have spoken in a language suitable to the occasion. In fact, however, the Buddha did not speak in two ways. Some of his words sound commonplace, but all outstanding teachers agree that when one becomes truly enlightened the Buddha's seemingly commonplace instructions attain a profound and weighty meaning. This is what Chōkei is emphasizing.

• *What is the Tathagata's language?* Hofuku starts a Dharma battle.

• *How can a deaf person hear it?* The superficial meaning is that a deaf person like you cannot hear it. However, the true listener is a deaf-mute.

• *I know you are speaking from a secondary principle.* The literal translation of the phrase which we have rendered as "secondary principle" is "a second head," which means a second step or measure, or even the second best—hence, an expedient or makeshift. The first principle is the essential point of Buddhism. Chōkei is saying that the Buddha spoke to ordinary, ignorant people in commonplace language that seemed to be rough and ready and not always quite correct, but that in fact the truly enlightened person realizes that every word of the Buddha was spoken from the first principle, hence Chōkei's assertion that the Tathagata does not have two languages. Hofuku knew this quite well and said, "Have a cup of tea." This was commonplace, but in reality most direct and to the point. Thus he approved Chōkei's words, though seeming to deny them.

• *What is the Tathagata's language?* If you say that, then tell me what you call the first principle.

• *Have a cup of tea.* "Good morning." "How are you?" "Have a cup of tea." These may seem to be ordinary, trivial phrases. But these commonplace words are not common from the enlightened point of view. Truly, they make up the first principle of Buddhism.

• *Who speaks from the first, who from the second principle?* Was Hofuku speaking from the first principle, and did Chōkei really fall behind?

• *Dragons do not lie in puddles; | Where dragons lurk, | Waves arise when no wind blows.* In Zen literature, dragons are often used to represent outstanding Zen monks. In an ancient legend, dragons are depicted as lurking in the depths of the sea, living among castlelike rocks and caves. When the moment comes, they rise to the surface and ascend to heaven, accompanied by thunder and torrents of rain. A dragon's movements in the depths of the sea disturb the water and an ominous whirlpool appears on the surface even though there is no wind. Setchō is suggesting that the seemingly simple encounter between Chōkei and Hofuku was just as remarkable.

• *Oh! You Ryō Zen monk.* Chōkei's personal name was Eryō, and he was generally called by the second syllable, *ryō*.

• *You've bruised your head on the Dragon Gate.* See Case 7. Setchō may seem to be saying that Chōkei was crushed by Hofuku's words, but in fact he is speaking not of Chōkei but to his disciples.

Case 96   Jōshū's Three Turning Words

MAIN SUBJECT   Jōshū said, "Clay Buddhas cannot pass through water; metal Buddhas cannot pass through a furnace; wooden Buddhas cannot pass through fire."

SETCHŌ'S VERSE
   Clay Buddhas cannot pass through water:
   The divine light illumines heaven and earth;

Had Shinkō not stood in the snow—
Many deceptions, many pretenses.

Metal Buddhas cannot pass through a furnace:
Men came to visit Shiko and found
The warning notice on the board;
But everywhere—the gentle breezes.

Wooden Buddhas cannot pass through fire:
I always remember how the monk Hasōda
Broke down the oven of sacrifice,
Whose god so long had bound himself.

NOTES   *Clay Buddhas cannot pass through water.* Clay Buddhas are clay
Buddhas. There is no need to deplore, regret, or boast of the fact of being
a clay Buddha. When it is immersed in water it will melt away. When it
is melted away, it is melted away. When it has come into being, it has
come into being; when it has disappeared, it has disappeared. Everything
is in motion and flux. Impermanency is the nature of things.
   • *The divine light illumines heaven and earth.* However, everything has
its own divine light, which makes heaven and earth shine brightly. Existence is a glorious thing. It has brightened the universe.
   • *Had Shinkō not stood in the snow.* Shinkō was the personal name of
the Second Patriarch. When he was born, a divine light shone through
the room, and his name derives from this (*shin*, divine; *kō*, light). The
story of his standing in the snow is related in the notes to Case 41 of
Mumonkan.
   • *Many deceptions, many pretenses.* If it had not been for the severe
training to which Shinkō and others like him subjected themselves, many
acts of deception would have been perpetrated by fraudulent so-called
teachers of Zen.
   • *Metal Buddhas cannot pass through a furnace.* A metal Buddha must be
a strong one. But everything has its weak points as well as strong ones,
its disadvantages as well as advantages. Metal Buddhas will melt in a furnace. When we are to fall, let us fall. Causation is not to be ignored. (See
Mumonkan, Case 2.)
   • *Men came to visit Shiko and found | The warning notice on the board.*
Shiko (800–880) was a disciple of Nansen. He put up a notice in front of

his temple which ran, "Shiko has a dog. It will have your head, your heart, your legs. The moment you hesitate, your life is lost."

• *But everywhere—the gentle breezes.* When you have once lost your life and then regained it, you will find that soft breezes blow gently through the whole world.

• *Wooden Buddhas cannot pass through fire.* Wooden Buddhas will be burned in fire. Each individual Buddha represents the universal Buddha. Each individual Buddha himself is the absolute one. The clay Buddha, the metal Buddha, the wooden Buddha, each has his individuality and personality. At the same time, they are all Buddhas.

• *I always remember how the monk Hasōda | Broke down the oven of sacrifice, | Whose god had so long bound himself.* The episode referred to here made Hasōda famous. One day, accompanied by his disciples, he went into a village shrine where there was an oven which the villagers worshiped as their tutelary god. Birds and beasts offered as sacrifices were killed and cooked in the oven. Hasōda struck the oven three times with his staff and said, "You were originally made of clay. Where could you have got this soul and godhead, which requires so much killing and cooking?" Thereupon the oven came tumbling down. From among the dust and debris appeared the figure of a man dressed in a blue costume and wearing a crown. He stood before Hasōda and, making bows, said, "I was the god of the oven. I was long subject to the effect of karma. Today you gave me instruction and I was emancipated from my life of suffering. Now I am in heaven. I have come especially to give my thanks." Hasōda said, "No-nature is your original nature. I have not given it to you especially." Then the figure disappeared. Hasōda's name (*ha*, break; *sō*, oven; *da*, down) was given to him because of this episode. His real name is unknown.

Case 97 The Diamond Sutra's "The Transgression Is Wiped Out"

ENGO'S INTRODUCTION   Even if now you hold fast and now you let go, you are not yet an expert. To infer three things from one example is not enough. Even if you can move heaven and earth, dumbfound the four quarters, crash like thunder, flash like lightning, upset the ocean, overturn mountains, and pour down like torrents of rain, you still fall far short of it. Is there anyone among you who can control the center of the heavens and the axis of the earth? See the following.

MAIN SUBJECT   The *Diamond Sutra* says, "If anyone is despised by others, even if he has committed some serious transgression in a former life and been doomed to fall into the evil world, the transgression in the former life is wholly wiped out by virtue of the fact that he is despised in this life."

SETCHŌ'S VERSE
  Holding the jewel,
  Merit is rewarded.
  Free from merit,
  The jewel reflects no more.
  Truly meritless,
  The heavens seek in vain.
  Gautama, Gautama,
  Do you know the secret?
  "Everything lies open,"
  Says Setchō again.

NOTES   *Engo's Introduction.* This is largely self-explanatory. For "hold fast" and "let go," see the notes to Case 4.

• *The Diamond Sutra says.* What is the sutra? This forms a koan. The answer is that the sutra is to be found in your own mind. Hōgen, the founder of the Hōgen sect of Zen, says, "Those who have attained Buddhahood are called the devotees of this sutra." When you are despised by others, for whatever reason, if you can hold on to your ordinary mind and remain unaffected by the actions of others, you are absolved of your previous transgressions.

• *Holding the jewel,* | *Merit is rewarded.* The jewel is Zen wisdom, which is granted only to the person who has earned it by his own efforts. But what is merit? True merit is attained when one becomes meritless.

• *Free from merit,* | *The jewel reflects no more.* | *Truly meritless,* | *The heavens seek in vain.* This is a reference to Sunyata (see Case 6).

• *Gautama, Gautama,* | *Do you know the secret?* Gautama was the name of the clan to which the Buddha belonged, and came to denote the Buddha himself. Setchō, of course, knows quite well that the Buddha was the first man to discover the secret; he asks the question here to emphasize his point.

• *"Everything lies open,"* | *Says Setchō again.* "Everything lies open to me" is Setchō's favorite expression when he comes to the ultimate secret of Zen.

Case 98 Tempyō's Two Wrongs

ENGO'S INTRODUCTION During the summer session I have burdened you monks from the five lakes with a great deal of talking. The diamond treasure sword cuts through all complications. Now, after all my instruction, you are left with nothing.

Tell me, what is the diamond treasure sword? Lift up your eyes and see the sharpness of the sword in the following.

MAIN SUBJECT When Tempyō went on a pilgrimage visiting teachers, he stayed with Sai-in. He always said, "Don't say you understand Buddhism. I find no one who can speak on it." One day Sai-in heard him and called, "Ju-i [Tempyō's personal name]!" Tempyō looked up at Sai-in. Sai-in said, "Wrong!" Tempyō walked a few steps away and Sai-in once again said, "Wrong!" Tempyō turned and approached Sai-in, who said, "I have just said, 'Wrong!' Who is wrong? Am I or are you?" Tempyō said, "I am." Sai-in said, "Wrong!" Tempyō said nothing. Sai-in said, "Stay here this summer and let us discuss the two wrongs." But Tempyō instead left Sai-in.

Later, when Tempyō was abbot of his own temple, he said to his disciples, "When I went on a pilgrimage it happened, in the course of events, that I was brought to see Abbot Shimyō [Sai-in's other name], who told me twice that I was wrong. It was not then that I was wrong, however, but when I first started south on my pilgrimage. I had already said it was wrong."

SETCHŌ'S VERSE

Zen people are too often frivolous;
They study much, learn much, but to no avail.
How deplorable, laughable, is old Tempyō!
You say you were wrong to make a pilgrimage:
Wrong! Wrong!
Sai-in's good words grow pale beside my "Wrong."
Once again Setchō says,
"Some monk may come forth and say, 'Wrong!'
Can you tell my 'Wrong' from Tempyō's?"

NOTES   *Tempyō* was, in Dharma lineage, Seppō's descendant in the fourth generation. He was a native of Honan Province in northern China. Little is known of him besides the story of the present case.

• *Sai-in* was a spiritual grandson of Rinzai. The sharpness of the death-dealing and life-giving sword (see *Mumonkan*, Case 11) is a favorite image in the Rinzai school of Zen. In this case Sai-in is shown to be a master swordsman.

• *Engo's Introduction.* In the original, these lines make a fine quatrain. In this verse, approaching the end of his comments on *Hekiganroku*, Engo presents his conclusion: I gave nothing and you have acquired nothing. It will take thirty years for one truly to understand this attaining nothing.

• *The summer session.* This is the summer retreat, which lasts ninety days.

• *The five lakes.* These are Payang, Tungt'ing, Taihu, Tanyang, and Chingtsao lakes. Poetically, they represent the whole of China.

• *A great deal of talking.* This means talking too much, which is deplored in Zen (see Case 8).

• *The diamond treasure sword.* Zen wisdom, which cuts off all delusive thoughts.

• *He always said, "Don't say you understand Buddhism. I find no one who can speak on it."* It is easy to criticize others. A shortsighted person often gets the idea that he knows everything and others do not.

• *Wrong.* It is not wrong to say, "I find no one who can speak properly on Buddhism," because no one can do so. But Sai-in categorically condemned Tempyō, saying he was wrong. Sai-in wanted to discuss this matter with Tempyō and make him understand the question thoroughly. But Tempyō told himself that he knew all about it, and would not stay to discuss the matter. However, knowing a topic conceptually is quite different from realizing it. In Zen practice we aim to realize things.

• *It was not then that I was wrong, however, but when I first started south on my pilgrimage. I had already said it was wrong.* It was said long ago, "Bodhidharma did not come to China, the Second Patriarch did not go to India." Zen is a matter not of coming and going but of truly realizing the spirit of Buddhism. But Tempyō, understanding this saying only conceptually and sticking to the idea, said that his pilgrimage was wrong but that as many others go on pilgrimages, so did he—but knowingly in his case. Poor Tempyō! He deceived himself and he deceived his disciples.

• *Zen people are too often frivolous.* There were in Setchō's day, as in any other generation, those who "mistook the bell for a jar" (see *Mumonkan*, Case 7) and talked big, as Tempyō did.

• *Sai-in's good words grow pale beside my "Wrong."* Setchō means that he has swept everything clear by saying, "Wrong! Wrong!"

• *Some monk may come forth and say, "Wrong!"* This "some monk" is Setchō himself. He secretly felt he was wrong in talking too much. But all Zen teachers knowingly do this wrong.

• *Can you tell my "Wrong" from Tempyō's?* This is self-explanatory, but Setchō had to add this line to conclude his verse.

Case 99   Chū Kokushi and the Ten-bodied Herdsman

ENGO'S INTRODUCTION   When the dragon calls, mists and clouds arise; when the tiger roars, gales begin to blow. The supreme teachings of the Buddha ring out with a silvery voice. The actions of Zen masters are like those of the most expert archers, whose arrows, shot from opposite directions, collide in midair. The truth is revealed for all ages and all places. Tell me, who has ever been like this? See the following.

MAIN SUBJECT   Emperor Shukusō asked Chū Kokushi, "What is the ten-bodied herdsman?" Chū Kokushi said, "Go trampling on Vairocana's head!" The emperor said, "I cannot follow you." Chū Kokushi said, "Don't take the self for the pure Dharma body."

SETCHŌ'S VERSE
"National Teacher" was forced upon him;
He made the name his own.
He helped the son of heaven
Trample on Vairocana's head.

With an iron hammer
He smashed the golden bones;
What else is left
In heaven and earth?

In the three thousand worlds
The lands and seas lie sleeping.
Who will dare enter
The dragon's cave?

NOTES   *Chū Kokushi.* See *Mumonkan,* Case 17.
• *When the dragon calls.* The dragon is a legendary being of mysterious power. When it calls out, mists and clouds form, and torrents of rain

descend to escort it to heaven. The attainment of enlightenment by a monk is here being compared to the dragon's ascent to heaven.

• *When the tiger roars.* The monk, whose spiritual actions often issue forth with the force of a gale, is here compared to a tiger.

• *Like those of the most expert archers, whose arrows, shot from opposite directions, collide in midair.* The literal translation of the original text is "as arrowheads collide in the air." This is a popular saying used to describe the activities of Zen masters. They may seem to contradict one another but invariably demonstrate the same truth of Zen.

• *The ten-bodied herdsman.* The herdsman is the Buddha; the ten bodies are his attributes. Various scriptures give different lists of the ten bodies. One set includes No-Attachment Buddha, Vowing-to-Save-All-Beings Buddha, Wisdom Buddha, Positive Buddha, Nirvana Buddha, Dharma Buddha, Mindful Buddha, Samadhi Buddha, Nature Buddha, and Easy Buddha.

• *Go trampling on Vairocana's head!* Vairocana is the Dharmakaya (Dharma body) Buddha, that is, absolute Buddha.

• *Don't take the self for the pure Dharma body.* It is a common Zen saying that your original self is the Dharma body itself. But now Chū Kokushi is denying this: "Don't take the self for the pure Dharma body." That is to say, your self is absolutely independent.

• *"National Teacher" was forced upon him.* It is a common saying that there is no name for the sage. But as one must have a label by which to be called, the title "National Teacher" was inevitably applied to Chū Kokushi.

• *The son of heaven.* A title of the emperor.

• *He smashed the golden bones.* The golden bones are the Buddha's bones. These have always been accorded the greatest respect. Shrines were built to contain them. Eventually the bones came to represent the Dharma itself. But Chū Kokushi smashed the golden bones with one blow, saying, "Trample on Vairocana's head!"

• *What else is left | In heaven and earth?* The whole universe was broken up.

• *In the three thousand worlds | The lands and seas lie sleeping.* This refers to the perfect silence and solemnity of the absolute.

• *Who will dare enter | The dragon's cave?* The dragon is said to keep the treasured gem (which represents the secret of the universe) under his chin, and to watch over it in his cave in the depths of the sea. The monks studying Zen are compared to the diver who goes to the bottom of the sea to wrest the gem from the dragon. Chū Kokushi destroyed what had been looked upon as the most sacred representation of Buddhahood. The nature of true Buddhahood must be sought in another dimension. Who will descend into this new dimension to fetch the jewel? That is Setchō's question.

Case 100   Haryō's Sword Against Which a Hair Is Blown

ENGO'S INTRODUCTION   We sow the cause and reap the results; starting carefully, we end in consummate perfection. From the outset nothing was kept secret. When I talked, I had nothing to give you. Some of you will say to me, "You have talked so much during the summer retreat, and now you say that from the beginning you had nothing to give us. What do you mean?" I reply that I will tell you when you have attained realization. Now, I ask you, is this simply because I do not fail to observe the first principle, or is there some real advantage in doing so? See the following.

MAIN SUBJECT   A monk asked Haryō, "What is the sword against which a hair is blown?" Haryō said, "Each branch of the coral embraces the bright moon."

SETCHŌ'S VERSE
>   To cut off discontent,
>   Rough methods may be best:
>   Now they slap, now they point.
>
>   The sword lies across the sky,
>   Snow glistens in its light,
>   No one can forge or sharpen it.

"Each branch of the coral
Embraces the bright moon"—
Marvelous!

NOTES *We sow the cause and reap the results; starting carefully, we end in consummate perfection.* Coming to the end of his comments on *Hekiganroku*, Engo delivers his epilogue.

• *When I talked, I had nothing to give you.* When the Buddha was passing away, he said he had not preached a word. Zen truth defies description.

• *You have talked so much during the summer retreat.* Communication is, of course, important, but true realization can be won only by your own efforts.

• *I will tell you when you have attained realization.* When you have attained realization, you find there is nothing that can be taught by others.

• *I do not fail to observe the first principle.* The golden rule of Zen is "Attain it by your own efforts." Imparting knowledge to others prematurely is strongly condemned in Zen practice.

• *Haryō.* See Case 13.

• *The sword against which a hair is blown.* The original text says *sui-mō-ken* (*sui*, blow; *mō*, hair; *ken*, sword), meaning that this celebrated sword is sharp enough to cut a hair blown against its blade. The sword represents Zen wisdom, which cuts through all worries and delusive thoughts.

• *Each branch of the coral embraces the bright moon.* You are intended to recite this line as an exercise in language samadhi. Then you will eventually reach a purified condition of mind in which you find yourself freed of all worries, including subconscious ones. It is as if they were cut off with a sword sharp enough to sever a hair blown against it.

• *To cut off discontent.* To be discontented means to be out of equilibrium. Though it may sound a commonplace thing, the ultimate aim of Zen practice is to recover the equilibrium of the mind.

• *Rough methods may be best.* Master painters want to paint, and master calligraphers want to write, like children, whose work is often naive and clumsy. The ancient philosopher Lao-tzu says, "The greatest skill is like awkwardness. The greatest eloquence is like stammering."

• *Now they slap, now they point.* Rinzai gave his disciple a blow, and Gutei lifted his finger (see *Mumonkan*, Case 3), as ways of teaching.

• *The sword lies across the sky.* Like the Milky Way, this great sword stretches across the sky.

• *Snow glistens in its light.* In the dark, stormy sky, snowflakes glisten in the light reflected from it.

• *No one can forge or sharpen it.* Since the beginning of time, long before human life began, this sword has commanded heaven and earth.

• *"Each branch of the coral | Embraces the bright moon"—| Marvelous!* Haryō's reply was splendid.

Genealogical Table

The table on the following two pages shows the master-disciple relationships, or Dharma lineages, of most of the Zen masters and other figures mentioned in *Mumonkan* and *Hekiganroku*, together with the numbers of the cases in which they appear. Italic numbers refer to cases in *Mumonkan*, numbers in roman type to those in *Hekiganroku*.

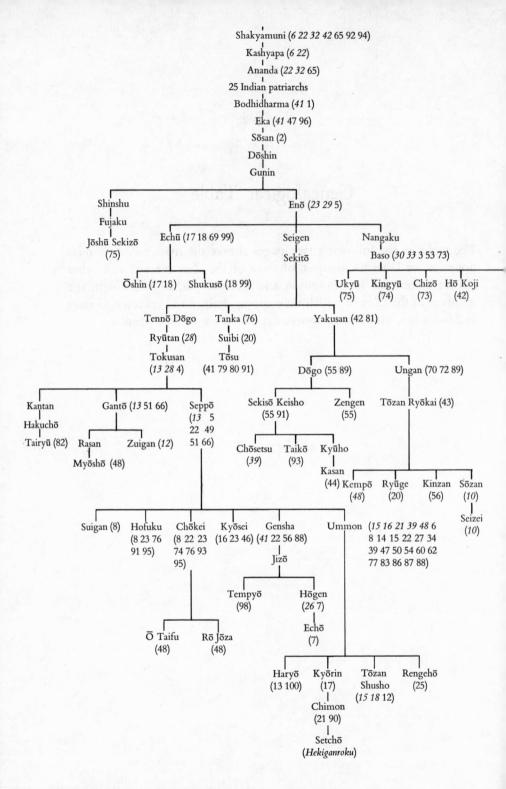

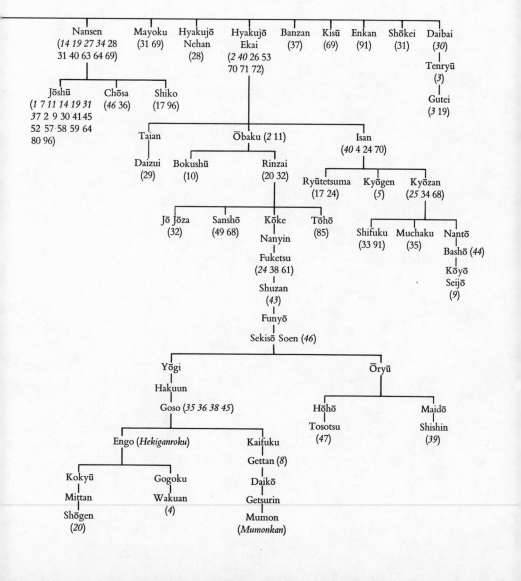

Nansen *(14 19 27 34* 28 31 40 63 64 69) Mayoku (31 69) Hyakujō Nehan (28) Hyakujō Ekai *(2 40* 26 53 70 71 72) Banzan (37) Kisū (69) Enkan (91) Shōkei (31) Daibai *(30)*

Tenryū *(3)*

Gutei *(3* 19)

Jōshū *(1 7 11 14 19 31 37* 2 9 30 41 45 52 57 58 59 64 80 96) Chōsa *(46* 36) Shiko (17 96)

Taian Ōbaku *(2* 11) Isan *(40* 4 24 70)

Daizui (29) Bokushū (10) Rinzai (20 32) Ryūtetsuma (17 24) Kyōgen *(5)* Kyōzan *(25* 34 68)

Jō Jōza (32) Sanshō (49 68) Kōke Tōhō (85) Shifuku (33 91) Muchaku (35) Nantō

Nanyin Bashō *(44)*

Fuketsu *(24* 38 61) Kōyō Seijō *(9)*

Shuzan *(43)*

Funyō

Sekisō Soen *(46)*

Yōgi Ōryū

Hakuun Hōhō Maidō

Goso (35 36 38 45) Tosotsu *(47)* Shishin *(39)*

Engo *(Hekiganroku)* Kaifuku

Gettan *(8)*

Kokyū Gogoku Daikō

Mittan Wakuan *(4)* Getsurin

Shōgen *(20)* Mumon *(Mumonkan)*

INDEX

The "weathermark" identifies this book as a production of John Weatherhill, Inc., publishers of fine books on Asia and the Pacific. Supervising editor: Suzanne Trumbull. Book design and typography: Meredith Weatherby. Production supervisor: Mitsuo Okado. Composition: Samhwa, Seoul. Platemaking and printing: Kinmei, Tokyo. Binding: Makoto Binderies, Tokyo. The typeface used is Monotype Bembo, the main text in the 12-point size, with hand-set Venice for display.